An
Entrepreneurial
University

An Entrepreneurial University

THE TRANSFORMATION OF

Tufts, 1976–2002

SOL GITTLEMAN

TUFTS UNIVERSITY PRESS

Medford, Massachusetts

Published by

UNIVERSITY PRESS OF NEW ENGLAND

Hanover & London

Tufts University Press
Published by University Press of New England,
One Court Street, Lebanon, NH 03766
www.upne.com
© 2004 by the Trustees of Tufts University
Printed in the United States of America
5 4 3 2

ISBNs for the paperback edition:
    ISBN—13: 978-1-58465-416-2
    ISBN—10: 1-58465-416-3

Library of Congress Cataloging-in-Publication Data
Gittleman, Sol, 1934–
    An entrepreneurial university : the transformation of
Tufts, 1976-2002 / Sol Gittleman.
       p.   cm.
    Includes bibliographical references and index.
    ISBN 1-58465-416-3 (pbk. : alk. paper)
    1. Tufts University—History—20th century.   I. Title.
    LD5393.G58   2004
    378.744'4—dc22   2004014581

TO TOM AND STEVE, *for making it fun*

CONTENTS

Preface *ix*

Prologue *xiii*

1 Tufts and the New American University *1*

2 The Coming of Jean Mayer

   The Accidental President *12*

3 Turning the Corner

   Consolidating the Mayer Presidency *45*

4 The Slippery Slope

   The Mayer Presidency, 1987–1992 *160*

5 The 1990s and the Changing World of

   American Higher Education *175*

6 The DiBiaggio Years, 1992–2001

   The Personal Touch *197*

7 The Coming of Lawrence Bacow *293*

8 Postscript

   A Walk on the Campus *305*

Selected Bibliography *319*

Index *323*

Academic histories can be very boring. University archivists and presidents have produced hundreds of volumes for the benefit of alumni and alumni associations who want to see the name of their favorite faculty member or dean in print.

The challenge for me is particularly great, because the document that follows has been preceded by two earlier volumes of Tufts history, written by Professor Russell Miller, a faculty member and historian who accepted the invitation of the Tufts Alumni Association to chronicle the history of this university. His first volume covered the period from 1852 to the centennial celebration. This was the Universalist Tufts, with four faculty and seven students on a hill in Medford, Massachusetts, created to educate fellow parishioners and soon ministers, always on a shoestring. Along the way, it added a medical school, dental school, and engineering program, none of which had sufficient resources and all of which had difficulty in gaining professional accreditation in these early years. The college staggered through the financial panics of 1873 and 1907 and the Depression of the 1930s, selling off land to survive. Volume II, written during the presidency of Jean Mayer, ended in 1983 and covered the presidencies of Leonard Carmichael, Nils Wessell, Burton Hallowell, and the early Mayer years. It was under Carmichael and Wessell that Tufts attempted for the first time to flex its intellectual muscle, to become, instead of a college, a university. The will was there; the means were not, and Tufts languished. Professor Miller told me that he should have been awarded the Olympic gold medal for skating on thin ice for his work on the second volume. President Mayer insisted on reading every word and made recommendations for change that Professor Miller had to fight off, while maintaining a good working relationship with his president. Russell Miller had also been a part of the earlier presidencies of Wessell and Hallowell and demonstrated a very sensitive discretion in dealing with people still very much alive.

It is now time for the narrative to move forward into the twenty-first century. There needs to be a re-examination of the rise of Tufts University under Jean Mayer that Miller was not able to address. It is truly a remarkable story in the annals of American higher education.

Russell Miller was also the University Archivist, and as such his histories reflect a view of an institution through its faculty meetings, minutes, and the formal events that were of interest to the living alumni of the institution.

I prefer examining this university from a perspective of my own career of nearly four decades as a faculty member and administrator, during a time when American higher education went through some extraordinary changes. I spent more than twenty of those years as Provost, serving three presidents. That experience provided me with an opportunity to work closely with three different leaders and to study the nature of American higher education from a very special vantage point as an eyewitness. I saw a university undergo dramatic change because of the vision of one man who was also capable of producing a happy anarchy in his management style.

These are the stories I would like to tell, and I intend to use my own voice. Someone once described the American university as a model of the incompetent leading the ungovernable, while somehow remaining the envy of the world. I have been on both sides as well as at the intersections, and I am not a detached observer.[1]

This book will be, then, a chronicle of an institutional metamorphosis at a time of remarkable change in this country's understanding of the university and its culture. I hope to appeal to the Tufts community, to the wider academic profession, and to anyone interested in the evolution of one of this country's great treasures: its higher educational system. Finally, I am pleased to share my personal delight in finding a profession that can provide such joy to the mind and spirit.

This is a book about people, and they should receive all the credit for its writing. Trustees emeriti Harvey Brooks, Matthew Burns, Allan Callow, Henry

---

1. Academic historians who have served as administrators often find themselves and their opinions very much a part of their text. See Martin L. Friedland, *The University of Toronto: A History* (University of Toronto Press, 2002), xi. Frank Rhodes, who served for eighteen years as President of Cornell University, characterized the often anarchic nature of academic governance in a more reasonable tone: "The American university remains an organizational enigma, whose loosely coupled structure and collegially based organization defy the established canons of management." Rhodes, *The Creation of the Future* (Cornell University Press, 2001), 14.

Foster, Nelson Gifford, Weston Howland, William Meserve, Ruth Remis, and William Saltonstall gave unstintingly of their memory. My friend and conscience Audrey Hale, Assistant Provost at Tufts and for more than four decades the repository of the university's historical memory, freely gave of her opinions, sharing her prejudices with a candor that only Audrey possesses. Betty Mayer opened her home to me, this warm and generous person. Carl Scovil, Jean Mayer's close friend and spiritual leader, shared recollections, as did Mason Fernald, an old Mayer confidante and an eyewitness to some of those early days of tribulation. Martha Pokras, who was there at the birth of the Veterinary School, could have written her own book but instead shared her thoughts with me. Steve Manos and Tom Murnane saw it all and were willing to go over both the hilarious and the painful incidents of their enormous contributions to Tufts. Gregory Colati and Anne Sauer opened the Tufts archives to me; Linda Dixon showed her usual generosity of spirit from the Trustees office. John Schneider led me to the University Press of New England and to Ellen Wicklum, an editor who encouraged beyond the call of duty. Research assistants Aysha Haq and Zachary Crowley helped bring order from chaos. Pat Pattullo read the first draft. He made good use of a red pen and a lifetime's reliance on the University of Chicago style sheet to remind me of grammar and syntax. My wife Robyn tolerated litter in our home that less tolerant spouses would have burned.

PROLOGUE

To understand the context and meaning of the chapters that follow, the reader has to understand me. I am a product shaped and directed by a very specific environment, one that only relatively recently found a voice in American higher education. Who I am is vital to the telling, and my personal journey accounts for what kind of book this will be. It has a special relevance to one university where I spent most of my academic life. I believe it also has meaning for those interested in the evolution of America's colleges and universities. Who I am is inseparable from that story.

While writing these words, I am preparing for my sixty-third consecutive year of school. Since kindergarten, I have known no other September experience. There has always been the late-August haircut, whether for elementary, secondary, post-secondary, or graduate school, or since 1961, full-time faculty status. The ritual of autumn in a classroom has been, during this time, uninterrupted.

At first sight, I had no business making a life in American higher education. But, when you give the idea a moment's thought, you realize that only in America do the children of immigrants become professors. My parents were East European Jews who came to this country as teenagers immediately after the end of World War I. My father had some small measure of a Jewish education; my mother could scarcely read Yiddish and never learned to write in English. My father had a better ear and spoke English without an accent. He took my brother and me to school, to the doctor, to the ball games. We grew up in Hoboken, New Jersey, where I cultivated my later interest in foreign languages by learning how to plead to my schoolmates, "Please don't hit me!" in several exotic tongues. We lived in one room behind the family candy store, which had no candy, because there was only enough room for a dozen telephones to take bets and calls from racetracks. "Bookmaking" did not refer to publishing or printing. My earliest education was focused on memorizing the names of horses and ball players, of jockeys and batting averages. At home, we had neither books nor music, culture nor art.

Yet, from my earliest memory, my mother pounded education into our heads. She did it the only way she knew how. Unable to read my report cards, she would look at them with mournful eyes and warn me, "Your brother is doing better." It seemed that my older brother was always doing better, no matter how hard I worked. (Jewish parents—or perhaps all parents—use fraternal competition to inspire their children. When I told this story to Steven Trachtenberg, President of George Washington University, he wondered if *his* father could have been married to *my* mother. He had had the very same experience.)

Getting good grades was important, but education took a second place to playing ball. Stickball, pinkball, stoopball, baseball, and anything that had as an object the hitting of a round ball against a wooden bat; this activity filled our days. Yet, when it came time to attend college, I had been conditioned. My older brother, four years my senior and therefore in a different world, attended first NYU, then startled the neighborhood by transferring with a friend to Ohio State, and took a Junior semester in Acapulco, where he played guard on the Mexican college basketball team. Our high school basketball coach had attended Drew University in Madison, New Jersey, during World War II. He visited my parents and told them that he wanted me to attend Drew with one of his basketball players and my best friend, Sidney Zwerling. He thought it wise that two Jewish ballplayers go to this Methodist college together. We were 1952 mid-year graduates (in those days the high schools graduated two classes per year), so when we traveled to Madison around Christmastime, we had our completed applications with us. Sidney met the basketball coach; I met the baseball coach and manager. The coach, a Latin and Greek professor, asked me what I wanted to major in. I said, "I came to play shortstop, not to major." The manager then said that he was a German professor, and that I should major in German, take care of the infield, and they would take care of me.

That was my introduction to German culture. I majored in German at Drew, played four years of baseball, went on to Columbia University for a Master's degree when it became apparent that I was not going to have a career in baseball (my only professional scouting report was as follows: "Nice kid. Can't hit, can't throw, can't run."), got married, went to Germany on a Fulbright scholarship, and enrolled at the University of Michigan in 1957 in the doctoral program in German and Comparative Literature. My wife Robyn, who was a freshman at Brooklyn College when we married, was accepted into the undergraduate college to continue her education.

We loved Ann Arbor. The University of Michigan was an intellectually stimulating environment. I found great mentors, developed an interest in German theatre, and caught for the Huron Bowling Lanes fast-pitch softball team. The University represented a combination of old and new values in higher education. When I approached the German Department with a thesis prospectus on the German dramatist Frank Wedekind, I was told that he was "too controversial" to serve as a topic. One of the plays ended with Jack the Ripper killing a prostitute; that placed Wedekind off limits. Besides, my mentor advised me that the senior members of the department had another topic in mind for me. It seems that the Chairman many years earlier had made a translation of Edward FitzGerald's *Rubaiyat of Omar Khayyam* into German, and the department had been looking for someone in nineteenth- and twentieth-century Anglo-German Comparative Literature to provide critical praise for this translation. When I asked the Director of Graduate Studies why I would take on such a topic, he answered "Because you will be out of here in eighteen months instead of five years." I accepted the topic.

At around the same time, in 1960, Jack Kennedy came to Ann Arbor and galvanized the campus with his Peace Corps address. In that year, Tom Hayden drafted the Port Huron Doctrine of the Students for Democratic Action, and the SDS was born. All of this in a town where the one black faculty member in Arts and Sciences, Caesar Blake, could not get his hair cut. He had to travel to Ypsilanti to find a barber. When the Free Speech Movement began in Berkeley in 1964, Ann Arbor was also ready to blow up.

In 1962, I had already come to the conclusion that big research universities were not for me. The primacy of research did not interest me. I applied to twenty-one New England liberal arts colleges and small universities. The job market in American higher education was expanding; this was perhaps the only time when there was a genuine shortage of college faculty. With the SUNY and California systems growing at an astonishing pace, there seemed to be four jobs for everyone looking for a position. But, Robyn and I wanted New England, something small without the pressure of "publish or perish," and close to our parents in the New York City area. Mount Holyoke College in Massachusetts was the first to offer me an Assistant Professorship, at $5,200, and I accepted without a visit to the campus. Within a year, we were ready to leave. South Hadley Center proved to be too small, by the second cocktail party we had met every faculty member, and our closest friend in the Classics Department had been told that he was being denied tenure because he had published too much, while teaching four courses each semester. In the meantime, my research on the controversial German dramatist Frank Wedekind continued, and my interest in the scholarly life, to my surprise, took hold. I wanted to write the first English-language monograph of Wedekind, and that research project got underway at Mount Holyoke. Early in 1963, I received a letter from Tufts University. They had not had a position available a year earlier, but now they did, and was I interested in coming. We were ready for Medford and Boston. In 1964, I became an Assistant Professor of German at Tufts, at the same salary that I had earned at Mount Holyoke in the second year: $5,600. Because I had published four articles, my teaching load was reduced to three courses per semester.

It did not take long to realize that Boston was an academic paradise. We lived on campus, had the last of our three children, shared a backyard with six other Tufts families and twenty-three children under the age of four, and thoroughly enjoyed ourselves. There was a strong commitment to teaching, but no one objected to scholarship, and there were a few recent arrivals in Economics and English who really advocated a breakout for Tufts as a university. The days of Tufts College, they said, were over. It was time to move forward.

My father had always said: Man plans, and God laughs. We thought we might be at Tufts for a few years. In 1966, the man who hired me in the German Department left for the University of Virginia. The Dean of the Faculty had three members of the department over age sixty whom he wanted to retire, and the remainder of my colleagues were also looking to leave. With little choice, Dean Charles Stearns appointed me Chairman of the Department of German, placed his hands on my head, and promoted me to Associate Professor with tenure. I had no peer review, no outside review, no review of any kind, but now I was suddenly a tenured member of the faculty and a departmental chair, at a time when departmental chairs were barons who presided and ruled. Just to make things more interesting, the Russian program was moved from Romance Languages, and I became Chairman of the Department of German and Russian.

For the next fifteen years, I did what I thought chairs were supposed to do: build empires. However, it was a rarity to do this in the field of foreign languages and literatures, especially in second-tier departments such as German and Russian. But, things were happening in the geo-political context that would have an influence on opportunities. We were still riding the Sputnik crest in Russian, then we added Chinese and Japanese, Hebrew and Arabic. After the publication of the Wedekind monograph, I began developing an interest in Yiddish culture, the world of my parents, and my next two books explored the emergence of Yiddish literature in Eastern Europe and the United States.

In 1980, four years after Jean Mayer assumed the presidency of Tufts, he was seeking a new provost to assume the position of chief academic officer of the University. Several of my colleagues suggested that I apply. After reading the job description, I demurred. What did I know about health sciences? The responsibilities were university-wide, involving supervision of the health sciences campuses in Boston and Grafton, where the Veterinary School was located. This was not for me.

In 1981, the search for a provost was re-opened, and the responsibilities had been divided. The administration would recruit for a Vice President for Health Sciences as well as a provost, whose main responsibilities would be for the Medford campus. I became a candidate for the modified provost's position, and President Mayer selected me. I began what I thought might be a two- or three-year term in this position. Given my experience in university-wide administration, I had no certainty of a long tenure. At least I would not have to worry about the medical, dental, or veterinary schools. On July 1, 1981, with Robert Levy, M.D., taking hold as Vice President for Health Sciences, I began my oversight of the Medford campus, with other university-wide responsibilities as yet not defined.

Bob Levy lasted eighteen months. After his resignation and departure for Columbia University, the three deans of the health sciences schools went to President Mayer and begged him not to appoint another Vice President for Health Sciences. "We'll take our chances with the Yiddish teacher," said Frank Loew, Dean of the School of Veterinary Medicine. The reasons for Bob Levy's failure as Vice President for Health Sciences were complex, but suddenly I found myself the consensus candidate to take charge of all the schools of Tufts University. For the next twenty years, I was responsible for the academic integrity of a complex small university with seven schools, more than eight thousand students, a thousand faculty members, and a budget that reached over $400 million. In that time, Tufts hired hundreds of faculty, experienced three different presidents, and transformed itself.

My announcement in September 2001 informed the Tufts community that I would step down as Provost at the end of the academic year. Twenty-one years made me the longest-serving provost at any American university. In August 2002, I was appointed the Alice and Nathan Gantcher University Professor, in my thirty-eighth year as a faculty member at Tufts.

Looking back at my immigrant parents, the life that we led, and our collective hopes and aspirations, I ask myself: Was any of this predictable or foreseen?

As best as I can see it, my father was right: Man plans, and God laughs. What I certainly did not realize was that, as I entered the profession, American higher education stood on the brink of enormous change.

An Entrepreneurial University

TUFTS AND THE NEW
AMERICAN UNIVERSITY

1

THE SHARED CULTURE

On December 29, 1962, Carl Bridenbaugh, University Professor at Brown University and outgoing President of the American Historical Association, gave his presidential address at the Association's annual meeting at the Conrad Hilton Hotel in Chicago:

> Here in Chicago, this evening, I propose a causerie, a sharing with friends and colleagues some of my thoughts about history and its possible future in a kind of Lakeside chat. I ask your permission to speak out loud. Or, perhaps, it is my duty as your President to report on the state of the profession and to suggest tentatively some measures to be taken for the benefit of ourselves and our posterity.[1]

Bridenbaugh then launched into a characterization of the academic environment in his discipline that he described as "high tragedy." He claimed that the state of affairs was not quite "the crumbling of a civilization round and about me," but what Professor Bridenbaugh goes on to describe in terms of a deeply sad nostalgia is the end of his world.

What world? Bridenbaugh tells us: "Today we must face the discouraging prospect that we all, teachers and pupils alike, have lost much of what the earlier generation possessed, the priceless asset of a shared culture."

As the 1960s dawned, this distinguished American historian looked back on a tradition in American higher education that was shaped in the countryside, villages, and small towns of colonial America and the United States. This was Protestant America, not without its struggles and contentiousness, but still possessing a common thread. The divisiveness stemmed from the indi-

1. Carl Bridenbaugh, "The Great Mutation," *American Historical Review* 68 (1963): 315–31.

TWO BARBARIANS AND A PROFESSOR OF BARBARIAN STUDIES

vidual denominations' desire for separation from each other, which led them to establish their own educational institutions under the flag of their religious preference. Harvard, Princeton, Yale, William and Mary, and the earliest post-secondary schools were dedicated to the moral and religious education of the clergy and parishioners. Brown was for the Baptists, Princeton for the Evangelical Presbyterians, later the Wesleyans were for the Methodists, and when Tufts was founded in 1852, the Universalist Church felt that it had its flagship institution, as well. As long as this remained a nation of immigrants, mostly from Europe and overwhelmingly Protestant, there would remain a common sense of purpose and destiny across the higher educational establishment. Within one generation, the German-speaking students at Moravian and those from Germantown who attended the University of Pennsylvania were answering questions in English. By the time the huge wave of Irish Catholics arrived in the 1840s, not much religious difference could be seen among the colleges. The appearance of large numbers of Catholics looking for higher education was enough to draw the wagons in a circle. The Catholic Church, for its part, preferred to keep its students to itself, and the founding of Notre Dame University (1842), Holy Cross (1843), and Boston College (1863) followed the Protestant model of separation whenever possible.

The genuine secularization and democratization of higher education in America came with the Morrill Act of 1862 that created the great public university system in this country. The Vermont Senator's legislation led to open doors for women as well as for secular and observant students who simply did not want any compulsory religious activities to mess around with their education. (Nonetheless, the American instinct for keeping distance between groups found the perfect device at the state universities: the fraternity system, which flourished because it still could discriminate.) The land grant idea even spread to the Afro-American population in the United States. Between 1862 and 1900, especially in the wake of the "separate but equal" doctrine validated by the Supreme Court in *Plessy v. Ferguson* in 1896, dozens of institutions were created that we now call "historically black," among them Tuskegee University, Alabama A&M, Delaware State, and Tennessee State universities.

In all of this frenzy of post-secondary growth in the United States, Professor Bridenbaugh's "shared culture" remained intact. American higher education was firmly in the hands of teachers and scholars trained in a common cause and common vision. For the most part, this vision was in the hands of Anglo-Saxons and Protestants, had a moral and ethical foundation, appreciated the historical destiny of the nation, and wrote histories that reflected this destiny. The recognition that a "native" American literary tradition also was taking root led to the acceptance of American literature as a distinct and unique American experience. Generations of scholars could feel secure.

THE OCTOPUS

The first hint of a new trouble came, as might be expected, from abroad. The German university model took hold with the establishment of Johns Hopkins University in 1876 and of a new benchmark degree that would transform American higher education and eventually lead to Bridenbaugh's malaise: the Ph.D. research degree. In an effort to emulate the German research universities, American scientists who were also leaders in education were eager to establish the first American research universities. Daniel Coit Gilman at Johns Hopkins, G. Stanley Hall at Clark University, and Charles W. Eliot at Harvard—all German-trained— were the enthusiastic champions of the new degree and its potential. By the turn of the century, many American academicians were troubled by what this new research agenda was creating. In a 1903 article, Harvard's William James deplored "the increasing hold of the Ph.D. Octopus upon American life."[2] Jacques Barzun repeated James' warning in 1945 and used the same metaphor: "The octopus has the young teacher in its grip and does not let him go."[3] Barzun was reflecting upon the impact that this degree, originally intended for the physical and biological sciences, was having on the fields of history and literature. Once the social "sciences" saw the added prestige and power given to their colleagues in the "hard" sciences, they rushed to emulate. It was only a matter of time before the humanities would look for some kind of methodological rigor to give them the same credentialing. (Bridenbaugh in his farewell address: "The finest historians will not be those who succumb to the dehumanizing methods of social sciences, whatever their uses and values, which I hasten to acknowledge. Nor will the historian worship at the shrine of that Bitch-goddess, QUANTIFICATION"(Bridenbaugh's emphasis).[4]

The research university was here to stay and was destined to play an increasingly important role in American society. Again, we learned from the Germans, who for the first time during World War I, combined the university, the state, and industry at the service of conflict. When Professor Fritz Haber won the 1918 Nobel Prize in Chemistry for research that had been the foundation of his war-related work on poison gas, it provided the model for the successful building of an atomic weapon in World War II. First in the fieldhouse at the University of Chicago, then on the desert of New Mexico, American academic scientists collaborated with industry and the government. A Tufts graduate, Vannevar Bush, fully understood the implications and the promise. He was the father of big science at the service of the state. His advocacy of federally funded science research represented the culmination of the new degree's prestige. It provided the environment for grantsmanship, first in the sciences, later in the social sciences and humanities, which further changed the landscape of higher education and added to Professor Bridenbaugh's unhappiness.

THE GREAT MUTATION

Of all the changes that he had been observing and that, from his perch, boded ill for the future of the profession, none disturbed Bridenbaugh more

2. Quoted in Theodore Ziolkowski, "The Ph.D. Squid," *The American Scholar* 59, (Spring 1990): 178.
3. Ibid.
4. Bridenbaugh, "Great Mutation," 326.

than the new faces that no longer shared the same culture or environment with his generation. His deep melancholy about "the urban-bred scholars of today" scarcely masked his discomfort with the backgrounds of the graduate students and newly minted Ph.D.s who in the early 1960s were pouring onto American campuses. The ethnic landscape was changing.

The changes were inevitable. The immigration that had been overwhelmingly Protestant came to an end in the 1840s, as the Irish Catholics came to America, but this population had little effect on the prospective pool of colleagues. Those Catholics who sought a career in higher education could see the handwriting; they gravitated naturally to those Catholic institutions where they would be welcomed.[5] All through the nineteenth century, the Catholic and Protestant immigrants came from literally dozens of predominantly European countries, while California saw an influx of Japanese farmers and Chinese coolie labor, to build the great western railroads.

But, nothing had prepared the campuses for the flood of immigrants who swept into the United States from the early 1880s and did not subside until the passage of the first national restrictive immigration laws in the early 1920s. From Southern Italy and Sicily came more than two million impoverished Italian immigrants, mostly peasant farmers. At almost the exact same moment in American immigrant history, an enlightened Russian Czar, Alexander II, was assassinated and replaced by the reactionary Alexander III, whose anti-Semitic Laws of 1881 made it clear to the East European Jews that they had no future in Czarist Russia. The only message they heard now was: Get out. Between 1881 and 1917, the Jewish population of the United States increased from 280,000 (0.6 percent) to 3,389,000 (3.5 percent). They left the filthy *shtetls,* the tiny villages and towns where they had been forced by the May Laws, they left the crowded cities, where most had been living illegally, they came with their children and their rags. Some could read, many were illiterate, and they came to America. Both the Italians and the Jews settled in the ghetto neighborhoods of the American cities that had been abandoned only recently by the Irish and other immigrant groups before them. A *New York Times* reporter described the Jewish Lower East Side of New York City in 1893:

> This neighborhood, peopled almost entirely by the people who claim to have been driven from Poland and Russia, is the eyesore of New York and perhaps the filthiest place on the western continent. It is impossible for a

5. See Peter Novick, *That Noble Dream* (New York: Cambridge University Press, 1988), 69n.

Christian to live there because he will be driven out, either by blows or the dirt and stench. Cleanliness is an unknown quantity to these people. They cannot be lifted up to a higher plane because they do not want to be.[6]

Before the century had turned, the children of these immigrants were pouring into American colleges and universities, scarcely one generation removed from the East European and American ghettos. They were alien in religion, culture, and custom to most other Americans. They also hungered for education. It was no wonder that Tufts President Elmer Hewitt Capen, when asked by the editor of *The American Hebrew* newspaper in 1890 to comment on "standards of conduct" of the few Jewish students he had known, answered: "The social characteristics of the Jews are peculiar. The subtle thing which we call manners, among them differs from the manners of Americans generally."[7]

President Capen's observations generally reflected the attitude of the vast majority of American educators toward all the aspiring immigrant groups who were trying to gain access to the elite institutions of learning. One of the few enlightened presidents was Woodrow Wilson of Princeton, who tried to abolish the eating clubs and to otherwise democratize his campus.[8] He failed, opposed by alumni, faculty, and trustees. During the academic year 1918–1919, when the percentage of Jewish students at Columbia was 21.2, at Tufts 18.9, at University of Chicago 18.5, and at Harvard 10.0, Princeton had a Jewish population of 2.6 percent.[9]

It would only be a question of one or at most two generations before these graduates of America's most distinguished undergraduate colleges would be knocking at the doors of the graduate schools and soon thereafter seeking academic positions in our universities. Young scholars, who, as Peter Novick characterizes them, "were all only one generation removed from the Eastern European *shtetl.*"[10]

By the time Professor Bridenbaugh was stepping down as President of the

6. Quoted from Allen Schoener, ed., *Portal to America: The Lower East Side, 1870 - 1925* (New York: Holt Rinehart, 1967), 58.

7. Stephen Steinberg, *The Academic Melting Pot: Catholics and Jews in American Higher Education* (New Brunswick, N.J., Transaction Books, 1974), 18.

8. See Marcia Graham Synnott, *The Half-Opened Door* (Westport, Conn., Greenwood Press, 1979), xi.

9. Ibid, Table 1.1, 16.

10. Novick, *That Noble Dream,* 341.

American Historical Association in 1962, the first generation of children of Eastern and Southern European immigrants had battered their way into the two most tradition-bound departments: History, particularly where the Americanists were holed up; and English and American literature. Nothing could stop this assault. To be sure, there were temporary victories for the traditionalists and champions of Anglo-Saxon hegemony. When two Italian anarchists were arrested and accused in 1920 of killing a paymaster in Braintree, Massachusetts, the Restrictive Immigration League finally got the weapon it needed to limit immigration. In 1922, President Abbott Lowell of Harvard was able to establish a quota system limiting the number of Jewish students accepted. Within weeks, Yale and other institutions followed.[11] Dean Frank G. Wren of Tufts reflected the prevailing attitude at a meeting of the Association of New England Deans held at Princeton in 1918, while the war was raging in Europe: "I find that more and more the foreign element is creeping in and now, because of the enlistments, the American boys are getting less and less . . . How can we get the boys of American parentage to come to college?"[12] Dean Sills of Bowdoin, at that time Acting President and soon to be appointed President, commented: "We do not like to have boys of Jewish parentage." The quotas lasted for about forty years, but enough of these students who did not come from "American parents" came to the universities and eventually became Professor Bridenbaugh's colleagues. These were "the urban-bred scholars" he felt were threatening the future of the academic Eden as he had come to know it. It made no difference if they were observant Jews or converts: They thought differently and would produce a kind of scholarship that would offend some. Susanne Klingenstein notes: "Even though the children and grandchildren of immigrant rabbis or ordinary observant workingmen would no longer keep the Sabbath or accept the dietary laws, their cultural interests and mode of perception would remain shaped to some extent by their ancestors' intellectual grammar."[13]

It was this intellectual grammar that eventually contributed to the revolution in thought and behavior on the college campuses of this country in the second half of the twentieth century.

11. See Daniel Oren, *Joining the Club: The History of Jews and Yale* (New Haven: Yale University Press, 1985).

12. Quoted in Synnott, *The Half-Opened Door*, 15. The following quotations are also from Synnott.

13. Susanne Klingenstein, *Jews in the American Academy, 1900–1940* (New Haven: Yale University Press, 1991), 136.

What was Tufts like in the early 1960s? When Professor Bridenbaugh was lamenting the state of his discipline, he was also commenting on the condition of American higher education, the quest for grants, the new standards of excellence, the retreat from teaching. Much depends on perspective. Historian Richard Freeland, in his history of Boston's universities, offers the following description:

> At Tufts, the problems were rooted in the difficulty of transforming an old, entrenched organization with limited resources. [President] Wessell, like [former President] Carmichael before him, could talk about scholarship, but altering the reality of a teaching-oriented faculty was another matter, especially given the policy of nonexpansion. In 1959 an accreditation team noted that less than half the faculty of Arts and Sciences possessed a doctorate and more than a quarter had only a bachelor's degree. Both numbers compared poorly with the universities Wessell hoped to emulate.[14]

What Freeland is describing was an institution stuck in its past, one not yet participating in the extraordinary changes that had begun sweeping over higher education. William James's research octopus had not yet gripped the faculty on the Hill in Medford, and Tufts lacked the financial resources as well as the will to bring about the changes necessary to compete. Psychologist Leonard Mead, appointed Director of Research, made it clear that research at Tufts "was strictly voluntary, and only an important adjunct to the primary educational mission of the College."

In most respects, Tufts maintained the common and shared culture that Bridenbaugh cherished, particularly in those departments charged with keeping the flame of tradition lit. The History Department did not hire its first non-Protestant until 1961, when the Greek Orthodox George Marcopoulos joined the faculty as a pre-doctoral Instructor. The first Jewish faculty member in history was Howard Solomon, who came to Tufts in 1971. There was none in American history until 1980.

The English Department had seen no need to diversify its faculty. The tradition of acquiring talent from the banks of the Charles River continued, and no one noticed any change when in 1954 Sylvan Barnet joined the Depart-

---

14. Richard M. Freeland, *Academia's Golden Age: Universities in Massachusetts, 1945 - 1970* (New York: Oxford University Press, 1992).

ment. What Professor Harold Blanchard, the Chairman, did not know was that Barnet was Jewish, even if his Ph.D., like *all* the Ph.D.s in the Tufts English Department, was from Harvard. Kenneth Myrick, Blanchard's successor, hired the first non-Harvard Ph.D.s in the English Department in 1961: Bernard McCabe from Stanford and Michael Fixler from the University of Chicago. McCabe was the first Catholic; Fixler the first overtly Jewish faculty member in the English Department. His father was a Hassidic rabbi, and Fixler brought the new intellectual grammar to East Hall. McCabe, who had a law degree in addition to his Ph.D., also had a brother who was a Black Friar monk engaged in a confrontation with the Church in Rome. But, it was not until the mid-1960s that the Tufts faculty began reflecting the changes that had come to other campuses somewhat earlier. When I arrived in the German Department in 1964, none of us were prepared for the revolution that awaited us.

PRESIDENTS, BOARDS, AND ACADEMIC FREEDOM

Presidents and boards of trustees mirrored the development of the American colleges and universities from their denominational roots. First clergymen, then businessmen, bankers, and lawyers of similar background made up the president's advisory council from the earliest times. When historian Charles A. Beard resigned from Columbia University to protest President Nicholas Murray Butler's efforts to silence any criticism of American involvement in World War I, he described in his letter of resignation the commonplace situation found on most campuses: "Having observed closely the inner life of Columbia for many years, I have been driven to the conclusion that the university is really under the control of a small and active group of trustees who have no standing in the world of education. . . ."[15] President Butler made his position very clear at the June 6, 1917, Commencement. After extolling Columbia's capacity to tolerate dissident opinions and the openness of the academic community, he said our entry into the war had changed everything: "What had been tolerated before becomes intolerable now. What had been wrongheadedness was now sedition. What had been folly was now treason."[16]

The Columbia situation represented the culmination of events over the

15. Richard Hofstadter and Walter P. Metzger, *The Development of Academic Freedom in the United States* (New York: Columbia University Press, 1955), 502.
16. Ibid., 499.

past decade where faculty had been first admonished, then disciplined, and finally fired for stating positions on issues that trustees or presidents found offensive. Already by 1915, the American Association of University Professors (AAUP) had established its organizational framework to seek protection and some measure of job security for faculty. Even the most distinguished teachers and scholars found themselves with furniture and books piled on the sidewalks, if they gave offense to trustee or president. The Columbia of Nicholas Murray Butler may have been the most egregious example, but there were plenty more. In the 1930s, that faculty had to sign loyalty oaths. Perhaps it was the outbreak of the next European war that prompted the AAUP to seek some sort of guarantee of protection for the faculty, and the result was the "1940 Statement of Principles on Academic Freedom and Tenure." At Tufts, the trustees first began discussing these principles in 1940, but it was not until 1958 that tenure as it has come to be understood, with formal probationary periods, became a fact of life. Most people believe that tenure has been with us forever. Actually, the institution has been with us for scarcely fifty years. The question to be discussed in subsequent chapters is whether it will survive the next fifty years.

Not all college or university presidents were cut from the mould of Nicholas Murray Butler. Most institutions of the first half of the twentieth century were led by men who enjoyed a strong collegiality with their fellow faculty members. Most came from the faculty, understood the culture, and served for many years. Most New England colleges and universities were led by people such as Joshua Lawrence Chamberlain, who had been a Professor of Rhetoric at Bowdoin College before enlisting in the Federal Army during the Civil War, who served as President from 1871 to 1883, and who taught every course in the curriculum except mathematics. These presidents were models of civility, for the most part, and they served a community of like-minded colleagues and fellow teachers. There was a strong sense of identity; everyone was alike, and an unchanging permanence that stretched from the nineteenth into the twentieth century suggested that this world would remain constant.

But, forces were at work. This generally idyllic world began seeing signs of destabilization as the United States entered World War I. World War II, the G.I. Bill, the changed emphasis on research, and a generation of young men and women who wanted to be part of the institutions that had excluded them earlier eventually would change the face of American higher education, and Tufts, as well. The great paradox of our times on our campuses today is the relentless, yet futile search for a civility and a community that will never return, because the world in which that civility flourished is gone forever. It represented stability, permanence, community, and to a considerable extent, mediocrity. It was recognizable, comfortable, familiar, and intellectually limited. People liked each other. Students were deferential, faculty were respectful, administrators paternalistic. Everyone got along. It was soon going to change.

THE COMING OF JEAN MAYER
THE ACCIDENTAL PRESIDENT

2

THE DARK YEARS OF TRANSITION

In 1973, Tufts was in a grim mood. The image projected by Presidents Carmichael and Wessell of a solidly anchored institution of higher learning had only a limited basis in reality. The Carmichael and Wessell years, between 1938 and 1966, produced generally satisfied and happy alumni, who even today look back with great nostalgia, particularly on the undergraduate institution they loved. But, the consistent and common theme for Tufts was straitened resources that left the university, as one historian of Boston higher education stated it, with "unanswered financial problems."[1] While through the years the Tufts community itself had demonstrated a consistent level of contentment and willingness to accept, the outside academic world viewed Tufts in a different light. Commenting on the university that Carmichael inherited from President Cousens, historian Richard Freeland notes that "the campus included two unexceptional colleges of liberal arts (one male, one female), both enrolling chiefly middle-class, commuting students, an undergraduate engineering program rated one of the weakest in New England, two once-independent and still quite separate professional schools in Boston, for dentistry and medicine, the second of which had been placed on probation by the American Medical Association in 1935, and the new Fletcher School of Law and Diplomacy . . . All these units were beset by financial problems."[2] A Divinity School was staggering toward extinction. By the time he left in 1952, Carmichael had been unable to bring about any appreciable change. He had increased enrollment to pay the bills, had raised no money at a time when other institutions were embarking on significant de-

1. Richard M. Freeland, *Academia's Golden Age: Universities in Massachusetts, 1945 - 1970* (New York: Oxford University Press, 1992), 206.
2. Ibid., 180.

velopment campaigns, and the tone of his final report to the trustees "was more apprehensive than celebratory."[3] He frankly stated that "the future usefulness of Tufts" will depend on whether it can solve its continuing financial problems. Carmichael had left Tufts with an endowment of $11 million. In 1928, the Tufts endowment had been $9.5 million. In the period between Cousens and Carmichael, the Tufts Trustees were overseeing the shrinking of Tufts resources at a time when fundraising was just beginning to take on serious dimensions in American higher education, and particularly in the Boston area.[4]

The Trustees did not want Carmichael to resign, but he had had enough. The Board of Trustees took the road of least resistance and handed the reins to someone very much like him, a former protégé from the University of Rochester, like Carmichael a psychologist. Nils Wessell, who had served in a variety of dean's capacities at Tufts, was for the Trustees a very safe bet. It is little wonder that Russell Miller stated in the official university history that "the presidential transition could not have proceeded more smoothly," nor is it surprising that in his inaugural address, President Wessell proclaimed his commitment to Carmichael's vision. He was warmly welcomed by the community.

President Wessell, before he resigned in 1966, had accomplished all he could, given the fact that there seemed to be a commitment on the part of the Trustees *not* to raise money. Tufts kept its sights low, the endowment continued to shrink in comparison to institutions to which it wished to compare itself. In an effort to enhance reputation, Wessell championed the name change from Tufts College to Tufts University in 1955, and in doing so oversaw the growth in Ph.D. programs to the point where Tufts offered in 1966 twenty-two different doctoral degrees with little or no status in the academic community. Our library and research resources were more in keeping with the smaller undergraduate colleges in New England. In order to produce revenue, President Wessell's only recourse was to increase enrollment. Fac-

3. Ibid., 185.

4. See Morton Keller and Phyllis Keller, *Making Harvard Modern* (Boston: Oxford University Press, 2001), 179–82. Harvard University set the pace for the rest of America as well as Boston. Between 1954 and 1969, Harvard established more endowed chairs than in all of its previous history. In the wake of this first major successful fundraising campaign at Harvard in the 1950s, 134 other colleges and universities started planned fundraising activities. Tufts was not one of them. College endowments are listed in *The World Almanac Book of Facts, 1929* (American Heritage Press, 1971), 390.

ulty salaries were still embarrassingly low, but few complained. In the 1959 self-study funded by the Carnegie Foundation, the report described a high level of faculty contentment. With few demands made on them, faculty members stayed on at Tufts for a period longer than one generally encountered in comparable institutions. Someone in the report managed to describe what he saw as "a happy mediocrity."[5]

No one wanted President Wessell to leave. He was enormously popular with the faculty and student body, who somehow managed not to notice how impoverished Tufts was. But, like Carmichael before him, Wessell had had enough. He had done everything he could to change the prevailing culture of the institution. He had allowed the creation of doctoral programs, in the hope of raising the status of Tufts, but there were no resources. He was fifty-two years old and had another career ahead of him.

Burton Hallowell came from Wesleyan University, where he had been a Professor of Economics and later Vice President for Administration and Finance. He arrived in 1967 and fell into a buzz saw. Within a matter of days, he discovered that Wessell had left him with a half-million-dollar deficit that was to grow into $1.5 million in two years. Hallowell did heroic work to keep this deficit under control. He was an able financial manager. But the college world was about to come crashing down on his head in the first few years of his presidency. It was the time of the great turmoil, and the Hallowell administration was rocked from its foundations. One will never know if Burt Hallowell would have reversed the presidential and trustee inertia when it came to raising money. Historically, the Tufts Board of Trustees hired presidents who did not want to ask for money, apparently because the Board did not want to give any. The idea of Board of Trustee leadership in fundraising was an alien concept to the Tufts community. Hallowell suffered through an indifferent stock market with an endowment that was going nowhere, and Tufts was falling further and further behind those elite institutions with which it wished to be compared. For their part, these New England colleges and universities looked upon Tufts as a poor relative. When the Consortium on Financing Higher Education (COFHE) was founded in 1974, Tufts was not invited to join, even though the earliest membership included every other New England college and university with which we had clear associations. The assumption could only be that Tufts had little to contribute. Remarkably, we were still able to attract good students, who were clearly stronger

5. Quoted in Freeland, *Academia's Golden Age*, 220.

than the institution. Tufts had gone from a college to a university without adding anything but graduate programs without resources behind them.

Hallowell, seeking advice on how Tufts might move out of the straitjacket of impoverishment, established two committees to examine the undergraduate educational experience and the general state of the university. In 1973, the University Steering Committee issued its report, *Tufts: The Total University in Changing Times*. The faculty, administrators, and trustee members had little vision to offer. The only models of college presidents that they could refer to were Carmichael, Wessell, and Hallowell. The 130-page document only confirmed what Richard Freeland stated in his analysis of Tufts of the early 1970s: Tufts, as an academic institution, might not be viable.[6] Every conceivable means of raising money was considered, from year-round operation to increased enrollment. As for fundraising, the sights were set so low that the amount suggested as a campaign goal would prove inadequate and have no appreciable impact. The New York consulting firm of Marts & Lundy was brought in to assess the fundraising potential and candidly told the committee that Tufts simply could not raise dollars sufficient for its needs. There were no wealthy alumni, and the rest of the alumni had never been asked and probably would not give. After describing the almost numbing list of needs in all schools, the failure to raise resources over the previous forty years, and the dismal prospects for raising money in the future, the report concluded that "the next five years, with all their problems, will be less difficult than the five or ten to follow."[7] Here was a snapshot of frightening futility projected through the year 1988. The in-your-face spirit of confrontation that marked the 1970s had eroded even the collegiality that had been a hallmark of Wessell's presidency. It was a dispirited institution with little sense of hope for the future. Burt Hallowell, a very decent human being who inherited financial troubles as well as a generation about to explode, never had a chance. When he announced his resignation in 1975, he did so with a sense of relief. He was just sixty years old, and like his predecessor, went on to another career.

Where was the university to turn next for leadership? Would this Board of Trustees, so historically incapable of producing the financial resources

6. See Freeland's chapter, "Evolution of the College-centered University: Tufts and Brandeis, 1945–1970."

7. *Tufts: The Total University in Changing Times*, a Report to the President by the University Steering Committee, January 1973, 13.

needed to move Tufts forward and unwilling to commit with its own resources, once again seek a president who could not imagine the magnitude of need for this starving university? Tufts in 1975 was living from hand to mouth, from payroll to payroll. The next president, looking at this Steering Committee report, could either revert to the timidity of his predecessors and set sights low enough so as not to strain the woeful development efforts of the past; or he could go where others had never gone in the history of the university.

It was time to change, or to leave. In the summer of 1975, my wife and I agreed that it might be time to look around for another university position. I had been at Tufts for eleven pleasant years, but there seemed to be little sense of where the institution was going.

Around this time, I had been approached by Dartmouth College as a possible Chair for the Department of German. But Boston had "ruined" us. After a weekend in Hanover, we left New Hampshire at a speed that violated every traffic law. We needed the city, and Boston was still the best choice.

THE SHOCK TO THE SYSTEM

In the year 2002, when I was about to step down as Provost of Tufts after twenty-one years, the daily student newspaper asked me in an interview if I could name the three most important events that occurred during my nearly forty years at Tufts. After a brief pause I gave them my list.

The first occurred in 1976, when Johns Hopkins Provost Harry Woolf, after having gone through the entire search process and having been offered the presidency of Tufts, eight days later declined to accept. No one could possibly have known the significance of his decision *not* to assume the presidency of Tufts. Next, a trustee delegation approached Jean Mayer, who had been rejected as a candidate, first in 1967 when Burt Hallowell was chosen, and then again in 1976 when the trustees selected Woolf. Now, weeks later, they had to go with hat in hand, embarrassed because the student press had already announced that Woolf had been the first choice. A trustee delegation met with Mayer at the Harvard Club in downtown Boston to ask him if he would accept the presidency. After a moment's pause, Mayer leaped from his chair and in his best French-American accent, proclaimed, "I'll do it!" In hindsight, that was the second most significant event in my time at Tufts.

The third most important event occurred three years later, during President Mayer's first evaluation, after months of turmoil, when the Trustees did not fire him, even after a vote reported to be eleven in favor of retaining, ten opposed, and eight abstentions. (I have three versions of the process in 1979 to re-appoint Mayer. He would laugh, years later, when he told me that the vote was 11 to 10, with eight abstentions. Another trustee told me that the vote was 14 to 13 with five abstentions. A third said that when a straw vote recorded seventeen "no" votes, he stopped counting and recalled that no final vote was ever taken. Mayer was re-appointed.) I hope that the chronicle of the following pages will help explain the selections I made of the most significant events in my time at Tufts.

Nothing in the previous 124 years of Tufts history could have prepared the university for the coming of Jean Mayer. He officially assumed the presidency on July 1, 1976, five years before I joined his administration as Provost. That half-decade was, arguably, the most tempestuous, chaotic, adventurous, and exciting period in the history of Tufts University. At the center of the whirlwind was Jean Mayer, obsessed with a vision of personal triumph that he intended to transfer to this university. He was consumed by his own optimism and the certainty that he would eventually succeed in attaining anything that he wanted. In 1967, he had been passed over as a candidate for the presidency of Tufts in favor of Burt Hallowell. Nine years later, he was back again as a candidate, and was once again rejected in favor of Harry Woolf. Then, as if by an act of fate, Woolf withdrew, and the Board of Trustees turned to Jean Mayer, finally. He had attained his first goal: the presidency of a university in the Boston area that had a medical school. No one on the Board of Trustees suspected what he had in mind, and I doubt if any of them understood the complex personality who had assumed the leadership of this somewhat unassuming and under-funded small university in Boston. Within a very short period of time, they would learn.

It is no wonder that the risk-averse search committee would have passed over Mayer as their first choice. Nothing in Jean Mayer's background would suggest similarities to previous Tufts presidents. He was born in Paris on February 19, 1920. His father, André, who was forty-five when Jean was born, was a famous physiologist and had an early interest in nutrition. He was also a French patriot, served in World War I, and undoubtedly communicated his dislike of the Germans to his son, which he actively nurtured for the rest of his life. Mayer came to science from both of his parents. His mother had been a laboratory assistant to the eminent Professor, who married her. She was a practicing physiologist in her own right. As an undergraduate, Jean Mayer first studied history, and then went on to the Sorbonne. The Second World War interrupted the family's life and Jean's education after he had completed his undergraduate studies. The family left for America, but Mayer returned to Europe to fight against the Nazis with the Free French. He was commissioned as a second lieutenant in the field artillery before being captured by the Germans in 1940. Mayer shot a guard, escaped from the prison camp, and joined the French underground. He was on DeGaulle's staff, attained the rank of major, and received fourteen decorations, including the Croix de Guerre with two palms, the Resistance Medal, and the Legion of Honor. Here was considerably more glory and adventure than one encountered in your typical New England college president, perhaps with the exception of Bowdoin's Joshua Lawrence Chamberlain, who anchored the left flank at the Little Roundtop at Gettysburg with the Maine Twentieth Regiment and has gone down in heroic history.

Mayer had married before leaving for France, and returned after the war to complete his graduate work in the United States in physiological chemistry at Yale, where he received his Ph.D. He took some time off in Paris to acquire his D.Sc. in physiology from the Sorbonne. He joined the Harvard faculty in 1950, serving as Professor of Nutrition in the School of Public Health, Lecturer in the History of Science in the Arts and Sciences, member of the Center for Population Studies, and Master of Dudley House. When he came to Tufts, he had been on the Harvard faculty for twenty-seven years. In the eyes of his Harvard colleagues, he seemed cut from a different, more dashing and adventurous model. One called him affectionately "the Little Prince."

The idea of "academic entrepreneurship" was a notion very few people in higher education had heard of. Businessmen might have understood the psyche of the visionary who is absolutely convinced that he cannot fail and who fearlessly takes risks in the face of dangers he dismisses. These high-stakes gamblers, when they encounter rules and obstructions, will ignore them, because their optimism and certainty have convinced them that the vision they see is the only goal.[8] For Jean Mayer, Tufts was an instrument placed in his hand, at the right time and in the right place, and he knew he would triumph. To speak to those people who knew him best before he came to Tufts and to those who dealt most closely with him in those early years, one encounters a picture difficult to get in focus. He was alternately described as infinitely charming, witty, duplicitous, ambitious, brilliant, intellectual, opportunistic, generous, vain, slippery, loyal, possessed of an inner

8. See the article by Daniel Goleman, "The Psyche of the Entreprenuer," *New York Times Magazine*, February 2, 1986, 30ff.

standard of excellence, and charismatic. One of his earliest and long-lasting acolytes was Stanley Gershoff, now Dean Emeritus of the Tufts Friedman School of Nutritional Science and Policy. Gershoff had known Mayer for forty years, mostly at Harvard in the School of Public Health, where they both served as faculty members. He loved him, but understood Mayer's single-minded ambition:

> In our early years as friends, Jean and I usually ate lunch with some of our colleagues. Then during a short period, Jean disappeared from our group. Boston had a number of fine private dining clubs, to meet influential people. Jean joined a number of them. He told me later that for a while he ate alone, but then he started to become friends with the members.[9]

Although he had spent most of his adult life in higher education, Mayer was singularly unwilling to deal with any of the trappings of traditional academic decision making, either as a faculty member or as an administrator. He wanted autonomy. He was accustomed to it in the laboratories that he ran in the Public Health School at Harvard; and he did whatever was necessary to maintain control over the enterprise he now led. To be sure, he had a Board of Trustees of more than thirty members, but he felt accountable only to a small number on the Executive Committee, and he successfully orchestrated them, at least at the outset, before they came to realize that this was no ordinary American college president. He had no intention of being weighed down by search committees. Not two months after his assumption of the presidency, he wrote to Henry Kissinger:

> (August 27, 1976) Dear Henry:
> Rumor has it that at sometime in the not too distant future, and whatever the outcome of the national election, you may decide that you want to lay down the mantle of Secretary of State which you have worn so successfully in the past years. In this connection I am writing to ask you whether you might be at all interested in the Deanship of the Fletcher School of Law and Diplomacy. . . . I am sure that should you be interested we could arrive at an agreement on such matters as salary and administrative help.
> Sincerely yours,
> Jean Mayer[10]

9. In Stanley N. Gershoff, "Jean Mayer 1920–1993," *American Society for Nutritional Sciences Journal of Nutrition* 131 (2001): 1651–54.

10. Archives of Audrey Hale, Assistant Provost for Faculty Administration, 1981–1995.

This kind of independent action was typical of what became "the Mayer Style of Management," which was generally marked by disinformation or non-information. He was often the only person who knew what he was doing. There was only one chain in his chain of command: his own. Years later, when I assumed the Provost's position, I tried to educate myself about what a Provost under Jean Mayer should expect. The outgoing first Executive Vice President in Tufts' history, Michael Hoffman, who had lasted less than a year, told me in June of 1981 that Mayer had no sense of rational planning, management, or organization. On his personality, he said that Mayer could not say "no" to anyone, with the result that he often told several people "yes" to the same job or proposition. "What some perceive as lying is really his inability to deal systematically with people in management situations." Hoffman, who had come from a corporate business background and had been brought in by the Trustees to bring order to the administration, simply capitulated. But, in 1976, in those early months of the Mayer presidency, no one had quite understood what was about to happen. Both Tufts and American higher education would see something transforming.

SCHLOSSBERG & CASSIDY

No one could have predicted the impact on American higher education that the meeting of two relatively obscure young Washington staffers had when they first encountered Jean Mayer in 1969. Mayer, after nearly twenty years on the faculty of the School of Public Health at Harvard, had established a reputation as one of the leading figures in the field of nutrition and public policy. He had learned how to deal with the seats of power in the nation's capital, and it was no accident that Richard Nixon appointed this lifelong Democrat as Chairman of the first White House Conference on Food, Nutrition and Health. This "conference" was not intended to be a week-long academic event. Mayer expected that it would continue for years, in order to advance a serious agenda dealing with the nation's health and preventative medicine through nutritional policy, something all very new both for the vast United States Department of Agriculture bureaucracy and for a medical establishment with very little interest in prevention and nutrition.

The Conference was well organized, and Mayer met two smart, young staff members who had experience in the often unfathomable maze of USDA programs, considered by many the most confusing and complex department of government in all of Washington, D.C. One was a lawyer, a recent graduate of Cornell, named Gerald Cassidy; his associate was Kenneth Schlossberg. Mayer soon discovered that Schlossberg and Cassidy had remarkable insights and access; their knowledge of the workings of USDA was very impressive.

In 1976, when now-President Jean Mayer of Tufts University was contacted by the recently established consulting firm of Schlossberg & Cassidy Associates, he had already come to appreciate the brains and energy of these two entrepreneurs, who shared the same capacity to move things that Mayer had. Mayer had assumed the presidency of Tufts only days before the call from Gerry Cassidy.

They had a proposition. With their knowledge of the USDA appropriation process and their connections within the agency and with congressional delegations who they worked with on agricultural issues, the consultants could identify vast sums of money, and with congressional connections reaching as far down as their personal relationships with staff members on Senate and House committees, they could direct large grants of dollars to a specific institution—or university—via a line-item appropriation, directed by a congressman who would order USDA to make this targeted appropriation.

It did not take President Mayer more than a moment to realize what an opportunity lay before him and his new university, more resource-poor than any he had ever encountered. He saw that in an instant Tufts could move from the list of also-rans and have-nots in higher education. He believed that he had ideas that were indeed marketable, but that, given the way federal dollars for colleges and universities were appropriated and awarded, Tufts simply was not competitive. He knew that the rich only got richer, and the poor were left outside the gates. There was no way that Tufts University, even with the academic innovations he was planning, could compete successfully for peer-reviewed grants with the giants of the land grant universities or with the private research universities of the Ivy League. He knew how the game was played at Harvard and at the other resource-rich universities; and he knew that Tufts simply could not play on the same field, with the same rules. So, as he did so often, he decided to make up his own rules. When he saw the opportunity presented by these two young entrepreneurs, he jumped at it.

They had started a consulting firm based in Washington, D.C., one that would cater specifically to the needs of universities that normally did not have access to peer-reviewed grants. Would Tufts be their first client? Without hesitation, President Mayer said yes.

Mayer assumed the presidency of Tufts on July 1, 1976. He met with the Executive Committee of the Board for the first time that summer. At that meeting, he presented a proposal to contract with the consulting firm of

Schlossberg & Cassidy. The Executive Committee's approval proved to be their most important affirmation of the Mayer presidency during his entire term as Tufts' leader. Nothing played a larger role in the transformation of Tufts under Jean Mayer's stewardship. As usual, it was a high-risk venture; the Board had no idea what was at stake.

Mayer's association with Schlossberg & Cassidy represented the historic beginning of what was to become a huge academic industry and opened a conflict that continues to this day in higher education research. The journalistic establishment reduced and simplified the issue and identified it with one word that indeed had some agricultural flourish to it: *pork*. Jean Mayer was the first university president who saw the potential for the development of worthwhile programs that would never see the light of day if they had to compete through the established peer review process and traditional funding provided by pre-determined budget commitments. But, Mayer saw another path: With leverage from congressional delegations, the agencies could be told that the money *should be earmarked for a certain university*. Mayer realized that, regardless of agency reluctance, once the Congress placed its muscle behind a project and insisted that the project be funded, no agency would risk the wrath of an appropriations committee chair, or the committee staff, for that matter. Both Schlossberg and Cassidy were exceptionally wired into these critical committees.

Some years later, the partners had a falling out, and Schlossberg & Cassidy Associates became Gerald Cassidy Associates, the most influential lobbying firm for universities in the country. Gerry Cassidy and Jean Mayer were kindred spirits. For as long as Jean Mayer was President of Tufts University, Cassidy remained a grateful friend. The ultimate beneficiary was Tufts, but the debate concerning what are now described as academic earmarks will continue. The amount of money allocated by this method rose from less than $17 million in 1980 to nearly $1.7 billion in 2001, by which time these earmarked funds represented nearly 10 percent of all federal funding for academic research.

THE VETERINARY SCHOOL:
GESTATION, BIRTH, AND FRAGILE LIFE

The creation of a Veterinary School at Tufts University might be recorded as Jean Mayer's most risky roll of the dice. It was his greatest act of defiance, and he did it against all odds.

The Commonwealth of Massachusetts was not a player in the evolution of veterinary education in the United States. With the Morrill Land Grant Act of 1862, the training of veterinarians got underway. Cornell University started teaching veterinary students in 1868, but its veterinary school was not founded until the 1890s. Iowa State had established a formal school in 1879, the first of the land grant vet schools to grant a veterinary degree. There was even a school to train black veterinarians at Tuskegee Institute under the 1890s Act, which established the separate-but-equal land grant concept. Although Senator Morrill represented the state of Vermont, New England was not quick to embark on veterinary education under the legislation he advanced. In 1854, a for-profit veterinary school was started in Massachusetts, the Boston Veterinary Institute, and it lasted six years. Then, in 1882, Harvard University took the lead for New England and opened the doors of a veterinary school, when it became apparent that for the most part, the land grant schools would serve only students from their home states. But, Massachusetts would not provide any state assistance, and the Harvard Veterinary School failed to gain an endowment. Two other states—New York and Pennsylvania—made significant contributions to their veterinary schools. The University of Pennsylvania Veterinary School had received free land and buildings, as well as a $158,000 endowment. The New York State College of Veterinary Surgeons at Cornell generated a $178,000 endowment and received free land, buildings, and a $25,000 subsidy from the state under the Morrill Act. The Harvard Veterinary School found itself dependent on a resentful medical school for facilities and unable to solve its deficit problems. It closed in 1907 after graduating 128 veterinarians, having fallen victim to a plot of the medical school faculty to abolish the separate school and to incorporate it into the Medical School.[11] When we examine the early years of the Tufts School of Veterinary Medicine, we see that the same medical school toxicity almost brought down the barely breathing vet school.

The most productive effort to that time came with the establishment in 1938 of Middlesex University, founded in Waltham, Massachusetts, which had as its main academic focus a school of veterinary medicine. It graduated 243 veterinarians before closing in 1947.

Clearly, there did not seem to be much of a future for veterinary medicine in Massachusetts or New England when Jean Mayer assumed the presidency of Tufts in 1976. Earlier discussions at the New England Board of Higher Education seemed destined for the wastebasket, even though the agenda

11. See Calvin W. Schwabe, *Cattle, Priests, and Progress in Medicine* (Minneapolis: University of Minnesota Press, 1978), 180ff.

item kept appearing. On April 21, 1972, NEBHE Executive Director Alan D. Ferguson added the following to his memo for "the Advisory Committee on Veterinary Medicine": "The agenda for the meeting will include discussion regarding pending legislation to establish state study commissions, the present fund-raising campaign, a public relations campaign, and a proposal for a feasibility and cost study for the establishment of a regional college of veterinary medicine."[12] But neither legislation nor funding emerged out of these discussions or occasional overtures from Massachusetts's governors to university presidents in the Commonwealth, asking about interest in a veterinary school for the region.

You can imagine the stunned response to now-President Mayer's announcement at his inaugural address in the summer of 1976 that one of his highest priorities was to be the establishment of a veterinary school at Tufts. Not only that, but Mayer informed the audience that veterinary medicine was on the edge of a tremendous revolution in research. By the 1990s, he asserted, veterinarians will be active in the fields of nutrition, marine and equine medicine, toxicology, public health, and environmental science.

He also had another motive. As the Master of Harvard's Dudley House, Mayer had watched generations of Massachusetts students fail to gain admittance to the out-of-state veterinary schools. Ninety-eight percent of New England applicants to the nation's veterinary schools were rejected because of state residency requirements. Of the thirty-eight New England students who were admitted to twenty-two veterinary schools, twenty-six were subsidized by Massachusetts at an annual cost of $221,000.

This was classic Jean Mayer. He had come to a university that had a history of conservative, cautious management, poor in resources, with no particular reputation for creative or innovative research, and he announced to the world that the institution was about to embark on a dramatically new academic adventure that had had a history of failure in New England; furthermore, he assured the listening audience that the journey was without peril, that the veterinary school would be a cooperative venture, with start-up and operating costs funded jointly by the six New England states. There would be no problem with the land, either. President Mayer was aware that the 1,100 acres of the Grafton State Hospital grounds near Worcester had been set

12. The meeting on May 10 was also attended by two representatives from New Jersey who wanted to be involved in any discussions regarding the development of a New England regional veterinary school.

aside by Governor Frank Sargent for some appropriate use. Sargent, who was one of the state officials advocating a regional veterinary school, made certain that the land would remain available after he announced the closing of the hospital and its activities in January of 1972.

Soon after his inaugural speech, the entrepreneurial optimist began rolling, while hypnotizing a Board of Trustees not really accustomed to such activities from a Tufts president. By August of 1976, not two months after taking office, Mayer had gotten Schlossberg & Cassidy signed to a contract, and they were actively working through the corridors of Congress, looking for earmark opportunities. The President also had found an ally on campus. During the interview process for the presidency Mayer had met a faculty member and Associate Dean of the Dental School, Thomas Murnane, and there was a chemical reaction that lasted for as long as Mayer was President of Tufts. Dr. Murnane had been a Tufts undergraduate before attending the Dental School and also acquiring a Ph.D. from Tufts in Basic Sciences. His entire academic life had been spent at Tufts, waiting for someone to come along who could inspire him. Tom Murnane possessed many of the same characteristics of optimism, guile, and charm that gave the Tufts President his unique persona. Together, they presented the Tufts community with an energy package seldom seen and rarely trusted. They moved with the speed of a whirlwind, or as others might say with less charity, a cobra. Once he became President, Mayer sent Murnane to the governors of the New England states with the plans for a regional veterinary school. At first, there was hesitant but modest commitment. The New England Governors Conference contributed two separate $100,000 planning grants. However, soon it became apparent that the New England states, as they had often in the past, would walk away from regional cooperation. Even though this cooperation had been the cornerstone of Mayer's pitch to his Board of Trustees, the states' abandonment did not deter him. By the summer of 1978, New England regional cooperation was dead. But, by that time, the work of Schlossberg & Cassidy had begun paying off. Thanks to the strong support of the Massachusetts congressional delegation, Tufts received in early 1978 a $10 million federal appropriation from the Department of Health, Education and Welfare for the construction of a veterinary school at Tufts University. In October of that year, the Commonwealth gave title to Tufts of a 634-acre parcel of land that had been part of the Grafton State Hospital. The price was one dollar. To those traditional Tufts Trustees, Mayer was either a magician or a madman; they were not sure which. Suddenly, they realized that they were in this venture alone, without the other New England states and with uncertain Commonwealth commitment, outside of the free land. When the preliminary figures came in by the fall of 1978, the cost of the school was to be $31 million, an unheard of figure for Tufts.

There was no slowing him down. By the fall of 1978, Mayer had himself a Dean of the Veterinary School, Albert M. Jonas, Professor of Comparative Medicine and Pathology at the Yale Medical School. Jonas was a veterinarian who had never been on the faculty of any veterinary school. Recruitment for students had begun for a charter class to enter in the fall of 1979, before the Board of Trustees had given final approval to establish the school.

In the meantime, neither the national veterinary nor the Tufts community could believe what it was witnessing. Obstacles were everywhere, and support around the institution was minimal. The deans of the veterinary schools at Cornell and Penn were actively campaigning against the establishment of a Tufts Veterinary School. They mobilized their alumni associations in New England and testified before Congress. These veterinary schools had for years enjoyed the contracts from the New England states and lusted after these students and dollars. Closer to home, the most unhappiness came from the faculty and administration of the Medical School, who saw resources so scarce as to be almost nonexistent going to a new school and a rival for attention. In spite of a background in public health, Mayer had arrived at Tufts with precious little credibility with the Medical School. Nutrition was a field that simply did not interest the clinical or basic sciences faculty of the medical profession, at Tufts or for that matter anywhere in the country. I remember my first interview as Provost with the Chairman of the Department of Molecular and Microbiology, while standing in front of the recently constructed Human Nutrition Research Center on the downtown Boston campus. "That building might as well be on the planet Krypton, as far as my department is concerned. We are not interested in human nutrition. No one down here is." That attitude basically represented the opinion of a great many in the medical profession across the nation in the early 1980s. In Mayer's first two years, his preoccupation with veterinary medicine and later nutrition really drove the Medical School faculty into a fury. While he was promising the Medical School all sorts of new monies and incremental faculty, every dollar he could get from the federal treasury seemed to pass through the Medical School and find its way to the Vet School or to Nutrition. There was rage downtown on the health sciences campus. When the Trustees finally approved the establishment of the veterinary school by a vote on October 28, 1978, the document still contained language that pointed to agreements with the other New England states, even though Mayer knew that by early October Maine, Vermont, and Connecticut had backed out completely. It also contained language underlining the Medical School's frustration, calling for the Chairman of the Board to appoint an ad hoc committee of Trustees to ensure "that any financing of a short-fall in donated funds will not impose an unreasonable burden on the Medical School and that it shall be the responsibility of the Executive Committee and the standing committees to work actively with the President and the University Administration in the development of the [Medical] School and to report thereon regularly to the Board of Trustees."

By September 1979, just over three years from his first announcement, Jean Mayer had created the Tufts University School of Veterinary Medicine. Dr. Murnane had worked out a relationship with the churlish Angell Memorial Animal Hospital in Boston to do small-animal teaching, even though both of them knew that research on animals would be anathema to any institution founded by the Massachusetts Society for the Prevention of Cruelty to Animals. It would only be a question of time before the relationship with Angell would collapse. The Basic Sciences faculty of the Medical School resentfully had agreed to take on the responsibility to teach the entering class of veterinarians, having been promised all sorts of benefits for the Medical School. Veterinary students would sit in the same classrooms with grumbling medical and dental students in the Basic Sciences' first two years of the curriculum. President Mayer was totally committed to the idea of "One Medicine": that all health sciences students could sit together in the same classroom for basic teaching. Mayer went so far as to establish Trustee language that created the "One Medicine" faculty, and placed the Basic Sciences faculty in all three schools. He ordered stationery that made the point clear: If you were a biochemist, microbiologist, anatomist, or physiologist, you were a faculty member in the Medical, Dental, and Veterinary Schools. President Mayer had not bothered to make explanation either to the acting Dean of the Medical School or to the faculty. He was asked to speak at a hostile meeting on the Boston campus, and everyone was certain that this would be the Great Confrontation. But everyone underestimated Mayer's capacity to charm an audience. When the President walked out of that meeting, he left a faculty believing in all of his promises. The $10 million construction grant had permitted work to start on a large animal facility on the Grafton campus, and an entering class had been recruited, along with a dean, faculty, and administration.

One could only look on in wonder at how this had all happened.

In the summer of 1981, a month after my appointment as Provost, two visitors came to my office in Medford. Although at the time I had no responsibilities for the health sciences campus, both these visits helped me to understand a world to which I had enjoyed no exposure. The first was Erling Johansen, Dean of the Tufts University Dental School. Robert I. Levy has just been appointed both Dean of the Medical School and Vice President of Health Sciences at Tufts, a new position with administrative oversight of all health sciences downtown in Boston. Dean Johansen had a request: Could he call me or visit from time to time? He hoped that the Provost would still be able to reach out to the Dental School, even though there was a Vice President for Health Sciences and a new reporting relationship. He sounded very apprehensive.

This was my introduction to the internal psyche of health sciences professional schools. The Dental School, which needed to have basic sciences taught to its students, had purchased from the Medical School the services of some faculty, rather than get too close to the Medical School. Sharing space, faculty, or facilities with the "M.D." community, academic dentists believed, could be fatal. Indeed, within the next ten years, this proved to be the case nationally, when some of the best dental schools in the country closed and had their research space gobbled up by hungry medical schools. At Emory, Washington University (St. Louis), Georgetown, Northwestern, Loyola University of Chicago, Oral Roberts, and St. Louis University, dental schools were closed. Economics was given as the reason, when any reason was given, but only two of these schools were showing modest deficits at the time. Right or wrong, the academic dental community believed that its research space was coveted by the neighboring medical schools at their institutions and this, they believed, accounted for their closings. Dean Johansen, now under the authority of an "M.D.," was looking for any port in a storm, and his visit to me was an effort to make certain that his dental school did not sink unobserved beneath the waves.

My second visit was from the newly appointed Dean of the Medical School and Vice President for Health Sciences, Robert Levy, M.D. Levy's appointment had made my acceptance of the Provost's position possible, since I really did not want to deal with the downtown Boston health sciences community. I had no expertise and did not have a strong interest in managing this part of the Tufts academic enterprise. Besides, President Mayer had already made it clear that he would be very "active" downtown.

Bob Levy had spent most of his career at the National Institutes of Health. He had a worldwide reputation in the research of blood lipid abnormalities associated with increased susceptibility to arteriosclerosis and blood lipid disorders. Jean Mayer had selected him personally, because Levy was one of the few but growing number of scientists who possessed the right letters after his name as well as an interest in the President's own field of investigation: nutrition.

But Levy had a problem, and he asked my advice. A delegation of Medical School faculty had asked him if it were really necessary for President Mayer to have a separate office on the downtown campus in Boston. They felt that the routine and regular presence of Jean Mayer in their lives would be a "problem" for them. I asked the Vice President what "the problem" was, and he said that he thought it was Mayer's field of nutrition, and that the general view of the Basic Sciences faculty, as well as a number of the clinicians, was that nutritionists at best were white-stockinged women who wore hair nets and put creamed corn on your tray in the hospital cafeteria. At worst, they were talk-show television hucksters who championed bad science and wrote newspaper columns. They probably knew that Mayer was a bona fide scientist, but he was a nutrition celebrity, as well. They simply did not want him around.

Soon after this meeting, I had my conversation with the Chairman of the Department of Microbiology referred to earlier, and it confirmed the growing sense in my mind that, to the scientists in the Medical School, nutrition was not part of their scientific world. The fact that President Mayer had advanced his nutritional agenda in his inauguration speech did not make any particular impression on them. Nor did the construction of a fourteen-story human nutrition research laboratory in the middle of the health sciences campus. It should have.

These events were part of my education in the labyrinthine mysteries of academic medicine, about which I knew nothing before becoming Provost in 1981. It had never even crossed my mind that the university telephone directory, which included faculty and staff from all the schools and campuses, would be a document destined to shed some light on these mysteries. During my first few days in office, I was looking up telephone numbers and noticed that some of the faculty had academic degrees listed after their names. This struck me as peculiar, because my academic culture of Arts and Sciences never attached "Ph.D." or whatever one had as a terminal degree after your name. It was always "Sol Gittleman" or "Professor Sol Gittleman." It did not take long to realize that my health sciences colleagues were the only ones in the university telephone directory who included the final academic degree. I called a friend in the Basic Sciences Department of Biochemistry, whom I knew had an M.D. degree (it was listed immediately after his name in the directory) for an explanation, and he informed me that no health sciences faculty would think it proper to omit the degree; that it helped inform the community who was a dentist, who was a veterinarian, nurse, Ph.D., and, he said "most importantly," who was an M.D. I asked my colleague: "Is the M.D. the top of the hierarchy?" "Oh, yes," he replied.

So there it was: the academic health sciences pecking order, with the M.D. on top and everything else falling in line. It was cultural, and it could even be institutional, as I noticed when I received my first copy of the Washington University (St. Louis) *Record*, the official university information newspaper. As I glanced through it, I noticed that *every* faculty member had the terminal degree letters after the name: law faculty, business, medicine, *and even Arts and Sciences.* I called yet another friend on their faculty, with whom I had gone to graduate school, and asked for an explanation. "We tilt toward Medical School practice in such matters of academic formality. The docs want their M.D. degree mentioned every time, so we have to conform in all university publications."

Now, here comes Jean Mayer, Ph.D., committed to the field of nutrition, which in the minds of most of the medical community at Tufts and the rest of the country meant very little scientifically and was represented in the Medical School and its primary teaching hospital, the New England Medical Center, by the Frances Stern Nutrition Center, established in 1918 to train nutritionists. By the 1970s, the Center was providing patient services in the various Tufts hospitals, and Professor Johanna Dwyer, an earlier Mayer assistant, had brought professional and scientific credibility to the field as Director of the Center, unrecognized as she might have been. In the official history of the Tufts University School of Medicine, *Century of Excellence,* no mention is made of the Frances Stern Center or of nutrition. They were invisible to the general medical community.

If there was any terrain on which Jean Mayer felt more secure than usual, it was when he was dealing with national nutritional issues. He did not need faculty allies at Tufts or anywhere. He was connected marvelously to the appropriate congressional committees dealing with the Department of Agriculture, and Schlossberg & Cassidy could do the rest. Within weeks of his assumption of presidential leadership at Tufts, Mayer was laying the groundwork in Washington, D.C., for a comprehensive nutritional agenda at Tufts that would dazzle the academic community in Boston and the country. He proposed that the United States Department of Agriculture fund the capital and ongoing scientific costs of a human nutrition research center operated at Tufts University to investigate the human nutrition requirements in the normal aging process. Mayer had convinced the Massachusetts delegation, and the delegation instructed the USDA: Do it. The Agricultural Research Service, the appropriate funding agency within the USDA, was furious. But, the ARS was helpless. All the wires had been placed, with the Senate and House committees coordinated by Schlossberg & Cassidy, who had very special connections from their White House Conference days with the committees dealing with nutritional issues.

What made it more aggravating was that Mayer was right. The lack of research into nutritional standards for an aging population was disgraceful, he said, and no other universities were picking up on this. Mayer was proving that earmarking could make scientific contributions to the country.

His activities also caught the attention of the Boston higher education community. As 1977 progressed, Harvard, Massachusetts Institute of Technology, and Boston University each in its own way attempted to inform the federal government that Tufts lacked expertise in the field of nutrition, and that only a four-university cooperative program could provide enough resources to guarantee success. Mayer had already recruited the key members of the Harvard School of Public Health's Department of Nutrition for Tufts, but the pressure from the other institutions continued. MIT tried in vain to get part of the proposed center placed on its campus.[13]

The Tufts medical community had not seen any new construction for basic sciences research in decades. Plans had been drawn up by generations of Medical School deans, with no results. One can only imagine the impact of an announcement in 1977 of a federal allocation of $2 million to make engineering and architectural studies for the construction of a USDA-owned and Tufts-operated USDA human nutrition research center on aging, a proposed fifteen-story state-of-the-art facility and laboratory. Shortly thereafter, it was announced by the Boston Redevelopment Authority that Tufts had acquired space at 711 Washington Street, adjacent to the health sciences campus in downtown Boston, for the building. Jaws dropped again when the $20 million construction allocation was announced, along with initial operating funds of $7 million for nearly a dozen research programs, covering investigation into lipoproteins, nutrition and aging; nutrition, aging, and cardiovascular metabolism; vitamin K–dependent proteins in hemostatis;

13. See Gershoff, "Jean Mayer 1920–1993."

nutritional epidemiology; bone density; body composition and nutrient needs; micronutrient absorption and metabolism; nutrition and eye lens function; and nutrition and free radical reactions—research that sounded very much like basic sciences activities, but focusing on nutritional issues. Mayer had lined up the exiled scientists from Harvard and MIT, and had even found a few jewels on the Tufts faculty who were willing and had been waiting, people like Norman Krinsky, a Ph.D. who had come to the Medical School in pharmacology in 1960, had published his first paper that year on Vitamin A and carotenoids, switched to the Department of Biochemistry in 1967, and now took full advantage of the collaborative opportunities in the Human Nutrition Research Center.

Yet, the Tufts President's agenda was even more complicated than that suggested by the research center in Boston. Mayer was at heart a public policy advocate; he wanted to make change in Washington, and for that he needed social scientists who would help him find a national and international forum. In November of 1976, a few months after his arrival, the Trustees approved the creation of a Nutrition Institute within the Arts and Sciences. It was in the Arts and Sciences where he felt he would place the social scientists and physiological psychologists whom he brought with him from Harvard. Their impact would prove to be enormous. A young Research Fellow from the Harvard School of Public Health, Robin Kanarek, joined the Arts and Sciences Department of Psychology in 1977. Mayer turned all of his grants over to her, and she instantly had more funding than the entire Tufts Department of Psychology! In June of 1977, Stanley Gershoff left Harvard, and within four years he would be named the first Dean of the only School of Nutrition— and one with a policy emphasis—in the United States. In May of 1981, the school was created by approval of the Board of Trustees, who had accepted in the past three years the establishment of two new schools, neither of which could look to any endowment. For Tufts, here was risk-taking on truly a grand scale. And there was still more to come.

THE MOST BEAUTIFUL WHITE ELEPHANT:
THE PRIORY AT TALLOIRES

In the autumn of 1976, Donald MacJannett was beset by worry. He was about to meet the new President of his alma mater, Tufts University, from where he had graduated in 1916. The eighty-year-old educator had been running private schools and camps in Europe for more than forty years, His first effort, the MacJannett School for Young Americans, was located outside of Paris. After opening a second school at St. Cloud, MacJannett purchased a plot of land on Lake Annecy in the Haute Savoie region in the village of Talloires, the site of an eleventh-century Benedictine monastery. It was here that his destiny would take him, and the MacJannett Camps—Camp L'Aiglon for Boys and Camp Alouette for Girls—soon established a reputation as a high-quality college-preparatory experience in Europe. He and his wife Charlotte attracted celebrity adolescents such as Prince Philip and Indira Gandhi, and only the Nazi occupation interrupted their activities. They spent the war years in the United States and returned to Europe in 1952, to renew their work.

In 1958, with the Benedictine buildings falling into ruins, the Priory where the monks had eaten was put on the market for sale. The building was a huge pile with a large main hall, and Mrs. MacJannet led the bidding and acquired the property for $10,000, along with enormous needs for reconstruction and rehabilitation, for which the MacJannets had no resources other than their considerable energy and wits. The camps finally closed in 1964, and it was about that time that Mr. MacJannet began asking Tufts presidents if they would be interested in acquiring a facility in an idyllic part of France that could serve as a potential European study center.

From the perspective of Tufts administrators and Trustees, this was the last thing they would have needed. European adventures in property acquisition by American universities were frightening to institutions with far greater resources than Tufts. Harvard University had just gone through the epic struggle to decide what to do with the bequest of one of its distinguished alumni, who died and left his European properties to his alma mater.

Bernard Berenson (1865–1959) was a Lithuanian Jew who graduated from Harvard in 1887 and became one of America's leading arbiters of taste in matters of Renaissance art and acquisition. He advised Isabel Stewart Gardner as she prepared to build the great Venetian villa in Boston's Fenway that would become the Gardner Museum and house the great collection, which Berenson helped create.

In 1900, Berenson moved to Europe permanently, and for the next fifty-nine years, until his death, he resided in a villa outside of Florence in the village of Settingnano. His villa, called I Tatti, housed his collection of books and photos, as well as art treasures acquired by Berenson during his European sojourn. Not even the Nazi occupation drove him out, and he was left unmolested. After his death in 1959, the probated will revealed that I Tatti and all of Berenson's holdings there were bequeathed to Harvard.

There was no endowment. Harvard, already far and away the most heavily endowed university in the world, was advised by its treasurer Paul Cabot to refuse the bequest.[14] Cabot was a huge force for financial stability and successful investment at Harvard. He was a founder of State Street Research and was considered the dean of institutional investors. He was eventually to serve for seventeen years as Harvard's treasurer. When Paul Cabot advised the Harvard Corporation to reject Berenson's gift, this carried more than considerable weight. But President Nathan Pusey wanted I Tatti, and although Harvard had no particular demonstrated interest in overseas holdings of this sort—very few Harvard undergraduates in the 1950s and 1960s took any time for study abroad—he was determined to turn Berenson's home into a center for the study of the Renaissance. The bequest was accepted over Cabot's objections, and the fundraising began.

The money for programs and endowment came in slowly. This type of facility was not one that appealed to the Harvard alumni, but eventually David Rockefeller's international interest provided the funds that became the nucleus for the I Tatti endowment. In those early years of the 1960s, I Tatti was considered one of Harvard's albatrosses.

With the history of I Tatti well known to all, Donald MacJannet made little headway with either Presidents Wessell or Hallowell. The last thing they needed was an unendowed, falling-down eleventh-century ruin in some mountainous region near the Italian border in France. His offer was rejected out of hand.

But Mr. MacJannet had three great loves in his life: his wife Charlotte, the campgrounds and Priory, and Tufts. He had heard about the new President, who was French. For Mr. MacJannet, this was his last and best opportunity. No guts, no glory. MacJannet met with Jean Mayer.

Mayer did not hesitate for a moment. He knew the region well, its staggering beauty and the reputation of its people. When from time to time he would regale me with war stories, President Mayer reminisced about "mon generale DeGaulle" and how DeGaulle said that only two countries really fought the Nazis: Yugoslavia and the Haute Savoie. Mayer had enormous regard for the people of the region, where some of the most ferocious fighting by French Resistance forces against the Germans and Italians took place. He told this octogenarian and loyal Tufts alumnus that he would be delighted to accept the property, and it was his intention to turn it into a European Studies Center to give Tufts a visible space on the continent. He accepted Mr. MacJannet's gratitude, as well as what the Founding Director Professor

14. See Keller and Keller, *Making Harvard Modern,* 251.

Seymour Simches described as "a large box filled with unpaid bills and back taxes."

One only can wonder what sorcery Jean Mayer indulged in to convince the Trustees, in May of 1979, to accept the facilities in Talloires for Tufts. By this time—we will chronicle the events shortly—a full-scale revolt against President Mayer had risen within his own administration and the Trustees were admitting that they could not control him. Nonetheless, the crumbling Priory—Mr. MacJannet did heroic maintenance by himself and with volunteers—was officially inaugurated as a Tufts University campus, with a tiny endowment. Tufts-in-Talloires joined the Veterinary School and the soon-to-be-named School of Nutrition as three financially unsupported educational ventures begun by the new Tufts President.

1979–1980: ANNUS TERRIBILIS

Approximately 20 percent of all college presidents, regardless of the care and diligence of the search process, are gone within three years. It makes no difference if an executive search firm has been used: One out of five presidential appointments prove to be the wrong choice. Problems can emerge almost immediately. Often there is no honeymoon period. The difficulties and confrontations most often are at the Board of Trustee level or with the faculty. Our academic trade journal, the *Chronicle of Higher Education,* has faithfully charted these failures over the past two decades or more. As Jean Mayer began the 1979–1980 academic year, no one could be certain of the odds that he would survive his third-year evaluation. The factors that caused his difficulties with the community may not have been unique in the annals of higher education, but very few presidents who were willing to confront the need for change at their institutions had Mayer's unique combination of academic vision and a willingness to take extraordinary risk, combined with the unwavering self-assurance of the confidence man who believes that he could never be caught. Generally, when presidents fail, the symptoms often are found in the failure of the search process, if the successful candidate does not get the opportunity to know about the institutional problems. (Burt Hallowell did not discover the structural deficit until a few weeks into his presidency in 1967.) In the case of Jean Mayer, it was the *institution* that received the surprise. Did anyone know of his plans and vision during the recruitment phase? He was, after all, rejected in favor of another candidate, turned to only out of an embarrassed need to get a president in place as soon as possible. No one involved in Jean Mayer's recruitment seems to recall plans for new schools of veterinary medicine or nutrition. His inauguration speech left the community open-mouthed. No one anticipated the enormous culture change that was about to descend on the Tufts community.

When it came, it was only a question of time before the reaction to this extraordinarily uncharacteristic Tufts President would set in. In his first annual report written in 1977 for the Trustees, President Mayer had stated: "If we stand still, we may die . . . Institutions survive by seizing opportunities rather than brooding at too great length upon their problems." In the first three years of his presidency, Jean Mayer did not stand still long enough to brood about anything, even though he faced some strong traditional icons. One of the two faculty administrators who represented Tufts as it had been were the Provost, Kathryn McCarthy, a physicist who has been a Tufts undergraduate and graduate student, who joined the faculty in 1946 as a twenty-two-year-old Assistant Professor. She moved through all of the academic ranks to Professor, became Chair of the Department of Physics, then Dean of the Graduate School of Arts and Sciences, before assuming the Provost's job under Burton Hallowell. She was the most respected faculty member and administrator in the Arts and Sciences. The other quintessential Tufts administrator was Dean of the Arts and Sciences Bernard Harleston, who was the only Afro-American faculty member when he became an Assistant Professor of Psychology in 1956. With the exception of two years spent as Provost at Lincoln University from 1968 to 1970, he had spent his entire academic career at Tufts, as had Kathryn McCarthy. Together they represented fifty years of Tufts continuity, tradition, loyalty, making do with whatever meager resources were at hand, and dedication to the liberal arts commitment with an emphasis on teaching.

On February 3, 1979, a headline story in the *Boston Globe* announced, "Tufts provost resigns in protest." Bernie Harleston hung on for another year. In March of 1980, he submitted his resignation as Dean of the Faculty of Arts and Sciences. In his final annual report that year, Harleston wrote: "I believe that we are at a crisis point on the issue of the management of change . . . I expect that the dominant mood among the returning upperclass students will be one of doubt and uncertainty, extending the disillusionment and disenchantment many of them felt during much of 1979–1980."

How did matters get to this stage with these two most respected colleagues whose values pretty much reflected those of the community? Simply stated, no one at Tufts had ever encountered anyone like Jean Mayer. Both McCarthy and Harleston were left bewildered by Mayer's style and the apparent willingness of the Board of Trustees to take the university to what they saw as the brink of both academic and fiscal collapse. Mayer's style was Management by Disinformation. He would rely on a very small number of trusted aides to move his projects forward, and simply did not inform either his Provost or his deans, particularly the Dean of Arts and Sciences. He called meetings without them, made promises that affected their budgets, announced the creation of new schools and fundraising strategies without consultation. He would promise the same money to several schools, move funds from one school to another with the abandonment of a shell-game artist. One administrator said that the same $50,000 gift from industrialist Henry Leir bounced from Arts and Sciences to the Fletcher School of Law and Diplomacy before finally coming to a soft landing to cover the deficit that was growing in the European Center at Talloires. In fact, deficits were everywhere, and Mayer's first three university budgets were in the red. These two Tufts loyalists, committed as they were to the undergraduate tradition of the college, were distraught at the creation of new and expensive professional schools. They simply did not buy into Mayer's vision of carrying the university forward on the shoulders of high visibility research in new fields.

But, more than that, it was a matter of style and emphasis. The President simply ignored those people on whom he did not rely, and at the same time he could mesmerize most of the faculty with the extraordinary impact he was having with the acquisition of federal funding, which, thanks to Schlossberg & Cassidy, was cascading into Tufts, albeit exclusively for the newly established professional schools. He told the faculty of Arts and Sciences: Don't worry; your turn will come soon. Some grumbled, but many were ready for change and were willing to take the risk.

There were other tangible signs of Mayer's impact. In the second year of his presidency, the acceptance of offers of admission to the undergraduate colleges bubbled to four hundred unexpected students over the normal return. The only feasible explanation was Jean Mayer's considerable national visibility. Here was a President whose eminence seemed to reflect on the university, and this did not miss the attention of some Trustees, who were willing to put up with what increasingly was being reported to them as administrative chaos.

There had been some critical changes on the Board of Trustees. Allan Callow, a distinguished Harvard Medical School–trained cardiovascular surgeon and a 1938 Phi Beta Kappa graduate of Tufts College, joined the Board of Trustees in 1971. It did not take him long to realize that his alma mater was falling further behind. He assumed the chairmanship of the Board in 1977, during Mayer's first year, and his initial shock came when he asked the Vice President of Development for a list of Tufts potential million-dollar prospects. The list never got past four names. Callow was stunned. He knew one of the names on that list: the President and CEO of the Dennison Corporation, a 1952 graduate of Tufts named Nelson Gifford, whom Callow called immediately after accepting the chairmanship of the Board. The new Chairman asked Gifford to join the Tufts Board, and the reply was no. Gifford explained that he was a businessman, had no patience with academics, needed to make his own decisions, and really was not interested. But Dr. Callow persisted, and Gifford reluctantly joined up in November 1978.

As Callow examined the sitting members, he focused on two long-timers to whom he was drawn. Warren Carley was a Ropes & Gray lawyer specializing in bonds investment. He graduated from Tufts in 1932 and had been on the Board since 1964. Weston Howland, Jr., was an investment banker who had no Tufts affiliation, but came on the Board in 1963. Carley and Howland were names known to everyone in Boston. These four were to hold the fate of Jean Mayer and the future of Tufts in their hands. Without their support, Mayer would never have made it past the first three-year appointment. It was to them that Kathryn McCarthy turned early in 1978, when she believed that Tufts had had enough of Jean Mayer.

All four of them were more than acquaintances of the Provost. They had known and respected her for many years. They knew that she represented the very best of the prudent caution that seemed appropriate for an institution as short on resources as Tufts was. Everything in their bones must have told them that these extraordinary three years of Jean Mayer were just too dangerous a course to continue. The picture painted by Provost McCarthy when she met with a small group of Trustees while President Mayer was in California was one that normally would have frightened these fiscally conservative New Englanders. Mayer had already prepared the way for a fundraising campaign that in Tufts terms could never succeed. Professional consultants, after examining Tufts' alumni giving, estimated that $22 million might be raised over five years from all parts of the university. The President dismissed this figure, reorganized the Development Division under his trusted assistant Tom Murnane, whom he appointed Vice President, and was prepared to announce a goal of $140 million, an astounding figure for a university that never had experienced a successful capital campaign. The deans were already furious when they discovered how much this campaign would cost the individual schools. McCarthy came to the meeting armed with considerable support from across the campuses. Students on the Medford campus had already marched to protest a 15.6 percent tuition increase, which Mayer was forced to reduce to 13.1 percent.

But, something told them that, as dangerous as the times might seem, this was to be a turning point in the university's history, and the exhilaration generated by Mayer's efforts was intoxicating. The rump group told the Provost that they would support the President. She resigned on February 2, 1978, effective immediately, the day before the story appeared in the *Boston Globe*.

This was not the end of Mayer's troubles. Considerable support arose within the Board for the Provost after her resignation when the reasons became public. A few Trustees resigned. Kathryn McCarthy represented Tufts' values, many felt, not this riverboat gambler who was endangering the viability of the university itself.

But the four critical Trustees had taken on the role of serving as the President's defenders, and their view that Tufts' future depended on the vision of the new President was to carry the day for Mayer. They also polled the faculty—actually making house visits on some—and discovered considerable support for President Mayer. Increasingly, it had become clear to more and more faculty across the university that there was a new energy and a new will. No one can remember what form the vote took to re-appoint the President. As I mentioned earlier, three Rashomon-like stories circulated of how close the vote was (if one was actually taken. There was much discussion. There is no record of a Trustee vote.)

Mayer was shaken when he returned from California and heard about the meeting with the Trustees and Kathryn McCarthy's subsequent resignation. I believe he genuinely did not know how deeply she felt about his leadership and direction. She returned to the faculty as a Professor of Physics. For the rest of his life, Mayer never could understand why his Provost felt that it was necessary to seek his ouster. Typical of his personality, he always greeted her with a courtly politeness as a colleague. He exercised all of his charm in an effort to win her over during his term as President. Professor McCarthy, who was to remain on the faculty for more than a decade, could not abide being in his presence.

MANAGING MAYER

It is difficult to imagine a board chairman in a more difficult situation than Allan Callow found himself in the winter of 1979. He had committed himself and the university to keeping a president who was arguably the most ungovernable free spirit among leaders in American higher education. Jean

Mayer really did not want to be accountable to anyone. He had spent down all the university reserves, created new schools, and was showing no signs of letting up.

Chairman of the Board Callow had to decide the best way to exploit his President's talent while at the same time assuring himself and his fellow board members that Mayer was under some control. Callow's support did not mean that he disagreed with everything that Kathryn McCarthy had charged. Jean Mayer was no team player. If he sought consensus at all, it was to convince others that he could not fail, even when his ability to distract people from looking at the results of his actions eventually caught up with him; and there were early signs that things might not work out as promised. Very little of the early assurances regarding the funding of the Veterinary School came to pass. The New England states' regional commitment had vanished, and Tufts was left holding a bag filled with a sizeable deficit. The arrangement with Angell Memorial Animal Hospital was showing signs of disintegrating, leaving the vet students with a possible future with no small animal facility for research or clinical activities.

When President Mayer informed Callow that he did not want to have a Provost to succeed Kathryn McCarthy, the Chairman realized that it was essential to keep some kind of restraints on Mayer. He told the President that there would be a Provost regardless of his wishes. To make the point, Callow asked the just-retired Dean of the School of Dental Medicine, Robert Shira, if he would serve as Acting Provost, since McCarthy's resignation was effective immediately. Shira, a retired Major General and formerly chief dental medical officer in the Army, accepted. When President Mayer found out, he was livid. He instructed the staff in the Provost's office that Shira would be in the Provost's office on the Medford campus only rarely, and that he would come in at most once a week to sign whatever documents needed a provostial signature. Mayer then ordered the Provost's office divided in half, reducing its size as he intended to reduce the stature of the office. Shira immediately countermanded the President's order and told the staff that he was working under instructions of the Board of Trustees. He accepted the reduced space in his office, but to make his point, Acting Provost Shira appeared in Medford as soon as his appointment was approved by the Board. Of course, Bob Shira had been a senior member of the university administration in his capacity as Dean of the School of Dental Medicine, had been on good terms with the President, and knew that the arrangement had to be stabilized. He soon made it clear to President Mayer that he was prepared to work as a loyal Provost to the President in what both acknowledged would be a temporary arrangement. In his two years in this position, Shira managed to serve Mayer and to win his confidence, even though Mayer knew that the Provost's marching orders came directly from the Trustees.

But, they still felt they needed a shorter rope, and in the summer of 1978 a Management Committee was established by the Board: It consisted of Callow, Gifford, Howland and Carley. They would try to keep their President under control, while allowing his creative juices to flow. Every penny of university reserves that had been carefully squirreled away by Burton Hallowell had been spent in the first two years of Mayer's administration. The fundraising campaign promised to put enormous strains on the individual schools, which were increasingly at the mercy of Mayer's decisions. The university budget was in deficit each of the first three Mayer years. He was meddling in individual salary decisions, chairing search committees, inviting candidates for faculty positions outside the search process, offering deanships, promotions, and tenure, creating and bestowing titles without any consultation, making commitments everywhere, and in general causing administrative chaos. He also wanted to make it clear that it was the President who would be making critical academic decisions, not the Acting Provost. On February 26, 1979, he wrote the following to the school deans, after the Trustees formally accepted Kathryn McCarthy's resignation: "It was the opinion of the lawyers on the Board that the intermediary review step between the deans and the President ought to continue and to be effected by someone with the title of Acting Provost . . . for the sole purpose of reviewing the appointments, promotions, tenures and leaves *before* they come to me." Mayer took charge of the search for deans in Medicine and Engineering, cutting out the Dean of Arts and Sciences, to whom the Engineering Dean reported. The handwriting was on the wall for Dean Harleston, who completely shared Kathryn McCarthy's view of the Tufts President. He held on for as long as he could, but finally submitted his resignation on March 4, 1980, not quite two months after the resignation of the Dean of the Medical School, Larry Cavazos.

The Management Committee had crossed the line. In spite of considerable opposition from others on the Board of Trustees, these four were going as far as they could with Jean Mayer. Yet, they were desperate to get the President under some kind of management control. Callow and his committee announced to the Board the creation of a new position: Executive Vice President, a senior administrator who would be selected by the Management Committee, astonishingly without presidential input. Jean Mayer could have cared less. There was no box big enough to contain him, and he knew it. Like

Kathryn McCarthy, Dean Harleston had gone to see Chairman Callow before submitting his resignation, in a last desperate hope that he could convince him of the present danger in following Mayer's path.

But, Allan Callow had experienced his own epiphany. After more than forty years of association with Tufts, he had come to the conclusion that any danger with this extraordinary President was better than the course taken by the university's leadership of the previous decades. Here was one of those remarkable acts of faith taken by Board chairmen from time to time in American higher education. Callow was prepared to risk everything with Jean Mayer, and he had gathered around himself a small number of powerful Board members who were also willing to ignore the voices of Tufts loyalists like McCarthy and Harleston.

There was nothing in the background of these four trustees that would have led one to expect this kind of response to the Mayer presidency. Everything about them suggested conservative and traditional prudence. A lawyer with a venerable Boston firm; a banker/financier with roots going back to colonial America; a business man and CEO of an old-line Boston company; and a medical man, not exactly your typical team of adventurers in higher education. Nonetheless, Mayer sparked something in them, and they were determined to see change at this institution.

They also understood the tiger whose tail they were holding. President Mayer played no role in the hiring of Michael A. Hoffman as Executive Vice President for Administration. In the letter the President sent to the Tufts community on May 27, 1980, he stated, "Mr. Hoffman will have overall responsibility for the administrative management of the University," but then offered a small dose of confusion by adding, "Specific information about certain areas of his direct operational responsibilities will be provided at a later date." With Robert Shira continuing as Acting Provost, the two senior academic and administrative officers of the university in effect were reporting directly to the Management Committee of the Board of Trustees.

Michael Hoffman came to Tufts from the position of Vice President and General Manager of the Electrochemicals Division of International Minerals and Chemical Corporation of Boston, and he was clearly an experienced general manager. Over three decades, he had held thirteen positions with five firms. In his first interview, he said, "I've never been as excited about a job in my life as I am this one." He knew Boston, had been a Harvard undergraduate, and at the age of fifty-six was fulfilling what he described as "a longstanding desire to get into academic administration."

Callow could not wait another second for Hoffman to come on board and straighten out the fiscal affairs of the university. The Management Committee literally was trying to run the institution, and that effort was doomed to failure. Most of the old-time Tufts financial people had remained in place and were being told to do things by Mayer that they had never experienced in Tufts' prudent history. On June 30, 1980, Callow wrote to Joseph Lambert, Secretary and Overseer to the Corporation, who was also under instructions to keep an eye on the President. Lambert had obtained access to some of the financial statements dealing with consultants hired by the President and the Development Division, and had sent them on to Callow: "As with so many things in the management side of Tufts, the printout you provided me concerning consultants suggests that there is little orderly process in the matter of hiring consultants. If I interpret the data correctly, I confess to being appalled that we have in a six-month period engaged consultants to the cost of $541,000." After some futile efforts to uncover the nature of these consultant expenditures, this physician-turned-part-time bookkeeper gave up. "I suggest that Mr. Hoffman be asked to review this entire process and following that, be instructed to make a report to the Management Committee." No matter how many people were watching the President, it was not enough. Lambert gets a pat on the back, but the Chairman's frustration is evident: "I commend and thank you for bringing this to our attention and at the same time am dismayed that this concern you expressed did not come to our attention from within the administrative staff." The letter was copied to President Mayer, Carley, Gifford, Howland, and Shira.

Hoffman was arriving just in time. The most experienced businessman on the Management Committee was Nelson Gifford, who ran Dennison Manufacturing, a major national producer of office machines and products. He had assumed as much direct authority over presidential spending as was humanly possible, going so far as to insist that he approve personally any request by the President over $5,000. But, this kind of micro-management by university trustees was impossible to maintain, and it was with the Board's collective sigh of relief that on July 1, 1980, Hoffman began taking operational control of Tufts University with instructions to manage the financial flow of dollars in all parts of the university budget. He had been handpicked by Gifford and enjoyed an unprecedented span of control. The Management Committee could feel at least some sense of relief, as the unnerving $140 million capital campaign was getting underway, the plans for a nutrition school were being drawn up, and new construction was exploding at the Veterinary School in Grafton and on the downtown campus with the Human Nutrition Research Center. The trustees had also given approval to the establishment of a school of basic biomedical sciences within the Medical School. With a $1.5 million gift, the Boston departments of biomedical sciences that had been administratively located in the Arts and Sciences in Medford became the Sackler School of Basic Biomedical Sciences. Characteristically, the money to name the basic sciences whizzed past the Medical School budget and went to the Veterinary School bottom line, to the fury of the Basic Sciences faculty who were expecting laboratory renovations. But the Management Committee felt assured that Hoffman could bring order without stifling the President. Here at last, they felt, was the right man.

Michael Hoffman submitted his resignation on January 10, 1981, not quite eight months into his first year at Tufts.

In spite of what might have appeared to be another shock to the system, in his very brief sojourn at Tufts University Hoffman had prepared the foundation for a stability that would allow President Mayer to fulfill his vision while giving the next Executive Vice President a chance to bring order to the enterprise. In his first and last annual report to the President (and to the Board of Trustees), Hoffman was diplomatic, but candid. He had already resigned when he submitted the report on June 30, 1981 and was serving his last day on the job. He stated what he had hoped to accomplish: "Determine and establish an organizational structure; improve the relationship and credibility between the Administration and the Board of Trustees (Note: seventeen trustees had voted against Mayer's re-appointment!); make the new organizational structure function . . . to ensure proper planning and management . . . Of these three objectives only the first can be said to have been completed successfully." He then laid out in his report a series of events that he described as "unpleasant and sometimes traumatic experiences." Clearly, Michael Hoffman had been just as ill-prepared by his business experience to deal with the Mayer administration as had been the Tufts Board of Trustees. How could a company or corporation exist if "there still appears to be something less than complete mutual confidence and trust" between the administration and its Board? This was not the world that Hoffman had expected when he stepped into higher education, and he stepped out as soon as he could.

3

Although Hoffman's unexpected resignation might have been viewed as another example of the President's capacity to produce administrative chaos, in fact it represented the beginning of the great metamorphosis and led to the brightest period of the Mayer presidency. In his brief tenure at Tufts, Michael Hoffman created a quality administrative infrastructure that provided the Management Committee the opportunity to find another Executive Vice President who *really* would be able to control the President while giving Mayer the range he needed to create the university he wanted. Gifford did not break stride for a second. He took charge of the search for Hoffman's successor as a one-man search committee. This time, however, he would look for someone with the right combination of brains and experience in finance and administration, but with some background in higher education or at least an understanding of what Gifford knew in his own heart was a mystery to him: the academic culture.

He found his person at the American Bar Association headquarters in Chicago. Steven Manos was the Assistant Executive Director for Administration and Finance of the ABA, ran a $40 million organization, was himself a lawyer and also had a Master's of Public Administration. He had served three years in the Navy as an officer, but what caught Gifford's attention was the fact that Manos had been an English literature major at the University of Minnesota, had graduated summa cum laude and was a member of Phi Beta Kappa: an intellectual!

After Manos had accepted the offer to come to Tufts, Gifford suggested that it might be a good idea to meet his new boss, although it was made clear to the Executive Vice President—elect that he would be reporting directly to the Board of Trustees, specifically to the Management Committee. Manos walked into the presidential office on the second floor of Ballou Hall in Medford, armed with answers to a dozen questions that he might be expected to handle. Mayer never asked one. Instead, he launched into a fifty-minute monologue of his plans for Tufts. When Steve Manos left President Mayer's office, he had a pretty good idea of what he could expect in his confrontation with an academic dynamo who was operating at top speed.

THE NEW PROVOST

The position of provost is perhaps the least understood academic office in American higher education. It came into existence within the past fifty years, as the activities of presidents became increasingly diverse and took the recognized leader of the institution more often away from the campus. Inevitably, there came a time, particularly at complex universities with a multitude of deans, when a chief academic officer directly responsible to the president was required. Deans have to report to someone, and as presidential responsibilities changed after the mid-twentieth century, that "someone" was identified as the provost, who sat between the president and the school deans and the non-academic directors or vice presidents. The provost took on even greater significance when universities turned to non-academic people as their presidents. From the faculties' point of view, if the president was going to be the ultimate judge in tenure decisions, that person had better have academic training. Otherwise, get someone in the office next to the president who *could* be trusted. In this scenario, the provost took on the primary academic decision-making authority. At most universities, the creation of any position that obstructed the deans' direct access to the president was unwelcomed, even unacceptable. Still, every Ivy League institution by the 1960s had filled the position of provost, with the exception of Harvard, where the deans simply said "no," and there was sufficient alumni leverage in the powerful medical, law, and business schools to block the appointment of a provost. It was not until the appointment of Harvard's first truly ceremonial president in 1991 that a provost was appointed, but the deans still refused to report to him. At the smaller Ivy League institutions, there was generally warfare between the Dean of the Faculty of Arts and Sciences (traditionally the most powerful academic office underneath the president) and the provost. To calm the nerves of medical school deans, universities would often join the title of "Provost for Health Sciences" or "Medicine" to the dean's title in order to protect the independence of the M.D.s.

At Tufts, the first provost appeared in the 1950s, in an effort to gain some control over the health sciences schools in Boston and the Fletcher School in

Medford, but also to give the Arts and Sciences faculty and the Deans of Liberal Arts and Engineering someone to report to other than the president. At that time, Fletcher kept the Tufts name as low-profiled as possible, never mentioning the two names in the same breath; and the last thing any of these schools wanted was another university-wide hand on the tiller. But Presidents Wessell and Hallowell saw the provost as an important layer of administration. The tradition was established, furthermore, that the provost would come from the Liberal Arts. When Kathryn McCarthy was named the fourth Tufts Provost in 1973, she had been a member of the Physics Department since 1946. When she resigned in protest of President Mayer's policies, she was in her thirty-third year as a member of the faculty.

Understanding why Jean Mayer selected certain people provides a valuable insight into this complex character. How do you explain his selection of a dentist and part-time administrator of the Dental School as the chief fundraiser of the university at a time when Mayer's entire future at Tufts depended on a successful campaign of staggering dimensions? Tom Murnane had absolutely no experience as a development officer, fundraiser, or administrator of a complex organization that included governmental affairs, public relations, publications, as well the planning and organization of campaigns in six schools, each with a different constituency and culture. Why did Mayer choose him? He was asked that question by a skeptical Board of Trustees, and the members got for an answer a brief lecture on the American Civil War. "Why did President Lincoln fire McClellan and hand his army over to an officer who in civilian life had run a dry goods store and seemed to have a drinking problem? He did it because he knew that Grant would fight!" This is what he wanted in his chief fundraiser: a person with energy and a willingness to do battle, to take risks, and to demonstrate a loyalty to the President. Mayer knew he could not fundraise by himself; he needed someone he could trust and who shared Mayer's spirit and fearlessness. He found this person in Tom Murnane. Murnane was one of very few people from whom Jean Mayer would take orders or advice, at least in matters of fundraising. He came to trust him as he trusted no one else.

In the case of many of his selections of deans, Mayer looked for a combination of characteristics that would serve a president who really considered himself *Dean of All Schools and Provost.* He looked for amiable academic personalities with a respectable research and teaching track record who would stay out of his way and take orders without making a fuss. He was generally not interested in academic leadership in his deans.

Nor did he want any more problems with a provost. He preferred having none, but once it became evident that the Board of Trustees would not permit him to operate without one, Mayer moved resolutely to cut down the provost's position to a size suitable for a president who considered himself the academic leader of the institution. Bob Shira was Acting Provost in his first year (when his office was cut in half, with the President's Assistant Mason Fernald sitting on the other side of a wall that divided the fireplace), and during his second and final year, a search began for what was now no longer to be "Provost and Senior Vice President," but instead "Provost and Academic Vice President." Mayer had already decided and had gotten Board concurrence that the health sciences would be the turf of a newly created "Vice President for Health Sciences," who would also serve as Dean of the School of Medicine. (Corporate titles began entering higher education when the boards of trustees started exercising more authority and wished to make universities more recognizable as well-run business entities. For the faculty's part, they had no idea what an "Academic Vice President" was.) The provost's reach would extend only to Medford, and to the three schools on that campus: Arts and Sciences (which included engineering), Fletcher in its own cocoon, and Nutrition, which was housed in three frame houses, safe from the contempt of the Medical School. For the first time in Tufts history, the search for a provost would include candidates from outside the university.

The Search Committee for the provost was chaired by Shira, who kept in touch with a parallel student committee. The three finalists were interviewed and the committees made their recommendations to the President. Two of the candidates were outside people, and I was the sole candidate from the Tufts faculty. The student committee rated one of the outside candidates as their first choice. Shira's committee recommended me. President Mayer called me to his office on April 23 to say that he was selecting me as his Provost and Academic Vice President with appropriately diminished authority and truncated responsibility. I set only one condition: that I be allowed to continue teaching each semester.

Why did President Mayer select me as his Provost? My administrative experience was limited. I had never been a dean and had served for fifteen years as a chairman in a department that at most universities enjoyed little stature and traditionally rarely provided university-wide leadership: German and Russian. But I had built the program to include Chinese, Japanese, Hebrew, and Arabic. Tufts had two modern language departments: Romance Languages and Literatures and ours, which Mayer told everyone was "Gittleman's United Nations." I was energetic, a builder, a popular undergraduate teacher, a reasonably successful scholar who had written three books, and the

President liked me, even though I was a German teacher, and he genuinely detested the Germans. He also knew that I was a Jew who taught an undergraduate course on Yiddish literature. His first meeting with me in 1976 went something like this:

> Mayer: So, you are Gittleman, the Chairman of the German Department. You know, I fought Fascism and killed Germans with my bare hands. I don't even like their language.
> Gittleman: Yes, President Mayer, but at least they didn't invent the word "Collaborateur."
> Mayer (after a short pause): Ah, you're right, you're right. You also do Russian in your department, no? Well, from my view, Asia begins at the Rhine.

Here was my new President, and he had no use for either the Germans or the Russians. He enjoyed all the prejudices of a nineteenth-century Frenchman, yet he was charming, and we liked each other from the start. But there was more to understanding his selection of me as his Provost. I could see his eyes light up when I asked to be allowed to continue teaching. For Mayer, a Provost who was out of the office teaching large classes of undergraduates was his ideal candidate. I also provided him with some cover for those McCarthyite critics who said that he was not interested in undergraduate education. For the kind of president who really wanted to be his own provost, my credentials and past history were ideal. He needed someone from the humanities in his administration, preferably someone with years of service at Tufts. I was a seventeen-year veteran of the faculty wars and had come up through the ranks. Mayer assumed correctly that I had no great administrative ambition, and that he would have a Provost at his back who did not wish to occupy the President's office in Ballou Hall. He saw me as no threat, someone who would stay out of his way. As a result, he passed up the opportunity of naming a prestigious outsider for the first time in appointing a Provost for Tufts.

On July 1, 1981, three new university administrators began their first day in new positions: Steven Manos, Executive Vice President; Robert Levy, M.D., Vice President for Health Sciences and Dean of the Medical School; and Sol Gittleman, Academic Vice President and Provost. Along with Tom Murnane, we reported directly to the President. Within eighteen months, Bob Levy had resigned. There would be no re-appointment of a Vice President for Health Sciences. Manos, Murnane, and Gittleman remained in place for twenty-one years, through three serving presidents.

Most of the more than four thousand colleges and universities in this country have a central administration organization that brings together, in a regular manner, the senior institutional officials—deans of schools and operational vice presidents—to deal with the issues that have to be planned and decided on in some kind of orderly fashion. In the first years of Jean Mayer's presidency, the Tufts system could be described as management by monologue. The only person who would have all the strings in his hand would be the President. It was this style that drove the previous Provost and the Dean of Arts and Sciences in desperation to seek Mayer's removal.

The four vice presidents who began meeting soon after July 1, 1981, came with different expectations and histories. Tom Murnane had been selected by President Mayer and enjoyed a relationship with him that was singular. No one was as close to the President. Although he supposedly reported to the Executive Vice President, President Mayer made it clear to Steve Manos that Development would report directly to the President. Tom was fully in tune with the Mayer presidency. Sheldon Wolff, Chairman of the Department of Medicine, had recommended Bob Levy, who like Wolff had a background as an NIH administrator and scientist. Levy had no concept of the unique eccentricities of Boston medicine, and soon discovered that his clinical faculty was completely owned by the principal Tufts affiliated hospital, the New England Medical Center, whose President and CEO, Jerome Grossman, M.D., was Jean Mayer's only rival for the center stage ever since he arrived from the Massachusetts General Hospital in 1979. Grossman and Mayer (described by one trustee as "two scorpions in a bottle") faced off against each other for more than a decade of confrontation between the hospital and the university. Jerry Grossman owned his clinical faculty, because he paid them. The clinical faculty of all the Boston teaching hospitals enjoyed academic appointments from one of the three medical schools in town, but almost all of their salary—and therefore their loyalty—was based on their clinical activities in the hospitals. When they published, they would often omit their academic title in favor of their hospital appointment. The Tufts basic sciences, having just been unified as the Sackler School, were also trying to strike out on their own independent path. Into this highly charged political situation came Bob Levy, a very nice and intelligent medical researcher and physician, without a clue to the politically charged atmosphere of Boston medicine or university life in general. Like so many medical school deans over the next twenty years, he would be devoured. He submitted his resignation in January 1983. He was never replaced as a vice president.

Steve Manos had been hired by Nelson Gifford and was accountable to him, although he nominally reported to the President. It was Vice President Manos's task to make certain that he had his hands on all of the university's financial controls. He was given a range of responsibility probably unprecedented in American higher education. He numbered among the first of a new kind of top non-academic officer: the Executive Vice President whose span of control was truly university-wide and did indeed have a significant influence over the academic finances of the institution. Frank Campanella at Boston College was perhaps Boston's most powerful Executive Vice President before Steve Manos. Others would follow.

Michael Hoffman gave me the benefit of his brief but intense period of service at Tufts toward the end of May 1981, five weeks before I officially became Provost. His first piece of advice: Get to the key trustees, who were Callow, Gifford, Howland, and Carley, the members of the Management Committee. They will support you. Second, develop a working relationship with the other senior vice presidents to re-establish the hegemony and seniority of the Provost. This is what the trustees wanted. Finally, keep President Mayer out of management affairs and restrain him as much as possible.

Within two weeks of my assumption to the Provost's position, trustee Howland called. I was to report to him once a month concerning the President's activities, and to inform him immediately if there were any presidential actions that might warrant trustee intervention.

For our part, we had no idea how we were to interact formally with the President, since he gave no indication of wanting to meet with us regularly, and he set up no routine orientation meetings with his most senior vice presidents before our start date of July 1. Having had little management and no corporate background, I did not know what to expect. Then President Mayer put on our calendars two dates a week apart, with the three new vice presidents. We received no agenda, and both meetings followed the same drill: President Mayer spoke non-stop about his plans for Tufts. It was a reprise of Steve Manos's first interview with him. Soon after, when the Executive Vice President suggested that the three of us should meet weekly without the President, I agreed with the most enthusiasm, since I had the most to learn. Bob Levy was not eager to come together too closely with the central administration, but he soon discovered the range of control that the Executive Vice President had, reaching right into the budgetary decisions of the health sciences schools. It had been Levy's intention from the beginning to create a parallel and independent organization of health sciences, mirroring the Provost's office. The President had assured him that he would be free to do this (another stake in the heart of the Provost's office). At the first meeting of the Troika without President Mayer, we had an agenda of issues that needed discussion and decisions. I informed the Health Sciences Vice President that, until the Trustees changed the bylaws, all his tenure cases in the basic sciences would come through the Provost's office and require my blessing; I also reminded him that the Trustee by-laws made the Provost, in the event of presidential incapacity, the Acting President. I had no intention of telling him how to run the health sciences campuses, as long as he understood that he was not going to set up an alternative organization to the Provost at Tufts. He assured me that President Mayer had given him a different impression; he was also beginning to understand that there might be more than one reality. When I suggested to Bob Levy that we might go together to the Trustees for clarification rather than to the President, he demurred and reluctantly accepted my interpretation, which was that there was one chief academic officer, and it was the Provost of the university. I took Michael Hoffman's advice to heart: Establish the authority of the Provost in spite of what the President wanted. He assured me that the Trustees would support me, regardless of what the President had promised anyone.

That was the first meeting. As the second meeting was about to begin the following week, the President walked in, looked at the list of subjects to be discussed, and informed us that henceforth he would chair all of these meetings, in person, and in his office. We could contribute to the agenda.

Inadvertently, we had forced him into regularly coming together with his senior advisors, and, as we were to discover, he would share information selectively. However, it did not take long for Steve Manos and me to exercise a kind of planning and management structure that the President could not thwart. Steve's Staff Council—made up of the several vice presidents and senior directors of operations—met weekly, and, most importantly, the Provost joined that group. I established a Provost's Council of the school deans to meet as close to monthly as possible. The deans, typically, did not want the Executive Vice President to attend. They were an untrusting lot and did not want non-academic administrators listening to their discussions. Fortunately, Steve Manos and I shared every shred of information for more than twenty years. The meetings of both committees, which continued for the entire Mayer presidency, were operational and psychotherapeutic. It did not take long for both groups to realize that they were dealing with a visionary and somewhat anarchic President who was taking Tufts onto another plane and a higher platform. We clutched each other for safety, but everyone knew that the ride was going to be exhilarating and in the long run productive.

The Mayer presidency had hit its stride. The only one who stumbled was Bob Levy. He needed more administrative sanity in his life and ultimately could not deal with the creative turmoil. In addition, as brilliant he was as a scientific investigator, he had little emotional intelligence in dealing with his health sciences constituencies. He was not prepared for the sullen paranoia of the dental faculty or for the "angst" of a Veterinary School located thirty-five miles away from any Tufts community and living on a shoestring. He made no effort to reach out to the dentists or the veterinarians who saw only an NIH-trained M.D. who exuded a benevolent condescension for any other set of letters after a name. In addition, President Mayer was building a facility around nutrition that no one downtown wanted. Sheldon Wolff, the Chairman of the eight-hundred-pound gorilla that is always the Department of Medicine in a medical school, had thrown in his lot with Jerry Grossman and the New England Medical Center. Levy had few resources, no power of persuasion, and little control over his clinical faculty. He was intelligent, earnest, and thoroughly unprepared to be Vice President or Dean of the Medical School. With his departure, President Mayer invited Tom Murnane to join the regular meetings; the Troika was in place for the next twenty years.

THE FIRST PRIORITY: RAISING MONEY

Of all the dramatic changes that have swept over American higher education in the last fifty years, nothing can match the extraordinary explosion in effort and energy put toward raising money for colleges and universities. What had been before the Second World War a homegrown and rather amateurish attempt to organize alumni giving to alma mater had become an industry staffed by teams of professional fundraisers who moved from campus to campus, following a flow of never-ending campaigns for more and more money. In the year 2002, twenty-one universities were in the middle of five-year fundraising phases whose goals were a minimum of $1 *billion*. More than forty institutions have endowments of more than $1 billion, and in spite of the current bear market, another twenty seem primed to join the club. Nearly three hundred colleges and universities, among which are numerous public ones, have passed the $100 million endowment mark. As mentioned earlier, it was Harvard University that set the tone for these activities in the early 1950s, and it did not take long for the pack to follow. The private universities and colleges that comprise the top one hundred endowments today began their campaigns. Between 1956 and the autumn of 1958, 134 colleges and universities raised over three-quarters of a billion dollars. The aggressive age of fundraising had begun.

But not at Tufts. I have often asked myself why, when almost every other sister institution in New England and the Middle Atlantic states had begun with various degrees of enthusiasm to organize themselves for the purpose of raising capital, Tufts did not. There seemed to be a sense among the administration and trustees of the 1950s and early 1960s that it was *impolite* to ask alumni to contribute to their alma mater. The idea of cultivating potential donors seemed alien to the culture. As late as the 1970s, the Vice President for Development was a teetotaler who did not serve alcohol in his home. I had been asked to participate in the cultivation of a donor in 1975, and we gathered in Belmont, Massachusetts, at the home of the head of Tufts Development. The donor was asked if he would like something to drink, and he asked for a Scotch and water. He was told by the hostess that "there was some cooking sherry. Would that do?" Something told me at that moment that Tufts was not really in the business of raising money.

In January 1976, Marts & Lundy produced a review of fundraising potential for Tufts. The needs assessment resulted in a list for an all-university campaign that totaled over $60 million for the most urgent needs. There was almost a pitiful request: "the most compelling specific need [being] $2,000,000 for the general maintenance to upgrade the physical plant . . ." There was not enough money to keep the campuses operating. Tufts had not had a campaign for fifteen years, and the two previous ones had both failed. The report stated that Tufts needed a minimum campaign of $50 million over five years, but "the present major gift prospects do not have the potential to support a successful $50 million campaign." Some of the comments coming out of the alumni focus groups who were interviewed spoke of fear and trepidation: "The goal is too large, $7.5 to $10 million would be a more realistic amount . . . $50 million startles me . . . it is way out of line . . . the goal should be $20 or $25 million or nothing at all . . . People would be scared off at $50 million . . . If it is assumed that a significant amount of the goal is to come from the Board, then $50 million is an unrealistic amount . . . [Note: Two Trustees said that they would not give anything to a campaign. Total Trustee giving in 1972 was just over $19,000!] . . . A goal of $50 million is unattainable . . . It is not possible to raise $50 million, not even $5 million a year for ten years . . ." There was, however, one lonely and prescient voice amidst the fear and trembling: "Tufts does not have anything the matter with it that $130 million would not cure."

This was the report that the newly inaugurated President Jean Mayer saw. He called Marts & Lundy back a year later. They had decided that $50 million was far beyond the reach of Tufts University. In fact, they did not believe that the alumni would sustain both annual giving and a capital gift in addition. They recommended a $12 million capital campaign without an annual fund, which would be halted during the duration of the capital campaign. If the annual giving were to be continued, the top figure that Marts & Lundy could recommend was $22 million for the entire university, with less than enthusiastic hope for success.

As optimistic as the new President was concerning his ability to take Tufts to a new level, he also recognized that his success in receiving the federal earmarks would drive any campaign to a greater goal. The federal government was requiring a 20 percent private match in several of the Schlossberg & Cassidy initiatives, and Mayer saw immediately that neither $12 nor $22 million was going to help. He met with the development team that he had inherited, told them, "Let's add a few zeros to the $12 million," and informed the stunned gathering that the campaign goal would be $120 million!

As he walked out of that meeting, the Vice President for Development was drafting in his mind his letter of resignation. When he received it, President Mayer knew that he could trust only one man to lead this unprecedented effort, which undoubtedly would shake the Tufts community to its foundation: He appointed Thomas Murnane Vice President for Development and turned the organization over to him. A month later, the School of Nutrition came into being, and the President instructed his new Vice President (and still member of the Dental School faculty) to add another $20 million onto the planning goal. On October 14, 1980, Tufts University officially launched an unprecedented $140 million capital campaign. Three Trustees had already resigned during the run-up and development of a nucleus fund.

As arbitrary as Mayer's process might have seemed, he realized that the needs of the university were enormous. He inherited a university endowment of barely $30 million, less than most of the New England liberal arts colleges with whom Tufts competed in athletics. We had the poorest endowed medical, dental, and veterinary schools in the country. Now there was a School of Nutrition with no endowment. Faculty salaries were not competitive, there were *no* fully endowed chairs in any of the schools, and facilities were sub-par. At the most recent accreditation, the health sciences library was ranked the worst of any accredited medical school in the country.

But, Tom Murnane set the tone. "The capital campaign will never end," he told the student newspaper on September 12, 1980, as he announced the kick-off; and it has not, more than twenty years later. When the Campaign for Tufts officially ended in 1984, the endowment stood at more than $59 million, and the campaign had raised $145 million, a staggering accomplishment for an institution with a history of failure in fundraising. Scarcely one year later, a nucleus fund was begun for a $250 million Campaign for Tufts II, which began in 1987. It, too, reached its goal. The Mayer presidency had raised over $400 million and had transformed Tufts University.

Nothing was orthodox in either of the campaigns. Tufts could not count on traditional alumni giving. The Tufts alumni had hardly been asked to support their institution in the past, so they could not be counted on to give at the start. Mayer and Murnane figured out another strategy. "The greatest sources of wealth are the parents," said the President, but he also turned to his own personal connections and mission, and he drew wealthy philanthropists with no previous connection to Tufts into his orbit.

Finally, there was the federal government and Gerald Cassidy, now leading Gerald Cassidy Associates, the most successful acquirer of targeted appropriations in the federal budget.

The money-raising professionals in Boston and around the country were stunned. There had never been a campaign like the first Campaign for Tufts. Everyone had known the history of Tufts fundraising over the past fifty years, understood the paucity of Tufts alumni and trustee giving, and in spite of Mayer's extraordinary success with his congressional earmark strategy, the fundraising community had not believed it would be possible between 1979 and 1984 to raise $140 million for Tufts. In professional development circles, Jean Mayer quickly became a legend. Normally, capital campaigns did not count grants from government sources, but Tom Murnane felt that he had no choice: The goal was so enormous for Tufts that he would have to count at least some of the federal dollars. Of the $145 million eventually raised in Campaign I, $27 million came from federal earmarks—$15 million for the veterinary school, $10 million for a new medical school building, and $3 million for a Fletcher School facility. (They might have counted all the USDA money earmarked for the human nutrition center, but Murnane and Mayer did not want to push this too far.) The alumni accounted for barely 20 percent of the total. In Campaign II, no government funds were counted in the $250 million raised.

In 1991, two scholars of academic fundraising selected "ten success stories" to illustrate the art of capital campaigns in American higher education.

The third example was Tufts, and the chapter was entitled "Not Afraid to Break the Rules."[1]

TRUSTEES: THE FINAL PIECE

At least seventeen members of the Board of Trustees had been ready to drop Jean Mayer as President in 1979. But the ones who counted the most were in his corner. The critical members of the Management Committee— Chairman of the Board Allan Callow, Westin Howland, Nelson Gifford, and Warren Carley—were judiciously augmented by other supporters who possessed the status to bolster the Mayer presidency. None was more prestigious than Charles Francis Adams, the ultimate patrician and the board member who, in a quiet yet regal fashion, exercised a commanding control over the Tufts Board of Trustees.

Charlie Adams was indeed special. Born in 1910, he was a member of one of the most famous families in America, the great-great-great grandson of President John Adams and the great-great grandson of President John Quincy Adams. His father had been the Harvard Treasurer for thirty-five years and had been appointed Secretary of the Navy in 1928.

Charles Adams was the kind of Boston Brahmin who Jean Mayer wanted to bump into when he joined those private clubs. He saw in Adams's Harvard roots—undergraduate and Business School—a link to the institution at which he himself had spent twenty-seven years and loved dearly. He was Chairman of the Board of the Raytheon Corporation, and as such a big player in the Boston business community. Everything about him suggested class and stature. His initial association with Tufts was not with the College or professional health schools, but with the School of Law and Diplomacy, which always saw itself on a much higher plateau than the university with which it reluctantly shared a geographical location. Fletcher barely recognized Tufts on its stationery. So, when Charles Francis Adams joined the Fletcher Board of Visitors in 1971, it seemed a natural association. An inherently polite and diplomatic gentleman, he accepted membership on the Tufts Board of Trustees in 1974 for a shortened term; and it was to Adams that Mayer turned during the difficult years of his university presidency—and Adams responded. He shared with the members of the Management Committee that same unexplainable belief that this new President represented

1. Margaret Duronio and Bruce A. Loessin, *Effective Fund Raising in Higher Education* (San Francisco: Jossey-Bass Publishers, 1991), 60–79.

perhaps an extraordinary opportunity for a university that required something extraordinary. He also genuinely liked Jean Mayer. When matters got dicey at Trustee meetings concerning a Mayer initiative, it only required a hand in the air from Adams to get the attention of the Board, and he would hold forth on the wisdom of Mayer's actions. The fact was that no one would challenge Charles Francis Adams, and he was in the President's corner and remained a loyal friend until his death in 1999.

Mayer required one additional validation from an ally on the Board, and that was to bolster the wisdom of his academic decisions. He needed an unimpeachable academic ally, and for this he turned again to Harvard.

Harvey Brooks was Benjamin Pierce Professor of Technology and Public Policy in the Kennedy School of Government and Gordon McKay Professor of Applied Physics in the Arts and Sciences at Harvard. Tall, courtly, and self-effacing, Harvey Brooks had an unimpeachable reputation in the Boston academic community as well as in the congressional halls and offices in the nation's capitol. Presidents asked his advice on issues of nuclear safeguards. His 1968 book *The Government of Science* laid out the pros and cons in the relationship between government and higher education. And he liked Jean Mayer. Brooks, who sat on literally dozens of boards, finally gave in to the Tufts President in 1981 and accepted an invitation to join the Board of Trustees. Instantly, the Tufts Trustees became an academically respectable body. Brooks was regularly in attendance during his six years of service and gave President Mayer his generous support. With Harvey Brooks in his corner, Mayer could silence a variety of critics in science and engineering who might question his policies and vision for Tufts.

As for the rest of the university community, that initial five-year period of turmoil had been less difficult to accept. Faculty as well as students saw early signs of a kind of change that they found galvanizing and for which they were ready. It was clear to them that this was a new kind of President for Tufts, and in spite of the bewildering new initiatives, they were willing to go along. They were willing to take the risk.

"THE PEACEABLE KINGDOM": FACULTY, STUDENTS AND CAMPUSES IN A TIME OF CHANGE

Edward Hicks executed his pastoral painting of harmony and prosperity hundreds of times in the 1830s and 1840s to reflect the peace and tranquility that he sought in an American society where God was in his heaven, and all was right with the world. It might even have represented the "shared culture" of Carl Bridenbaugh's academic paradise, where a paternalistic respect and mutual admiration characterized the state of higher education in America at the mid-nineteenth century.

However, by the 1970s, Hicks' painting reflected neither the mood of campus nor country as Jean Mayer assumed the presidency of Tufts. Within a few months, Jimmy Carter would become the American President, and both of these leaders had to deal with a mood and culture specific to their times. There was a complementary chaos in country and university; and the world, as well, was in a malaise. The reaction to the war in Vietnam created a chilling numbness for the generation of the 1970s.[2] It cared mostly about forgetting the euphoria and excess of the 1960s and lost itself in a more self-centered quest. The young people of post-Vietnam America looked around them and saw failure. Every continent was in turmoil. The United States was still trying to extricate its troops from Thailand in 1976. There were riots in Soweto, Madrid, the Philippines, Istanbul, Pakistan, assassinations in a dozen countries (including Afghanistan), and natural disasters killing thousands. In July of 1977, the new Israeli government of Menachem Begin had begun to implement its settlement policy in the West Bank, and riots erupted in Nablus and Ramalah. International terrorism had already begun, and there were hijackings, kidnappings, and political murders in every year of Carter's term. Looking back from the twenty-first century and the messianic fervor that has swept the world, two events in particular should have been given a special mark of attention. In November 1978, a charismatic, apocalyptical cult leader named James Jones led his followers to a camp in Guyana, South America, where more than nine hundred adults and children committed suicide in preparation for the end of the world by drinking Kool-Aid laced with cyanide. In January of 1979, the Shah fled from Iran, and the country was in the hands of the Shiite leader, Ayatollah Khomeini. The Islamic revolution had begun. In November of that year, the hostages were seized at the American embassy in Teheran and remained prisoners for 444 days, released only after President Reagan assumed the presidency in January 1981.

The world's economy was in shambles. What we now call "stagflation"— slow growth with repeated bouts of high inflation—had gripped the economy of most nations, including the United States. The British pound had

2. See Christopher Lasch, *The Culture of Narcissism* (New York: W.W. Norton, 1978), 4–5.

fallen to under two dollars for the first time in history, and Prime Minister Harold Wilson resigned. It was a global recession that was to last until the early 1980s. In Africa, starvation threatened millions.

Nothing marked this grim four-year period in America as much as the energy crisis. In March 1979, the Three Mile Island reactor melted down, shaking the nation's confidence in nuclear energy. With the Middle East in flames and an OPEC oil embargo at work, the leap in oil and gasoline prices in the United States drove President Carter's approval rating down to 30 percent in the national polls.

The campus mood across the country reflected the worldwide anxiety. Nothing seemed to work. The liberal and more aggressive activists on the left on the college campuses who had had the field to themselves during the 1960s now began to see their work undone. After a generation of hectic progress in the civil rights movement, the nation seemed to seek a new direction. In July 1978, the Supreme Court came down with its Bakke decision, which, while not prohibiting any use of race in admissions to the University of California Medical School at Davis, said that the set-aside of sixteen spaces for students admitted through a "special admissions program" for minority students was unconstitutional because it involved a quota. Mr. Bakke, who said he was more qualified than the students accepted under the special program, was admitted. A glance at the Supreme Court made it clear that the fragile liberal coalition around Justice Brennan was getting old. Brennan and Thurgood Marshall could be gone shortly, and President Carter did not have enough political authority to get like-minded jurists approved. Justices Burger and Rehnquist would form the new coalition, it was felt, and indeed, this proved to be the case over the next two decades. The liberal and radical student activists had faded into the background, more worried in the 1970s about grades than ideology. As the 1980s opened, the wave of student activism broke out of the conservatism movement.

As for the faculty nationally, their success in the anti-war effort had given them a real sense of empowerment, and that translated into a desire for a more formal adversarial role in dealing with the administration. The large state systems had already unionized. Now, the major initiative of the later part of the 1970s was the effort to unionize private universities. The faculty at Boston University had found its perfect adversary in President John Silber, and the AAUP chapter there was busily getting ready to establish a bona fide faculty union. Faculty activists were delighted when the National Labor Relations Board had found in favor of a petition to organize made by the fac-

"I've been invited to address a conference of professors of twentieth-century American literature who are sleeping with their students."

ulty of Yeshiva University in New York City in 1975. To the NLRB, the faculty did not have sufficient authority to be considered managers or supervisors, as Yeshiva University contended. Around the nation, and particularly at Boston University, the faculty eagerly moved forward, even when the Second Circuit refused to enforce the Board's order, and the case moved to the Supreme Court.

What has since become known as "the Yeshiva Decision" set back faculty unions at private universities for two decades and left the professoriate without a cause. In 1980, the Supreme Court affirmed the opinion of the Second Circuit that faculty have managerial authority. John Silber informed the embryonic faculty organization at Boston University the next day that it was out of business, and efforts to establish faculty unions closed down all over the country. Eventually, faculty would turn to supporting other unions on campus, for clerical workers and custodians, and now, in the twenty-first century, for graduate students and teaching assistants.

At Tufts, Russell Miller captures the pervasive pessimism in his second volume of Light on the Hill. The faculty saw only "a gloomy future . . . Problems were raised but never satisfactorily solved . . . Recommendations were made, but nothing was ever done about them . . . In many ways the work of the Committee on Undergraduate Education [part of the 1973 report "A University in Changing Times"] was an exercise in futility."[3] He described two university-wide reports as "the most widely unread documents ever generated at Tufts" and in his analysis of the Graduate School of Arts and Sciences Miller states, "Tufts did not have the faculty, library, laboratory facilities or financial resources" to maintain a viable program.

It was against this background that Jean Mayer appeared at Tufts in July of 1976 and set out his improbable agenda: buoyant, optimistic, and refusing to accept any of the dark realities confounding the world, the country, and the campus.

THE STUDENTS: ALTERING THE MOOD

President Mayer found his theme for dealing with the undergraduate population after he saw a headline in the *Tufts Observer,* the primary student publication and news organ, on September 17, 1976, barely a week into his first semester at Tufts: "Admissions selectivity reaches all-time low." Tufts was admitting one out of every two students who applied. This article appeared in the same edition that printed his entire inaugural speech, in which he proposed that Tufts create New England's only veterinary school and, in passing, he laid out an agenda to deal with worldwide famine. Two weeks later, the President held a student press conference in which he announced the first $10 million federal grant for the establishment of a human nutrition research center.

Mayer gave the students the same message that he gave the faculty: Stop suffering from an inferiority complex, and get going. That is exactly how he handled his immediate concern: student pride in the institution. He had every reason to take this course. In the previous year, a series of articles written by undergraduates expressed various degrees of disillusionment, the end of student activism, the failure of the 1960s to make permanent change, and closer to home, a sense that Tufts, because of persistent budget cuts, was "stagnant and declining."[4] One persistent reporter retrieved the five-year campus master plan from 1972, which projected at least four new buildings on the Medford campus, including a long-awaited campus center, drama center, and research/classroom buildings. By the fall of 1976, none had materialized, and none were anticipated.

3. Russell E. Miller, *Light on the Hill: A History of Tufts College, 1852–1952* (Boston: Beacon Press, 1986), 381–86.
4. *Tufts Observer,* January 30, 1976, 10.

The capacity of the new President to alter the mood of the student body was one of the great paradoxes of the Mayer presidency. In actual fact, he really did not possess any reliable instincts in dealing with college students and their academic priorities. President Mayer often boasted of his service as Master of Dudley House at Harvard and the House courses that he offered, but he did not understand the undergraduate curriculum particularly well. His first remarks to the faculty of Arts and Sciences suggested that Tufts ought to cease giving credit for elementary foreign language courses. "Everyone should speak some basic second language, we should not give academic credit for Berlitz learning," he told me in an early meeting with departmental chairs. He understood little about foreign language courses and teaching methodology, although he considered himself an expert in just about every subject. Twenty-six years at the Harvard School of Public Health had not prepared him to deal with undergraduate education, but he had an opinion about everything. In an interview with the student press during his first months, he attacked the Experimental College for permitting peer teaching. The "Ex. College" was a creation of the 1960s that empowered students to explore new ideas with faculty regarding curriculum and academic innovation. It had a policy board made up of equal numbers of students, faculty, and some administrators who approved courses taught by outside people with expertise that the faculty did not possess. These "Visiting Adjunct Part-time Faculty" were lawyers, physicians, union organizers, small business owners, advertising executives, and stockbrokers who offered street-smart knowledge that the faculty did not have to enrich the curriculum. From time to time, a student, even an undergraduate, who had, for example, an expertise in numismatics, would offer a course. Students could only give grades of Pass/Fail to other students. The Ex. College also became the testing ground for new languages. Chinese, Japanese, Hebrew, and Arabic started there, showed staying power with student interest, and were accepted into the curriculum by the faculty. Korean and Armenian had a chance, were offered, but demonstrated no capacity to maintain interest among the larger student body and were dropped. Currently, Hindi-Urdu is being tried out.

The Ex. College was most useful as a pressure valve where students could let off steam and get a sense of empowerment in an area usually reserved for faculty. The four student members of the eight-person Board were given full voting rights, and a two-thirds majority was required for all major decisions. Here students' political activity and their demand for alternative educational opportunities could be absorbed. The university's Afro-American Studies and Women's Studies programs were started in the Experimental College.

Peace and Justice Studies had a home for ten years in the Ex. College before the faculty of Arts and Sciences voted to take it over. It also was an innovator in creating peer-advising programs that gained national recognition. Mayer had no idea of the popularity of the Ex. College among Tufts undergraduates, and he never fully understood innovation in American higher education. He was a classically trained European with an elitist belief in that tradition. But, when he saw the firestorm his remarks caused, he wisely accepted an invitation to meet with the Ex. College Board, and he smoothed things over. Although he was never a cheerleader for the Experimental College, he learned to keep a respectful distance.

His true genius was in taking charge of the campus mood and the alumni alienation that he inherited, and, through the strength of his own personality, transforming the atmosphere. In October, he entered into an agreement with MIT, Harvard, and Wellesley to permit Tufts students to join the ROTC and train in Cambridge. Nothing had caused as much bitterness among the Tufts alumni as the elimination of the ROTC program in 1969. Actually, Tufts did not eliminate the program; the faculty simply de-recognized the military courses and withdrew academic rank and title from the military teachers. Without these, the Department of Defense pulled its people out of campuses all over the country. Administrations had no choice in the matter, because the faculty had purview over curriculum and academic appointments. But MIT was a land-grant school, and as such its faculty had no choice in the matter: Land-grant institutions were by law obliged to serve the ROTC or be in danger of losing all federal support. Regardless of the political will of the MIT faculty, no one was going to risk the loss of *all* government money. Mayer gave two reasons for joining up with the three Boston universities. "The country must be defended," and he genuinely believed that Tufts students with military training represented the best officer material. There was also a more pragmatic need: "Right now we have damn little money for scholarships," he told the student press. There was some grumbling from one or two faculty, but the students were accepting, and it made the new President an instant hero with the older alumni.

It was his national visibility that changed the mood at Tufts. "Mayer puts Tufts in the national spotlight," the *Observer* headlined on November 19, still in his first semester. "If Jean Mayer has done nothing else for Tufts, he has certainly put the university on the map by making headlines across the country." Three weeks later, editor-in-chief Jeff Kindler wrote: "The end of Mayer's first semester here allows us the opportunity to pretend, for a moment, that the dust from his whirlwind has settled temporarily and to evaluate the beginning of his tenure at Tufts . . . What emerges is a picture of a man who has no doubt where he is leading the university." Kindler then quoted *Boston Globe* editor Thomas Winship, who earlier in the week had presented the Tufts President an award at the Golden Globe ceremony: "Jean Mayer is *the* college president to watch in the country today." For the undergraduate students, watching their President meant watching their university, and their pride of institution leaped forward. The student newspaper even supported a 9 percent increase in tuition. Kindler laid it out: "The student body of 1977–1978 will be asked to finance the future. As collateral, the university offers diplomas that may be worth much more twenty years hence. The student is being asked to look beyond his four years here. It's a gamble, but a worthy one. It will result either in a big payoff or the loss of all the chips."

The effect of Mayer's presence could be seen as well as felt. The new Dean of Admissions, Michael Behnke, announced in April of Mayer's first year a significant increase in applications. In the year-end wrap-up, the *Observer* editors—like all student journalists much more eager to carve up a university administration—gave him a resounding vote of approval: "Few can questions the success of his first ten months as Tufts tenth president. Hopefully, the future will confirm the great expectations he has encouraged."

The honeymoon would not last for his entire term of presidency. There were many incidents during the sixteen years he served when the students savaged him for his statements and actions. His acceptance of the gift of the Ferdinand Marcos chair for the Fletcher School took place during his second year. Again, his traditional instincts and historical roots betrayed him. Imelda Marcos had worked with him on some very tough issues of world hunger, and they had traveled together. Ferdinand Marcos was the most decorated war hero in his nation's history, and that resonated with Mayer's values. Above all things, Mayer considered himself a historian, and he assumed that the students would understand what it meant to fight fascism and to defeat the Japanese and the Germans in World War II. He paid little attention to the contemporary dictatorship in the Philippines.

It seemed almost that the undergraduates were drawing a new energy and advocacy from the President himself. In bringing vitality and renewed internationalism to the campus, he sparked student activism. The campus papers were filled with Mayer's speeches about solutions to world hunger and the need for action. Ironically, he lit the candle of campus engagement. Soon after the Marcos incident, students began organization for divestment in South Africa.

And they forgave him, because he was bringing eminence and attention to their university. The campus was happily stunned by the increase in the acceptance rate of the class that arrived in September 1977. Instead of the 1,050 entering freshmen that had been planned for, 1,422 had accepted the offer of admission! The yield had gone from 31 percent to nearly 40 percent, and the campus was swamped with students. The university had to rent two floors of the Sheraton Commander Hotel in Harvard Square and set up a shuttle bus service to transport the students to the Medford campus. Newspaper headlines talked about "the Mayer Effect." There was also a dramatic fall-off in transfers and withdrawals. The momentum was building, as applications to Tufts increased 15 percent annually in Mayer's first three years. While he was generating $500,000 annual deficits, the editorial board of the *Observer* seemed delighted with his activities: "During much of the month President Mayer could not be found in his office. He was in Indo-China and Rio. As Vice-Chairman of the President's Commission on World Hunger, [he] led a four-man commission to Vietnam. In Rio he spoke at the major plenary session of the XI International Congress on Nutrition." In a special December supplement, the editors wrote: "The national publicity, new programs and new facilities generated by Mayer have been the number one cause of the leap in Tufts popularity."

In his toughest year, his third, he weathered the resignation of the two most popular faculty members/administrators in the Arts and Sciences. Kathryn McCarthy was admired; Bernie Harleston was loved. On the announcement of her resignation, Provost McCarthy told the faculty, "The struggle is just beginning," but other than the article telling of her resignation, the campus media made no editorial comment. When Dean Harleston resigned, a genuine outpouring of enormous affection came from students all over the campus, and the Dean made it clear that it was his differences with the President that caused him to step down.

But no one took up the gauntlet. The students looked around, saw construction, new programs, and energized fundraising. They were also listening to their parents, who were being told at home by friends that Tufts had a very exciting President.

The President could also get lucky. In the first issue of the *Observer* in September 1979, the year of the presidential evaluation, editor Neal Shapiro (in his adult life twenty years later head of NBC News) warned: "In many ways, things have never been better at Tufts. The University continues to expand, to receive national attention and to attract a higher quality student. Yet Tufts has run at a deficit for three consecutive years, the campus is overcrowded and students and administrators are starting to wonder . . . Observers say that this could be the crucial year, crucial for Tufts and crucial for its president, Jean Mayer." One month later, the headline in the October 12 issue trumpeted in bold letters: "CORMACK AWARDED NOBEL PRIZE." Alan Cormack, a Tufts physicist, had been awarded the 1979 Nobel Prize in Medicine. In 1963, Cormack had developed mathematical algorithms that the scientific community saw as having no particular value. He did not even bother seeking a patent. But his and other contributions to the field of nuclear medicine eventually led to computed tomography (CT), magnetic resonance imaging (MRI), positron-emission tomography (PET), and all future body-scanning technologies that have revolutionized diagnostic medicine. His great friend and fellow physicist, Kathryn McCarthy, had done the laborious work of nomination and advocacy all during the previous years. But, it was Jean Mayer who stood next to Professor Cormack at the Tufts news conference. For all intents and purposes, this was another feather in the cap of the Mayer presidency. The students loved it, Tufts had its first Nobel Laureate, and it happened during the presidency of Jean Mayer. At the end of this, his third year as President, he was re-appointed, but by the thinnest of margins.

His personality and optimism fueled his resiliency. He weathered two building occupations in the years between 1982 and 1985, once when he reversed a positive tenure decision of a popular, politically activist sociologist, and again when the Trustees were slow in responding to South African divestment. In early November 1979, while on the way to tour refugee camps in Cambodia, he had an attack that was diagnosed as a coronary. The President was rushed to a hospital from the airplane, Mrs. Mayer joined him, and in the issue of the *Observer* where this story appeared, Chairman of the Board Allan Callow gave what sounded somberly like a eulogy for a lost leader when he said, when questioned about the President's illness, that Mayer's contribution over the years to Tufts had been profound. However, the illness proved to be no more than a reaction to a vaccination, and he was in his office one week later. He was back, with the same élan. Soon after, he announced that the student Campus Center in Medford would be his highest priority, and in 1980 he secured an anonymous $1.5 million gift to name the campus center after his much beloved wife. When the Betty Mayer Campus Center's cornerstone was placed in the ground in 1984, President Mayer was delivering on a promise made by five previous Tufts presidents. From that point on, he could do no wrong.

When his persistence, optimism, and luck were aligned in the heavens, everything fell his way. For ten years he had been pursuing the Frank W. Olin Foundation for a building grant. The F.W. Olin Foundation gave two grants a year to private colleges or universities, worked closely on the design and construction, sent their own architect, paid for everything down to the last shingle, turned the key, and handed it to the university. For nine years, President Mayer, who did not enjoy begging foundations, gave the F.W. Olin people proposal after proposal for a building for chemical engineering, nutrition, biotech, and was routinely turned down. His last proposal got to the final six selections, but again was rejected. Furious, Mayer instructed his foundation people to take the consolation $50,000 given to applicants who made the semi-finals. Without his permission, I called the Olin office and asked if Tufts could have one more chance. They agreed, and I went to the President, begging for one more crack at Olin. He threw his hands up in disgust, said he did not care, just keep him out of it, he was through with "these obnoxious people," whereupon we organized a proposal for a modern language and culture building, a theme that Olin had never previously funded. Mayer was delighted when he called me with the news that Tufts was getting the Olin Center for Culture and Language in the 1989 foundation appropriation.

By the early 1980s, the mood of the nation had swung to the right, and President Mayer was a rare university president willing to use the bully pulpit of his office. He picked his spots, kept close contacts in both political parties, and when he saw an opportunity to speak out, he did. On a December 26, 1983, "Face the Nation" television interview, he was asked to respond to President Reagan's comment that the reports of great malnutrition in America were "grossly exaggerated." He endeared himself to the students by replying: "Well, I am sure that there are many things that the President knows that I don't know, but nutrition does not happen to be one of them." In 1986, he received the National Society for the Prevention of Blindness Award, and in his acceptance speech urged a fifteen-year campaign to combat blindness, and remarked that funding for neurological research "seems to be more realistic than the Strategic Defense Initiative." Senator Kennedy called the next day to congratulate him. Jean Mayer, who often said that modesty was not particularly a virtue, took his university with him into the limelight, and the student body was quick to realize it. His pride became their pride.

Years later, as he approached the end of his presidency, Jean Mayer was past seventy years of age and was far removed from the culture of the Tufts undergraduates. Those later generations of students were not even aware of how this grandfatherly gentleman with the charming French accent had transformed their university totally.

THE FACULTY OF ARTS AND SCIENCES:
"THE GREAT MANIPULATOR"

In the spring of 1978, Leila Fawaz was a newly minted Harvard Ph.D. in Middle East history, with two job offers in the Boston area where her husband practiced medicine. She thoroughly enjoyed her interviews and meetings with the Department of History at Boston College. The reception at Tufts had been less cordial, and she was very sensitive to this kind of emotional chemistry in a department. Her first instinct—which she followed—was to accept the offer at Boston College. Hoping for validation from her closest mentors in Cambridge, she asked two distinguished Harvard historians, Harry Hanham and David Landes, if they thought she made the right choice. They made the same point: "Go where Jean Mayer is President; also, the Fletcher School," Hanham said, and Landes concurred.

The image that his two former Harvard colleagues had of Jean Mayer was to prove prescient in the years to come for the Tufts community, but also for the wider academic world, which typically did not anticipate the swing in mood in the nation that would result from the landslide victory of Ronald Reagan. Eventually, some academic leaders would have to emerge and challenge the new criticism coming out of the nation's capital and elsewhere. William J. Bennett was appointed Director of the National Endowment for the Humanities in 1981 and served until 1985. He was succeed by Lynne Cheney, who served until 1993. In that period, academics in general were to be exposed to an assault on their profession that had not occurred since the hot blasts of H. L. Mencken, who delighted in hammering the university community.[5] Mencken's tone and challenge were taken up by a whole generation of aggressive conservatives who were no longer willing to sit back in what they saw as a culture war, with the prize being the hearts and minds of the American public. This was to be a top-to-bottom effort on the part of the more conservative voices of higher education who had felt marginalized by the generally overwhelming liberalism found on the American campus, particularly in the humanities and social sciences. Ronald Reagan had empowered them. At the student level, a new and strident conservative journalism was to lead the way. In 1980, the *Dartmouth Review* announced the first call to battle, and two years later, Tufts' *Primary Source* published its first edition. Characteristically, the less pugnacious Tufts conservatives immediately tried to distance themselves from Dartmouth's already nasty tone. The first *Pri-*

---

5. See, among others, "The Groves of Academe," in *Prejudices,* Fifth Series (New York: Alfred A. Knopf, 1926), 133–41.

mary Source editor, Danny Marcus, announced, "the *Dartmouth Review* makes an impact by being shocking. It's bad journalism. Our goal is not to be like that. We are not Ronald Reagan's newspaper."[6] More than twenty years later, both magazines are still going strong.

From his seat at the NEH, Bennett was able to articulate the issues that he found generally on campuses all over the United States in the early 1980s. He was blunt and made his opinions clear: Faculties were out of touch with the majority of Americans, and they preferred to ignore President Reagan's landslide mandate; a relatively small percentage of faculty had captured the quorums of Arts and Sciences meetings and were pushing through a highly political and ideological agenda; most faculty did not want to be bothered, and preferred to avoid faculty meetings; the "liberal elite" had turned into "an adversary culture" and were attempting to force these ideas down the throats of an unsuspecting student body and their parents, who were being told, Bennett said, that "America is sick and corrupt."[7]

Here was a former faculty member who had taught at Williams and Boston University, openly critical of American higher education. Furthermore, he spoke with the authority of a newly elected president who, it was being predicted by liberal academic economists, would lead the country into deeper economic crisis, but instead oversaw an expansion of almost eight years of consistent economic growth. (Just before the second Reagan landslide in 1984, the Tufts campus voted nearly 60 percent for Senator Mondale. The campuses *were* generally out of touch with the American voter. Bennett quotes Cornell Professor Werner Dannhauser: "Show me a college professor and I will show you someone who mocks Ronald Reagan."[8]) The culmination of Bennett's initial slam at the state of American higher education came with Allan Bloom's *The Closing of the American Mind* in 1987, the first of the published jeremiads denouncing the American university.[9] It was hard to ignore the criticism, because Bloom's book became an instant best seller and remained so for two years. He was followed by even more belligerent attacks that also caught the ear of the America public. In 1988, Charles Sykes authored another best seller called *Profscam,* even more scathing in his denun-

6. *Tufts Observer* 17, September 10, 1982, 3.

7. See William J. Bennett, *The De-Valuing of America* (New York: Simon and Schuster, 1992), 13–52.

8. Ibid., 159.

9. New York: Simon and Schuster, Allen Bloom, *The Closing of the American Mind* (1987).

ciation: "Almost single-handedly, the professors—working steadily and systematically—have destroyed the university as a center of learning and have desolated higher education, which no longer is higher or much of an education."[10] Social critics like Roger Kimball and Hilton Kramer joined in; dissatisfied academics such as Chester Finn, Bennett, and Cheney expressed harsh criticism of the liberal professoriate, and the National Association of Scholars gave an organizational home to the conservative voice that demanded to be heard.

It was a time when leaders of American universities needed to step forward, and Jean Mayer was never reluctant to take up the challenge. He also loved the center stage. The faculty of Arts and Sciences, regardless of the disagreements that it would have with him, realized as quickly as the students that this presidency was going to be an exciting ride. Mayer had the same effect on faculty morale as he did on students' self-esteem. He galvanized them, manipulated them, and in the end changed the faculty's perception of itself.

The Arts and Sciences faculty at Tufts reflected all of the stress, strain, tensions, ideological battles, and changes that were buffeting higher education in the 1980s. I can scarcely recall a faculty meeting that President Mayer did not chair. There was only one place he wanted to be, and that was in front of the faculty, telling them of his plans and stating his opinions. He was impatient with faculty process and what he saw as an endless conversation. After one long and futile meeting, he told them: "If the First Amendment had been put before this faculty, at least two members would have reasons to table it."

He was also surprisingly quick to understand the need to protect the traditions of great undergraduate teaching that he had inherited, and that had not necessarily been part of the culture of his previous employer. Harvard certainly had the occasional great undergraduate teacher, but rarely did that person, by the 1970s, make it to tenure unless he had demonstrated that international research reputation that Harvard so cherished. The Harvard tenure procedure was reasonably familiar to those outside it. When a candidate came up, he was not considered a candidate per se for the position. He was one of a cohort of candidates for an open spot in the department, and the search would involve listing the top five or ten candidates around the world. The most impressive widely reputed scholar would receive the offer, and more often than not, the incumbent in Cambridge did not get the nod. As in the other great research universities of the United States, the preoccu-

10. Regnery Gateway, Charles Sykes, *Profscam* (Washington, D.C.: 1988), 4.

pation with grants, federal funding, and scholarship in general had led to what Page Smith had identified as "the flight from teaching . . . The talk is always about teaching 'loads.'"[11]

Tufts had a different tradition. Although Mayer, no sooner had he set foot on campus, announced that the road to reputation and eminence was through expanded research, he had been around long enough to realize that Tufts' greatest strength was still as a teaching college where undergraduates received most of the attention of the faculty. What he wanted to bring about—and which he ultimately did—was to make it a teaching institution where everyone did research. From time to time, he and I had some great battles about this balance. Tufts had a beloved three-person Geology Department, with a tradition of undergraduate teaching that went back for generations. The members traveled to the poles with their students; climbed mountains, and hiked up and down cliffs all over New England and the national parks. They did not do much research, but they sent countless students on for graduate work. Soon after I became Provost, the President instructed me to start building a department of petrochemical geologists with a graduate program that would lead to serious federal funding. He needed convincing that this was not the place to tamper with a Tufts tradition. To his credit, he listened and learned to respect the older generation of great teachers that he inherited who might not have enjoyed scholarly reputations. He knew that the Economics Department had one nationally known scholar of the Soviet economy, Frank Holzman. But, he also knew that the students flocked to Professor Dan Ounjian, a great advisor and teacher who had gone to Tufts College and was the incarnation of the "Mr. Chips" image. Ounjian never published a refereed article, but the quality of his teaching sent generations of Tufts undergraduates to some of the best doctoral programs in the country. It was to Dan Ounjian that Mayer turned when he needed action from the Economics Department. The President never showed anything less than great respect for those people whom he knew could lead the faculty in the direction he wanted. Mayer was the Great Manipulator, and no one seemed to mind. People like Ounjian were everywhere in the Arts and Sciences: Seymour Simches, Georgette Pradal, and Martine Loutfi in French; James Elliott and John Gibson in Political Science; Jerry Collins in Drama; Bob Dewald in Chemistry, who besides being a great teacher was the rare chemistry faculty member with a research group and NSF funding; Zella Luria, Walter Swap,

11. Page Smith, *Killing the Spirit: Higher Education in America* (New York: Viking Press, 1990), 1–6.

Marty Zelin, and Lucille Palubinskas in Psychology; Jesper Rosenmeier in English; Howard Hunter in Religion; Bert Reuss in Geology; Jack Zarker in Classics; George Marcopoulos in History; Ben Perlman in Mechanical Engineering; Jim O'Leary in Engineering Graphics and Design; Sylvia Feinburg in Child Study; Norton Nickerson in Biology; and dozens of others, all committed, scholarly, and well versed in their fields, but whose primary reputations were made as teachers. Their great contribution was in the classroom and coffee shop. They were five-day-a-week faculty members, and if you needed them on weekends, they were available.

In the pre-Mayer days, Tufts also had some newly arrived, future academic stars who eventually grew to national scholarly eminence. Sylvan Barnet in the English Department had come to Tufts from Harvard in the early 1950s, like so many new Ph.D.s not wanting to leave the Boston academic world. He had other interests, such as collecting Japanese calligraphy; Boston's museums and collections meant a great deal to him. He and his two graduate school partners, William Burto and Morton Berman, became an academic industry. "Barnet, Berman, and Burto" editions of introductions to literature and writing style represented no less than the entire college division of Boston-based Little, Brown and Company. If the Tufts name was known to anyone in Kansas or Mississippi, it was because these first- and second-year college texts were adopted everywhere in the country. Barnet was also editor of a very popular Shakespeare series and dozens of other anthologies and collections. His introductions were erudite and readable. In addition, Barnet was a superb teacher of Shakespeare in the largest lecture classes in the university.

Sometimes, you are lucky. John Fyler took a position in English in 1971 because, of the one hundred schools he wrote to, Tufts was the only one to offer him a job. He went on to become an eminent Chaucer scholar who also managed to teach Old English to generations of excited undergraduates studying Beowulf. The classicist Peter Arnott had arrived at Tufts from the University of Iowa before Jean Mayer, with a reputation as the country's leading anthologizer of Greek and Roman plays in English translation as well as perhaps the world's great classical puppeteer. His one-man performances of the classical repertoire drew enormous crowds wherever he performed. He had tired of the Midwest and sought a position in Boston. The Department of Philosophy was a little jewel of a department with an enormous reputation, built by Hugo Bedau, who recruited Norman Daniels from Harvard and Daniel Dennett from UC Irvine. Bedau was already the leading anti–death penalty voice in academic philosophy; Daniels, earlier part of the anti-war movement as a Harvard graduate student who spent some study time behind bars, became one of John Rawls's great interpreters on compensatory justice; Dan Dennett moved into areas of cognitive science and became a philosopher about whom other philosophers write books. All of them were also superb teachers of undergraduates. T. J. Anderson was arguably the most noted Afro-American academic interpreter of Scott Joplin. Miriam Balmuth was an internationally acclaimed archaeologist of Sardinia. The Drama Department, with Arnott, Kalmin Burnim, and Laurence Senelick, had an eminence in dramatic literary criticism that was unique among theatre departments across the country. Tony Smith in Political Science had established himself as one of the most promising young Ph.D.s to come out of Harvard. He had two other job offers, in Montreal and Washington, D.C. He wanted to remain in Boston, and has gone on to become one of the most distinguished political scientists of his generation. Jeff Berry came in 1974 from Johns Hopkins and set a high scholarly standard from the outset among the Americanists in the Political Science Department. Madeline Caviness, in Art History, was yet another of the Harvard B.A., M.A., Ph.D.s who wanted to remain in Boston when she came to Tufts in 1972, to a department with no scholarly aspirations. It quickly became clear that her work in medieval stained glass windows would draw international attention. John Conklin in Sociology likewise had received his graduate training in Cambridge. "I was excited by the prospect of staying in the Boston area." He did not want to find a new apartment, so Tufts was the perfect choice. That he became a prolific author of some of the most frequently adopted textbooks in sociology as well as a leader in criminology scholarship demonstrated once again that gems were to be mined at Harvard, if only it were done with care.

Even in athletics, not one of Mayer's great commitments, he inherited exactly what he needed. Rocco ("Rocky") Carzo took over as varsity football coach in 1965 after a career in Division I sports programs and soon became Tufts' Athletic Director. He wanted something else, as well, and he found it in Jean Mayer, who eventually wanted to push a nutritional health initiative all over the campus. Carzo adopted the President's agenda, became a champion of wellness and physical fitness and could be found during endless summers cavorting with a pack of students and faculty around the hills of the Tufts European Study Center in Talloires.

Although Mayer strengthened significantly the international thrust of the university, Tufts already enjoyed a reputation in modern foreign languages and literatures, particularly in German and French, where the critical acclaim for the writings of Ron Salter, Alan Clayton, and Christiane Romero extended across the Atlantic. None of these young scholars came to Tufts for research facilities, libraries, or graduate students, none of which were at hand. Boston was the great attraction before Mayer's coming. The tiny Faculty Research Fund routinely paid out much of its money for Widener visiting library cards at Harvard. The Tufts library collection was virtually useless. Eventually, they would need a catalyst to keep them at Tufts. They found it in their new President. He also wanted the faculty publishing in eminent presses, preferably university presses. He saw an opportunity in the newly formed University Press of New England, a consortium of about a dozen small but eminent colleges and universities, led by Dartmouth. He sent an entrepreneurial engineer, Professor Percy Hill, to Hanover to look things over, and Hill reported that UPNE was an opportunity. Tufts officially joined the consortium on July 1, 1979, with the Tufts President leading the cheering.

Tufts Arts and Sciences also had some programs in place that needed exploitation and were perfect fits for Mayer's strong international commitment. With his interest in world famine and hunger, his vision for Tufts' role was a global one. Not every university he might have led would have presented him with the opportunity that the school in Medford offered him. There were only two departments responsible for the teaching of modern languages: Romance Languages, and the department that the President called "the Department of Everything Else": German, Russian, Chinese, Japanese, Hebrew, and Arabic. Before his arrival, these departments had created strong relationships with European universities. A French program in Paris was started in 1964 under the leadership of Professor Seymour Simches, then Chairman of the department. I had done my student Fulbright year in 1956 in the German university town of Tuebingen, in the southwest corner of the Federal Republic, on the edge of the Black Forest and not far from Strassbourg. When I arrived at Tufts in 1964, my first determination was to establish an exchange program with Tuebingen, which started that same year. Today, forty years later, both programs continue to flourish. The Tufts-Tuebingen relationship is the oldest existing program between a German and an American university. In the abstract, the President saw the Tuebingen program as an important part of his strategy. In reality, he wanted nothing to do with the Germans. During his presidency, he received a stream of invitations to visit Tuebingen or any other part of the German higher education system. To the best of my knowledge, he never set foot in Germany again after the surrender of the Third Reich. He had a long memory.

Mayer saw the opportunity inherent in the inchoate international agenda that Tufts already had, and he embraced it. No previous Tufts president traveled overseas as extensively as he did. Talloires immediately became a focal point for international meetings on a variety of world health and nutrition issues. The Tufts students in Germany and France were joined by a newly created Spanish program set in Barcelona, and they began gathering at Talloires for their orientation. Later in Mayer's presidency and with his encouragement, historian Martin Sherwin established a relationship with faculty at Moscow State University who wanted to explore with Americans the evolution of research that led to the atomic bomb and the political implications of the Atomic Age. Sherwin's interests eventually led to simultaneous classes in Moscow and Medford taught via a "space bridge."

The final piece was the International Relations program, which inevitably became the largest of all undergraduate majors. He realized that the Fletcher School was hemmed in and needed space. The President instructed Schlossberg & Cassidy to seek funds for Fletcher expansion. With eighteen months, they had linked Tufts with another university in an earmark that made two congressional districts happy and provided facilities grants for the expansion of two schools of advanced international relations. Fletcher was one of them. He also saw an opportunity to drag Fletcher closer to the rest of the university by building into the grant application office space for an undergraduate program in international relations. It was created at the President's urging in 1977 by the faculty of Arts and Sciences with some input from the Fletcher School, not as a separate department, but as a program to be run by committee. Normally, faculty committees running academic programs could produce a nightmare, but in this case the results were profoundly important for the university. The IR major and the extensive conferencing both fit into the undergraduate summer program at Talloires equally well, and the President was in the middle of everything. Junior Year Abroad applications increased because of the strong foreign language requirement of the IR major. The seniors who returned from these overseas programs—as many as 30–40 percent of the junior class was studying abroad—immediately applied for Fulbright scholarships. Within three years of Mayer's arrival at Tufts, the university was sending proportionately an extraordinary number of Fulbright award winners overseas, generally back to the countries where they had spent their junior year. Tufts was blessed with extraordinary directors of the programs in Tuebingen, Paris, and Madrid. Bob Asch became an institution and legend in Tuebingen; "Der beste Amerikaner" they called him in the local newspaper. He, Virginia Remmers in Paris, and the Berenguers in Madrid were twenty-year veterans who gave unimaginable stability to these programs and created generations of loyal Europeanists with Tufts degrees.

When the Cabot Intercultural Center at Tufts University was dedicated in 1980 as the new home of the Fletcher School of Law and Diplomacy, the Director of the Undergraduate Program in International Relations occupied a suitable part of the sixth floor.

What appeared as an explosion of Tufts' international activities in the Arts and Sciences was not missed by Tom Murnane, who established an International Advisory Board of Overseers comprised mostly of Tufts parents and previous undergraduates now living abroad. This proved to be a very focused and generous group, attentive to their own geographic interests, but willing, as it proved, to endow chairs in Greek and Aegean Studies, Eastern Mediterranean Studies, and Iberian Studies, and to fund a wide range of programs in international affairs.

But Mayer's first priority in Arts and Sciences was with the faculty. He saw the strengths of the undergraduate faculty and he saw the glaring weaknesses. There were science departments with scarcely any federal funding. Biology and Chemistry were in deplorable shape. Labs were fitted with broken hoods, the facilities were dilapidated, and the faculty, some of whom were admirable teachers, could not compete for federal grants.

Mayer, who never waited for deans, started calling into his office departmental chairs, and gave them orders: When you do searches, look for potential scholars just as much as you would look for teachers. Look particularly for biologists and chemists who could be funded. He smacked his lips as he pointed to the Physics Department, which had maintained for the previous twenty years a considerable grant from the Atomic Energy Commission, succeeded by the U.S. Energy Research and Development Administration, later the Department of Energy and ran a strong high-energy research program with a group of scientists who, for Tufts, were a complete anomaly. There was nothing in the Arts and Sciences remotely like it. The indirect costs returned to the university from this one activity were greater than the aggregate from all the other departments of Arts, Sciences, and Engineering. (From 1957 to 2003, this small number of astonishingly influential particle physicists led by Professors Jack Schneps and Rick Milburn brought in nearly $23 million in grants to Tufts, never missing a funding cycle!) He also instructed Frank Colcord, Dean of Arts and Sciences, and Fred Nelson, Dean for Engineering, that the bar was going to be raised for tenure, because that was the only way to move forward: The faculty needed a push. He made it clear to me when I became Provost in 1981 that he did not like faculty-elected committees on tenure and promotion, because they usually reflected the faculty's instinct to elect the weakest scholars it could find to run for office. Indeed, within three years of Mayer's arrival, the faculty elected a committee completely made up of associate professors who were a long way from promotion to the final rank. The President played a very active role in the tenure cases. He read everything and went over every case meticulously. He was absolutely certain that he knew more about *everything* than any candidate in the humanities or social sciences. "What can she tell me about George Sand that I don't know?" he would ask. He also got a perverse pleasure in telling the faculty that he overturned a committee recommendation, when in fact it was his Dean or Provost who took action.

But, the idea was not to overturn faculty recommendations; it was to bring in candidates who were so good that we could all agree to their tenurability. This was where his influence was felt. In his view, the Biology and Chemistry departments were critical in setting the tone. They should include excellent teachers, fine mentors for both undergraduates and graduates students in research, and above all: be fundable. This was a challenge, because Tufts was not a major producer of Ph.D.s. These two departments had to teach literally thousands of undergraduates every semester. Graduate education and research took second place, and there was a time in Mayer's early years that no one in Chemistry was funded. The German and Russian Department, on the strength of one grant from the National Endowment for the Humanities, had more indirect costs coming to the university than Chemistry!

Mayer insinuated himself into the hiring of new faculty. Even the candidates who were being interviewed for positions had felt the difference. Professor June Aprille, who came to Tufts in 1978 and became a leader in the research associated with Reyes Syndrome, sensed that "it was clear that Tufts was in the process of hiring a different kind of faculty—one that was more research oriented while still being dedicated to fine teaching. I came to Tufts for the opportunity to do research and teaching at a high level, an opportunity that was created, I believe, by Mayer's vision. The hires around my era seem to have begun the transformation . . . You could see that there were going to be different standards for tenure and promotion." She recalled vividly Mayer calling her into his office where a foundation head had mentioned that they were considering her for a grant. "He personally helped like that to get us going. He was very inspirational." Aprille became one of the best-funded researchers in Biology, was an outstanding teacher of undergraduate and graduate students, soon became departmental chair and recruited the next generation of biologists for Tufts. Perhaps her greatest contribution was as Principal Investigator of a grant awarded by the Howard

Hughes Medical Institute in 1989 for five years called the "Undergraduate Bioscience Education Initiative." The $1.5 million was exclusively for undergraduate research and provided for three new tenure-track positions that eventually became four, three of whom were eventually granted tenure. In 1994, Hughes gave a second $1.8 million award for the same purpose.

Chemistry, when Mayer arrived, was little more than a wasteland. By 1981, the department had almost doubled its size. One of those new appointments, then Assistant Professor David Walt, who over the next twenty years would become one of the university's most productive scientists, now required Mayer's intervention. He had been hired with the expectation that a high-field nuclear magnetic resonance spectrometer, an NMR device, would be available to him. When he arrived, there was no spectrometer and no plan to acquire the $300,000 piece of essential equipment. Three junior chemistry faculty members walked into Mayer's office and told them of their dilemma, that their research programs could not even begin without the critical machine. Mayer called in Dean Frank Colcord, who stood in front of the young scientists as Mayer told him, "Buy it." Walt clearly remembers thinking: This is where I can build my career. This man will make it happen.

The bar had been lifted in the sciences. But, Mayer took his classical French education very seriously. For him, the center of the academic universe was the history department. Martin Sherwin had only just arrived from Princeton as a diplomatic historian, having won acclaim for his study of the dropping of the first atomic bomb on Japan.[12] The President wanted to meet him, and Sherwin and his wife Susan, who happened to be on campus, found themselves in Mayer's office. Sherwin recalls "his clear intention to do whatever he could to build up the quality of the History Department. The President was committed to the idea that history was at the heart of education." Nearly thirty years later, Susan Sherwin remembers that first meeting. When the President was talking to a young faculty couple, he was on stage: "He talked a lot about history and his own background . . . He was effusive and delighted that we were at Tufts . . . There was never an occasion in which I was present that Jean Mayer did not lift the level of the exchange and bring something interesting, even fascinating, to it. I remember every moment we were in his presence."

President Mayer also caught on quickly. He had come from an academic tradition in science of high-powered competition. He ran a tough lab for

12. Martin Sherwin, *A World Destroyed: The Atomic Bomb and the Grand Alliance* (New York: Alfred Knopf, 1975).

twenty-six years at Harvard's School of Public Health. Tufts surprised him. He said at his first faculty meeting: "Forgive me if I misspeak from time to time. I have spent my entire academic life at Yale and Harvard, and I am not accustomed to being at an institution where the people actually seem to like each other." That remarkable sense of cordiality had always been a characteristic of Tufts, going back to earlier presidents. Historian Richard Freeland had warned that it was also a reason for Tufts' lack of progress back in the 1950s and 1960s: The place was just too comfortable. Jean Mayer did not try to change that culture, but he did add the right amount of vinegar to the recipe to perk things up. This high-powered scientist-president allowed the civilized atmosphere to prevail. Maryanne Wolf, Professor of Child Development, inspirational teacher, and one of the world's leading experts on reading disorders, came to Tufts in 1980 with her new Harvard doctorate. "I was very intrigued by Tufts, in part because of Jean Mayer and in part because it reminded me of a small town where everyone could get to know everyone, just like getting to know you and Jean in those days. The real question becomes: why did I stay, and the reasons are the same." The transformation and re-focusing of the Arts and Sciences faculty was perhaps the most significant event of the Mayer presidency. It truly was destined to become a great teaching faculty where everyone did research. Mayer did not see the completion of this evolution, but he was there at its creation.

THE FLETCHER SCHOOL OF LAW AND DIPLOMACY: DOWN FROM OLYMPUS

My own undergraduate experience at a small liberal college exposed me early in my academic career to the unique intimacy of the American college experience. I knew the entire faculty at Brothers College of Drew University, called "university" because of the Methodist seminary that shared the oak forest, but in reality nothing more than a tiny college adjacent to a little divinity school. My graduating class numbered seventy-five. The Philosophy Department had one member. Faculty meetings were held in a small dining room. There is nothing like the American college experience anywhere else in the world for getting to know everyone on campus.

On the other hand, the American research university has evolved into a series of silos, with thick walls to separate school from school. Derek Bok's experience as a new faculty member at Harvard Law School was typical: "One of my reasons for choosing to teach rather than practice law was the thought of mingling with scholars from a wide variety of fields. I had looked forward to spirited lunches at the Faculty Club with archaeologists fresh from digging in exotic lands and astronomers brimming with theories about life on other planets. Alas, nothing could have been further from the truth. The Law School, filled as it was with friendly colleagues, seemed cut off from the rest of the University as if by a vast moat."[13] Law schools historically have cut themselves off from their parent universities whenever possible. Law librarians had been instructed by the American Bar Association Academic Committee to report directly to the Dean of the Law School, and not to some central university librarian. Law schools often will hold their commencements independently of the university ceremony, and if it is possible to have the school located on another campus, away from the rest of the university; that would be the best of worlds.

Bok's experience could find an echo in any number of schools or departments at a university. Traditionally, the medical school has limited communication with other health sciences, particularly keeping the dental school at a distance. A department of medicine by itself can permit internal politics to divide it into fiefdoms. Those who are not cardiologists have been known to describe that specialty in their department as "the third rail: touch it, and you die." If there happens to be a veterinary school in a university, it is usually located in some isolated rural area, far from other schools, and in any case, they deal with animals, not humans. Business schools have been known to build their own libraries and athletic facilities, for the exclusive use of their faculty, students, and staff.

Then there is the issue of sheer size. The American research university has generally evolved into a behemoth. Some of the state institutions have become communities with more than sixty thousand students and concomitant numbers of faculty and staff. Even the Ivy League has institutions whose enrollment reached over twenty-five thousand students with departments numbering hundreds of faculty. That elusive sense of "community" very quickly reflected Professor Bok's disappointment. In some cases, you do not even know everyone in your department.

Universities such as Tufts were scaled-down versions, but still demonstrated a complexity that could result in the silo effect. Geography also played a role. When Jean Mayer arrived in 1976, he found a medical and dental school in Boston along with a Tufts undergraduate and graduate program housed in a unit historically called the Boston School of Occupational Therapy. On the hill in Medford, there was the undergraduate population in lib-

13. Derek Bok, *Higher Learning* (Boston: Harvard University Press, 1986), 1.

eral arts and engineering numbering around 4,000, the mostly part-time 1,000 students in the Graduate School of Arts and Sciences, and the 220 students and 20-plus faculty—many part-time—in the Fletcher School of Law and Diplomacy, the oldest such graduate professional school in country, founded in 1933. The total population of Tufts was a manageable 6,500-student body. Historically, the Fletcher curriculum was an amalgam of political science, government, international law, and economics. The school had been created from the loftiest ideals: to counteract the isolationism that dominated attitudes in the United States since the failure of Congress to ratify the Treaty of Versailles and to join the League of Nations. The Fletcher mission was to help America see its world responsibilities, to play a role in what some saw as a dangerous world that would require this country and its people to engage in a struggle for freedom. Intellectually, one might have reasonably expected a measure of synergy with the appropriate departments in Arts and Sciences. But history took a hand in how the school and the university viewed each other. Fletcher seemed to have two missions: educate future foreign service officers; and stay as far away as possible from any identification with Tufts University.

First, the history: When the Fletcher School was created in 1933 through an endowment left ten years earlier by Austin Barclay Fletcher, it was stipulated that the bequest be used to establish a school of law and diplomacy. Boston already had every conceivable kind of law school related to the needs of the American Bar Association. When Harvard's Law School Dean Roscoe Pound went to President Cousens with the idea of creating a school of international affairs and law to combat the isolation of the United States in the 1930s, they quickly reached agreement. The result was the first school giving a graduate degree in international relations. There would be no American law degree as such. Harvard students could take courses at Fletcher, Fletcher students would be permitted to register for law courses at Harvard, and Harvard and Tufts would jointly administer Fletcher. The endowment would remain at Tufts. After the first year, the basic agreement was modified to vest full administrative responsibility in Tufts.

That might have been the last agreement jointly arrived at by the two institutions for the next twenty years.

In the period between the founding and the end of World War II, the academic playing field where Fletcher was administered look more like an uneven battlefield. From the beginning, nine of the eleven faculty at Fletcher in 1933 were part-time lecturers who had full-time Harvard appointments. Tufts simply did not have the resources for advanced graduate work in international relations. Tufts College contributed one course, from the Chairman of the History Department, Halford L. Hoskins.[14] President Cousens tried to recruit a dean, but the endowment did not throw off enough funds to make taking a position at Tufts attractive, even if there was a Harvard connection. Hoskins served as Acting Dean, and when Cousens could not convince anyone to take the position, he gave the permanent deanship to Hoskins, over the objections of newly appointed Harvard President James Conant and the rest of the Harvard faculty. From that point on, the Harvard faculty simply ignored Hoskins. "The Harvard people taught what they wanted, when they wanted to, without seeking approval from the School's dean," wrote Timothy Brown.

The school opened in 1933 with twenty-one students, five of whom came from Harvard. None held Tufts undergraduate degrees. As far as these students were concerned, they were studying at Harvard, but unfortunately were located geographically in Medford. They used Harvard's Widener Library, were taught by Harvard faculty, and enjoyed a self-imposed isolation from the rest of the Tufts campus, which until 1955 was, after all, merely a college. The Fletcher administration avoided using the Tufts name on stationery whenever possible.

Over the next forty years, this strange relationship continued, with the Fletcher students wholeheartedly identifying themselves with Cambridge, cross-registration of students overwhelmingly out of balance and tilted toward Harvard, and a sense of alienation on the part of the Tufts community who systematically were excluded from Fletcher activities. Fletcher's institutional identity and the allegiance of its faculty, staff, and students had little or nothing to do with Tufts University. One wonders why Harvard, a preeminent research university already developing its own strength in international fields, bothered to maintain the agreement with Tufts over those forty years. By 1943, only a decade into its existence, Fletcher did not look viable. The endowment was drying up and disappearing, student enrollment had fallen, and there were not enough funds to recruit a decent faculty.

But, for the first time in the uneven relationship between Fletcher and Tufts, the field tilted in another direction. The Arts and Sciences had recruited two young diplomatic historians who proved to be both fine scholars-

14. These events and the subsequent historical narrative are taken from an unpublished Master's degree from the Harvard School of Education, written by Timothy Benjamin Brown in 1991, *Initiating Professional Education in International Education: The Fletcher School of Law and Diplomacy, 1923–1943.*

teachers and able administrators. They took an interest in Fletcher, which by that time was in no position to turn a back. Harvard had no doubt decided that the Fletcher School would fail by itself, without need of Harvard delivering the coup de grace. Dean Hoskins, after ten years of an unhappy administration, abruptly resigned, giving three days notice on June 27, 1944. Professor Ruhl Bartlett, who was Chairman of the History Department in Arts and Sciences, took over as Acting Dean and served for a year until the appointment of Robert Stewart, a graduate of the first Fletcher class with a Harvard Ph.D. who had enjoyed a State Department career in European Affairs. Stewart was quick to see where the academic quality of the faculty was situated: on the other side of the campus. He appointed Bartlett to a tenured position at Fletcher immediately, and also brought over to the Fletcher faculty from History Professor Albert Imlah. Bartlett and Imlah gave instant academic and intellectual credibility to the Fletcher faculty. Stewart served for eighteen years as Dean. His tenure represented the only sustained period of intellectual excellence that Fletcher enjoyed during most of its first half-century of existence. He still could afford very few full-time faculty. As late as 1960, Fletcher had only three full-time appointments. Yet, these three full-timers served at a time that the Fletcher School exercised its greatest academic and intellectual authority. Surrounded by part-time Harvard and MIT lecturers, these three became, as one testimonial described the one living emeritus in 1981, "the soul of the Fletcher School of Law and Diplomacy." They were Leo Gross, George Halm, and Ruhl Bartlett. All three had come to Tufts via the undergraduate college. Two were refugees from Nazi Germany. They left an unforgettable mark on generations of Fletcher students.

Of the three, Leo Gross was the most beloved by his students. An expert in the field of international law and organizations, Gross came to the College in 1941 and in 1944 was appointed to a full-time professorship at Fletcher. He retired in 1980, but taught part-time for several years after that. He died in 1990. He received his doctorate from the University of Vienna in 1927, came to the United States in 1930, and stayed. For Jewish academic refugees from Hitler, there was not much of a job market, and Gross worked for various private and public agencies, including the League of Nations and the State Department. He lectured occasionally at Fletcher from 1941 to 1943 until enough funds were scraped together to make him a full-time appointment. He was a great authority on international law and organizations, an advisor to nations, after World War II a scholar welcomed everywhere in the world, but most important to his Fletcher life, a most admired teacher and mentor. He was elected to the American Academy of Arts and Sciences in 1958.

George Halm brought an even stronger international reputation for his scholarship when he came to Tufts College in 1937. He had arrived in the United States two years earlier, another refugee from Nazi Germany. Halm was not a Jew. He was a "Wunderkind" economist, receiving his doctorate from the University of Munich at the age of twenty-three, and appointed to his chair at Wuerzburg at twenty-seven. His articles and books were published and circulated all over the world. When Hitler came to power, it was known that Halm would have "a problem" at Wuerzburg, because his wife Lore was Jewish. It took him two years to settle his affairs, and he left for America in 1935. His first academic position at Tufts was in the College Economics Department, which would only provide him a Lecturer's title, then immediately promoted him to Assistant Professor, but not until 1942 did Halm become an Associate Professor. By that time, Fletcher realized what it had in its midst and offered Halm a Professorship in International Economic Relations. Halm, Gross, and Bartlett collectively gave the Fletcher School an instant scholarly reputation, which it previously did not have. Halm was elected to membership in the American Academy of Arts and Sciences in 1955.

Halm, Gross, and Bartlett were clearly academicians shaped by their times. Two were refugees from fascism. Bartlett was a Wilsonian historian who viewed the triumph of American democracy and the defeat of the Axis powers as the turning point of world events in the first half of the twentieth century.

By the time Jean Mayer came to Tufts, the Fletcher School and its faculty had assumed a completely different scholarly orientation and enjoyed a wholly new reputation. The generation of the Second World War was elderly and on the verge of retirement. A new, cold war had begun, and the Fletcher School was very much a part of it.

The Dean of Fletcher was Edmund A. Gullion, not an academic, but rather a career diplomat and former Ambassador to the Republic of the Congo. He assumed the deanship in 1964, and soon after proclaimed himself "an unqualified supporter of American involvement in Vietnam." He was also about to transform the faculty and the school.

After the conclusion of World War II and the beginning of the Cold War, schools such as Fletcher began taking on a role unusual in American higher education. These advanced professional schools of international affairs—years later formed into an organization called the Association of Professional

Schools of International Affairs, or APSIA—took on a strategic role in rela-tionship to the security of the United States. Those located in Washington, D.C, particularly the schools associated with Georgetown University and Johns Hopkins, enjoyed a relationship with governmental agencies that could be interpreted as blurring the lines between disinterested scholarship and national purpose. Johns Hopkins School for Advanced International Stud-ies, SAIS, was located in the nation's capital rather than in Baltimore for that very reason: to be close to the action. This relationship to government pol-icy also was reflected in the kinds of people that these institutions sought to bring on board as faculty. They were not traditional scholars of political sci-ence, economics, or international affairs, but rather "practitioners" of the art of government who might author works that reflected the political orienta-tion of their previous government service, either as consultants to federal agencies or in many cases as former full-time government employees, up to ambassadorial or secretarial rank. As a consequence, historically—right up to the current times—the faculty at these "outposts" of governmental policy generally did not produce those scholars who were advancing knowledge in the fields of study. That remained the task for the less employable and more traditionally trained Arts and Sciences faculties; the significant scholarship in these areas came from that quarter. Only in the field of economics, both international and domestic, did the government turn to the Arts and Sci-ences for the best and the brightest rather than to these more applied and Washington-oriented practitioners. Rarely would one find the university's star economist on the faculty of an APSIA school, the exception being Prince-ton's Woodrow Wilson School and the School of International and Public Affairs at Columbia (SIPA), where the Arts and Sciences faculties were merged with the professional schools.

Fletcher's leadership over the previous eighteen years before Edmund Gullion's arrival in 1964 had been coming from the traditional academic ori-entation of Dean Robert Stewart, who, although he had been in government service, had a doctorate and was considered by his peers to understand the scholar's world. Dean Gullion did not, nor did he have a particularly good instinct for the academic sensibility. His entire career was in the diplomatic service, starting as a Vice-Consul in Marseilles in 1937, with subsequent ser-vice in Salonika, London, Algiers, and Helsinki. The young diplomat was trained by Dean Acheson and Robert A. Lovett, two of the first-line builders of American post–World War II strategy. He was at the epicenter of many of the great U.S.-U.S.S.R. confrontations, commencing with his appointment in 1949 to the American Embassy in Saigon. Gullion left as Charge d'Affaires in 1952, just as the war in Indochina was intensifying. His diplomatic apex came with his appointment as Ambassador to the newly independent Republic of the Congo in 1961. Gullion was right in the middle of the events in the aftermath of the Patrice Lumumba murder. He served for three years in Africa's hottest Cold War nation, with the CIA by all accounts very actively involved in trying to destabilize or stabilize a government and to move it away from the Soviet orbit. His activity in this underdeveloped, mineral-rich former colonial country, then in the midst of an ideological struggle between the Soviets and the Americans, very much affected how he saw his role as Dean of the Fletcher School.

Dean Gullion presented striking similarities to Ambassador Gullion. He was clearly Chief of Mission of the Fletcher School and set its course by determining its political direction. He had been on campus a very short time when he announced his position on the American presence in Southeast Asia. In the fall of 1964, this was a certain way to drive a wedge between Fletcher and the rest of the university. He did not bother with any of the academic niceties of open searches. Between his arrival and departure in 1978 he had found considerable financial resources and added nearly a dozen faculty members, many of whom had been associated with him over the years. He was a passionate believer in containment of the Soviet Union as a strategic objective of American foreign policy, and to that end he recruited Uri Ra'anan in 1966. He had met Ra'anan in Europe years before and endorsed his aggressive anti-Soviet position. Field Haviland had been with the Brookings Institution where he had met Gullion, who had promised to write a book for Brookings about the experience in the Congo. The book never materialized, but Haviland received an invitation to join the Fletcher faculty in 1968, to succeed Leo Gross in the field of international organizations, although Professor Gross was not ready to leave. Haviland remained at Fletcher for another fifteen years and never extricated himself from this marginalized role.

The Dean had several strategies in mind, all emanating from his global vision. He had seen in the Republic of the Congo what USAID programs could accomplish in pulling the native population toward a particular view of the world. To that end, he wanted to establish at Fletcher an international development program and brought in a close subordinate from the Congo mission, Robert West, who set up the Fletcher Program in International Development Studies.

In 1971, Professor Robert Pfaltzgraff came first as a part-time visiting faculty member, then the next year as full-time from the Political Science Department at the University of Pennsylvania. Pfaltzgraff was a different breed. He was already a very productive scholar, and his research interests in European security were exactly what the Dean was looking for. He was recognized in the field of international relations theory, and Gullion knew him from conferences on arms control in which Pfaltzgraff had participated. Above all, he was an indefatigable and energetic organizer and had already created an independent think tank called the Foreign Policy Research Institute that produced policy pieces and conference papers dealing with issues of Soviet containment. Here was both a high-quality academic and a practitioner who would gain access to like-minded congressmen and serve as a consultant to governments. The NATO people thought very highly of him as well. In his first full-time year at Fletcher, Pfaltzgraff established the International Security Studies Program and a few years later he brought the Philadelphia-based think tank to Cambridge, Massachusetts, as the Institute for Foreign Policy Analysis. Within a short time, every other academic program at Fletcher came under the shadow of the Security Studies program. Pfaltzgraff and Ra'anan became a formidable tandem, and by the early 1970s the Fletcher Image was carved in ideological stone, as far as many in the academic community were concerned. The firebombing of Dean Gullion's office in March 1971, not necessarily an act committed by someone in the Tufts community, characterized the chasm that existed between Fletcher and the rest of Tufts. Feelings on both sides of the gulf were running very high. Fletcher wanted nothing to do with Tufts, its administration, or its student body. From the perspective of the Arts and Sciences, Fletcher was a walled fortress surrounded by an impenetrable ideology.

As is often the case, neither side completely had a handle on the truth. Several eminent young scholars on the Fletcher faculty were able to keep clear of the other politicized groups, and Dean Gullion should be given credit for expanding the Fletcher curriculum. Benjamin Cohen was a brilliant young political economist whose international interests drew him to Fletcher in 1971. Alfred Rubin came in 1973 as a specialist in international law and quickly became one of the world's leading experts on international piracy and the law of the sea. Rosemarie Rogers, an émigré from Austria, was an internationally recognized scholar in the field of refugee movement. The Dean also realized that in the future, international business would find a place in the Fletcher curriculum and made the first move in starting the International Business Transactions program.

But the Dean's most important appointment came in 1973. By this time, he had granted tenure to a half-dozen faculty who had produced uneven scholarly results in areas marginal to mainstream political science and international relations. Pfaltzgraff, Cohen, Rogers, and Rubin were the only contemporary Fletcher scholars whose works could be found on syllabi at other universities. Gullion recognized that he needed either an academic dean or someone to free him up for activities more in keeping with his skills of diplomacy, namely, raising money. He saw the needs of the Fletcher School and was willing to put his energy to this task. He was the first Fletcher Dean to get out of his office for the purpose of raising money. (His successor did even better.) Gullion went to the Luce Foundation and applied to the National Endowment for the Humanities for funds to establish a chair in Civilization and Foreign Affairs. He knew the person he wanted, and he shaped the job description to fit.

John Roche was one of the more remarkable figures in the Fletcher community over the past three decades. He was in every sense a Renaissance man. He was very smart, shrewd, had an utterly unscrupulous side, demonstrated unwavering loyalty to friends and relentless contempt for enemies or just people he took a dislike to, and just when you thought you knew him for a scoundrel, he could be completely disarming. He was a sharp academic politician who had swum with the sharks and played a senior advisory role in the Lyndon Johnson White House. The Beltway Roche was a constant Johnson loyalist during the grimmest days of the Vietnam War, and when pressed hard by publishers, who were dangling enormous advances to write a memoir of his times with Johnson, refused to produce the standard insider's gossip. He took many of LBJ's confidences to his grave. After leaving Washington, D.C., Roche returned to Brandeis University, where he became Chairman of the Department of Political Science and later Dean of the Graduate School. He had come out of earlier faculty days at Quaker Haverford as, in a description by one of his colleagues there, "an authoritarian left-leaning socialist," but Stalin and World War II had begun the process of moving Roche's ideological compass heading. By the time he had become President of Americans for Democratic Action, he had swung close to Gullion's orbit of anti-communist containment. He became too conservative for Brandeis, and when Fletcher offered him the Luce Professorship in Civilization and Foreign Affairs, he jumped on board. It was not for several more years under a new Dean that Roche actually gained the title of Academic Dean, but in Gullion's last five years, Roche fulfilled the role of gray academic eminence. He had enormous energy, was a charismatic teacher, for a time wrote a national column that infuriated his old liberal buddies, exercised a stinging tongue on most of the academic community for whom he had open contempt, and became a fixture on several State Department advisory committees. At the same time, he was enough of a nonconformist to irritate his more hawkish colleagues, and on domestic matters, he never abandoned his socialist roots. He could speak some Yiddish and fit comfortably into his Brooklyn Irish-Jewish neighborhood until the day he died. He also understood academic quality and soon realized that help was needed at Fletcher.

Jean Mayer was astute enough as a scholar to observe, after he settled into the Tufts presidency, that the Fletcher School was living on its reputation. Gullion had tenured nearly a dozen faculty without serious peer review, most of whom were consulting and not producing anything resembling a distinguished body of scholarship. Pfaltzgraff, Rubin, Rogers, and Cohen were the exception. Mayer would read the doctoral dissertations coming out of Fletcher and express considerable unhappiness to anyone in earshot. He also did not appreciate what he considered Fletcher's standoffish independence. He put himself on the search committee for the new Dean when Gullion announced that he intended to step down at the end of the 1978 academic year, after fourteen years as Dean. The President wanted someone with at least a sense of what constituted a university. He found someone who had the university in his genes.

Theodore Lyman Eliot, Jr., became Fletcher Dean in 1979. He was the last living American Ambassador to Afghanistan. His successor was assassinated. Ted Eliot's academic pedigree could be found in his roots. He had relatives who had served as presidents of Harvard and Washington University in St. Louis. While he did not have formal academic credentials, his two degrees were from Harvard, and he understood the dynamics of a university. Eliot possessed the patrician style that President Mayer so admired from his Harvard days. The six foot seven inch Eliot proved to be a wise shepherd for Fletcher, a great dean, and a good personal friend. We were drawn together by a mutual interest: baseball.

I had been Provost for three days in July 1981 when the Fletcher Dean made an appointment for a courtesy call. I had known that his great-grandfather had been the President of Harvard and an uncle had led Washington University. It was with some anxiety that I walked into my office to find Dean Eliot sitting on the couch, waiting for me. He stood up, and I was looking straight ahead at his belt buckle. For an instant, the differences in our backgrounds seemed like a canyon, and I had no idea how to begin the conversation. The new Dean took care of that. While shaking my hand, he looked over my shoulder at an autographed picture on the Provost's fireplace. "Is that Louis Tiant?" he asked, recognizing the former Red Sox Cuban pitcher. When I acknowledged that it was indeed Louie Tiant, Eliot continued, "Are you interested in baseball?" I told him of my life-long passion for the game and of my membership in the Society for American Baseball Research. He asked me to wait for a moment, that he had to rush down to his campus house. He returned ten minutes later with an album of the 1938 Boston Braves. We spent the next hour going over his pictures, and we have been close friends ever since.

Eliot inherited a faculty that was 90 percent tenured. He put John Roche in place as his Academic Dean with instructions to broaden the curriculum in history and culture, move into regional studies in Asia and the Middle East, and to avoid any more awards of tenure. By the time Ted Eliot announced his resignation in 1985, all of these conditions had been met.

Dean Eliot understood the resources available at a university, but he also inherited alumni with a historical antagonism and a view that Fletcher was vastly superior to the rest of Tufts University. President Mayer was going to change that perception very quickly, and during the Eliot deanship Fletcher moved closer to the rest of the Hill. John Roche and I crafted a document we called "The Treaty of Packard Avenue" (the street that ran between Fletcher and the rest of the campus). Roche realized that the strength in history, political science, and culture was in the Arts and Sciences, and we arranged for a series of joint, dual, and adjunct appointments of faculty from the undergraduate colleges. Some of the Fletcher faculty felt threatened and balked, but Roche pushed forward. Included in the arrangement was the use of Fletcher students as teaching assistants in undergraduate economics and political sciences courses, since neither department had a doctoral program. Within a year of Eliot's arrival, Fletcher students were teaching hundreds of undergraduates and were offering courses in international subjects in the Experimental College.

The Mayer-Eliot relationship was delightfully antagonistic. The Dean knew that the President would be enormously helpful in Washington with appropriations, and indeed one of Mayer's very first strategies was to acquire a new facility for Fletcher. Eliot took on the private fundraising part of this enterprise and he proved to be a superb advocate for Fletcher—and the university. Together they were a very effective pair of internationally focused advocates for the school.

But they were an odd couple: the tall, very elegant and dignified Dean whose Harvard credentials and Brahmin stock gave him access by birth to every private club in Boston that Jean Mayer wanted to join; and the short, foreign-born President who ardently wanted to impress the likes of Theodore

Lyman Eliot, Jr. Their clashes occurred usually on issues of fundraising strategies. Eliot, a confident advocate fully aware of his considerable strengths, thought he knew how to open the pocketbooks of his alumni as well as those in the foundation and corporation world; he surely had a commanding persona. Mayer considered himself and his development team the source of all wisdom on the topic; and he wanted to direct the Fletcher campaign. Eliot insisted on the Dean's prerogatives, was willing to cooperate, but demanded a certain amount of autonomy. In the face-off, the President blinked, Eliot won considerable independence, and together they brought the Fletcher physical plant and endowment to unimagined levels.

The Dean had toiled as a professional Foreign Service officer during the Cold War and was no admirer of the U.S.S.R. But he lacked Gullion's ideological tunnel vision and was frustrated in his efforts to broaden the base of Fletcher's foundation support. "I couldn't get Ford Foundation money for anything." His strategy in dealing with the dominance of the International Security Studies Program and its nationally known and not universally admired focus was to expand Fletcher's offerings in directions that would serve the school in the future and possibly dilute the ISSP. Besides capturing part of the time and commitment of the best of the Arts and Sciences faculty, he made some critical appointments in international business that developed the program that Gullion had started. The platform for Fletcher's next two-decade push into the international business and finance curriculum was constructed under Eliot's direction. He understood the potential competitive disadvantage of a school like Fletcher if it did not compete successfully with the American business schools that undoubtedly would be moving toward a more international agenda. The Cold War was still the center of world attention, but the Fletcher curriculum was already moving in other directions. Eliot also secured a million-dollar endowment from Edwin Land, the founder of Polaroid, for a chair in Japanese history that brought John Perry from Carleton College to Fletcher.

Eliot took steps that were in concert with the university and its leader. When Mayer finalized the $6.7 million combined grant and long-term, low-cost loans from HEW in September 1979 that were to provide for a new Fletcher building, the Dean instructed John Roche to work out the space needs of the undergraduate international relations program in the facility to be designed. The three-hundred-seat auditorium would be used for large undergraduate classes primarily, but also for Fletcher gatherings and conferences. He used all of his enormous diplomatic skills to educate the Fletcher students, who had passed a resolution banning Tufts undergraduates from any seats in the Fletcher Ginn Library at *any* time. The Dean asked them if they would mind being banished from the Cousens Gymnasium, the university's recreational space that was heavily used by Fletcher students and carried financially without any contribution from Fletcher on the Arts and Sciences budget. On second thought, undergraduates might occupy empty chairs, said the Fletcher Student Council. We worked out an appropriate compromise that allowed Tufts undergraduates the use of the Fletcher library facilities at any time other than exam periods, when the space would be reserved for Fletcher students.

President Mayer saw enormous university potential in Fletcher, and Eliot reciprocated. Mayer invited collaboration between Fletcher and all of the other schools, particularly in the health sciences. He wanted international programs developed in health and nutrition, global food resources, and any other health-related issues that could maximize Fletcher's reputation and organizational strengths in dealing with social infrastructures. The light bulbs went on in Fletcher and the School of Veterinary Medicine at a university-wide meeting held at Fletcher of faculty who had come together to share research interests. Professor Al Sollod of the Vet School stood up and informed the gathering that his research interests were in the area of African animal disease prevention and the development of a serum to prevent Rinderpest, the cattle disease that had plagued the world. Professor Dirck Stryker of Fletcher turned around to listen to Sollod, then said he was an economist interested in local African livestock development and establishing societal and village infrastructure in sub-Sahara Africa. The result of this chance meeting was a $14 million grant over more than five years from the USAID to support joint research efforts seeking to provide technical support to the pastoral people of the Sahel, the nomadic Twareg people of Niger. This was an unprecedented cooperative effort by two schools that had to learn each other's culture, style, and structure. It was agreed that Fletcher would initially be the primary manager of the grant. Without the two deans, Eliot and Frank Loew of the Veterinary School, this project would have been doomed. It worked only because the two schools were willing to knock down their traditional and historical walls, and they had the leadership to make it happen.

Eliot was indeed a breaker of walls, if it could help Fletcher. He was also tired of the carping about Tufts that he had heard since his arrival and was determined to create a generation of students who would begin to think more in turns of Fletcher as part of a university. When he reached his goals, he was prepared to step down, because his eyes were turned to another world. During the third year of his deanship, my first as Provost, at one of our frequent conversations, Eliot took out his wallet and showed me his driver's license: it was registered in California. "Some day I will come to you and tell you that I am leaving. Pat and I will move closer to our children. That's our goal." That message came in 1985. By then, Fletcher was in a new building shared with thousands of undergraduates who were routine daily visitors, and Eliot had shoved the Fletcher school to the center of Tufts University's image and mission. He shared Mayer's international vision and felt that the best place for Fletcher was at the heart of the university. Not one faculty member had been granted tenure during Eliot's deanship, but his hiring had set the course for the next decade.

The President had always been in the middle of deans' searches, at times even serving as chair of the committees. But the Fletcher School had exercised its traditional sovereignty even over Jean Mayer. He and Provost McCarthy sat on the committee that brought Ted Eliot to Tufts, but the alumni association and the faculty insisted that a Fletcher faculty member chair the committee, and the President relented. By 1985, some major steps had been taken to exercise stronger centralized presence. The schools continued to have great autonomy, but there was no doubting Steve Manos's span of control over their finances and budget discipline. Tom Murnane had a strong hand on the overall development activities, although Fletcher was more satisfied than the other schools, because the Dean had wrestled some of the fundraising activities away from central administration. Now was the time to inform the Fletcher community that they could remain sovereign, but ultimately they would acknowledge and accept their role within the university. President Mayer knew that I was determined not to get another career diplomat, that it was time to break the cycle and to show how flexible and interdisciplinary Fletcher really was. The search committee recommended by the faculty was a model of political correctness: two from security studies, and one from every other discipline in the Fletcher curriculum. The only difference from previous committees was the appointment of the chair, who, they were informed, would be the Provost. There was only modest protest from the alumni association. It was also made clear that I would take three candidates to the President, who would make the final decision. The committee did its work during the one-year interim deanship of John Roche, who also had served as Acting Dean for the previous search; and the mold was broken.

Although one of two candidates recommended was in the field of security studies, I made the final selection, and the President concurred. Jeswald

Salacuse had been the Dean of the Law School at Southern Methodist University since 1980, where he also taught international business transactions and international economic development law. He had received his law degree from Harvard, and spent most of the next seventeen years in Africa and the Middle East as the Ford Foundation's advisor in establishing the basis of law in the Sudan, Zaire, Lebanon, Egypt, Saudi Arabia, and Jordan. He authored the definitive two-volume study of the legal systems of all the francophone nations of Africa. Salacuse was a significant legal scholar, had a native command of French, a good working knowledge of Arabic, Spanish, and Italian, vast international experience, and had run a complex academic enterprise. His credentials were perfect for the Fletcher deanship. The alumni association howled in protest.

The President received the first of the irate phone calls from Fletcher alumni, unhappy that a diplomat had not been chosen. He told them that at this particular moment it was more important to have a scholar to raise the standards. My calls came from alumni associations, who insisted that I appear at hastily called meetings to explain myself. I declined all such invitations, but informed the membership that they were welcome to my office at any time for an explanation.

Jes Salacuse was a genuine academic. He understood academic collegiality, the empowerment of committees, the raising of faculty standards by consensus. He established a strong tenure and promotion committee and told them what appropriate academic standards should be for a school as eminent as Fletcher. He did not need an academic dean. He was his own. The faculty awarded him tenure as Professor of International Law. In addition, he possessed academic street smarts to a significant degree, and knew how to govern the ungovernable. He was transparent in his conversation, direct and willing to say whatever had to be stated, but in a congenial way. He was completely without ideology and was determined to prepare the Fletcher School to face the challenge of competing with the great business schools of the nation to train future generations of global executives. Salacuse, who served as Dean for eight years, through the collapse of the Soviet Union, had the capacity to take a curriculum strongly directed toward a confrontational agenda between super powers and redirect it for a world that was changing where he stood. The ground was shifting underneath these schools of advanced international relations, and their leadership required an agility that the Fletcher Dean fortunately possessed in abundance. The early outrage of the alumni vanished. Even those strong supporters of the International Security Studies Program did not rise up when an ad hoc Tenure and Promotion Committee, under the watchful eye of the Dean, turned down the tenure candidacy of the program's junior member. Meetings were called inviting faculty and students to protest, but the Dean and the committee held their ground, and Professor Ra'anan abruptly resigned his Fletcher appointment, after twenty-one years, before the spring semester began in 1988. By that time, the program had already added another more balanced senior appointment in Richard Shultz, who fit comfortably into the overall Fletcher curriculum. Both Pfaltzgraff and Shultz made a smooth transition to the new global arrangement after the U.S.S.R. broke apart, and they understood their role within a significantly expanded Fletcher curriculum. They became driving forces in curriculum revision and have led the way into the twenty-first century by championing programs such as Humanitarian Studies, Human Rights and Conflict Resolution, and International Environment and Resource Policy, while watching the international economic and business curriculum grow. Ironically, in the post–September 11, 2001, world, security is once again very much part of global affairs, but the Fletcher ISSP is now one program in a highly diversified curriculum.

There were no confrontations with President Mayer. Salacuse was a university dean in every respect. He had cordial relations with all of the schools and built bridges particularly with Arts and Sciences, nutrition, and environmental programs. Fletcher drew even closer to a university that was getting stronger every year. Increasingly, the Fletcher School took pride in its relationship with the rest of Tufts University. Salacuse was very quick to understand what the Tufts President was projecting as an image for the collective institution.

Nothing is as important in the job description of a Provost as the hiring of the deans. After that, you try to stay out of the way. Years later, Dean Salacuse reminded me of my words when he arrived to take over: "We brought you here to build." Ted Eliot deliberately held back on the granting of tenure. He did not like what he saw in the candidates on his arrival, certainly did not appreciate the number of tenured positions granted by his predecessor, and was determined to leave a better opportunity for his successor. Jes Salacuse took every advantage. First, he put in place a more rigorous system of faculty evaluation and would tolerate only the best scholars on a standing Tenure and Promotion Committee, even if he had to use Arts and Sciences personnel to do it. He got rid of an ad hoc system that was vulnerable to manipulation. Lawyer that he was, he put in a clear guide to contract renewal. At the end of his service as Dean, 70 percent of the faculty were Salacuse hires. He also built joint degree programs with two other schools outside of Tufts:

WILL WORK FOR
HUNDREDS OF THOUSANDS
OF DOLLARS

Dartmouth's Tuck School of Business Administration and Bolt Hall, the law school at the University of California at Berkeley. He was also "presidential," had he chosen to go on in higher education administration. But when he told me that he was stepping down as Dean as of September 1, 1994, it was to return to the faculty "for the best job in the world: a Professor at Fletcher."

THE SCHOOL OF MEDICINE: A MATTER OF TRUST

The Fletcher School's early and subsequent alienation from its university was more a function of class-consciousness, a sense that Fletcher was by any measure a superior institution than the university to which, in the Fletcher community's opinion, it unfortunately had been attached. That attitude died off as the older alumni disappeared. Students who have attended the Fletcher School over the past twenty years have enjoyed a different experience from those who were exposed to the Brahminism of the first fifty years. As Fletcher and Arts and Sciences moved closer, a much more shared faculty and common agenda made this alteration in attitude inevitable. The more recent Fletcher deans and faculty had little patience for the rigid sovereignty that separated them from the rest of the university, their fellow deans, and their colleagues in economics, political science, or history. They became one campus, basically one intellectual culture. There was also one President, and Jean Mayer left no doubt in anyone's mind, including the deans, faculty, staff, and students of the Fletcher School, that he was the President of the whole university. Granted, there will never be perfect harmony. Professional graduate students at Fletcher are considerably older, and show at times little patience with what they perceive as the political immaturity of undergraduates. But, the standoff alienation of earlier generations is gone, and Tufts presidents and Fletcher deans since Jean Mayer fully understand that there is one hill in Medford with no border crossings.

In that respect, the graduate professional schools of international relations that shared a campus with other parts of their universities made a reasonably comfortable adjustment to academic collegiality, whether at Columbia, Princeton, Harvard, Georgetown, or Tufts.

Schools of medicine are something else. Academic humor is replete with jokes about presidents of universities and their medical schools. Every year, so the story goes, the presidents of Harvard, Princeton, and Yale have a photo taken together. Only one is ever smiling: the one without a medical school. Another university president has a recurring nightmare that eventually drives him to a psychoanalyst. The nightmare has him president of a university with *two* medical schools. And so it goes.

Scholars who write about the history of American medical education inevitably come to the vexing issue of relationships and loyalties. Historically, medical schools, hospitals, and eventually medical centers have existed in various states of alienation from their universities and from each other. The more aggressive and visionary university presidents simply grabbed the wandering medical school by the throat and shook it until it surrendered. For forty years of his presidency, Harvard's Charles Eliot chaired virtually every faculty meeting at the Harvard Medical School, to the consternation of many senior faculty members. Eliot, like other university presidents, was determined to make the medical school part of the university, no matter what the medical school wanted.

Most of the 125 medical schools in the United States have been, at some time and to various degrees, in a state of war with the universities they belong to, and, in more recent times, with the affiliated hospitals with whom they share a clinical faculty. The teaching hospitals, whether owned or not owned by the universities, have had their share of conflict with them. After all, they have leaders who are also called "President." Personalities, status, and power have played a role in many of these confrontations, which continue to this very moment. Some of the recent Boston hospital mergers involved Harvard teaching hospitals, and the implications of the merger between Massachusetts General Hospital and Brigham and Women's had a far-reaching impact on the teaching of Harvard medical students as well as the other Harvard hospitals that were supposed to be part of any coalition. Harvard Medical Dean Dan Tosteson gathered the five "major" hospitals together for talks, but the MGH and Brigham and Women's leadership secretly broke away and created their own alliance. The last people to know about this merger were the Dean of Harvard Medical School and the President of Harvard University.[15] The culture of civility that had bound the physicians and medical community in Boston was shattered by the strains of the financial crisis of the 1990s. At one dramatic moment, the New England Medical Center was in crisis. Its high-profile President had resigned; no one seemed capable of staunching the flow of red ink. A merger was needed, and the NEMC physician-administrators turned to their colleagues at sister institutions for aid and comfort. Boston medicine was an intimate community; everyone seemed to have trained with everyone else, were mentored by the same legendary giants, and shared a common culture. Instead, what they found was cold-blooded economics and the hope that NEMC would close and go out of business. These recommendations did not come from the green-eye-shaded accountants, but from fellow physicians who were now competitors. NEMC survived, did find a merger partner, and has weathered the storm. But, the sense of community among people of medicine had been damaged and may never be restored completely.

No part of the academic community has experienced such perilous times as those physicians among our colleagues who also want to be called "Professor," but whose lives are infinitely more complex than those of the rest of us. No one in higher education has been forced to face such issues of loyalty and allegiance, as have the academic health professionals over the past thirty years. Up to and through the end of World War II, the image of the physician, the compassionate family "Doc," in the minds of the American public shone brighter than any other profession. Drs. Kildare and Marcus Welby were fictional icons totally accepted by the vast majority of Americans, and they reflected well on the institutions that produced them: the American medical school and hospital. But the public was unaware of the change that was coming over these institutions and their mission, which had been almost

15. See the article "Mr. Fix-it" in *Boston Magazine,* January 26, 2003.

exclusively the education of medical students and patient care in an environment of great self-esteem. Soon, however, Kildare and Welby would be giving way to a new type of physician, one who, besides his M.D. degree, might also possess a Ph.D. in Microbiology or Molecular Biology and whose primary interest was research. They would be spending time in the laboratory, writing grants, courting grateful patients, or consulting with pharmaceutical companies, rather than sitting at the bedside or making house calls. Hospital heads soon abandoned the image of the beloved Dr. Gillespie, played by Lionel Barrymore in a wheelchair in a dozen extraordinarily popular films, in favor of a corporate-model physician who preferred to pronounce on issues of national health policy while running advertising campaigns for the hospital. Coming out of World War II, the entire enterprise of the health sciences medical world exploded in a wave of federal funds generated through the National Institutes of Health. Medical schools once had viewed their world as the intersection of three activities, with medical education at the center. Research and patient care took second and third place behind the primary purpose of the medical school, which was the education of the next generation of physicians. But, as the research agendas made enormous amounts of money available, the hospitals that previously had served as a branch for the education of the medical student saw opportunities to establish independent research agendas of their own, in competition with the medical schools. Simultaneously, the patient care enterprise also blossomed into a huge money-making activity. The medical schools needed the hospitals more than ever to prepare the physicians of the future, and the clinical faculty who worked primarily at the hospitals seeing patients gradually had less and less time to work with students. To this end, the need for hospital affiliations was a driving force to make the medical schools a part of an integrated medical center, where clinical facilities were at the disposal of the medical students, who were being trained by clinicians with research agendas, patients, and a hospital administration that owned their loyalty and increasingly controlled their income. As long as the tense equilibrium could be maintained and the money flow remained uninterrupted, whatever problems might be lurking beneath the surface were held there. But, in the 1970s, the federal government pulled the plug on the funding, by which time the medical schools had been drawn away from their universities and were strengthening ties, when possible, to their primary teaching hospitals. At stake was the loyalty of a clinical faculty, who were being asked to see more and more patients and, if necessary, conduct more and more research, independent of the medical school, from which their academic title originated. In Boston, where traditionally the universities did not own their hospitals, issues of loyalty became even more dramatic, because clinical income, the principle source of salary, came from the hospitals, not from the medical school or university. The hospitals insisted, therefore, that the research dollars and indirect cost recovery generated by these physicians who were simultaneously professors at the medical school and staff physicians in the hospitals should be passed through the hospital systems, not the medical school. This was another battleground.

However, in the last two decades of the twentieth century, the inherent instability finally was driven to the surface by the crisis in managed care. What we discovered was that the medical community, when wounded and in pain, could not cure itself. When the hospitals, squeezed by insurers and HMOs, started hemorrhaging dollars in the 1990s, the system of mutual benefit and tolerance broke down, and it was every physician, medical school, and hospital for itself. In all of this, where was the university? Historian Kenneth Ludmerer asked those questions: "Could a hospital ever be a real part of a university if its primary obligation were to patient care? Could a medical school remain true to university values if its activities in patient care became too demanding?"[16]

No one had prepared a generation of dedicated academic physicians for the pain and suffering felt by their profession. Whether located at a medical school, hospital, or medical center, no one seemed able to cope. Since 1980, the tenure for medical school deans has been 3.5 years. One who lasted five years and had been warned by friends to stay away from medical administration noted, "The most poignant caution came when one of my colleagues pointed out that the word *dean* is but one letter from *dead*."[17] Deans were overwhelmed by a sense of helplessness, an inability to bring order to the lives of their colleagues and stability to their students' education. A retiring president of a surgical association, in his presidential address, agreed with a colleague who "held that the only dean who was ever good for anything was Gunga Din (pronounced *dean*), Kipling's regimental water carrier for, at least, he gave you a drink of water."[18] What one saw in these last few decades of the twentieth century was the loss of control felt by the academic health sciences

16. See Kenneth M. Ludmerer's magisterial and aptly named *Time to Heal: American Medical Education from the Turn of the Century to the Era of Managed Care* (New York: Oxford University Press, 1999), 21.

17. Samuel Hellman, M.D., "A Piece of My Mind," *JAMA*, 280, no. 19 (November 18, 1998): 1657.

18. Henry Buchwald, M.D., "Presidential Address," *Surgery*, 124, no. 4 (October 1998): 595.

community, a plummeting of morale and a growing sense of despair. The HMOs, the M.B.A.s, generally people with different letters after their names, were running the lives of the M.D.s, whether in medical schools or hospitals.

And, yet, in spite of all the malaise, this had been an astonishing time for medical discovery and progress in the academic medical community. Since the end of World War II, a medical revolution had occurred, at the center of which was Boston, a relatively small town with three medical schools, nearly two dozen teaching hospitals, and a tradition of medical teaching, research, and patient care second to none. The research reputation was driven by the Harvard Medical School, in the 1930s already a national resource and by the 1970s a titan, affiliated with hospitals generally acknowledged as among the best in the world. The other two medical schools, Tufts and Boston University, were the little kids on the block and trained general practitioners for New England. At this watershed moment, Jean Mayer became President of Tufts and looked for some academic health scientists who had no time for despair and who wanted to be part of a university that in 1976 found itself with a new president interested in lifestyle, aging, and wellness as determinants of health and illness, rather than just medical intervention. Tufts Medical School was about to undergo its own revolution.

The Tufts Medical School was very much in the same penurious condition as the Arts and Sciences had been for the past decades. In 1950, the school had moved from its original Huntington Avenue site, where it had been located since 1901, to its current Harrison Avenue location, across the street from the New England Medical Center. It converted an eight-story, totally inappropriate garment factory into classrooms and laboratories. This and the few adjacent buildings were to remain the research facility for the medical school for more than fifty years, arguably the worst medical research space in all of American higher education. No matter what renovations were attempted, it always remained a factory. But there was synergy with the institution across the street. The hospital now could offer professorial rank to its clinical staff, and the New England Medical Center—NEMC—was able to recruit through the years some outstanding clinical chiefs. When Joseph Hayman was appointed the first full-time Dean of the Medical School in 1953, in the sixtieth year of the medical school's existence, he demonstrated what could be done, even in the face of poverty. During the thirteen years of his leadership, he appointed nineteen of the twenty-two department chairs, found enough funds to renovate a few labs, and attracted some young researchers.

It was also not an accident that Tufts Medical School could compete for some excellent students during the immediate post-war years. Tufts was one of a handful of medical schools—and the only one in Boston—that did not have a quota for Jews or Catholics.[19] From 1920, medical school admission policies mirrored those of the private undergraduate schools in limiting the number of East European Jews and Catholics. Historian Ludmerer provides some startling numbers: "By the late 1930s and early 1940s, rigid quotas were found throughout medical education. In the early 1940s, 3 out of every 4 non-Jewish students were accepted, in contrast to 1 out of 13 Jewish students." Jews, Irish, and Italians came to the garment factory, to the New England Medical Center and to the Tufts University Medical School, and were grateful. They helped create its character, much of its excellence, and the willingness to accept a different model of medical culture. Years later, when Tufts Medical School was competing for students with the best medical schools in the country, I was always astonished to hear, when they selected Tufts—still in the rabbit warren of a garment factory in the most run-down section of Boston—that they chose Tufts because of the extraordinary friendliness and warmth they felt when meeting the faculty. When Joe Hayman stepped down in 1966, he had recruited a nucleus that would form the intellectual core for the next thirty years. He brought in Professor Count Gibson and established a Department of Preventive Medicine in 1957. Into that program came a young Fellow named Mort Madoff. Hayman created a Department of Community Medicine and in 1965 recruited Jack Geiger. Gibson and Geiger would be the leading forces just a few years later in establishing pioneering community health centers at Columbia Point in Boston, and then in Mound Bayou, Mississippi. The Dean brought in a young Canadian biochemist named David Stollar, an M.D. basic scientist, in 1964, the same year that Lauro Cavazos came as Chairman of the Department of Anatomy, and James Morehead was among his first hires. A year later, John Harrington was appointed a Clinical and Research Fellow in Medicine. Norman Krinsky came in 1960, first in Pharmacology, then moved to Biochemistry. The Dean wanted a Department of Microbiology and recruited Dr. James Park as its first chairman. Park recruited Elio Schaechter, Eddie Goldberg, Andy Wright, and Abraham Sonnenschein. In 1968, the department name was changed to Molecular Biology and Microbiology, and Park recruited Dr. Victor Najjar to hold the first Massachusetts American Cancer Society Chair in Molecular Biology at Tufts. When Najjar stepped down, he was succeeded by Dr. John Coffin, who currently holds the chair. The chain forged by Dean Hayman is still intact. The people he brought to Tufts would become chairs of depart-

19. See Ludmerer, *Time to Heal,* 63–64.

ments, deans of the Medical School, and the great teachers; in spite of the medical wars that threatened to overwhelm the profession in the last decades of the twentieth century, the Tufts community in that garment factory never lost its unique humanity. To be sure, relations between hospital and Medical School administrations during the Wessell presidency turned acrimonious as each institution battled for hegemony. Neither had the financial resources to do so. But the scientists on both sides of Harrison Avenue were by nature collaborators. By 1975, a young molecular biologist named Michael Malamy was training M.D. Fellows from the Department of Medicine. He also published with clinicians from Medicine. Andy Wright and Andrew Plaut tightened the links between Microbiology and Medicine and are working together productively into the new millennium. The Cancer Center at NEMC helped to recruit outstanding young molecular biologists to the basic sciences: Naomi Rosenberg, Brigitte Huber, and Coffin all needed the active existence of a basic science–clinical synergy, and they made it happen. The scientists were the matchmakers themselves.

Through the 1960s and early 1970s, Tufts Medical School remained a poor relative in Boston. Harvard University did not dominate the universities and colleges in the Boston area in the same way that the Harvard Medical School exercised authority over the other medical schools in the city. Those of us in the Arts and Sciences, for example, assured ourselves that we taught better and more often than colleagues in Cambridge, and that our mission, even among senior faculty, was to teach undergraduates. There was a huge diversity among the dozens of institutions. Harvard was big and rich, but it was engaged in different activities in different ways. The medical schools, however, did the same thing and competed for the same grants from the same federal agencies, who were obliged to fund the best proposals, which, in Boston, with rare exception, came from the well-equipped faculty at the Harvard Medical School and its affiliated hospitals. The rich got richer. Although Tufts had some superb individuals in both clinical and basic sciences positions, the physical plant made it almost impossible to take the school seriously. The Tufts Medical School routinely received the minimum three-year accreditation from the Liaison Committee on Medical Education (LCME) and was reminded that it had the worst library facility among *all* of the American medical schools. To be sure, there were dreams of new buildings and modern research facilities. The desks of more than one dean were filled with blueprints and a lingering hope that, alas, when once stuffed inside a drawer, would never see the light of day.

Still, the Medical School was not moribund scientifically. Something unique about the school and its spirit made a noticeable impact on young faculty who had worked at other medical schools in and out of Boston. Tufts Medical School managed to hold on to some superb young scientists because it was a civil place to work. The faculty actually liked each other. In spite of the garment factory, the appalling facilities, and dreadful library, the Department of Microbiology and Molecular Biology under Elio Schaechter's leadership built up a cadre of young investigators who, miracle of miracles, competed successfully for NIH funding against the giants of medical research across the river. Many faculty members at Tufts Medical School could have left for more attractive positions at any time, but they chose to stay, because they had found something that had become all too rare in the cutthroat atmosphere of big-time medical research: people they liked to be with. Scientists in adjacent labs talked to each other, ate Chinese food together, and were pleasant colleagues. Schaechter was one of those rare basic science departmental chairs who shared power and looked for consensus. Everything was a discussion, all decisions were collaborative. It was a commune. To this day, more than thirty years later, the members of that department try to keep the salary differentials as small as possible. Elio Schaechter has long since gone to California to write books about mushrooms in a well-deserved retirement, but the rare atmosphere he created is still there.

And now came a new President, with a secret: He really *was* interested primarily in the Medical School, and he intended to let the downtown community know this. Having served as Provost with three Tufts presidents and been witness to many different presidents at other institutions, I have had some opportunity to observe the variations that emerge in presidential leadership and the reactions from the faculty. Some presidents do not wish to engage, are by nature delegators, stay away from the faculty, and hope that their provost and deans can lead. These are ceremonial presidents, and they can be very effective with alumni, students, staff, town/gown relations, and just about every kind of nonacademic in the community. The faculty can be indifferent to this leadership style, as long as the money keeps rolling in. They insist on noninterference from these presidents in matters of academic policy. Since such a president would never dream of interfering with faculty prerogatives, this is a relationship that can work. There is considerable fundraising activity, but no fundamental challenges or threats to any part of the academic enterprise. Faculty and deans become prime movers. However, when a nonacademic president becomes intrusive in academic matters, decides to make over the faculty, clear out the dead wood, and bring a kind of corporate efficiency to the enterprise, war can ensue. Examples of this kind of disaster can be found throughout the annals of higher education. Often, the paradigm is the result of a chairman of the board who says to himself, "I can run this institution. It's no different than my business, and less complicated at that." Fatal words.

Another kind of president has come to the institution for the purpose of making change. Much depends on where you sit on the campus, as well as presidential temperament, in determining your response. This academic change maker can be very exciting for a faculty if the times are right for movement at a university and if the president has the emotional intelligence to pull it off with the diverse academic community. There are times when a school wants attention and become resentful when the president is distracted by his interest elsewhere in the university and ignores what some would say is the most important part of the institution, if it happens to be your part. In Jean Mayer's early years at Tufts, this reflected the attitude of the Arts and Sciences: "Why wasn't the President paying more attention to us, instead of spending all of his time with the health sciences? Didn't he realize that the Arts and Sciences were the heart and soul of Tufts," they complained. They wanted this president's attention, because it had become apparent that President Mayer was not a delegator or passive leader. He was out there, making things happen, and the Arts and Sciences faculty, unaccustomed to such activity, wanted the happenings to occur for its benefit. Still, the Arts and Sciences, accepting as they were of Mayer's academic background and international reputation, never gave him an academic appointment. Such was the uncertainty that scientists in traditional biology or chemistry departments had of the field of nutrition. What is it, they wondered. Not until the School of Nutrition became a reality did Jean Mayer have any academic recognition by a Tufts faculty.

How, then, did the object of Mayer's attention respond to this president who had come to Tufts because it had a medical school? After an initial period of bewilderment came the hope that perhaps they could keep him at arm's length. You might recall that I discussed earlier Dean and Vice President Robert Levy's puzzled response to a request by a delegation of his faculty to keep the President from coming downtown to the Boston health sciences campus. No one offered an academic appointment to this distinguished Yale-trained physiologist who had run a federally funded laboratory at Harvard for twenty-six years. The School of Medicine at Tufts could find no natural place for a nutritionist in their faculty. But that would not keep President Mayer from involvement in the health sciences.

A New View of Health

What could the Medical School faculty make of Jean Mayer's inaugural speech in 1976, when he spoke of a new day for nutrition at Tufts? Where was nutrition on the radar screen downtown? There was the Frances Stern Nutrition Center, run by the first-rate scientist Johanna Dwyer, who had trained with Mayer at the Harvard School of Public Health, but in the minds of the majority, this was not mainstream medical research or basic science. They were not overly concerned when the Nutrition Institute was established in Medford and Professor Stanley Gershoff joined the faculty of Arts and Sciences from Harvard in June 1977 as its Director. What no one foresaw was a vision that was to stretch over twenty-five years and culminate in the nine-story Jaharis Family Center for Biomedical and Nutrition Sciences, dedicated in Boston on the Tufts campus in 2002, with the School of Nutrition on the first two floors with space for cross-disciplinary collaborations, and the rest dedicated to biomedical research. The generous philanthropy of Trustee Michael Jaharis was built on the financial foundation of nearly $7 million from the federal government that, ten years after his death, validated Jean Mayer's vision of the symbiosis between nutrition and biomedical research. A few of the more venerable basic scientists moving into the new space might give a nod of thanks in the direction of Mount Auburn Cemetery, where lay buried a former president who was responsible for finally getting them out of the garment factory.

None of the ultimate beneficiaries could have had an inkling of any idea in 1976, when Mayer placed the first building blocks of his plan in place. Within a few months of his accession, Tufts was awarded a federal allocation of $2 million to make engineering and architectural studies for a national human nutrition research center. Working with the Boston Redevelopment Authority, Tufts then acquired a parcel of land at 711 Washington Street, right in the middle of the downtown health complex, and disbelieving eyes read of a $20 million construction grant and watched as, in what seemed to be a blink of an eye, fourteen stories of construction girders rose out of a parking lot normally used by "business women" plying their trade in what historically had been called the Combat Zone. The indignant ladies were replaced by a large sign linking Tufts University's name with the United States Congress and the Department of Agriculture, in what was to be a series of state-of-the-art laboratories dedicated to the study of human nutrition and aging. It did not take long for the Medical School faculty to hear that the Center was funded initially with $7 million of operating dollars that eventually would grow to a $12 million annual appropriation supporting over 50 scientists and 150 technicians and staff.

The general disbelief was mixed with a certain amount of grumbling. What was nutrition's relationship to disease? What role did nutrition play in the education of medical students or the treatment of sick patients? Why was Jean Mayer bothering with side issues in medicine and research, when the Medical School had such terrific needs? The answer to some of these questions came with the appointment of the Center's founding Director, Hamish Munro, a distinguished medical doctor, Professor of Nutrition at MIT, an internationally known protein biochemist who had an early interest in molecular biology, and a member of the National Academy of Sciences. It was clearly the President's intention to fuse nutrition onto biomedical research as a uniquely Tufts contribution. He would accomplish this with world-class scientists whom Munro would recruit. The first generation of scientists brought to the Human Nutrition Research Center on Aging were a combination of brilliant interdisciplinary investigators, many with M.D. and Ph.D. degrees. No one in the Medical School could challenge Munro's medical reputation. He even organized the laboratories in the Center to focus on the body's organs. Mayer saw the opportunity that an aging population provided; he understood that Americans were going to live longer and grow older. He convinced "Tip" O'Neill, the Speaker of the House and a close personal friend, that "Tufts Nutrition" was destined to stand tall, right next to "Tufts Medicine." The Medical School did not see it immediately, but here was the future course set by the new President of Tufts University.

If Mayer's attention to nutrition science caused some unhappiness among the Medical School population, his interest in veterinary medicine resulted in a howl and no little bitterness. After the initial shock when he announced at his 1976 inauguration his intention to establish a veterinary school at Tufts, the downtown faculty managed to organize itself into a common voice, and that voice said: The last thing Tufts needs is a veterinary school. The Dean of the Medical School at that time was Lauro Cavazos, who served from 1974 to 1980 and who would have a distinguished career after leaving Tufts as President of Texas Tech University and later as Secretary of Education during the Reagan presidency. He was not a physician, but he was an experienced medical school administrator and former Chairman of the Anatomy Department in the basic sciences. He got his first baptism of fire in the early years of the Mayer presidency. The Dean had been completely left out of any discussions concerning the building of the Human Nutrition Research Center and the creation of a veterinary school that was supposed to use Medical

School basic scientists to teach the veterinarians. But what sent Cavazos over the edge was a phone call he received from the chief administrator of one of Tufts major teaching hospitals in 1977, asking Cavazos "when the money was being transferred that President Mayer promised us for our teaching." It seemed that the Tufts President, on his own, had been visiting the teaching hospitals, conferring with administrators and division chiefs, and making promises that the Medical School would have to make good. Cavazos made an appointment for 8:00 A.M. the next morning, met Mayer in his Medford office, closed the door, and told the Tufts President: " If you want to be Dean of the Medical School, that's all right with me, just let me know." Mayer assured him that he had no such intention and promised better communication. When Cavazos left for Texas Tech in 1980, he knew as little of Mayer's intentions and plans as he did in 1977, and the whirlwind had not yet subsided.

There was literally no support for a veterinary school among the medical faculty. Mayer assured them that resources hitherto unavailable would be forthcoming when the veterinary school money started coming to the university. From the viewpoint of the Medical School, that never materialized, even when new hires in the basic sciences were made. Several times in the course of these first few years of the Mayer presidency, he would appear before an angry faculty of basic scientists and clinicians, ready to tear him apart, yet somehow he continued to work his magic. The faculty miraculously emerged from these meetings assuaged, mollified, and reassured. They had no idea what the President was creating, but they somehow continued to go along. In order to increase the size of the basic sciences, President Mayer announced to the medical, dental, and veterinary schools, without consultation with the deans, his idea of "One Medicine," that students from all three of the health sciences schools could be sitting together in one classroom, sharing the experience of basic sciences instruction. There would be one basic sciences body, he told them, with faculty from all three schools being members of the appropriate department. The first two years of veterinary education would be given downtown, in space currently occupied by the Medical School. Cavazos demanded to know where the space was. Work it out, said the President, who assured the Dean that funds for renovations would be forthcoming and that Mayer had already secured a $1.6 gift for basic sciences improvements. In October 1979, forty-one veterinary students began their education on the Boston campus, in space now shared with the Medical School, already cramped and starved for classrooms, laboratories, and money.

Indeed, there was a $1.6 million gift, from the medical entrepreneur Arthur M. Sackler, whom the President had met through a common friend, Professor Louis Lasagna, an internationally recognized pharmacologist with close ties to the pharmaceutical industry. Lasagna, at the Medical School of the University of Rochester, had created the Center for Drug Development with funds donated by Sackler and others and was recognized as the "Father of Clinical Pharmacology" for his contributions to the field. Mayer informed everyone downtown that this money was the first that would provide resources for much-needed improvements—and it was never seen again. Whether Mayer intended it or not, the Trustees immediately applied these funds to the mounting deficits of the Veterinary School, and the downtown campus never saw any of this money.

"Hospitality" was not an operational concept when the veterinary students found themselves sitting among the medical students in histology, biochemistry, physiology, and pathology. It soon became apparent that *everyone* was going to be unhappy. The Medical School faculty thought that the entire idea of One Medicine was no more than a fantastic Mayer conspiracy to provide the Veterinary School with courses and a faculty at no or little cost. The veterinary faculty saw immediately that insufficient comparative aspects were being taught in classes taught by Medical School faculty, who did not want to go the extra mile in supplementing their lectures. For their part, the veterinary students resented lecturers who emphasized only human physiology, microbiology, and diseases. Finally, the medical students simply announced that they were not interested in animal models. The cultures clashed irreconcilably. When the Veterinary School administration wanted to hire teachers to fill out their curriculum, which required accreditation from the American Veterinary Medicine Association, the basic sciences chairs vetoed appointments in their departments unless these new hires would be of use in the ongoing research agendas. Cavazos took an instant dislike to the first Veterinary School Dean, Al Jonas, whom Mayer had recruited from Yale Medical School. Jonas, intelligent, irascible, and lacking in the diplomatic and interpersonal skills needed to gain acceptance in this explosive environment, was fired by Mayer in the spring of 1981 (or, rather, was fired by Provost Shira. The President simply did not have the stomach for face-to-face confrontations).

To make matters more confusing, Mayer announced that the Ph.D. programs in the five basic sciences departments, logistically attached to the Arts and Sciences faculty in Medford, would now be located administratively in Boston and formed into the Arthur M. Sackler School of Biomedical Sciences as a school with degree-granting authority, but no budget of its own. The Medical School would fund it. Mayer was single-handedly—and generally without consultation—making wholesale changes in organization and curriculum in the health sciences schools. The Medical School carried the brunt of the burden, without compensation. This was too much for Cavazos, who announced his resignation. In June 1980, President Mayer appointed Murray Blair as Acting Dean of both the Medical School and the Sackler School. Blair, a pharmacologist and Ph.D., fit the Mayer mold and would stay out of the President's way.

Thus, was the Sackler School given life. The faculty could not believe that Tufts would name a school for a gift of $1.6 million that was immediately delivered to another school of the university, but there it was. The trustees dutifully voted approval of the Sackler School on July 1, 1980. The school of basic biomedical sciences at Tufts was born. For its entire history, the Sackler School would try to figure out what its relationship was to the Medical School. As Mayer conceived of One Medicine, all of the basic scientists were now faculty members in three schools: medical, dental, and veterinary. They reported to chairs who were also now the chairs in three schools, each of whom reported to three deans, which, in effect, meant that they reported to no one. It looked like anarchy. Marty Flax, the Chairman of the Department of Pathology, commented in disbelief: "It was all done by mirrors!"

Yet, in the midst of this apparent chaos, equaled by a similar administrative confusion that was gripping the Arts and Sciences, the presidential magic began to work. In 1977, with the help of the two previous chairmen of the Department of Medicine, Sam Proger and William Schwartz, Mayer recruited Sheldon Wolff from the NIH as the new Chairman of Medicine at Tufts and Physician-in-Chief at the New England Medical Center. Wolff was one of the nation's most highly regarded scientists, and Mayer "worked him over" until he accepted the Tufts and NEMC position. Shelly Wolff was also one of the most energetic builders of scientific programs in the country, as well as a superb mentor. He brought to Tufts some of the best and brightest young medical scientists from the NIH and built a new kind of intellectual relationship between clinical and basic sciences at Tufts. Scientifically, the hospital and the medical school moved closer together, as both began expanding their research agendas. Mayer prodded and poked the scientists on both sides of the street, and with the creation of the Sackler School with the term "biomedical sciences" in its title, the faculty for the first time built an M.D./Ph.D. program. Now, programs in Immunology and Neurosciences demonstrated the value of interdisciplinary clinical–basic science research.

Graduate students in Sackler were the immediate beneficiaries. They now had a home. Before Sackler, doctoral students in the basic sciences were registered in the Arts and Sciences in Medford, which diminished their feeling of connection to the Medical School. They had little connection with Medford, either. With the creation of the Sackler School, despite its lack of resources, graduate students in the Medical School were provided with a strong departmental and interdisciplinary home. By 1981, the quality and quantity of Ph.D. applicants to the Sackler was clearly improving.

The Tufts image in health sciences was changing. The name seemed to be everywhere. In 1979, the Tufts Health Plan was established as a not-for-profit health maintenance organization (HMO) by Morton Madoff, with Jean Mayer's blessing and Trustee approval for the use of the Tufts name. Mayer continued his globe-trotting advocacy of nutrition issues, famine relief, and worldwide food distribution; in the United States he took on all problems related to hunger and nutritional needs of the population both rich and poor. He was arguably the country's most vocal and visible advocate on these pressing national concerns. His column appeared in dozens of newspapers nationwide.

Two Scorpions in a Bottle

There was little doubt that the President enjoyed his notoriety, and once the Board of Trustees—or at least the four horsemen who had decided that they would ride this president for better or worse—had committed to him, Mayer's expansive personality filled whatever space was available, particularly downtown where he felt his reputation in nutrition would make the greatest impact. He loved the attention of the nation and particularly of Boston, appearing with regularity on the local prestigious public television and radio programs. Christopher Lydon, a local PBS personality, could not get enough of the Tufts President, who would pronounce on any health-related issue. The news and publicity associated with the federally funded nutrition building, the Sackler School downtown, and the Veterinary School out in Grafton placed Mayer and his university in the center of the Boston conversation about health. As mentioned earlier, he and his congressional friends successfully had fought off the efforts of other local schools to get a piece of the action in nutrition. The Boston academic heavyweights were not accustomed to having Tufts University standing in the limelight, especially since both Harvard and MIT had made alterations in programmatic activities to downplay their nutrition programs. The other great academic personality in town, Boston University President John Silber, turned his attention to issues of higher education in general, and both Tufts and B.U. gained enormous visibility in the marketplace. The Massachusetts congressional delegation gave them the spotlight, and there was enough room for two. Space, however, would have to be made for others.

In 1979, the New England Medical Center appointed a new leader, not as an Executive Director, but as a President, Executive Director, and Chairman of the Executive Committee. In an act almost as daring as that taken by the Tufts Trustees, the hospital Board in effect turned over every aspect of management and governance to Dr. Jerome H. Grossman. His appointment meant that he was President of the corporation that owned the hospital, Chairman of the Executive Committee of the Board of Governors that ran it, and Chief Executive for Operations. Grossman was destined to become Boston's first all-powerful hospital ruler. He shared authority with no one.

Jerry Grossman had come from the Massachusetts General Hospital, and in much the same fashion that Jean Mayer used Harvard as his model and challenge, Grossman was determined to carve out for the New England Medical Center a unique identity that would bring it out from underneath the shadows of the powerful Harvard teaching hospitals: MGH, Beth Israel, Brigham and Women's, Deaconess, and Children's. He came with unique talents. In 1979, his career-long focus on information technology in health care delivery was years ahead of its time. He understood managed care and was an early participant in the Harvard Community Health Plan, whose automated medical record system he developed. In 1969, Grossman created Medical InformationTechnology (Meditech), a pioneer organization in the development of integrated hospital information systems. He was a visionary, an entrepreneur, and an energetic change agent who wanted better things for the institution that he now was leading unequivocally, almost without accountability.

It is difficult to imagine how much New England Medical Center and Tufts University School of Medicine might have accomplished, had these two remarkable leaders been able to tolerate each other. As it was, this proved to be a Golden Age for both institutions, in spite of the fact that hospital, medical school, and university were in an uninterrupted state of conflict.

Rarely had I ever met two more similar individuals who disliked each other so intensely as did Grossman and Mayer. Each had a similar goal: to control the other's institution. Jerry Grossman took his title of "President" very seriously, and he felt that there was room for only one such designation in the relationship between his hospital and Tufts. That being the case, he preferred severing all relationships with the Tufts name, going so far as to have the traditional form "Tufts-New England Medical Center" removed from the Dental School tower in the middle of the night in the early 1980s. He also discouraged his clinical faculty from using the Medical School professorial titles in their publications.

Where the Tufts medical faculty saw Mayer as chaotic, they viewed Grossman as ruthless. Since he provided the overwhelming number of dollars of salary for his clinical faculty, he demanded their loyalty, and he tolerated little in the way of opposition. Mayer could charm his way into faculty hearts. Jerry Grossman used other weapons more effectively. Above all, he demanded and got the loyalty of the Department of Medicine, the single largest contributor to research dollars in the health sciences and, under Shelly Wolff's guidance, a place where basic scientists and clinicians enjoyed a genuine synergy. Thanks to a grateful patient, the hospital was able to renovate elegant space for Wolff's department. When Medicine moved into the Tupper Building, all $4 million of research money went with it, leaving the Medical School out in the cold. The rivalry and bitterness did not disappear when Jean Mayer left the presidency in 1992. Every year from 1979 to 1995, the annual report of the Dean of the Medical School—no matter who it was— echoed Dean Henry Banks in 1985, when his opening sentence read: "The major problem that remains is that of our relationship with the New England Medical Center. At this writing there is no progress in this regard." If Grossman could do damage to the Medical School, he would do it. When it came to medical school accreditation, he could be his most mischievous. By 1986, the tenth year of Mayer's presidency, the downtown campus had blossomed with two new extraordinary Tufts constructions. While there had been only tepid enthusiasm for the Human Nutrition Research Building, the medical school community finally realized that President Mayer could deliver on his promises when they saw the completion of the eight-story Arthur M. Sackler Center for Health Communications, a building that provided desperately needed classrooms, office space, and a state-of-the-art library. Dean Banks could not wait to go through the accreditation review with the Liaison Committee for Medical Education, the LCME. Everything, he felt, had changed in his medical school, and this 1945 graduate who had been selected by Mayer because of his loyalty as much as his reputation as an orthopedic surgeon, was ready to show off.

Imagine his crushing disappointment when Tufts Medical School received its by-now routine three-year limited accreditation, because of a "disruptive relationship with its primary teaching hospital." The LCME report was otherwise completely laudatory and filled with praise for the new facilities, research expansion, curriculum, and student enthusiasm. But one interview with the hospital president was all it took. Only when an exhausted and worried Board of Governors, in what seemed a different time and different age, saw New England Medical Center approach the edge of ruin in 1995, did Jerome Grossman leave; and only then did the healing begin.

In spite of this rivalry and the associated turmoil, hospital and medical school from 1981 to the end of the decade enjoyed a period of unprecedented prosperity and growth. Basic sciences research, with the appointment of new leaders, made huge strides. Mayer's friend Louis Lasagna was appointed Dean of the Sackler School in 1984, along with a new Chairman of Physiology, Irwin Arias, an M.D. researcher with a worldwide research reputation in the physiology of the liver. David Stollar, another rare consensus builder, in Biochemistry, Bryan Toole in Anatomy and Cellular Biology, Moselio Schaechter in Molecular Biology and Microbiology, Henry Wortis in Immunology, and Barbara Talamo in Neurosciences recruited some of the best young researchers in the country who were ready to join a biomedical enterprise that seemed on the verge of an intellectual explosion. By the time Pharmacology broke off from Biochemistry in 1986, Richard Shader and David Greenblatt led the nation in citations in the field.

At Jean Mayer's tenth anniversary as President, the Medical School had also been transformed, even to the extent of taking on the international focus that Mayer wanted each of the health science schools to assume. As his first decade as President was coming to a close, both the Medical School and Dental School were negotiating with the United States Department of Treasury to transfer technology to a start-up medical and dental school in Saudi Arabia, at King Abdulaziz University. The agreement between the two universities, brokered by a government agency under the auspices of the American-Saudi Commission on Economic Cooperation, lasted for thirteen years and was a model of cross-cultural scientific cooperation. With an annual budget of $1.2 million, Tufts sent a stream of faculty to the Arabian Desert. On the Tufts side, we had an entrepreneurial Ph.D. in science who was appointed Dean for International Affairs at the Medical School. Adel Abu-Moustafa was an Arab, a scientist, and a deal maker. Tufts sent women, Jews, Christians to this new health sciences campus in Jeddah without a hitch and built two first-rate faculties of medicine and dentistry. Abu-Moustafa could handle almost any cultural and scientific problem. Only once did he need help, when the Saudi government insisted that women faculty could not drive when they came to Saudi Arabia. I called a meeting of three women who represented the female leadership of the contingent about to leave and asked them if they would mind being driven around the country. After a short, tense silence, the senior female scientist said: "The hell with it. Let them chauffeur us around."

The road still to travel would not be traversed in Jean Mayer's lifetime, but there is no doubt who paved it and prepared the way. When in 2002 the first purpose-built research facility in the 110-year history of the Medical School was dedicated by Dean John Harrington, it represented the fulfillment of Jean Mayer's dream for medicine—and nutrition—at Tufts.

THE SCHOOL OF DENTAL MEDICINE: FINDING A LIFESAVER

The medical education community went through some difficult times in the first ten years and beyond that overlapped the Mayer presidency of Tufts from 1976 to 1991. Many hospitals associated with universities closed their doors permanently; others were sold off before horrified eyes to for-profit organizations. However, other than a rare merger of two medical schools, all 125 medical schools survived.

Such was not the case with schools of dental medicine. Over the last three decades, eight dental schools closed their doors. Of the fifty-five that remain today, several are in danger of going under, and enrollment reductions over this period are equivalent to the closing of another fifteen average-size dental schools. Gone are the dental schools at St. Louis University, Oral Roberts University, Emory University, Georgetown University, Fairleigh Dickinson University, Washington University-St. Louis, Loyola University of Chicago, and Northwestern University. Do themes emerge from this list? Almost all had been associated with medical schools; three are Catholic institutions; and they are all private. Several were in states where currently the only remaining dental school is the lone state institution. Financially, they were not universally in difficulty. What ultimately brought about their demise was the perceived irrelevance these schools had to the academic and intellectual enterprise of the parent university and, at best, the indifference of their medical schools or medical centers.

In the higher education community, this was a unique Slaughter of the Innocents. No part of the academic enterprise had seen such a significant meltdown of a field of study or of professional training in modern memory. Even in the 1990s, when some trustees and presidents took it into their heads that Sociology was no longer a discipline with a focus or mission and motions were brought before the faculties of some distinguished universities to eliminate these departments, the rest of the Arts and Sciences rallied around their besieged colleagues, and the aggressors, whether right or wrong, re-treated. What happened to the academic dental profession was unique, as some of the most prestigious private institutions in the country, at times with an almost ferocious speed, shut down their dental schools, dispersed the dazed remaining students, grandfathered a few of the tenured faculty, and gave the labs to the medical schools. Morale within the surviving dental community plummeted to unprecedented depths.

There is a striking contrast to observe in the historic attitude of loyalty and affinity to a parent university between medical schools and dental schools. The medical schools in the United States wanted to be left alone, free from entanglements with university administrations or Arts and Sciences faculty who, in the eyes of the academic M.D.s, had no idea what life was like in a medical center or medical school. A few even completely severed the re-lationship. The Baylor College of Medicine, stating that it could not compete for federal grants because of the Christian mission of Baylor University, in 1969 broke away completely. Today, when one asks the parties about the re-lationship or affiliation either historical or current between the two Baylors, the answer is a terse reply: "There is no relationship or affiliation."

Schools of dental medicine, on the other hand, eagerly sought a warm and nurturing place nestled safely within the university bosom. They wanted to belong, to be accepted and embedded into the security of a university as well as, it had been hoped, a medical center. From the earliest nineteenth century, roots of proprietary for-profit independent dental schools, barely one gen-eration removed from the local barber-as-tooth-puller, dental schools ar-dently wanted the official blessing of university affiliation and proximity to what they perceived as the legitimacy of medical schools (even though some of these were no better than their for-profit dental school counterparts, as the famous Flexner Report on medical education pointed out in 1910). From the outset, the dental profession with its academic aspirations was beset by an anxiety that never left it.[20] Advancement in science, research, and discov-ery only enhanced the reputation and eminence of the practitioners of the medical arts. As medical research led to more and more discovery and better health, the public's esteem and its sense of the magic and majesty of the medical profession only grew greater. On the other hand, fluoridation drove

20. See Marilyn J. Field, ed., *Dental Education at the Crossroads: Challenges and Change* (Washington, D.C.: National Academy Press, 1995), 1–34.

some of the dental profession into hysteria. Some dental practitioners viewed this enormous public health advancement as a doomsday warning to their profession. The roller coaster cycle of dental school enrollments over the past thirty years, after the self-proclaimed Golden Age of Dentistry in the post-war boom of the 1950s and 1960s, is a reflection of the enormous uncertainty felt by non-specialist practitioners who worried whether the profession would be able to survive in a world that promised the elimination of cavities. The everyday dentist had become accustomed to prosperity with caries. Ironically, it was World War II that confirmed this belief when it became clear that the single greatest problem associated with the physical condition of potential draftees was bad teeth. Nearly 10 percent of those declared unfit for duty suffered from poor oral health. Dental schools nonetheless were generally not interested in research on prevention during the post-war period. The 1995 Institute of Medicine report states, "It is not surprising that dental schools figure little in the most important oral health research of that period, that is, investigation of the oral health effects of fluoride."[21]

This flight from research in the mid-twentieth century was another factor that separated dental schools from medical schools, which were really just gearing up as research centers with the enormous new amounts of NIH funding. Dental schools simply were not involved significantly in scientific investigation.

Even as the twentieth century came to an end, research at dental schools was not a high priority. Whatever space was available was given over to the clinical practice of the faculty, in order to supplement faculty salaries that were not competitive with practice in the outside world. As matters currently stand, hardly any dental students opt for a career in academic dental medicine, somewhere between 0.5 and 1.3 percent of the four thousand annual graduates who were polled in the year 2000.

Boston academic dental medicine was, like its medical counterpart, different. Some states had one dental school, the public institution. The city of Boston had *three*, all private. The Commonwealth of Massachusetts had none. As was the case with the three medical schools, Harvard was unique even in dentistry. It admitted a tiny class of thirty-five students who were destined to enter the profession as researchers and academic faculty. From the beginning, the Harvard dental program, founded in 1867 as the first university-based dental school in the country, was in close affiliation with Harvard

21. Ibid., 54.

Medical School. Some dental faculty would say too close. Today, the Dean of the Harvard School of Dental Medicine reports to the Dean of the Harvard School of Medicine, which makes the point for Harvard that dentistry is only a branch of medicine. Boston University is the newcomer, with origins dating back to 1958 as part of the Boston University School of Medicine. The dental program became the Boston University School of Graduate Dentistry in 1963. In 1972, it began giving the Doctor of Dental Medicine degree, with classes of approximately 150 students and a separate identity from the Medical School.

The Tufts School of Dental Medicine traced its roots back to 1868 and the Boston Dental College, one of the primitive proprietorial enterprises that dominated the preparation of dentists in this country. Conversations between the Boston Dental College and the Tufts Medical School had begun in 1897 and trustees of Tufts and the dental college authorized a union on March 14, 1899; at that point the Tufts School of Dental Medicine came into independent existence, on the usual Tufts shoestring. The shoestring might have been the symbol of the Dental School, whose entire endowment as late as 1963 was an inconceivable $10,000. As the Dental School emerged from a period of general prosperity for the profession, its own future looked very much in doubt. Even Tufts official historian Russell Miller had to admit that matters looked bleak: "President Wessell [1961] expressed grave doubts about the future of the dental school, which in his view was turning out mere technicians . . ."[22] Be it as it may, these "technicians" represented four out five of all New England dentists.

There was something as a value-added, however, which gave the Tufts Dental School a special identity. It was a sense of community responsibility that found a place and a voice. A Department of Social Dentistry was established in 1961 through the efforts of Professor and later Dean Louis Calisti, who was trained in public health and knew about the unmet needs of the general public, especially the poor. He became Dean in 1963 and soon joined forces with Jack Geiger and Count Gibson to provide dental services for the pioneering neighborhood health center at Columbia Point. Over at Boston City Hospital, a team of residents and interns under the charge of the Tufts Chief Resident of Oral Surgery, Tom Murnane, were seeing over one hundred indigent patients every day in outpatient clinics. When the city could pay, it did. When it could not, the Tufts dentists took care of the poor, regardless.

22. Miller, *Light on the Hill*, 364.

Inevitably, the Tufts commitment in medicine and dental medicine to that part of the community not being served in the 1960s and 1970s—the very young, the very old and the very poor—could not be sustained. The Dental School had a nonexistent endowment, inadequate facilities, and the initial commitment on the part of the federal government to support these efforts weakened. Gibson and Geiger became disillusioned, and left Tufts Medical School. Columbia Point eventually closed its doors.

These were difficult times for the Dental School. As bad as the facilities were in Medford and in the Medical School, the Dental School was operating in an environment at best called primitive. Calisti realized that he had to build a new facility, or close the doors. He alone among all of Tufts administrators was willing to coordinate a federal grant submission with a capital campaign. He successfully negotiated the Health Professions Teaching Facilities Act for a $6 million grant, to be matched by Tufts. Alas, the campaign for a new dental building bogged down almost immediately, and only through the assumption of enormous debt could the new dental tower at One Kneeland Street be constructed, and then only as a fragment of what had been intended. The building was dedicated in April of 1973, eight years after the initial project start, when there was another president and dean. In the meantime, national enrollments were plunging; the environment for the profession had turned hostile, and the first of the dental schools, at St. Louis University, had shut down. Tufts School of Dental Medicine had every right to worry that it might be next. It fit the profile perfectly.

But when Jean Mayer came to Tufts in 1976, it was in the School of Dental Medicine that he found his warmest reception, not because they were desperate to find favor in the eyes of the new President, but because it was in the Dental School that Mayer found interest in nutrition and prevention. He also found people whom he liked.

The Dean was Robert Shira, who took over in 1972, a year after Lou Calisti had been recruited to the University of Maine to establish a medical center. When Calisti left, Dr. Thomas Murnane was named interim Dean for 1971–1972. Here were two people—both dentists—who Jean Mayer found very much to his liking. The relationship with Tom Murnane was almost paternal. There was an instant bond of trust, and the two became inseparable for all of Mayer's presidency, and beyond. Bob Shira was a military man, and they understood each other completely. Shira had served as Assistant Surgeon General and Chief of the United States Army Dental Corps. He also understood the politics of medical centers: for ten years he had been Chief of the Dental Service at Walter Reed Medical Center. After a career in the military that spanned thirty-three years, Shira retired with the rank of major general. He respected leadership and the chain of command. Mayer soon realized that if you told the Dean of the Dental School to do something, he would do it. When it came time to find an interim Provost in 1979 after the defection of Kathryn McCarthy, he and the Board of Trustees turned to the recently retired Dean of the Dental School.

In 1976, Shira had already been Dean for four years and was making limited headway in alleviating some of the anxieties of his gloomy professional colleagues. An indefatigable optimist like Mayer, the Dean had a military bearing and enormous energy. He was also a wonderful raconteur and after-dinner speaker, and bore none of the characteristic pessimism of his profession. He turned to the alumni, gathered them in, established new clubs and fundraising goals and started bringing new money into the operating budget of the Dental School. It was also his interest in oral health services, prevention, nutrition, and public health that brought him together with his President. What Jean Mayer also knew about the dental school of his new university was that it had a tradition of leadership in nutrition education that went back thirty years.

Dr. Abraham Nizel was a practicing dentist when he came to the faculty of Tufts School of Dental Medicine in 1946. His scholarly interest was in nutrition and its impact on oral health. By the mid-1960s, he had developed a model for integrating nutrition assessment and counseling into the dental practice. Nizel got to the Frances Stern Program in Nutrition at the New England Medical Center and made an ally by bringing the Frances Stern students into a clinical dental rotation. Nizel planted the seeds, and one of the first to take root was a Frances Stern Master's candidate, Carole Palmer, whom he hired in 1969. As of this writing, thirty-four years into an affiliation with Tufts, Professor Palmer is still on the faculty at Tufts Dental School and serves as the central force in the modeling of nutrition programs for dental education nationwide. Their first grant from the Nutrition Foundation was to establish "A Model Nutrition Teaching Program for Schools of Dentistry and Dental Hygiene." By the time Nizel retired in 1986, Johanna Dwyer, trained by Jean Mayer at Harvard, had taken over the Frances Stern program and was working closely on research projects with other Tufts dentists, notably Athena Papas, a dentist with an MIT Ph.D. in oral biology and a strong commitment to nutritional research. Before coming to Tufts in 1974, Papas had worked at MIT closely with Hamish Munro, destined to become the first Director of the Tufts Human Nutrition Research Center. Even before the HNRC building was completed, Papas was working with Munro-appointed scientists Robert Russell and Robert McGandy on nutritional research studies. Today, nearly thirty years later, Tina Papas, Professor in the Tufts School of Dental Medicine, is working with HNRC scientists on Vitamin A and bone loss.

Nizel, Palmer, and Dwyer had introduced Tina Papas to the Tufts President soon after he arrived. She reminded Mayer that he had lectured in Munro's oral biology program at MIT. While still at Harvard, Mayer had read Abe Nizel's books, *Nutrition in Clinical Dentistry* (1960), *The Science of Nutrition and its Application in Clinical Dentistry* (1966), and *Nutrition in Preventive Dentistry: Science and Practice* (1972). Before he ever set foot on the downtown campus, President Mayer knew where his initial base of operation would be: the Dental School.[23]

This would prove to be an astonishingly exhilarating experience for a school with no experience at sitting in the center of health sciences activity on an academic campus. Shira and Nizel welcomed the President with open arms, and Mayer reciprocated. His first speech to the Dental School faculty was one of assurance. He told them that as long as he was President of Tufts, its dental school would enjoy the prestige that it so richly deserved. The faculty loved it.

And they needed it. The mid-1970s was a difficult time for the profession, which had not yet shaken off its image of "drill, fill, and bill." The practitioners who were in business for themselves for the most part were worried that the dental schools were creating an oversupply of competition. They were also angry at the effort of dental schools to build up the clinical practice on campus, which the non-academic dentists saw as a direct threat to their income. Furthermore, on private university campuses across the United States, administrators were beginning to examine the relevancy of their dental schools within the medical center context of the health sciences. Financially, the Tufts School of Dental Medicine was as shaky as the rest of the university when Mayer arrived. Administratively, Bob Shira was approaching retirement age and would be stepping down as Dean. The appointment of his successor was critical to the future survivability of the Dental School. The crushing debt, which resulted from the failed campaign for the new building, threatened the school's finances.

There was also a crisis in the curriculum. In the early seventies, it looked as if there would be a shortage of physicians and dentists in the country, so

23. See the foreword by Jean Mayer to the 1989 edition of Abraham E. Nizel and Athena S. Papas, *Nutrition in Clinical Dentistry* (Philadelphia: Sanders, 1960).

the federal government looked for ways to get more health professionals into practice faster and passed the Health Professions Act. Washington offered financial incentives—capitation in the way of extra dollars for each student graduated in three years instead of four—and the Tufts Dental School, desperate for any additional income, took the bait. The first accelerated three-year class graduated in 1975. The government made up the lost year of tuition and added new monies on top of that. The impact on year-round teaching became immediately clear: Whatever research that might have been underway died under the pressure of an uninterrupted 132-week curriculum. The faculty was teaching all the time, right through the year. Then, within a few years, it became apparent that there would *not* be a shortage of health professionals, and within a decade the government withdrew the capitation and financial incentive program, and left those schools that had bought in to the three-year curriculum twisting in the breeze, with a year's less tuition for their troubles. The new Dean would also have to address this enormous administrative and programmatic headache: to continue the three-year accelerated program and give up completely on any hope for a research life at the Dental School; or go back to the traditional four-years of instruction, which would require a phase-out of one while installing the second. In either case, the faculty would be going through an extended period of pain and suffering. The school would need a leader with grit, determination, and a thick skin. It found one.

There was something about Erling Johansen that Jean Mayer liked immediately, when he met the new Dean who took charge of the Dental School in 1979. He had spent five years living in Nazi-occupied Norway during World War II. The war represented a bond for several of the faculty, and Mayer always drew close to these people. Among his favorites in the Dental School was the Chairman of Oral Surgery, Hristo (Chris) Doku, a passionate and patriotic Greek-American with vivid memories of the German occupation of his homeland, and Helmi Vogels, a Latvian-American who had come to the school in 1950 as a Research Associate in oral pediatrics after a childhood of suffering first under the Nazi tyranny and then under Soviet occupation. Johansen had been part of a group of twenty-two Norwegian students who were brought to this country immediately after the war to offset the shortage of dentists resulting from the Nazi occupation and the closing of the Norwegian dental schools. He graduated from Tufts Dental School in 1949, and went on to a distinguished research career in academic dental medicine at the University of Rochester, where he got his Ph.D. in Pathology in 1955. President Mayer loved to hobnob with the Cambridge-Harvard Yankees, but it was not surprising that he felt very much at home in this comfortable European environment with a group of people who shared a common historical fight against fascism and talked about it often among themselves. They were of the same generation, held the same memories, and all spoke with marked accents. This academic salon that President Mayer discovered in the Dental School was made up of professionals who, in 1976, had known each other for decades. Johansen, who had graduated from the Dental School nearly thirty years earlier, was very much a part of it when he returned, and Mayer was welcomed into their midst.

Erling Johansen was the Dean who served the longest number of years in the Mayer presidency, from 1979 to 1995 on into the DiBiaggio years. It was a time of great turbulence in the dental profession and in dental education. He persevered, endured, and the Tufts School of Dental Medicine survived and even prospered, because Johansen had the temperament of a survivor. If the Third Reich could not defeat him, no adversity in his profession was great enough to bring him down.

Nothing came easy. From the moment he assumed the deanship of the school, the profession both inside and outside of academic dentistry went into a tailspin. The post-war Golden Age for the practicing dentist saw an increase in applications to dental schools from 4,644 in 1959 to 15,734 in 1975, a leap of 239 percent. Then came the fear of fluoridation, competition from clinical practices in the dental schools, significant professional bad-mouthing by dentists themselves who discouraged young people from entering the field, and applications plunged to 4,996 in 1989. In 1981, there were 1.2 candidates for every opening at an American dental school. Not much selectivity. Then, on top of the challenge of merely finding sufficient students, Dean Johansen had to face the issue of quality. The average college grade point of many dental school applicants in the 1980s in sciences courses was considerably under a B average. The thought of taking C-grade students into professional health sciences sent a shudder through the faculty that was also felt in the other health sciences. The Dental School at Tufts did not have its own basic scientists. It purchased services from the basic sciences faculty of the Medical School and, starting in 1980, from the Sackler School. With President Mayer's Utopian dream of One Medicine, with all basic sciences classes containing medical, dental, and veterinary students, the dental students found themselves struggling mightily to keep up in classes with the highly selective medical and veterinary students. The veterinary students were tolerant; the medical students were not. After complaining first about the use of animal models, they turned their scorn on the inadequately prepared dental students.

This was humiliating for Dean Johansen, and inevitably for the Dental School faculty. In his first year as Dean, the Tufts scores on the National Board exams were deplorably low in both clinical and basic science sections.

On top of these woes, Dean Johansen had to deal with the public policy mess caused by the Health Professions Act, which was repealed just in time for the Dental School to face another budgetary crisis. Just as Dean Shira had to service two different curricula—of four and three years—Dean Johansen was faced with the reverse—going from three back to four. Like Dean Shira before him, he had two classes with two separate curricula running simultaneously between 1981 and 1984. If he had hoped to begin a research agenda, it would have to be without space, since six of the nine departments had no research space, equipment, or facilities.

He was running two different classes with different curricula; there were insufficient operatories and patients, so that at one point nearly 60 percent of the graduating class could not be certified for a May commencement. Student morale was dreadful. Thefts and disappearances of equipment were endemic, and an underground student newspaper, *Tufts Luck*, greeted the Dean upon his arrival.

Erling Johansen took one long look at the dental school that might have been a candidate for closing, and, using all of those qualities that went into the Norwegian national character, stubbornly attacked all of his problems. He jumped on the Mayer fundraising bandwagon, went after every opportunity from his alumni, and to the surprise of everyone, he began raising money. In his first few years as Dean, he added operatories, named everything in sight, and soon had enough facilities to train his students in time to complete their courses. He instituted a strict security system and cut down on the equipment loss by 88 percent in the first year. He met regularly with the class officers, listened to their problems, gave them a forum, and the underground newspaper disappeared. He hammered away on the national test scores, and the Dean was able to report to the President after two years that the scores had improved dramatically. No one thought that Johansen would be a particularly good fundraiser, but he stopped at nothing to increase the Annual Fund giving and jumped into the capital campaign with both feet. He renovated enough space in the incomplete dental tower to provide some research facilities for his faculty, who at first did not believe that research could ever come back to the Dental School. When the Dean began turning down candidates for tenure because of insufficient research, the faculty knew he was serious. By 1981, fifty research projects were underway.

When Bob Levy announced his resignation first as Dean of the Medical

School in 1983 and five months later from the Vice Presidency of Health Sciences at Tufts, it was the Dental School Dean who led the delegation to urge that there be no Vice Presidential replacement to oversee the health sciences in Boston. Erling Johansen was fiercely proud of his profession and respectful of it. He considered himself a first-rate basic science researcher and took umbrage at any slight; he did not like being supervised by a Vice President who was also the Dean of the Medical School. Bob Levy made it clear that the Medical School was the center of health sciences on the downtown campus. It certainly might have been true, but the courtesies of the health sciences community have to be exercised in subtle and appropriate ways, and Dean Johansen had had enough of reporting to an academic physician.

President Mayer concurred, and I became the immediate supervisor of all health sciences school deans. This was just what Dean Johansen wanted: the opportunity to be woven tightly into the fabric of the university. He had no illusions about the difficult times to come, and he wanted his faculty to know that they could count on the President and his team to make the right noises and signals. I attended more dental faculty meetings than I did for the combined medical, veterinary, and nutrition faculties. President Mayer could be a powerful cheerleader and would say whatever had to be stated, whether he believed it or not. At an early Dental School faculty meeting, he described the Tufts Dental School "as one of the finest in the nation." He knew better, but he knew the importance of the message, from which he never wavered.

During the mid-1980s, with private dental schools all over the United States closing their doors, TUSDM relentlessly held on and continued to strengthen itself. It also became a family affair. Inge Johansen formed a Women's Club of dental wives and was a constant supporter. She was really the first of a kind, the first spouse who became a part of the campaign strategy for the school.

There were always setbacks. To take advantage of the Talloires facility, the dental faculty held a continuing education program in the Tufts European facility for fifty participants from seven countries. It was initially a terrific success, and the school invested considerable effort and dollars into the program. It all came crashing down with airliner explosions blamed on Libya in 1986, when a large delegation of Italian dentists cancelled at the last moment, costing the school hundreds of thousands of dollars. But, that year, when four dental schools closed and the profession as a whole was experiencing a national fit of anxiety, the Tufts Dental School received its first-in-history unqualified maximum ten-year accreditation. It seemed as if the rest of the dental community was beginning to believe President Mayer's words.

THE SCHOOL OF VETERINARY MEDICINE:
A SPECIAL WILL TO SURVIVE

On February 7, 1977, a headline in the *Boston Globe* announced, "Tufts Veterinary School Gets Go Signal." Just seven months earlier, Jean Mayer had announced his intention to start a veterinary school. He had convinced Governor Dukakis to transfer a 582-acre site of the recently closed Grafton State Hospital to Tufts for $1.00. A month later, thanks to Senator Kennedy and the other members of the Massachusetts congressional delegation, $10 million was obtained to construct the Hospital for Large Animals.

I tried earlier to give readers some idea of the frantic pace, energy, and improvisation that led to the creation of the Veterinary School at Tufts University. President Mayer and Tom Murnane simply would not turn from the target, and with the philanthropic help of trustee Henry Foster, they made it happen. At least, they made the start. It would take more than the vision of these three to make it endure.

The Vet School was blessed with a particular kind of good fortune at the outset: there were wildly enthusiastic students whose most fervent dream seemed about to be realized, after years of disappointment and frustration. With no more than twenty-seven veterinary schools in the country at the time, New England students were among a large number of would-be veterinarians who had been closed out from opportunity. Now, in an extraordinary turn-around, they had been given a chance. Nothing was going to deter them or diminish their joy. The adrenaline rush overcame every reality. Not even the streets of Boston piled high with occasionally uncollected garbage could upset the first class of forty-one V'83 candidates—twenty-four men and seventeen women, none from the Tufts undergraduate colleges—who had been selected in 1979 from over four hundred applicants. First-year student Steven Rowell remembers his wife's first comment when she stepped out of the car in front of the downtown Vet School office and found herself, not in the imagined rolling fields of central Massachusetts, but instead surrounded by urban blight: "You brought me from Santa Fe for this?" But it did not matter. Nothing mattered. Not the stares of the medical and dental students in the combined classes, followed by the "oink" and "moo" noises when the faculty tried to use some animal models. When one talks to these professional veterinarians more than twenty years later, the same emotional high and bonding emerge out of their conversation in describing those first semesters. Many of them were country-bred, not at all accustomed to the urban grime of this particular part of Boston where the health sciences were located. But they simply refused to allow any negative vibrations to get in the way. What difference did it make if the anatomy labs were not ready? Or if the instructors seemed one class ahead of the students? For this first year's class as well as the several that followed, the adventure was so compelling that they chose to ignore the academic, geographic, or social difficulties. All they cared about was sharing this excitement with each other. They even felt sorry for some of the medical students who complained when the initial exams placed many of the veterinary students at the top, with more than a token number of medical students finding themselves in the lower portion of the class curve. To this day, the Veterinary School Class of 1983, those who were there at the Creation, consider themselves the Chosen People.

They also found themselves blessed from the very beginning of the school with a remarkable group of dedicated staff, some of whom, now in their third decade of service to the Vet School, carry on that tradition. Martha Pokras, one of the original administrative staff members, early on took over the nonacademic management of the school with a level of professionalism usually reserved for M.B.A.s. But she was much more than that. Whenever problems personal, domestic, or academic emerged, the students ran to her. She was what every dean prays for: the ultimate problem solver. This surrogate older sibling institutionalized that role and was literally wedded to the school, since she was married to one of the students in the second class.

The earliest faculty of those first few years threw themselves into the struggle for education and survival. Those basic sciences faculty who were enlisted to teach veterinary students along with the medical and dental students showed various degrees of sincere cooperation, indifference, contempt, and hostility. The only basic scientist/vet who had been part of the Tufts downtown faculty was Irv Leav, a well-funded researcher who had NIH support and was considered an anomaly by his colleagues, whose image of the veterinarian was someone with horse pictures in the office and low scientific standards. There was also the anger directed against President Mayer for moving forward with the Vet School when the Medical School had such enormous needs. Leav took the battering, but he had some allies. David Stollar in Biochemistry, and the chief of Endocrinology in the New England Medical Center, Seymour Reichlin, were always supportive where others were not. Out in Grafton, where the students really wanted to be, Dean Jonas had recruited a cohort of veterinarians who were eager to start something new. They were adventurers, risk takers, and loved students—some a little too much. They were willing to come to a start-up veterinary school that the trustees had decided would have no tenured faculty. This was a condition that the larger trustee body held fast to: no tenure in Mayer's new schools.

The students had inoculated themselves against hostility and inconvenience, whether it was coming from other students and faculty at Tufts or Angell Memorial Animal Hospital, an MSPCA-sponsored organization which, with some concern, had signed on to provide small animal teaching facilities for the new Vet School. For large animal work, the school had purchased the practice of veterinarian George Looby in Woodstock, Connecticut, and he hired clinician George Saperstein to join him as faculty in that teaching service, until the Amelia Peabody Large Animal Pavilion opened in Grafton in June 1982. They remained a strong part of the backbone of large animal teaching for years to come.

Outside the walls of the student euphoria and excitement, Dean Al Jonas was in a constant state of war with the other schools as well as Jean Mayer's administration. It simply was not working. He had a confrontational personality with a short fuse that could be lit by any number of frustrations. It was time for a change. Mayer, with the recommendation of Trustee Henry Foster, the most committed board member, turned to a Johns Hopkins Medical School veterinarian who had been serving on the Tufts Vet School Visiting Committee. On February 1, 1982, Frank Loew took over as Dean. The final piece was now in place.

From the beginning, there was a great deal about Frank Loew that attracted the Tufts President. The new Dean's earlier work actually had been in nutrition and nutritional toxicology. His early research helped establish the safety of what is now called canola oil, which had been considered toxic to people and animals. Loew also worked on an important disease of cattle related to vitamin B-1, thiamin. He was not a traditional "cow doc" or "swine doc." He worked internationally, spending a good part of the years between 1972 and 1976 in Cuba, where the disease related to B-1 deficiency was rampant. Early in his career, he became interested in the treatment of laboratory animals and the ethical use of animals in experimentation. It was no accident that he shaped the character of what was to be eventually identified as the most animal-sensitive veterinary school in the country.

Like Mayer, Loew was a Renaissance man: a medical intellectual, and an antiquarian who had written books on several historical topics. And he was charismatic. More than anything else, it was Frank Loew's ability to lead and to bring together a community around his vision for the school that provided the will to survive. When he arrived, it was not a community. Al Jonas had recruited some excellent faculty. Irv Leav was already in place and led the design of the basic science curriculum, the first two years. Jim Ross chaired the Department of Medicine out in Grafton and set the highest standards for clinical faculty in teaching, research, and service. Tony Schwartz brought the Surgery Department immediately up to speed, and together they hired most of the great Grafton-based faculty: Sue Cotter came with her prestige from Angell to the Department of Medicine; Larry Kleine was a highly regarded radiologist with expertise in small animal radiography. Al Sollod was also brought in before Frank Loew arrived to build a program in international veterinary medicine. Carol Reinisch came from Harvard/Dana Farber with strong connections at the Woods Hole Institute to run the Comparative Medicine Department. There was a high-quality nucleus, waiting for someone to start a chain reaction.

Frank Loew was a shrewd psychologist who understood the challenge faced by a new school in a university culture that had no previous encounter with this species of health professional and did not want one. Jonas had been on an equal footing with the other two health sciences deans, and he could not make the communication work. Frank Loew would now operate under the authority of a Vice President for Health Sciences who was also the Dean of the Medical School. Coming out of Johns Hopkins Medical School, he knew the culture and would work with Bob Levy as well as under him, as needs be. But the Dean of the Veterinary School had two offices and could escape to the wide-open spaces of Grafton, where the true heart of the Vet School was beating. In Boston, he mastered the clash of civilizations and waited patiently until he would leave the city and eventually move all of his students to the country, where, everyone in the school agreed, they really belonged.

Trustee Henry Foster showed no small amount of courage in suggesting that Loew become the next Dean of the Veterinary School. His wealth came from his position as CEO of Charles River Labs, Inc., the nation's largest provider of high-quality rodents for medical experimentation, founded by Foster and soon, in the words of a business magazine, to become "The General Motors of laboratory animals." Foster knew of Loew's commitment to animal welfare and, as much as possible, to an environment in the veterinary school that would be as free as possible from the use of animals in any experiments. While Foster's industry saw Frank Loew and his followers as adversaries, he was committing himself heart and soul to a new Dean whose publicly stated goal was to curtail the business led by his greatest beneficiary. But, for Henry Foster, the welfare of the Tufts Veterinary School was his most focused concern, and he advocated for Frank Loew, even at the cost of alien-ating his own business associates. Foster saw very clearly where Loew was headed, with the appointment of Andrew Rowan, viewed by most traditional veterinarians and Foster's associates as a leading anti-vivisectionist, to the Vet School faculty. Most old-time vets, graduates of the land grant schools, were not interested in issues associated with companion animals and did not see the changes coming in the veterinary student community. Loew con-vinced his benefactor that change was inevitable, and to his enormous credit Henry Foster kept his faith with the new school. The earliest admitted stu-dents were committed to the idea of teaching veterinary medicine without sacrificing animals of any kind. The core (required) third-year surgery course involved all students practicing on anesthetized, "purpose-bred" dogs, that is, animals raised and purchased for use in teaching and/or research. The students did a minor surgery, from which the animal awoke and recovered, and then a major procedure immediately after which the animal was eutha-nized while still under anesthesia. Within a few years of his arrival as Dean, Loew could see where the students were heading. He, along with course director John Berg, helped the students make a thoughtful, informed, yet passionate request to come up with an alternative procedure, which they did. It was clear that Tufts would lead the nation in reducing or eliminating the use of animals, while never compromising the quality of the learning expe-rience. Animal welfare and issues associated with animals as friends and companions to the humans with whom they shared the planet became a sig-nature program of the school in Loew's tenure as Dean. Foster's courage in defending something he basically did not agree with was remarkable, but he loved the Vet School more than he did his livelihood. The Tufts Center for Animals and Public Policy was destined to take veterinary medicine into very new territory.

Like Jean Mayer, Frank Loew had some things figured out on his own and would move with singular stealth toward his goal. He did not believe, as Mayer did, that the relationship with the Angell Memorial Animal Hospital would endure, and from the very first moment of his arrival at the Vet School he began courting Henry Foster with this in mind. In 1985, university ad-ministrators and trustees, town and state officials, and congressional digni-taries gathered in Grafton for the dedication of the Henry and Lois Foster Hospital for Small Animals, a $3.6 million facility that brought the veteri-nary students back from Boston's Angell Memorial to the central Massachu-setts campus. Loew negotiated a peaceful separation from Angell without bad feelings.

Nothing was as masterful as Loew's dealings with the Commonwealth. In his first year as Dean, he stunned the Massachusetts higher education community when it was announced that the Tufts School of Veterinary Medicine would receive an initial $3.3 million appropriation from the Commonwealth, in spite of bitter opposition from the state university system and its flagship institutions in Amherst and nearby Worcester, where the University of Massachusetts Medical School was located. The public university system in Massachusetts jealously guarded its prerogatives, having suffered for centuries with the inferiority complex caused by a tradition of powerful private universities and colleges in Massachusetts. There was nothing like this preeminence of the private higher education sector in any of the other forty-nine states of the nation. The idea of appropriations to any of these private institutions, no matter what the reason, was to be fought at all costs. It made no difference that the Commonwealth of Massachusetts had been one of the prime movers in seeking some university to take the risk of establishing a veterinary school in Massachusetts, perhaps as a regional New England entity. Soon after Tufts and Jean Mayer stepped to the plate, much of that initial support melted away, and it was not until Frank Loew began working over the legislature that hope for a subsidy returned. From Tufts' perspective, the university was doing an enormous service to the Commonwealth at a remarkably small cost. The $3.3 million initial appropriation, vital as it was to the school's survival, was smaller than any other state's appropriation to its veterinary school. In fact, over the years, the amount has risen and fallen with the whimsy of the legislature, having been completely wiped out on several occasions. But, it was Frank Loew who nailed that first historic money. He and President Mayer established a very special relationship with then-Senate President William Bulger, who was an unfailing supporter of the Tufts Vet School.

Frank Loew and his school were self-starters. In his second year as Dean the massive $14 million Niger project with Fletcher took off. Loew wisely gave the credit where it was due, to Al Sollod, his Director of International Veterinary Medicine and an experienced African researcher. He and Fletcher's African agricultural economist Dirck Stryker were the principal investigators and initially came together without any assistance from the university. The two Deans agreed that Fletcher would be the manager of the grant, the largest in Tufts history. But, the President did not like to give up center stage. One Saturday about three months into the grant during the Veterinary School Dean's second year at Tufts, Frank Loew received an unusual Saturday morning phone call from President Mayer with a request to meet him out at Grafton that afternoon. When Loew got out to the Vet School administrative building, Jean Mayer was waiting, with the Director of Grants and Contracts, Carla Ricci. Also present, at the President's request, were Sollod and Stryker. Mayer got to the point immediately: This was the biggest and most important grant in Tufts' history, and it should be run out of the President's office. Henceforth, he announced, Carla Ricci would serve as his Deputy in all formal matters involving the grant and necessary sign-offs. The Dean managed to keep Al Sollod under control; Stryker kept his cool, and when the day was over, nothing much had changed, except that the President would be more in the center of things. It was Al Sollod who made the greatest contribution over the next five years, arranging for overseeing Jeff Mariner's development of a heat-resistance vaccine to combat *Rinderpest,* the deadly disease of cattle.

As clever an orchestrator and Machiavellian manipulator as Mayer was, he met his match in Frank Loew. While the President was trumpeting the brilliance of his One Medicine idea for the Boston campus, with a vision of medical, dental, and veterinary students sitting in common classes of mutual respect, the Veterinary School Dean was bristling under the burden of hostility he felt from the Medical School faculty, who never ceased complaining about their teaching of veterinary students without sufficient (in their eyes) compensation. But, he was a cool diplomat, talked One Medicine, while planning to get out of town as soon as possible. In his first years, he spent the bulk of his administrative time in the Veterinary School's Dean's office on Harrison Avenue, cheek to jowl with the Medical School. He hated it, but since the first two years of Vet School teaching was done in Boston, he had little choice. He also knew what he needed: facilities and faculty, initially to teach his second–year courses, and eventually all of his students in Grafton. He needed laboratories, classrooms, and above all, high-quality basic scientists who wanted to work independent of Medical School space and who preferred the 582-acre site in pastoral Grafton. He recruited Sawkat Anwer in 1983 out of a post-doctoral appointment in Germany. Anwer, a superb basic scientist who worked on diseases of the liver, was funded for 75 percent of his effort by the NIH, greater than most of the Boston-based scientists, and was immediately given a joint appointment in Biochemistry and Medicine. He was the building block for a basic science effort, which was destined for Grafton. Loew's message to the downtown basic scientists: I can find people just as good as you are.

He also needed great teachers, and One Medicine was not the answer. After a few years of patching together the anatomy teaching with visiting or retired faculty from other schools, Loew hired Amarendhra Kumar from the University of Florida, who immediately established himself as a legendary teacher as well as an accomplished artist, drawing symmetrical diagrams on the chalkboard with both hands at the same time!

Loew was a superb marketer. He always referred to his institution as "the dandiest little veterinary school in the country," but he was not going to be satisfied until it was the *best* veterinary school in the country, a daunting task, given the traditions of Penn and Cornell and the financial stability of the other state veterinary schools. He threw himself into the challenge and became the quintessential school cheerleader for all of the Vet School activities. He worked the local community, invited anyone and everyone out to Grafton to enormously popular open houses, went out of his way to invite students, staff, and faculty from all over Tufts to bring the kids and join in the festivities.

In 1985, he moved his office out to Grafton, determined to make the Vet School one of a kind in the country. The "animal welfare" program, led by Andrew Rowan, quickly inspired the student body to a new appreciation of the scientific study of animals and animal issues dealing with their behavior, comfort, and uses. Rowan was an excellent communicator, the students loved him, and the Center for Animals placed Tufts at the front of various national debates on the use of animals, even in entertainment. For the first time, a veterinary school became an advocate for animals. Tufts Vet School even had an animal psychologist in veterinarian Nick Dodman, whose books received enormous exposure on national network television. There was nothing like this anywhere else in academic veterinary medicine in the United States.

The Dean knew that, given the meager resources he had to work with, the school could not be all things to all people. It could not compete with the giant academic veterinary institutions, so Loew looked for targets of opportunity. The Niger grant gave Al Sollod and another younger, internationally oriented veterinarian, "Chip" Stem, the opportunity to develop a full-fledged program in International Veterinary Medicine. They also carried within them the evangelical passion of the animal welfare people. The Tufts Vet School had its share of true believers who felt that they were out there saving the world. At times, you could believe it. Years later, some of these veterinarians were the only people allowed to cross the cease-fire lines in the bloody civil war in the Sudan as they inoculated cattle on both sides of the conflict with the same vaccine developed during the Niger Project.

One of the founding faculty members, Chuck Sedgwick, founded and ran a wildlife clinic. He brought along a graduate from the second class, Mark Pokras, whose energy carried Wildlife Medicine forward as a program that was instantly popular with applicants and then students. The clinic was rife with "good news" animal stories and appropriate photo ops for the press of wounded eagles and little kids carrying a frog with a broken leg, asking, "Mister, can you fix my frog?" There were also nice connections to Massachusetts state environmental agencies, the U.S. Fish and Wildlife Service, and the EPA.

Loew arrived at Tufts just as biotechnology was taking off in the early 1980s, and he saw the opportunity. Karl Ebert was the leading faculty investigator at that time and moved the Vet School into transgenic sciences, setting the stage for Eric Overstrom's later cloning work. Here the Dean was thinking strategically. He believed that the Commonwealth would see biotechnology as an eventually attractive source of revenue and would want the Vet School to be a player in the development of this industry. He was right.

Some of the earliest advocates of the school were from the Hamilton, Massachusetts, horse set, and Loew thought it wise both scientifically and politically to develop a program in Equine Sports Medicine. A small program had been in place when Loew arrived, but the Dean saw it as a unique opportunity for the study of equine gait and lameness.

These were the Signature Programs, a combination of offerings unlike any other in American veterinary medicine. In addition, Tufts also focused on leading in the development of oncology and emergency and critical care medicine for animals.

Of all the deans I had worked with, no one had the determination, energy, and vision of Frank Loew. He also was a complicated personality and did not take insult easily, expected respect from the other health sciences, and wanted to be appreciated. The only times I thought we might lose him were after his appearances before the Trustee Committee on Administration and Finance, where the Trustees took out their frustration at the inadequate funding they were giving the school by tearing into the Dean, whose management of scanty resources and high maintenance of morale was truly inspirational. Loew would come out of those meetings with steam hissing from his ears. Mayer did little to protect him, and the Dean had to take care of himself, with whatever protection I could provide. Gratitude was another of his qualities. He never forgot anyone's assistance.

By the President's tenth year, the Tufts School of Veterinary Medicine had already produced more veterinarians for the Commonwealth of Massachusetts than all the combined efforts of the previous century. The scientific and educational reputation of the school was superb, and it received in its first try an unprecedented full seven-year accreditation in 1986. The school was soaring. To be sure, it was a half-built bridge. The funding was uncertain. Mayer and Loew were hard-working fundraisers, and individual buildings could be renovated one at a time, as dollars became available, but there was no appreciable endowment, and it was the entrepreneurial spirit of the Dean that kept the faculty, staff, and students in a constant state of excitement. They loved their Dean, and they loved their school.

NUTRITION: THE SEARCH FOR LEGITIMACY

At the 1969 White House Conference on Food and Nutrition that Jean Mayer had organized and run, the panel on deception and misinformation agreed that Adelle Davis, self-proclaimed as America's most celebrated nutritionist, was probably the most damaging source of false nutrition information in the nation. Davis (1904–1974) trained in dietetics and nutrition at the University of California at Berkeley and took a Master of Science in Biochemistry from the University of Southern California. She had bona fide scientific credentials, wrote popular books, and was perceived by the medical community as a quack.

Adelle Davis was the best credentialed of a long line of sensational individuals who had caught the attention of the general public in the United States as nutritional advocates. They appeared at a time when film, radio, and later television provided an exposure that fit perfectly into the needs of a country looking for simple answers to its problems of health. They were all called "nutritionists," and they all became millionaires. Bernarr Macfadden was internationally famous during the first half of the last century proclaiming his doctrine of "body love," natural foods, outdoor exercise, nudity, and the natural treatment of disease. He denounced the medical establishment while the medical community branded him a charlatan. He inspired millions of people all over the world. Macfadden connected himself to the nineteenth-century food faddists-turned cereal makers, Charles W. Post and W. K. Kellogg when he opened a health sanatorium in what had become the nutrition capital of America,—Battle Creek, Michigan—home of the huge cereal empire that Post and Kellogg had built on a platform of healthy foods such as Grape Nuts and Graham Crackers (named for Sylvester Graham, an early-nineteenth-century primitive nutritionist with a cult following). Macfadden wrote nearly 150 books with titles such as *Strength from Eating, Making Old Bodies Young, The Miracle of Milk, Diabetes: Its Cause, Nature and Treatment, How to Gain*

Weight, and *How to Reduce Weight.* When he died in 1955 at the age of eighty-seven, several of his obituaries identified him as advocate of good nutritional habits. No such comments appeared in any medical journals.

Like Macfadden, Carleton Fredericks (1910–1987) had no scientific training other than the required courses for his English major at the University of Alabama, but that did not prevent him from writing on the jackets of his twenty-seven books: "America's Foremost Nutritionist." On the basis of a Ph.D. in communications from NYU in 1955, be began calling himself "Dr. Fredericks." The title of his doctoral thesis was "A Study of the Responses of a Group of Adult Female Listeners to a Series of Educational Radio Programs," which happened to be his own broadcasts on station WOR in New York City. He was for decades one of the most popular radio personalities in America, giving out "nutritional therapy" instructions to millions of listeners. His radio spots were syndicated all over the nation. He attacked the medical profession relentlessly, gave advice about vitamin supplements, denounced the use of sugar, and ridiculed anyone who disagreed with him. Gayelord Hauser (c. 1895–1984), described by James Harvey Young as "a suave and talented performer," was Hollywood's nutrition consultant during the 1920s and 1930s.[24] He advocated the use of five "wonder" foods—skim milk, brewer's yeast, wheat germ, yogurt, and blackstrap molasses. His books were best sellers. Hauser lectured in every corner of the United States, presenting his material as courses with an academic form and content to them. He looked like an academic, he sounded like an academic, and the listening and viewing public bestowed enormous popularity on him.

Macfadden had his greatest impact in the mass media in the form of short subject films, some of which were banned for obscenity and public nudity. But the public, who made little distinction between quackery and science, took his subtitled nutritional advice seriously. At times, even earnest academics apparently had some difficulty in distinguishing one from the other. Social historian Young's study of quackery, published in 1967, made no mention of Adelle Davis, who just two years later was branded by the White House Conference on Food, Nutrition and Health as the nation's most dangerous purveyor of nutritional misinformation.

It was Davis who was dubbed "the high priestess" of self-promotion.[25] Be-

24. James Harvey Young, *The Medical Messiahs: A Social History of Health Quackery in Twentieth-Century America* (Princeton: Princeton University Press, 1967), 340.

25. Stephen Barrett, M.D., and William T. Jarvis, ed. *The Health Robbers: A Close Look at Quackery in America* (Buffalo: Prometheus Books, 1993), 367.

fore she died in 1974 of cancer, Davis was a talk-show phenomenon. From Dinah Shore and Merv Griffin to Johnny Carson, she moved as a national icon of nutritional expertise, unchallenged in spite of the official condemnation of the White House Conference. Her most popular book, *Let's Eat Right to Keep Fit,* stayed on the best seller list even after the medical community performed a detailed, page-by-page analysis of her errors.

Who could blame the public for being confused? Jean Mayer was publishing a book at the same time with the title *A Diet for Living.* It had on the paper jacket the title of "Dr. Jean Mayer," although he was not a medical doctor, identified it as a book club selection and the author as the writer of a widely syndicated newspaper column; in general it sounded very much like the promotional activities of the "others." That the author was a faculty member at Harvard's School of Public Health and had run a scientifically productive laboratory for more than two decades did not distinguish him in the eyes of the public from the rest of the nutritional pack. Nor did this public have a clear understanding of "nutrition" as a science. It seemed to be a field that was not yet complete. The word "vitamin" was only coined in 1911 and it was as late as 1926 that vitamins B, C, D, and E had been found to be necessary for good health. Work on amino acids, minerals, and their relationship to well being was going on in the 1940s. The Food and Drug Administration, established in the first decade of the century, was racing to keep up with the scientists as well as the charlatans, who seemed at times to be winning. The genuine scientists did not know how to promote or to compete. In September 1928, the American Institute of Nutrition was founded, and the first issue of the *Journal of Nutrition* was published that month. The first scientific meeting was held in New York City at the Cornell Medical College in March 1934. They needed to catch up with the nutritional entertainers who held the hearts and minds of America.

Before he became the Tufts President, Jean Mayer the scientist had taken on those who, he knew, were deceiving the nation. Ironically, Jean Mayer the entrepreneur used many of their same marketing devices to sell his reputable books and to spread his gospel. When he arrived at Tufts, he also had fences to mend in the medical community. They had taken the brunt of the counterattacks by celebrities like Hauser, Fredericks, and Davis, who had labeled them all "pill pushers" and tools of the pharmaceutical firms.

Here came Jean Mayer, himself a public nutrition personality, and one with an agenda. From the first, the Tufts medical community was guarded in its reception. They knew that Mayer was a good scientist, although they made clear distinctions between Harvard's Medical School and its School of

Public Health, where Mayer had served for twenty-six years. The faculty of the Tufts Medical School, which included the clinicians at NEMC, watched Mayer very carefully as they prepared themselves to measure the quality of the people he would bring in to staff an initiative in nutrition.

If there was one single appointment that was of the greatest significance in the early years of establishing the scientific viability of nutrition as a health science at Tufts, it was that of Hamish Munro as the first Director of the Human Nutrition Research Center on Aging (HNRCA). He was a brilliant scientist, a physician who did seminal work on protein metabolism, and later in his career he was among the first to recognize and conduct studies on nutrition and genomics. He had been at MIT when the newly appointed President of Tufts orchestrated a task force through his congressional contacts to consider the establishment of a human nutrition research center dedicated to the study of aging. A year later, with considerable help from Schlossberg & Cassidy, now under contract for Tufts and working the halls of Congress, the Agricultural Appropriations Bill of 1978 earmarked for Tufts University, Medford, Massachusetts, one of the country's six human nutrition research centers, owned by the federal government, but staffed and operated by the university. Once the appropriation was cleared, Mayer went after Hamish Munro, who began his tenure early in 1980. This charming, witty little Scot brought a sly humor and wit with him. Already in his sixties, Munro took it upon himself as a final calling to do for the aging population of the United States that which no one else had thought of doing: providing some nutritional measurements for the rest of their lives and gaining a better understanding of the role of food and nutrition in preventing the chronic diseases of aging, such as cancer, cardiovascular disease, brain disease, diabetes, and eye disease. With his arrival at Tufts, nutrition was given instance scientific credibility. Here was a senior MIT scientist with an international reputation who had left Cambridge to come to Tufts. This was clearly a new day.

There was more to come. Munro hated administration and recruited two Associate Directors who were first-rate scientists, Robert Russell, also a physician, and Jeffrey Blumberg, a Ph.D. But it was Munro who made the critical decision to organize the Center by focusing on the body's organs, and to that end he did not hire the "usual" nutrition-trained scientists, but reached out to investigators trained in biochemistry, dermatology, endocrinology, pharmacology, and medicine and directed them to bring their expertise to bear on the mission of the Center: nutrition and aging. Among those earliest arrivals were Allen Taylor, who worked in nutrition and vision; Simin and Mohsen Meydani, in nutritional immunology and vascular biology; Alice

Lichtenstein in cardiovascular nutrition; Beth Dawson-Hughes, in calcium and bone metabolism; along with Russell, who ran the gastrointestinal nutrition lab; and Blumberg, who was chief of the antioxidant research lab. Ernie Schaefer joined them soon after as chief of the lipid metabolism lab. Instantly, the quality of basic science research at Tufts made a leap forward. A sense of grudging stubbornness persisted among some of the Tufts people in the Medical School who were not ready to announce faith in the gospel of disease prevention. They reflected the same reluctance of the medical community all over the nation, the vast majority of whom also were not interested in the relationship of nutrition to disease prevention. To this day, more than twenty-five years after Munro and Mayer pioneered in their research center, very few of the 125 American medical schools have clinical nutrition programs fully developed or integrated into medical school thinking or the curriculum.

There were other obstacles, as well. In these first years of earmarking, the federal bureaucracies, unaccustomed to this direct intrusion into their activities, bridled at the orders they were being given by the congressional delegations, who were all trying to clean up large appropriations for their districts and states. Members of Congress sent out bulletins and press releases to all of their constituencies announcing which school had been funded for which project. The federal departments would not dare do battle with entrenched and powerful committee chairs, so they sucked it up as best they could. But there was a vengeful meanness about the Department of Agriculture (USDA) and the Agricultural Research Service (ARS). They had to appropriate the money, often without additions to their budgets, but they could hold to the letter of the language in the appropriations. Whenever possible, the ARS made life miserable for the HNRCA administration. Above all, the government officials wanted to make certain that no other part of Tufts could exploit the resources of the HNRCA. The facility—all fourteen floors—was essentially cut off from the rest of the university. Classrooms were not available for general use. Since it was government-owned and Tufts-operated under the agreement, the agency could exercise a considerable amount of control over the building, once the money had been released. The auditorium could not be used for any functions other than the Center's, and ARS tried to cut off any research that even hinted at not being mission-related. Instead of taking the broadest interpretation of aging, which arguably was the life cycle, the bureaucrats took the narrowest. It was only when the agriculture personnel realized how remarkable was the research coming out of the Center that they let up a bit. Reluctantly, the people at the

ARS in Beltsville, Maryland, on streets called Anthrax Highway and Pesticide Road, came to understand what a nutrition laboratory like the HNRCA located in the middle of a health sciences campus could accomplish. The dissemination of nutrition research results could "infect" other health science schools and teaching hospitals. It was not long before the Tufts School of Dental Medicine and even the School of Veterinary Medicine saw the potential for inter-school research. Joint appointments sprung up like mushrooms. In his last report to the President before he retired as Center Director in 1983, Munro wrote: "For the first time in the history of modern science, a coordinated effort to increase the quality of life of the aged through nutrition was launched." Elected Washington officials saw votes in an aging population who were being serviced finally through congressional initiatives, and they were not about to permit government agencies to obstruct beyond an acceptable level. Eventually, both the USDA and ARS let up in their pressure on Tufts. After five years of Center operations, medical school students were able to use some Center classrooms and faculty could hold joint seminars in the auditorium. This was considered a major breakthrough.

The real problem came with the relationship with the other part of nutrition at Tufts, the School of Nutrition. Mayer always had a two-pronged idea. The social science policy entity—the School—should have a direct role in the dissemination and interpretation of the research done at the Center. Mayer had brought Stanley Gershoff from Harvard to establish the School of Nutrition on the Medford campus. He wanted the School kept initially at arm's length from the health sciences, and in those early years Nutrition reported to the Provost, not to the Vice President for Health Sciences. After Bob Levy left in 1983, all the schools reported to the Provost.

Mayer's idea was to have the close relationship between the Center and the School make possible the education of a new generation of nutritionists through the appointment of Center scientists to the School faculty and the participation of students under their guidance, doing research at the Center. He was seeking to create the next generation who would look very much like himself: bench-working scientists who understood public policy.

But the ARS was not interested in education nor in making Tufts a unique health sciences institution, with nutrition as its center; and it was *most definitely* not interested in advancing the cause of a school dedicated to nutritional social science and policy. The USDA had visions of congressmen from a butter- or beef-producing region outraged at some statement or data coming out the Tufts School of Nutrition—the only nutrition school in the United States—that might reflect badly on their home states or districts.

This was anathema for the D.C. or Beltsville agriculture bureaucrats. So, they insisted that a wall be built between the Center and the School. Stanley Gershoff, the founding Dean, with Mayer a primary mover in drawing up the initial federal grant that funded the Center, saw the downtown Boston nutrition facility as an extension of his School, as the laboratory arm of his nutrition empire. This was not to be. Hamish Munro, besides being an impish wit, was also a consummate academic politician and took particular delight in playing the role of government informer. He wanted no part of Gershoff and his school. Whenever possible, Hamish would drop a nonlethal but poisonous dose of hemlock into the ears of the government officials stationed at the Center for oversight, telling them at every opportunity when a School of Nutrition social scientist showed up in his building. I knew that Munro was making trouble and told the President, who brushed it off. He had known Hamish for years and had seen him operate on his colleagues at MIT and Harvard. "He cannot help himself. You show him a back and put a knife in his hand, and Pfft!" Nonetheless, Mayer got his revenge. When he believed that the Center's reputation nationally had been sufficiently established, he announced Munro's retirement before Hamish knew about it.

The School of Nutrition was performing in exactly the way Mayer wanted. Schlossberg & Cassidy added language to the enabling legislation that permitted science-track graduate students to work in the Center on stipends provided through the School, and in addition gave academic rank to the HNRCA scientists. This also infuriated the people at USDA, but Mayer simply went around them directly to the Massachusetts congressional delegation or to Jamie Whitten, Chairman of the agriculture appropriation sub-committee. The School's faculty was going to make policy on any issue they chose. By 1983, the *Tufts University Diet and Nutrition Newsletter* had become the most visible publication of its kind in the country, and it spoke out vigorously about fads, nutritional issues, cholesterol, eggs, meat, and all sorts of products whose producers were also clients of the Department of Agriculture.

The School of Nutrition also did not limit its activities to the United States. Mayer wanted an international focus and he encouraged Gershoff to work abroad. Beatrice Rogers and Marian Zeitlin, two young social science researchers who joined the faculty in the early years, scarcely sat still for a moment. Zeitlin worked all over Central America, and Rogers' first big research project for the School was as Principal Investigator on a two-country study of the impact of price policy on food consumption in the Dominican Republic and Mali. She took graduate students with her and set up field stations and residences for Tufts in these countries. She used the Dominican

Republic data to analyze the impact of female headship of households on food consumption and the nutritional status of children. Later, she joined Zeitlin in Honduras looking at the relative cost effectiveness of providing food or cash in maternal child health and in school feeding programs. When the people at USDA saw projects like this coming out of the School, they moved mountains to keep these faculty out of the Center. Munro delighted in telling the on-staff USDA watchdogs whenever Rogers met with one of her graduate students in an HNRCA office. Gershoff would complain to Mayer, who went right to his Washington connections, and some staff person from a congressional committee would then threaten the USDA with a cut in appropriations. It was war, but the science went forward and was gaining a great deal of public visibility. HNRCA scientists were being interviewed everywhere on television, National Public Radio, the *Today Show, Good Morning, America,* and all the pre-cable network stations. Along with the *Newsletter,* the School of Nutrition encouraged nutritional communication throughout the nation. Jeanne Goldberg had been one of President Mayer's ghostwriters for his syndicated column on nutrition and continued that work as a faculty member at the School. In time, after Mayer's retirement, she established a Master's degree in nutrition and communication.

Of all the successes in his first decade as President of Tufts, perhaps nothing rivaled his accomplishment of associating the Tufts name with the gold standard of nutrition research and policy in the country. Jean Mayer gave Tufts University a unique and singular identity. When Irwin Rosenberg came to the HNRC as Director in 1986 from his position as Chief of Gastroenterology in the Department of Medicine at the University of Chicago Medical School, this solidified the position of nutrition in the medical community downtown. At Chicago, Rosenberg was also Director of the NIH Clinical Nutrition Research Center. His eminence as a physician, scientist, and researcher in the field of nutrition rivaled that of Munro. He also had a stronger international, public health and policy orientation, having started in the 1960s in East Pakistan/Bangladesh and eventually worked on issues of nutrition and infection with respect to cholera. Rosenberg's credentials in biochemical nutrition placed him at the forefront of the emerging nutritional sciences, ranging from vitamin deficiency to malabsorption of nutrients and complications of gastrointestinal disease. He was the perfect candidate to see Mayer's goal to its conclusion, and before he was finished, Irv Rosenberg had made the marriage between medicine and nutrition a happy one. Some years later, when he became the first Director of the HNRC who was also responsible for the School of Nutrition—we named him Dean for Nutrition, to keep the ARS from making too much trouble—Rosenberg had fulfilled Mayer's vision. He had given coherence to nutritional science and policy and had draped them with both a national and international mantle recognized everywhere in the world.

THE TOP OF THE MOUNTAIN

When he submitted his tenth annual report in November 1986 to the Board of Trustees, Jean Mayer could look back on a university he had transformed, and he knew it. The *New York Times* had interviewed him a few months earlier, for the Sunday, June 8, 1986, edition. He was telling the public what he would shortly tell his Board. The article was a combination of accurate historical journalism, self-promotion, and unabashed pride of accomplishment.[26] The reporter had a good hook into what Tufts had been and what it had become, growing from a "sound, middle-aged university that seemed forever in the shadow of Harvard and MIT" into an institution that "has broken new ground with centers for the study of environmental management and aging, and graduate programs in nutrition and veterinary medicine. And it has acquired an international flavor that leads college guides and surveys these days to describe Tufts with such words as stylish, excellent and hot."

This was Jean Mayer at the peak of his success, a leader, at age sixty-six, with energy, vision, and ego. The reporter had described him as "a charming but not necessarily modest man." The Tufts President could be forgiven for a slight re-writing of history. "I had to replace every dean and every vice president because they were not performing as I expected," said the man who never bothered who was dean or vice president if he did not have to, and who much preferred docile non-leaders who would stay out of his way. Jean Mayer, entrepreneur *extraordinaire* and Lone Ranger, had more administrators resign on him or threaten to resign out of frustration than he ever fired. In this expansive interview, he talked about his war record, how he helped liberate "a couple of concentration camps," his gamble in establishing both the veterinary and nutrition schools, the remarkable success in fundraising and concluded that "this is a very different university than it was ten years ago."

This was the triumphantly self-confident president who, in effect, said to the Trustees in November of his tenth year as leader: I told you so, didn't I? Even the precarious financial foundation of the Veterinary School appeared

26. "Jean Mayer's Decade at Tufts: A Stamp of Passion," *New York Times,* June 8, 1986, 54.

to have stabilized somewhat, as the state appropriation reached a figure in excess of $5 million. He even puffed himself up as a fiscally responsible CEO at the end of his introduction: "Finally, I am happy to report something that is no longer 'news': for the seventh year in a row, the university has achieved an operating surplus." He did not add that the Board of Trustees had forced this discipline on him through the instrument of Steve Manos, one of the most powerful executive Vice Presidents in American higher education.

At any university, a president with this record of accomplishment would have had every reason to point to a decade of extraordinary accomplishment. For Tufts, it was nothing short of a miracle. The $145 million Campaign for Tufts was a staggeringly unprecedented success, given the pace of progress over the previous century. New buildings had sprouted everywhere, the endowment had doubled (it still had a long way to go), the donor base had more than doubled, and total fund-raising achievement from 1976 to 1986 when compared to 1966 to 1976 showed a 468 percent increase, from $31 million over a decade to $176 million. At the center of the whirlwind of accomplishment was this President; and in his own mind, he was clearly not done.

After ten years as President, Jean Mayer was not looking toward any finish line. The only position that might have taken him away from his university presidency would have been a call from Washington to take over the Department of Agriculture, and that call never came. Tufts had proved to be the perfect instrument for him. He had demonstrated admirable patience in waiting for what he wanted: a presidency in Boston. Harvard had been beyond his reach. He had been an unsuccessful candidate at Boston University when John Silber was selected, and had been passed over *twice* by Tufts, only miraculously to get the call after Harry Woolf's change-of-mind. Now that he had what he wanted, the thought never crossed his mind to give it up. The idea of "completion" was alien to him. There was always something else to build. He had undergone serious bypass surgery, had a gall bladder removed, and had been ordered to give up hang-gliding in Talloires, where he routinely jumped off a 2,000-foot cliff, but he thought of himself as indestructible and assumed he was irreplaceable. After all, he had taken Tufts to heights never dreamed of by his predecessors. He concluded his ten-year review at the end of the 1986 annual report with the following observation: "The hopes for the next decade rival or surpass the accomplishments of the last. Together we will continue to brighten the 'light on the hill.'" There was no thought in his mind that he might not be the leader to take Tufts through the next decade. After all, it was not unprecedented for some presidents to enjoy a career of two decades or more heading one institution, especially in Boston. The surest way to guarantee the continuation of his presidency was to begin another fundraising campaign, and he instructed his acolyte Tom Murnane to begin putting the pieces in place for a $250 million effort, this time without counting the federal contribution. For the next campaign, the alumni would be prepared appropriately to give, as well as the Board of Trustees, who had undergone a tectonic shift under the careful orchestration of Tom Murnane.

Murnane suffered all during his years as Senior Vice President for Development because of his closeness to Mayer. The faculties dismissed him as a nonintellectual and concluded that he was useful only as a slick academic Irishman who could get close to the politicians on Beacon Hill. He was given no credit for raising much of the money, when in fact it was Murnane's charm and visceral intelligence that located and identified many donors. The President was a great talker and not much of a listener. He overwhelmed his audience with the power of his ideas, but he was never allowed to travel to major donors alone and was generally accompanied by his indispensable Vice President for Development. Like Mayer, Murnane operated best unencumbered and with a minimum of constraint. Neither could really manage a bureaucracy and had little interest in doing so. But, like Mayer, Murnane wanted control and that meant a centralized Development effort, and the deans fought him. No matter how much money he brought in, they were convinced that they could do better, if their fundraising efforts were uncoupled from central administration. Still, as great a contribution that he made as a moneymaker, it was his careful stewardship of the Trustees that prepared the way for the second and grander fundraising campaign, from 1986 to 1991.

Of all the structural changes that took place during Jean Mayer's presidency, the metamorphosis of the Board might be recorded as the most significant. It took place at a time when college and university boards all over the country were coming to grips with their authority and responsibilities. For Tufts, out in the cold of fundraising for so many decades, it was critical to get Trustees who did not reflect the traditional parsimony when it came to philanthropy toward the university.

Board of Trustees: A Geography Lesson

The make-up of private college and university Boards of Trustees during the first two centuries of American higher education was predictable. Their religious calling drove the institutions, and trusteeship meant serving on a board to oversee the development of the moral character of the students and faculty. Philanthropy and endowment came later toward the end of the nineteenth century when prominent businessmen and alumni made their way to the boards. Most institutions were somehow positioned to take off when serious fundraising began in a big way in the post-war and affluent 1950s. Tufts was not.

The theme that runs through the two-volume history of Tufts executed by historian and faculty member Russell Miller is financial stress. Granted, there *never* is enough money for institutions to satisfy themselves, but in the case of Tufts College and since the mid-1950s Tufts University, the inability to raise money was the dagger aimed at the institution's heart. The Board of Trustees chose to ignore what could have proved a fatal danger. As soon as Mayer and Murnane teamed up, they turned their attention to Board membership. Not everything they encountered was a disaster. During his tenure, President Wessell recognized the changing dynamics and character of the student and faculty population as diversity began altering the nature of the Tufts alumni. Still predominantly a commuter school whose alumni remained in the area, the Tufts Board was overwhelmingly local, but it did begin in the 1950s to look a little less Protestant. It had long ago given up the requirement for Universalist presidents, but during the 1920s and 1930s, with the unspoken but rigorously applied quota system in the undergraduate colleges, ensured close control on the number of Jewish and Catholic students admitted. It was President Wessell who recognized the opportunity, and took it. President Mayer inherited a Board that had no history of giving, but had some potential, which Tom Murnane noted immediately. Louis Berger was CEO of a major international construction firm and a 1936 graduate of the College of Engineering. Alexander McFarlane was a 1934 graduate and Chairman of the Board of CPC International Inc., an international leader in the food industry. Irene (Eisenman) Bernstein was one of the handful of Jewish women (four per class for the next two decades) admitted to Jackson College in 1934, who mysteriously were assigned in double rooms as each other's roommates. Jackson bigotry continued right through the war years into the post-war period. In 1946, Roberta Sheer found herself rooming with one of the four Jewish girls admitted to her class. The other two were down the hall, also roommates. Years later, as Bobbie Burstein, married to Tufts overseer Maxwell Burstein, she would meet regularly with the other three to reminisce about those extraordinary times of racial and ethnic profiling at Tufts. This practice at Jackson College continued right into the 1950s. Ruth Lubarsky, later Trustee Ruth Remis, had no difficulty finding the other three Jewish first-year women in the class of '54—they were all on the same floor. Berger and McFarlane, during the Mayer presidency, would make gifts of endowed chairs and Irene Bernstein and her husband David, not a Tufts graduate, renovated an entire floor of the library in the 1980s, but their philanthropy before Mayer was minimal. Mrs. Bernstein told me years later that she was delighted finally to be asked to make a significant gift to Tufts, because earlier no one had brought up the subject of giving. The Burstein and Remis families became lifelong major donors to Tufts, as their children and grandchildren attended in very different, less prejudiced times.

Clearly, Tom Murnane had a strategy: move beyond Boston and, if possible, outside of the country. There was no question that the international agenda of the President would pay benefits, and this agenda should be reflected in the Board. He needed a willing President as well as a Chairman who accepted the idea, and this he had in both Allan Callow, who was Chairman until 1986, and in his successor, Nelson Gifford. Callow and Gifford were critical to any successful reshaping of the Board. It was not enough that they should just "go along." They had to be willing and aggressive salesmen and work with Mayer and Murnane. They enlisted the aid of the other Board player from a previous presidency, Weston Howland, Jr., who had no Tufts affiliation but had been brought on in the early 1960s in an effort to bring some financial stability to Tufts' shaky existence. You may recall that it was these three who cast their lot and the future of Tufts with Jean Mayer; and it was their willingness to see the Board's center of gravity shift away from Boston and its Protestant traditions that made change possible. It was Murnane's plan, but without them, it would never have happened.

When the Second Campaign for Tufts began in 1986, the Board, like Tufts itself, had been transformed. It was these Board members whose names would appear on buildings and endowed chairs and who would be responsible for a significant percentage of the $250 million target. Tom Murnane orchestrated this membership strategically. Some of the most important additions were not alumni. He needed one Trustee totally dedicated to the future welfare of a school that had no alumni, the Veterinary School, and Dr. Henry Foster was a willing enthusiast. Murnane had met him and introduced him to the President during the early days of Vet School planning. For the next twenty-five years, Henry Foster's dedication to the Vet School never wavered, and he even tightened his relationship to Tufts when his grandchildren came to Medford in the 1990s.

Placido Arrango and Issam Fares came to Murnane's attention when their children were enrolled in the undergraduate college in the early 1980s. Both were internationally connected, philanthropic, and gave Tufts a visible presence in Spain and the Middle East. Shirley Aidekman was also a Tufts parent, had a commitment to the university through her children, and loved the arts. Joseph Neubauer, Israeli-born of German parents who fled the Nazis, had come to Tufts in 1959 on scholarship, was now Chairman and President of what was at the time called ARA Services, Inc., now ARAMARK. His daughter had matriculated at Tufts, and Neubauer, possessing his own ferocious intellect and with no patience for mediocrity, liked what he saw in Jean Mayer and decided to stay for the ride. He came onto the Board in 1986.

Murnane also paid careful attention to his local constituency. He added John Cabot, William Saltonstall, and Hester Sargent, members of three venerable Boston families who liked the new President. Bill Cummings, a 1963 Liberal Arts graduate who as President of Cummings Properties had control of nine million square feet of real estate in the Greater Boston area, was a prominent Catholic layman, in Boston a very important constituency. Years later, Cummings played a critical role in convincing the Archdiocese when Tufts appointed a first-in-the-nation Catholic priest as university chaplain of a secular university. In addition, Murnane looked for people who would respond to the President's charisma and at the same time also brought a new sense of involvement to development activities. He wanted people who would ask others. This was a critical new aspect of Trustee involvement. Ed Merrin, Class of '50, was a prominent New York City art dealer who was very involved in Jewish philanthropy. He and Murnane looked for potential in people with a track record of asking others as well as giving themselves; and they found what they were looking for in the New York City Jewish community. Here was a tradition of stepping up to the table and getting others to do so, as well. Nathan Gantcher, Liberal Arts '62 and James Stern, Engineering '72, both Wall Street financiers, were on the board by 1983. It was Ed Merrin, through his connections in the art world, who earlier had helped recruit Placido Arrango. Now he brought on Shirley Aidekman and Nathan Gantcher. Jonathan Tisch A'75 joined the next year. Gantcher eventually became Chairman of the Board, succeeding Nelson Gifford in 1995; Stern succeeded Gantcher in 2003. During the chairmenships of Callow, Gifford, and Gantcher, Tufts University raised $1 billion, an amount that would have been inconceivable to earlier generations of Trustees. At this writing, the campaign that will commence at the outset of the new millennium under Chairman James Stern will be for $1 billion.

The fundamental focus of the Chairman and the Board had shifted during these past twenty-five years. Under Gifford, Gantcher and Stern chaired the Development Committee, and because of their ability and willingness to raise money quickly became the most dynamic duo on the Board. When Gantcher became Chairman, Jim Stern took on the Development effort himself.

For what was officially called "The New Campaign for Tufts," announced in 1987 in the *Wall Street Journal, New York Times, Washington Post,* and *Los Angeles Times,* there was extraordinary symbolism in the names of the leadership. The Co-Chairmen of the Campaign were Nathan Gantcher and Weston Howland, Jr.; the Chairs of the Capital and Annual Funds were Nelson Gifford, newly appointed Chairman of the Board, and Roslyn (Schwartz) Berenberg, Vice-Chairwoman of the Board, and another of those Jewish Jackson roommates whom the Dean of Women thought "would be more comfortable with their own kind." This Board reflected the two worlds of Tufts and what had happened to the university during the Mayer years, the years of maturing, of growing up. Gifford and Howland were in the process of acknowledging a new heritage for Tufts. To be sure, there were few people of color on the Board, and none of these had great philanthropic means. But, for the foreseeable future, the name of the game regarding Board membership was "Give"; and the center of gravity had moved from parochial Medford and Boston to other east coast cities, California, and Europe. In every respect, Jean Mayer had prepared himself and his university for the next decade of his leadership. It was not to be.

*An American Faculty, the 1950s. President Wessell addresses the Arts and Sciences: all white,
nearly all male.*

President Nils Wessell, 1953–1966. No one wanted him to leave. He knew it was time.

President Burton Hallowell, 1967–1976. He arrived to encounter a deficit and a whirlwind of student unrest.

Provost Kathryn McCarthy. She admired Hallowell, but not Jean Mayer.

Nelson Gifford. He was reluctant to become a Trustee. His decision to support Jean Mayer was critical.

Bernard Harleston, Dean of Arts and Sciences. He and Provost McCarthy believed that President Mayer was ruining Tufts.

Allan Callow, Chairman of the Board of Trustees in 1976. He and Gifford were Mayer's strongest supporters and the risk-takers.

The future Tufts President. A youthful Jean Mayer fights fascism and Hitler's Germany.

Jean Mayer, 1976. The transformer arrives, and Tufts begins shaking on its foundations.

Jean Mayer, 1990. Not mellowing after fourteen years.

The President and Betty Mayer. A most gracious lady.

The third leg of the Troika: Sol Gittleman, Provost, with the Director of the Experimental College.

Vice President Tom Murnane. A dentist who raised a billion dollars.

Executive Vice President Steven Manos. No one knew how much power he had.

Frank Colcord, Dean of Arts and Sciences, 1980–1987.

Hamish Munro, first Director of the Human Nutrition Research Center. Superb scientist and first-class troublemaker.

Fred Nelson, Dean of Engineering, 1980–1995. Like Colcord, nice guys whom Mayer chose.

John Roche, Fletcher Academic Dean, power broker and consummate politician, here sitting with Senator Kennedy.

Stanley Gershoff, first Dean of the School of Nutrition. Mayer loyalist and friend.

Edmund Gullion, Dean of the Fletcher School of Law and Diplomacy, 1964–1978. The Diplomat as Dean.

Theodore Eliot, Fletcher Dean, 1979–1985. No one was granted tenure during his deanship.

155

Jeswald Salacuse, Fletcher Dean, 1986–1994. Like Eliot, he wanted to be a part of the university.

Trustee Henry Foster. The savior of the Veterinary School.

Albert Jonas, first Dean of the Veterinary School, 1978–1981. He fought the other health sciences and lost.

Martha Pokras, Executive Dean, Veterinary School. No matter who was Dean, she was indispensable.

Joe McManus, Chief Financial Officer, Veterinary School. Another nonacademic who was vital for school survival.

Frank Loew, Dean of the Veterinary School, 1982–1995. The closest reincarnation of Jean Mayer.

Robert Shira, Dean of the Dental School, 1972–1979; Provost, 1979–1981. Forced on Mayer by the Trustees, he won the President's trust.

Erling Johansen, Dean of the Dental School, 1979–1995. He laid the foundation; tenacious, courageous, an academic bulldog.

157

Lonnie Norris, Dean of the Dental School, 1995–present. Humanized an abrasive faculty and built for the future.

Patricia Campbell, Executive Dean of the Dental School. This new breed brings management skills that the faculty accept.

Robert Levy, Dean of the Medical School, 1981-1983. Brilliant scientist, terrible people skills.

Henry Banks, Dean of the Medical School, 1983–1990. A Tufts loyalist who believed in Mayer.

Louis Lasagna, Sackler School's First permanent Dean, 1984–2002. Mayer's personal pick.

Jerome Grossman, 1979–1995. Hospital President, CEO, Chairman. Mayer's Medical Nemesis.

THE SLIPPERY SLOPE

THE MAYER PRESIDENCY, 1987–1992

4

Economist John Kenneth Galbraith once expressed the paradox of the entrepreneurial personality: "The great entrepreneur accomplishes his act of conception at the price of his own extinction."[1] One wonders at what point the key Trustees at Tufts began thinking that too much of Jean Mayer's brand of dynamism was not healthy for the university.

Certainly, the national and Commonwealth economy were factors. What was most remarkable about Mayer's accomplishments at Tufts was that he succeeded in the face of uncertain economic times. The stock market crashed in 1983, but soon the Reagan tax policies produced strong growth until 1987, along with a considerable increase in deficit spending, which helped to create, in the public mind, a roller coaster economy. In October of 1987, the stock market plunged 500 points from 2200 to 1700, and the national mood began to turn somber again.

The problems began with the Veterinary School. At Tufts, 1987 marked the high point of Vet School stability, which meant for President Mayer the best of times. Frank Loew and Tom Murnane had gotten the state appropriation over $5 million for the first time, and, although the cost-of-living increases were not regularly part of the process, the sporadic increases were of enormous help and a real morale booster for the school. Even though the Commonwealth contributed only 13 percent of the school's total budget—a much smaller percentage than any state or quasi-private vet school (such as Penn and Cornell)—there was a feeling of stability and optimism. The Board of Trustees, which had earlier made Frank Loew's life miserable, was less aggressively abrasive and critical. Instead of taking out their hostility on the

1. Daniel Goleman, "The Psyche of the Entrepreneur," *New York Times Magazine,* February 2, 1986, 63.

President about what seemed to be a permanent Vet School deficit, they had gone after the Dean. There was no question, even from the Trustees, that the Vet School was the best and most frugally managed of all the Tufts schools, but there was no way that any veterinary school could manage without major subsidies. Now, however, they saw the potential that Loew was developing for business in the biotech industry out in Grafton, and they bought into what Governor Dukakis was calling "The Massachusetts Miracle." This was also giving the governor ideas, and in the fall of 1987 he appeared on the Grafton campus—at his own invitation—where his optimistic speech cautioned one of the faculty to comment: "Is this guy running for President?" Indeed, he was.

In February 1988, he became a candidate. Before the year was over, the Massachusetts Miracle had turned into the Massachusetts Mess, and Dukakis was a beaten and humiliated politician. With the state economy again in trouble, so was the Vet School appropriation. When the newly elected Governor William Weld took office, he line-itemed the Vet School appropriation down to *zero*. The Trustees pounced immediately, and the administration was instructed to prepare a plan outlining the risks entailed by the university, in the event that we close or not close the School of Veterinary Medicine. These things can never be kept secret, and rumors began flying all over the campuses from Grafton to Boston to Medford. In downtown Boston, there was a considerable amount of "What did I tell you!," that it was never a sustainable idea, one of Mayer's follies. *Schadenfreude* was very much in evidence.

Mayer, Murnane, Loew, and their Beacon Hill lobbyist Jack Brennan got access to Weld and made a hard-nosed sell for the Vet School and the biotechnology industry. Weld, to his eternal credit, understood the benefits to the business community and restored most of the cuts, to the shock of many, who were already preparing funeral orations for the Veterinary School. Loew had to do enormous damage control on morale among his faculty and staff. Students had some awareness of the threat to the school, but the old-timers had begun feeling some sense of security, and the shock of seeing just how fast they could be abandoned and made to feel fatally vulnerable, left them shocked.

The whole experience took a great deal out of Jean Mayer. He realized that at the first sight of serious financial trouble, the Trustees would not support "this little jewel." He had, however, also come to realize that when he really needed an ally, Senate President William Bulger could be counted on, even if the Trustees proved to be fair-weather friends. In spite of twelve uninterrupted years of surplus, even with the deficits of the Vet School, at the first sign of a serious threat to the bottom line, the Trustees reverted to a need for financial stability almost immediately. Tufts had come a long way in ten years, but they were in no mood for further risks, and suddenly the Vet School looked vulnerable. A decade ago, risks were necessary. Ten years later, it was time to consolidate the enormous gains their President had brought about.

But Jean Mayer was not ready for consolidation. The new Governor of the Commonwealth looked like he could be counted on to support what Mayer insisted was the perfect example of public and private cooperation in veterinary education, and now the President could turn his attention elsewhere, to an idea perhaps even *grander* than anything previously conceived of. He wanted projects on some large scale. After the nutrition and veterinary programs, President Mayer had worked with Gerry Cassidy to bring a Center for Environment Management via an EPA earmark to Tufts, and then a program for Chinese government officials funded by the USIA to study at the Fletcher School. Neither was of the scale he liked. For his next grand gesture, President Mayer turned to the downtown campus, and his conception was one of such size and complication that it dwarfed the scope of both the nutrition and veterinary schools.

President Mayer had found himself out-gunned and out-maneuvered by President Grossman of the New England Medical Center. Jerry Grossman had unprecedented powers of financial control over the hospital and its apparatus. His enormous success and apparent financial wizardry won him the complete confidence of his board and several of the members of the Tufts board, who also served as either governors or trustees of the hospital. Jean Mayer had a difficult time gaining the loyalty of the clinical faculty, and his medical school deans shared this frustration. Sheldon Wolff had virtually taken the Department of Medicine out of any control of the Medical School and had moved into research space owned totally by the New England Medical Center. Wherever the university turned, there was Jerry Grossman, who seemed to delight in making life difficult for Tufts Medical School. The deans were convinced that he hindered our accreditation, and Jean Mayer was also certain that any candidate for the Dean of the Medical School who talked to the President of NEMC would not remain a candidate for long. The hospital was gobbling up all the available research space downtown, and the Tufts President needed a way out.

Mayer proposed the solution in several meetings of the Board of Trustees during the 1989–1990 academic year. The idea was staggering. The President conceived of a separate for-profit entity, the Tufts University Development Corporation (TUDC), which would acquire air rights over various portions of Boston real estate, at the Massachusetts Turnpike or the South Station transportation hub. Over these sites would rise two million square feet of construction, which would include six to eight hundred thousand square feet of prime research space, to be shared by pharmaceutical companies attracted to Boston and their new partners in research, the Tufts University School of Medicine and the School of Nutrition. Jean Mayer would provide the linkage through his connections. In addition, there would be a 675-room hotel, a 700,00-square-foot office tower, and twelve hundred parking spaces. The President assured the trustees that there would be no liability to Tufts since "a corporate veil" would separate TUDC from its vulnerable non-profit and chaste university namesake. The President told the Tufts Board of Trustees that here was a way to guarantee the future viability and independence of the Medical School *at no risk to the university.* This was a song they had heard before.

Remarkably, it was a proposal that met with considerable approval from a small but solid number of the Tufts Trustees. There were real estate developers and builders who saw the imaginative scope of the plan and thought it visionary, just as President Mayer had impressed them with his vision nearly thirteen years earlier. It was risky, but in its imagination and grandeur, a truly futuristic image presented itself. Most of the board were terrified, others intrigued.

Even for the plan's supporters, one question loomed. Could Jean Mayer, now nearly seventy years old, with failing health for several years and buffeted by events both of his own doing and the action of others, carry this plan forward? Here he was, the builder of half-bridges, of a world-class veterinary school and a unique nutrition school, neither with an endowment, neither complete within the original conception. But, then again, "completion" was not a word within his vocabulary. Here he was moving on to another wondrous idea, but one that he could scarcely hope even to approach fulfillment. One thing was certain: He would never let go on his own initiative. For others on the board, the thought, no doubt, had been planted: It was time to think of transition, perhaps to a more stable platform.

Intellectually, President Mayer remained the same restless spirit. Physically, the job was taking its toll. Eventually, his effort at trying to serve as seven deans, a provost, *and* the President of the university began wearing him down. He allowed me to run the Fletcher School search for a Dean in 1986 that resulted in the appointment of Jeswald Salacuse, but he insisted on running the searches for all health sciences deans. When Henry Banks announced his retirement as Dean of the Medical School in 1988, President

Mayer informed me that he would be chairing the search committee personally. He assured the Board that Tufts Medical School was now in a position to attract an outstanding candidate from around the country. He placed his own stature on the line and suffered an unaccustomed humiliation. After more than a year of frustration, the search ended in failure. He could never reconcile his differences with President Grossman, and without a joint effort, no sane candidate would take the job. After nearly two years of acting deans and no hope of finding a dean from outside, I suggested that he appoint someone from inside whom he trusted and liked: Morton Madoff, a physician and Professor of Community Health, a capable manager who had the ability to be nasty to everyone, including the hospital president. This search demonstrated to the trustees of both school and hospital that Jean Mayer's stature was not enough to attract a medical school dean from the outside.

New problems and distractions kept appearing. Around the same time that Henry Banks stepped down, we were advised by federal authorities of a complaint stemming from claims made public by a research assistant in the Medical School charging that a faculty member in the Department of Pathology, Assistant Professor Thereza Imanishi-Kari, had engaged in research fraud. The allegation quickly found its way to a congressional committee chaired by Congressman Charles Dingell. The case was complicated by the fact that the original research was done while Imanishi-Kari worked at MIT in the lab of Nobel-Laureate David Baltimore.[2] When Baltimore, irate at the intrusion of Dingell's committee and the charges made by his staff, aggressively defended himself and his science, the investigation turned political. Dingell went after everyone associated with Baltimore, MIT, and Tufts. Enormous pressure was put on President Mayer to put distance between Tufts and the suspected faculty member, whose department remained steadfastly supportive. Dingell threatened to cut off all federal funding for Tufts, and the trustees began to buckle. Even student opinion was convinced of the charges against the Tufts scientist, and letters appeared in the undergraduate newspaper urging that Tufts separate itself from the beleaguered pathologist. Mayer anguished over this. His instincts told him that the investigatory process was more like a lynch mob. He had met enough congressional staffers to know how these people sometimes made their reputations: by tearing down someone else's. But, he was caught between the medical school faculty supporters, the wavering Trustees, Dingell's bullying, and a genuine desire to see justice done.

2. See Daniel J. Kevles, *The Baltimore Case* (New York: W. W. Norton, 1998).

We found a way out. Professor Imanishi-Kari was placed on administrative leave, with pay. The tenure clock was stopped, she kept her laboratory, and until the charges against her were settled, she would exist in a state of academic suspended animation. If found guilty, her relationship with Tufts would end immediately. If she were vindicated, she would return to her department without prejudice. In the meantime, no federal agency would dare to fund her, as long as Congressman Dingell was investigating. Still, without NIH support and no federal agency willing to accept her applications, she did apply successfully to the American Cancer Society and kept herself going until she was eventually cleared of all charges in 1996. However, during the final years of Mayer's presidency, the case remained unsettled, David Baltimore was forced to resign his presidency of Rockefeller University, and some of Mayer's connections in the nation's capitol backed away from any confrontation with the powerful Democrat congressman from Detroit, whose seniority had him wired into the top echelons of power in Washington. University circles, right up to their presidents, discussed Congressman Dingell as yet another third rail; touch him, and you perish. President Mayer, torn between his need for final proof concerning the professor's guilt or innocence, agonized over his decision. In the end, he placed some distance between Tufts and Tereza Imanishi-Kari, while still assuring her that exoneration would result in complete restitution and the continuance of her career at Tufts. Some Trustees were unhappy and took this decision as caving in to faculty pressure. Today, Professor Imanishi-Kari is a tenured member of the Department of Pathology at the Tufts University School of Medicine.

It was a time when university presidents, no matter how eminent and successful, were proving to be vulnerable. Along with Baltimore's fall from grace came the demise of Donald Kennedy's twelve-year presidency at Stanford, amidst unsubstantiated but glaringly public charges of misuse of research funds generated as indirect costs. The press was filled with stories about lavish spending on presidential yachts. Kennedy simply gave up. A faculty who did not appreciate the publicity about research fraud associated with their president pushed out Baltimore.

Normally, Mayer loved the kind of limelight that high profile and public exposure gave the university. He would proclaim, "All publicity is good publicity," even if it involved a sensational murder case. In 1982, Tufts accounting auditors began an examination of the grants held by Associate Professor William Douglas, a tenured member of the Department of Anatomy. Douglas was a respected researcher who habitually prowled the notorious Combat Zone of downtown Boston and had become enamored of a prostitute named Robin Benedict, whom he placed as an assistant on his grant.[3] He embezzled money for her. After the fraud had been uncovered, Douglas was suspended, and while the process of figuring out how to organize a case for dismissal was being discussed, Douglas was arrested for the murder of Benedict. He was subsequently convicted, although the body was never found. For those of us who were caught up in the newspaper stories, with the usual faculty ambivalence concerning dismissal of *anyone*—short of murder—and the business of figuring out what to do with an issue of academic fraud and misconduct, these were time-consuming events. The Tufts President turned it into a history lesson for the Board of Trustees that he happily linked with Harvard, where in the previous century another faculty member and anatomist had committed murder and similarly disposed of the body. He had been hanged, Mayer reminded the Board, but the Harvard faculty at that time also had difficulty coming to a decision about dismissal. Mayer's interest in the Douglas case was also amusingly professional, since the Tufts professor had at one point reached a weight of 317 pounds and the nutritionist President kept asking me for reports on the hearings we were holding and the defense that Douglas, along with several colleagues and Tufts faculty, was mounting to account for his embezzlement. He passionately proclaimed that the strict diet on which he had been placed had resulted in his strange behavior. Douglas had brought a psychiatrist and endocrinologist to support his argument. The murder charge, his arrest and conviction pushed all of the academic discussion into the background. In the two years that the case was part of the public record in the Boston and national press, the President seemed to enjoy his reports about Douglas to the Trustees, which he never failed to include. He would comment on the issues of diet, weight loss, and use his expertise to advantage.

When it came to reporting to the Trustees on the confrontation with Congressman Dingell, President Mayer was much more guarded, defensive, and hesitant. He had been bruised, saw danger, and expected criticism from the Trustees, which he heard. What defiance of Dingell threatened was a total loss of federal funding. This was not an isolated case of fraud or murder. The threat presented by this powerful congressman endangered the entire university, and the Trustees made certain that their President fully understood their concerns. Some were very unhappy that Imanishi-Kari, even under limiting terms, could still call herself a Tufts professor.

3. See Teresa Carpenter, *Missing Beauty: A True Story of Murder and Obsession* (New York: W.W. Norton, 1988), 15–85.

In retrospect, one Trustee decision during this period should have alerted Mayer that the board was focused on transition, even if the President and his closest associates were not. Soon after the board recognized the President's decade of extraordinary leadership, he informed me that the Executive Committee strongly urged him to appoint a leader for Arts and Sciences, which at the time included Engineering, with a vice presidential title. This would be an executive academic position, still reporting to the Provost, but as such would give this "dean" an eminence greater than the deans of the sister schools at Tufts. None of the Troika wanted this and neither did the President, but the Board of Trustees had its way. The incumbent Dean, political scientist and Professor Frank Colcord, said that he would stay on until an appointment was made. The faculty of Arts and Sciences saw the enhanced position as recognition of their position as first among equals in the university, and applauded the Trustee decision.

This also demonstrated the evolution of a national phenomenon: the growing authority of university boards of trustees and their corporate relationship to the President, or as they more frequently called the leader of the university, the CEO. There was a new focus on what the board saw as its primary responsibility: finding the right CEO. The evolution of Board authority came right out of the for-profit sector, where increasingly the Chief Executive served at the pleasure of a board, indeed, was selected by the board chairman. The academic tradition of faculty search committees to participate in presidential selections was a totally alien concept. But, as faculty strength also grew in the second half of the twentieth century, the faculty was taking its responsibility as a prerogative of shared governance. It wanted to be involved and heard. In a future presidential search at Tufts, these two forces were destined to clash.

The thought that the first Vice President for Arts, Sciences and Technology—the official new title—might be the right person to succeed Jean Mayer as President might have only existed in the mind of Nelson Gifford, but he was Chairman of the Board, was a very business-oriented CEO of a major corporation, had figured out how long he would stay on as Chairman of the Board, and felt a keen responsibility to make certain that the presidential succession would be handled smoothly. In the world he came from, there was a fixed retirement date for the Chief Executive Officer, and Chairman Gifford had done the arithmetic for President Mayer.

But this was not a screening for a future president. As a consequence, when the President instructed me to run the search for a new leader of the Arts and Sciences, my sights were set on just that, not on presidential succession. Tufts did not have a tradition of selecting world-class scholars as their leader in Arts and Sciences, and I believed this was the most important characteristic of the right candidate. The faculty/student/staff search committee chaired by me accepted that standard, and the person selected as the first Vice President for Arts and Sciences at Tufts was Robert Rotberg of Massachusetts Institute of Technology, a historian with an international reputation and the author of a recently acclaimed biography of Cecil Rhodes. He was the unanimous choice of the search committee, and President Mayer concurred. Although he had only minor administrative experience at MIT, he served on the Board of Trustees at Oberlin, seemed to understand the higher educational culture, and certainly knew quality.

Bob Rotberg had a reputation for being charming as well as tough and abrasive, with uncompromisingly high academic standards. In my false security as a reasonably good mentor, I believed that I could emphasize the first of these characteristics and soften the others. I was wrong. President Mayer got hold of Bob early in the game, and told him to take this faculty and make it even better, and that the only way to accomplish this was by being tough. My advice had been to go slowly at first, win their confidence, and then raise the bar of quality. Within six months of taking on the job in 1987, Vice President Rotberg had alienated a significant and vocal minority of the faculty. The Tufts chapter of the American Association of University Professors went for his jugular. Within three years, he was gone, appointed President of Lafayette College. During the struggle over his survival as Vice President, some Tufts faculty had gone directly to the Board to voice their complaints and suggested that it was the President who was responsible for Bob Rotberg's abrasiveness. It became apparent to the Board that there would be no mentoring from within, no help from the President in preparing for his successor, because he did not want a successor. When Jean Mayer turned seventy late in 1990, the Board acted.

At a meeting of the Troika in the winter of 1991, President Mayer informed us that Chairman Gifford had told him that it was time to formalize the succession. President Mayer seemed accepting, since "I will play a major role in selecting my successor, and I will be named Chancellor of the University." He put on a very brave face. It was clear to me and to my colleagues that President Mayer did not want to relinquish his position, and, if at all possible, he would hold on to as much authority as he could, as John Silber successfully did some years later at Boston University. President Mayer felt that he had time to get organized, to find the perfect President of Tufts for the perfect Chancellor. In a second *New York Times* interview with Fox Butterfield on April 1, 1992 ("Tufts President Helps His University Stand Tall Amid Giants of Academe"), Mayer told the reporter that he would retire at the end of the 1993 academic year. In his own mind, this would give him more than a year to play a significant role in finding his successor. True to form, he took the initiative. For Jean Mayer, the perfect successor to his presidency would be someone of enormous eminence, preferably scientific, a Nobel Laureate, who had limited administrative experience and would have to rely on a wise Chancellor for advice and counsel. With this strategy in mind, he asked me to visit with Dudley Herschbach, Professor of Chemistry and the Baird Professor of Science at Harvard. Herschbach shared the Nobel Prize in Chemistry in 1986. I was to urge him to consider being a candidate for the presidency of Tufts. Professor Herschbach was a lively conversational companion for an hour, expressed delight that his friend Jean Mayer would consider him a worthy candidate, but declined. He said that he had no concept of what a university president would do. He had no way of knowing that his sense of his qualifications would have been the ideal job description written by Jean Mayer for his successor.

What President Mayer did not know when he gave that April, 1992 interview to the *New York Times* was that the search process would be completed in the next month with a president selected and ready to take on his duties in September, a year earlier than Mayer had planned. The key board members sensed Mayer's need to control every part of the process, if possible. He also—and quite justifiably so—felt that his presidency had set the scene for a truly eminent next president for Tufts. There was no question in the minds of those who spent the better part of our days with him that he would consider the selection of the next president as a validation of the Mayer legacy. As unhappy as he might have been to step aside, he was determined to let the academic world know how he had transformed the university, and what better way to validate that fact than by securing a successor of truly great eminence? If, in doing so, he could also secure his influence as Chancellor, all the better. The Nobel Laureate with little or no administrative history seemed the perfect model.

It is not certain what the Board of Trustees had in mind when they secured the services of an executive search firm, nor what orders the firm had been given. These executive search firms have been one of the more controversial legacies inherited from the corporate traditions. All of these companies—the biggest and best known are Heidrick & Struggles and Korn Ferry International—started out in the corporate world assisting for-profit boards in the search for the CEO of their dreams, or even for people on slightly lower rungs of the corporate ladder: COOs, CFOs, and the newest incarnation, the CIO. It was inevitable that these organizations would turn their attention to "the educational practice," as the literature describes it. One of the senior staff personnel is assigned to each institution, for the purpose of securing the best possible applicant pool.

Chairman of the Board Nelson Gifford would reserve for himself and the Executive Committee the final selection, but he empowered a large, twenty-one person screening and review committee made up of trustees, faculty, deans, staff, and students, chaired by trustee Brian O'Connell, a Washington-based nationally known alumnus who had dedicated his career to organizing non-profits as a national force. The universal sentiment from those members who served was that the leading staff person from the executive search firm was inept. Word got out quickly that the applicant pool, as it rounded itself down to the final few, was not as distinguished as people had hoped. Four candidates were interviewed, and there was no consensus. There was general knowledge of the four finalists. Their names were released to the public, and the *Boston Globe* published them on April 23, 1992 ("Four Finalists Selected for Tufts President"). The Tufts community was reconciled to the selection of one of them.

But not Nelson Gifford. He saw his most critical role as Chairman of the Board to select, before he stepped down, a candidate who could manage the remarkable enterprise that Jean Mayer was leaving behind. Gifford participated in the interviews of the finalists and sensed the lack of unanimity. He did not like any of the finalists, either.

John DiBiaggio had a problem. In 1992, he had been President of Michigan State University for seven years. A Michigan native, this was the perfect culmination of a career in higher education administration, where he had spent his entire academic life. Trained as a dentist, he became an Assistant Dean at the University of Kentucky Dental School in 1967, Dean of Dental School at Virginia Commonwealth University from 1970 to 1976, Vice-President for Health Affairs and Executive Director of the Medical Center at the University of Connecticut from 1976–1979, and assumed his first university presidency at the University of Connecticut in 1979. He left UConn for Michigan State in 1985. He was one of a handful of dentists who had attained the top of the pyramid in this status-sensitive world of higher education. He had experienced the wars associated with the politics of the state university system and big-time college athletics. At the University of Connecticut and Michigan State, he had seen it all: aggressive alumni demanding national recognition in athletics, politically elected boards of governors with a dozen different agendas, and admissions standards often tailored to the needs of a myriad of constituencies. He was a savvy swimmer in the shark-infested waters of this world. He loved it, had attained a position of leadership in the National Collegiate Athletic Association, was active in trying to reform renegade and often out-of-control coaches, and was a regular attendee at the over-the-top sporting events associated with this life. He was made for managing the enormous bureaucracy of a large state-supported enterprise like Michigan State, where success in the athletic programs gained the greatest visibility. In the Wolverine State, he valiantly dealt with the generally accepted academic superiority of the University of Michigan as best he could. Nothing he could do would change that reality, but Michigan State was getting its share of the academic limelight. As he approached age sixty, John DiBiaggio seemed set for the rest of his academic life.

But at Michigan State he took a stand against a successful football coach who also wanted to be Athletic Director. President DiBiaggio did not think this was in the best interest of the program, and said so. The AD was himself a savvy political animal, got to the governing board of the university, and convinced them that he was more important than the President. DiBiaggio's decision was overridden, and he took this as a signal to look elsewhere for another presidency, but stealthily. He did not want anyone to discover that he was willing to leave, particularly if it should be for another state university with very vivid "Sunshine Laws" of public disclosure.

At some point in the unhappy process of the presidential search at Tufts, John DiBiaggio's name came to the search and screening committee. He apparently had been willing to let his name circulate among private institutions, because he could trust the confidentiality of the process. The faculty on the committee took one look and concluded that this was not a good match. But Nelson Gifford was not deterred. He had asked around, and sources close to other Big Ten university presidents had told him that the Michigan State leader was among the best sitting university leaders in the United States. The example of Harold Shapiro, first President of the University of Michigan and then of Princeton, satisfied him that a move from big public to elite private was not out of the question, and Shapiro, along with James Freedman, who had gone from the University of Iowa to Dartmouth, was a supporter of his Michigan State colleague. Both Shapiro and Freedman gave strong endorsements, and DiBiaggio became the stealth candidate of the Tufts Chairman, who had made up his mind about the four finalists: None of them would be the next President of Tufts University.

Now, the question became one of timing. The Tufts community knew that there were four candidates, but Nelson Gifford knew that there was a fifth. Besides the *Globe* announcement, the names of the known Tufts finalists also appeared in the *Chronicle of Higher Education* for May 6. By this time, President Mayer realized that the timetable was out of his control. He had thought that he would be in office until the end of the next academic year, but the search had been accelerated. The Executive Committee of the Board had met with the three finalists—one had withdrawn after his name appeared—and now, in the spring of 1992, they would meet with an unannounced fourth candidate, in secrecy. John DiBiaggio met with the Executive Committee of the Board at the Ritz Carleton Hotel in Boston, along with some members of the search committee, and as fate would have it, Dean Louis Lasagna of the Sackler School in all innocence casually mentioned to President Mayer that he had seen "an old acquaintance."

When Mayer discovered that John DiBiaggio had been meeting with the Executive Committee, he went into a rage. He remembered what he believed was the then-President of the University of Connecticut's opposition to the Tufts Veterinary School and considered DiBiaggio unsuitable. He was also vain enough and justifiably proud of what he had accomplished for Tufts to expect an academic or intellectual giant to succeed him. President Mayer had his sources on the search committee and knew that DiBiaggio's name had come up, but the candidacy had gone no further. Chairman Gifford, at this point, realized that he had an unhappy sitting Tufts President who wanted to control the search and would, if necessary, poison the water around any candidate of whom he did not approve. Gifford had to move fast, even if it meant not sparing the feelings of his out-going President. At this point, Jean Mayer was completely cut out of the succession. At the May 1992 Trustee meeting, the Chairman of the Board announced that he wanted an executive session and to the astonishment of all of us, asked the President to join all the other non-Trustees outside while the board met. Mayer, who was also a Trustee, nonetheless dutifully went outside to wait downstairs in the Mugar Lounge with Tom Murnane, Steve Manos, and me, while Gifford informed the Board that John DiBiaggio had agreed to become the eleventh president of Tufts University. When we heard the applause downstairs from the Trustee meeting, none of us had any idea who had been selected. The President, still witty and smiling while suffering, softly sang the words of a Gershwin tune: "They're writing songs of love, but not for me." We were called back upstairs to complete other Trustee business, but Chairman Gifford did not announce to us the name of the new president. He briefly turned the meeting over to the Vice Chair and quietly asked Director of Communications Rosemarie van Camp to follow him outside. He gave her the name of the new president and instructed her to tell no one at Tufts. He told her to get in touch with her counterpart at Michigan State University to create a joint news release about the new appointment that would go to the media Sunday afternoon—after the Saturday night black-tie dinner for honorary degree recipients, after the Sunday morning commencement ceremonies, and after Gifford would have told President Mayer of the decision on Sunday afternoon. On May 17, Commencement Day, a press release was sent to the *Boston Globe,* the *Boston Herald,* the *New York Times,* and all electronic media announcing that effective September 1, 1992, John DiBiaggio would assume the office of the Presidency of Tufts University. The first call Rosemarie van Camp received from a student reporter in East Lansing was to inquire about the seating capacity of the Tufts University football stadium. When she told him, there was a long silence over the phone.

Jean Mayer, after sixteen years as president, became the first Chancellor of Tufts, with independent responsibilities designated by the Board of Trustees. He would concentrate his efforts on the development of the research space in Boston, where the Chancellor's office was located.

Four months later, on January 1, 1993, at the age of seventy-two, Jean Mayer died suddenly. The Mayer era of Tufts history was over. When Steve Manos called me on New Year's Day to tell me that Jean Mayer had suddenly dropped dead, I thought of the lines from Shakespeare's *Richard II:* "For God's sake, let us sit upon the ground and tell sad stories of the death of kings . . ." It was sad that he was gone, but I never was certain he could live as a marginalized Chancellor, in a Boston office, out of the limelight of the presidency. Like the hero of his youth, Charles DeGaulle, this Frenchman, too, needed to be at the center of things, he needed to be the man of action, the agent of change. Looking back on the Mayer presidency, I am struck by how this one man had been able to transform an institution. He arrived at Tufts in a time of uncertainty for the university, when the faculty felt shaken by the events of the 1970s that had left us weakened, vulnerable, and lacking in the confidence to move forward. There was a sense of paralysis, as we watched ourselves slip into a kind of frumpy mediocrity, without the resources or the will to pull ourselves forward. The 1973 self-study document *A Changing University in a Changing Times* had said it all: The next five years will be tough, but the ten years after that will be worse. This was a feeling shared by everyone in the Tufts community. Then came Jean Mayer, unexpected, not passionately wanted, in many ways an accidental president who had been passed over twice before. He arrived, caused chaos, provided enormous leadership, energy, and vision, barely survived, and then went on to create *his* Tufts University. But he could not stop creating, and the Trustees needed a pause, something Jean Mayer was incapable of. He was above all a paradox, simultaneously among the first and last of a kind: the first of a new breed of academic entrepreneurs who combined high-level intellectual credentials with a political instinct that placed the American university right in the middle of congressional policy and the national limelight. At Tufts, he was the ringmaster, once even appearing dressed in high hat and tails leading an elephant at a Ringling Brothers circus in the Boston Garden. At the same time, he represented a style of American college and university presidents who were becoming increasingly rare: the genuine academic leader, in charge of the intellectual enterprise from start to finish. He was president of only one institution, for which he was one of a kind.

THE 1990S AND THE CHANGING WORLD
OF AMERICAN HIGHER EDUCATION

In many ways, the passing of Jean Mayer was symptomatic of what was happening in American higher education. He had come to Tufts in 1976. In that year, *U.S. News & World Report* was just another news magazine running unsuccessfully behind *Time* and *Newsweek*. The *Chronicle of Higher Education* was a struggling publication hungry to increase its meager advertising revenue. The Association of Governing Boards (AGB) of Universities and Colleges had just succeeded in attracting the first private, elite institutions to its membership and now looked hopefully to the future. By the time Jean Mayer left the Tufts presidency in 1992, the American university had undergone a profound metamorphosis in form, content, and attitude. Jean Mayer was the last Tufts president who had no computer in his office. He drove his own automobile (to the danger of everyone on the road, I might add). He had no lawyer to negotiate the terms of his employment. The for-profit boards that he served on were positions that came to him because of his scientific eminence and were not part of any written agreement with his Chairman of the Board to guarantee additional compensation. He had no university credit cards, no membership in country clubs. He lived in the run-down president's house that had not been renovated for the nearly sixty years of its existence. When the heat went off in the Cousens Gymnasium, the temperature also dropped in the presidential bedroom on Packard Avenue. Betty Mayer always left an extra blanket at the end of the bed. The Tufts President paid scant attention to *U.S. News and World Report* and mentioned it only once in an annual report; nor did he read the *Chronicle of Higher Education* or *Trusteeship*, the journal of the AGB.

Even the presidential spouse was built from an older model. When asked in a Tufts inauguration publication in 1976 to describe herself, Betty Mayer said, "I'm just a housewife." Betty van

Courtesy Nate Beeler.

Heusen was a child of the Depression, born in Somerville, Massachusetts. She did three years of college work at Radcliffe and Vassar before dropping out to get a job on a weekly newspaper in Weston, Massachusetts. Before coming to Medford, Mrs. Mayer completed her undergraduate degree in the Harvard Extension program. She met Jean Mayer in 1941, when she was a secretary in the Department of Physiological Chemistry at Harvard, and he was a twenty-one-year-old French artillery officer having escaped from Vichy France and taking courses with some of his father's colleagues in Cambridge. The senior Mayers had been advised earlier to get their children out of France in the event of a German occupation. Mme. Mayer was Jewish, and the children would be threatened by Nazi racial laws. Betty van Heusen and Jean Mayer were married in March 1942, as Mayer was shipping out with a Free French unit from Halifax, Nova Scotia. She stayed with him through good times and bad until his death, having five children, a quiet, calm, even reticent but utterly beloved wife and mother. She was the consummate understatement. Betty Mayer wore her modesty with remarkable dignity, and every student who ever met her discovered her gentle and gracious nature. In Dudley House at Harvard, where Professor Jean Mayer had been headmaster and she officially associate master, she poured tea, helped with all sorts of personal problems of the students, and won the hearts of Harvard commuters who called Dudley House their home away from home. She was the dedicated volunteer, and when her children were grown she gave of her time to organizations like Church Women United and UNICEF. When she became the President's Wife at Tufts, Betty Mayer brought that same modesty with her. Her children helped with the move from Cambridge. She did not want staff in the President's House, preferred picking up the phone herself. The house would do as is, repairs were not necessary. She could manage with the heating system.

President Mayer was satisfied, as well, for this was not the age of the imperial presidential estate or the trophy house, nor of the off-campus presidential residence or the invisible spouse. The Mayers did not entertain. They were seen on campus every day, she often in jeans, walking their dog, and Betty Mayer was a fixture at student events. But, other than the occasional reception and rare dinner for development purposes, the President's House was their home to live in. It was not a house really prepared for any significant social undertakings, and it was not their style to do so, in any case. Tom Murnane, the Vice President for Development who knew how to raise money, devised alternative means of fundraising that did not require personal presidential entertaining. Mayer was a national and international figure and activist, and he did not use the presidential residence as his launching pad. He did not cultivate donors; they cultivated him. As for Betty Mayer, a private but committed presidential spouse, this was the way of life she could tolerate. She attended to the most trivial student gatherings while being involved in every aspect of the Tufts community. She loved students, faculty, and staff, and they reciprocated wholeheartedly. She was what so many previous presidential wives had been at Tufts and at other New England colleges and universities for generations. But this tradition was coming to an end, along with the accepted role of the American college and university president. Being the academic and intellectual leader of an institution was not going to be enough. Universities were reaching a level of complexity that required, in the eyes of their boards, a new set of virtues.

By the 1970s, beginning at the large land-grant public institutions, boards of trustees and regents were looking for a different kind of president and spouse.[1] The biggest state universities of the 1950s and early 1960s were large, but they were manageable with enrollments initially around twenty thou-

1. On the presidential spouse, see Joan Clodius and Diane Magrath, *The President's Spouse: Volunteer or Volunteered* (Washington, D.C.: National Association of State Universities and Land-Grant Colleges, 1984).

sand, even as exponential growth was about to take off. Someone in the style of Clark Kerr at California or Robben Fleming at Michigan could be directly responsible for the academic integrity of the institution and still manage to get their arms around the increasing activities of the president. John Silber, at private Boston University from 1971 to 1996, saw himself as this kind of president: the leader in every respect, a first-rate scholar who was dead certain he knew more about many things than most faculty, much like Jean Mayer, who was a friend. That he stayed on for more than twenty-five years as President of BU in total control and continued as Chancellor is an example of trustee satisfaction with a president who was willing to play very hardball with the faculty and exert a maximum of presidential authority. Like Silber, Kerr and Fleming were also able to keep the lid on the athletic programs and to maintain some semblance of academic standards. But, increasingly, big-time athletic empires were winning the hearts and minds of alumni, who measured the president by the number of wins and, heaven forbid, losses. Regents had to uncover presidential candidates who were willing to go along with the explosion in athletic interest and, when pragmatically necessary, were willing to hand over control of athletics to the athletic directors, who had become enormously empowered. To chronicle this change, one need only examine the extraordinary influence and rise to power of the National Collegiate Athletic Association in the last thirty-five years of the twentieth century. The NCAA became the guardians of authority and academic standards, as the coaches gradually replaced the university presidents as the standard bearer of the institution. Alumni remember the golden ages of "Bear" Bryant at Alabama, Bobby Knight at Indiana, and Adolph Rupp at Kentucky when they might not recall the name of the university president. The alumni were voters, as well. Boards of trustees or regents saw the handwriting on the wall and deeply breathed the highly charged atmosphere of state politics; they were generally elected to their positions by popular ballot and understood the importance of a successful athletic image.

Through the last decades of the century, the land-grant institutions grew enormously, some reaching enrollments of sixty or seventy thousand students on a single campus. Academicians like Fleming or Kerr, who had come up through the tenure ranks and had served as president or chancellor of only one institution in their careers before retiring, no longer seemed to provide a sufficient pool of candidates. They also showed some geographic limitations. Kerr had his career on the West Coast; Fleming had risen through the ranks in the big state institutions of the Midwest. Both were national figures, but with a peculiarly regional flavor. Their salaries, modest by today's standards, were still higher than their most successful coaches. There were hints of things to come, however, in the academic fields that served as a springboard for their administrative careers: Fleming was a Professor of Labor Relations and was an expert in mediation and negotiation. Kerr came to Berkeley in 1945 from the University of Washington as an Associate Professor in the School of Business Administration. Regents were already starting to look for management and marketing, rather than academic, leadership.

Eventually, some distinguished private universities were caught up in the athletic frenzy. The 1980s and 1990s saw big-time professionalism creep into programs at Georgetown, Stanford, and Duke, with the salary of the basketball coach dwarfing the compensation of the president. These elite private institutions played by the same rules as the other NCAA Division I-A public powerhouses, governed by what is called Proposition 48, which sets the acceptable SAT score for an entering first-year student at a *total* of 800, verbal and math combined. That is, on average, 600 points lower than the general applicant to these institutions. Any presidential candidate contemplating coming to these schools would have to confront this issue at the interview stage. One would have to make a commitment to a big-time athletic program and not face the question of whether an entering basketball player at Duke or Georgetown, admitted by a different academic measurement standard, could handle the rigorous first-year curriculum while participating in what is arguably a full-time job run with complete professionalism by a staff that will be measured only by success. Presidents at some very distinguished universities in the 1980s found themselves caught in the trap of big-time athletics. Northwestern University, always the academic standard bearer of the Big Ten Conference but the athletic doormat, decided in the late 1980s that national recognition in athletics was the path to follow. That meant a change in admissions policy and a profound shift in the university's focus. Within a short time, the football program was producing a Rose Bowl participant, and the entire athletic program was flying high, until four former Northwestern football players were indicted on charges of lying to federal grand juries investigating sports betting at the school during the 1993 and 1994 seasons. A former Northwestern football player admitted that he had run sports betting operations at Northwestern and the University of Colorado. Others who pled guilty of betting and fixing games were football players at the University of Notre Dame, and basketball players at Northwestern.

Some serious presidential soul-searching must have taken place at a distinguished educational institution like Northwestern when such corruption was uncovered. However, scandals like these at the great public and private universities that have bought into big-time athletics are routine and will remain so. Like so much else in this country, institutions do not have much memory. At Boston College, a gambling scandal among the players seemed to occur in every decade, whereupon the sitting president/priest would institute reforms, followed by an expansion of the football stadium or the field house. Nothing really changes. Rarely will a university president take the unpopular stand of diminishing the status of an athletic program. In the 1980s, Father John Brooks, President at the College of the Holy Cross in Worcester from 1970 to 1994, decided that his institution would be improved without the ancient athletic rivalry with its Jesuit sister school Boston College and announced that athletic scholarships were going to be drastically reduced, while academic standards would be raised across the board. The alumni howled. Within two years, Holy Cross's SAT scores shot up two hundred points, and its academic reputation enjoyed the highest level in its history. The Rev. Brooks was yet another of the rare transformers in higher education who viewed big-time athletics as an impediment to academic excellence. It had been nearly five decades since President Robert Maynard Hutchins of the University of Chicago argued that nonacademic pursuits such as intercollegiate football had nothing to do with higher education, at which point Chicago abandoned what has since Hutchins' time grown into the enormous, near-professional enterprise we have today, allegedly managed by university presidents.

Seeking the right president to deal with the extraordinary issues of a major athletic program became an issue for those institutions having to live with this priority. At a private institution such as New York University, rocked as it was by gambling scandals in its basketball program in the 1950s and 1960s, athletics was reduced to the so-called Division III level, without scholarships for athletes. These kinds of institutions hold no interest for Las Vegas point spread or other big-time gambling activities. But the trustees at NYU were still trying to push the envelope, and in 1981 found an individual who proved to be nontraditional and transformational. John Brademas had served as United States Representative in Congress from Indiana's Third District for twenty-three years (1959–1981), the last four as House Majority whip. During his time in the Congress, he had written or helped write most of the federal legislation enacted during that time concerning colleges and universities. To be sure, he had impeccable academic credentials. He was a Rhodes Scholar, earned his Ph.D. at Oxford, and by the time he retired from the presidency of NYU in 1992, he had been awarded forty-seven honorary degrees. Nonetheless, he was a politician, and a defeated one, at that. But his connections in Washington were also impeccable, and the Brademas presidency became another model for trustees and regents to examine, as he took NYU to a new and competitive eminence in New York City and the nation. By the time his presidency was over, Columbia University was looking over its shoulder, in no small measure due to John Brademas. He was a potent fundraiser and extraordinary ambassador for the university. He delegated authority to his deans and marketed his institution. "The Branding of NYU" became a case study for professionals interested in the selling of the American university. By the 1990s, as governing boards with a strong sales orientation became increasingly interested in marketing their academic "product," trustee meetings routinely heard presentations from marketing consultants whose expertise was "changing the image and position of your institution." What was meant by "position"? The answer: your place in *U.S. News and World Report* college rankings.

Some social historian of higher education more versed than I in the psychological nuances of national movements will be better equipped to chronicle the phenomenon of this magazine's impact. The amount of print, publication, energy, time, strategy, and resources dedicated to addressing the *U.S. News* rankings probably can never be accurately tabulated. Whether an institution applauded, attacked, tried to ignore, or otherwise dealt with the annual fall appearance of the college rankings edition, higher education was held captive by it and the other publications that tried to capitalize on Americans preoccupation with lists and competitive advantage. Dealing with an improvement or a drop in the rankings became yet another preoccupation for the president, along with figuring out how *U.S. News* computed its data and then coming up with countermeasures. Institutions were actually tailoring admissions strategies and resource allocations to respond to the *U.S. News* methodology. Any good news became a highlight of the endless number of glossy marketing publications that crossed the desks of higher education administrators all over the country. "Tops in regional comprehensive category!" "Among the top thirty in best bargains in the Midwest!" chortled one school after another. Some colleges and universities—generally those in the very top level of rankings—formed Coalitions of the Disdainful and sent out newsletters or press releases announcing that they officially were going to ignore the offending edition, even as alumni interest in this academic pecking order increased and parents of prospective students hungered to get their children into a "Top Twenty-Five" or "Top Fifty" school. The one thing that was certain was that the publishers of *U.S. News and World Report College and University Rankings* had struck gold and were delighted in the extraordinary notoriety.

One issue of one magazine had stood an entire educational establishment on its head. As presidential candidates were being interviewed on campuses all over America, branding, marketing, and image consumed considerable segments of the discussion with board members, along with organizational issues that were accompanied by new mantras: Total Quality Management; Process Re-design, and Process Re-engineering. None of this represented the language of the Academy.

These conversations were not limited to the also-rans, second-tier, or have-nots who sought some means of raising their profile or ranking. In selecting its presidents, Dartmouth College in many ways epitomized the thinking at the board level in testing new models of presidents. John Kemeny, president from 1970 to 1981, was one of those transformational leaders in American higher education. He was a Hungarian by birth, a Jew, a distinguished mathematician on the Dartmouth faculty, co-inventor of the BASIC computer language. President Kemeny pioneered in the student use of computers. He was an intellectual giant. He was also quintessentially a faculty member, taught two courses a year, and during the days of rage on the college campuses kept Dartmouth at a reasonable temperature.

Apparently, that was not good enough for the Board of Trustees, who, after what seemed to be a reasonable search, found no adequate candidate and selected their own Chairman, David T. McLaughlin, as the fourteenth president of Dartmouth College. The alumni, skeptical when Kemeny had been appointed, were delighted with this total Dartmouth Man (as he was described in the college literature). He earned his B.A. in 1954 after a distinguished undergraduate career with membership in Phi Beta Kappa, Green Key, Palaeopitus, and Casque & Gauntlet. He continued at the Amos Tuck School at Dartmouth for his M.B.A., which was awarded the next year. His career as a business leader led him back to the Dartmouth Board of Trustees in 1971 and he became its Chairman in 1977. The Dartmouth Board evidently did not want another academic to succeed President Kemeny. Instead, they turned 180 degrees to select their own Chairman, who at the time was the CEO of the Toro Company, manufacturer of lawn-mowing equipment. Dartmouth had a previous president with a business background, Ernest Martin Hopkins, who served with great distinction through two world wars from 1916 to 1945. The Dartmouth Board believed it was, once again, time to bring the wisdom and discipline of the business world to Hanover. The Board had no doubt that President McLaughlin would be an enormously potent Dartmouth fundraiser. It seemed, to them, the best of all possible choices. The faculty did not agree, and the six-year term of President McLaughlin's presidency was marred by often-acrimonious confrontations.

But the selection of David McLaughlin did reveal the process of thinking that the Dartmouth trustees and other governing boards nationally were engaged in, namely, that one needed a modern manager to manage, regardless of the peculiarities of culture that the academic sandbox presented. They believed that the modern-day complexities of the contemporary American college or university required a modern-day CEO, like David McLaughlin, and he agreed. But, for all the Dartmouth background and preparation that this Dartmouth Man enjoyed, it was not enough to make it work

McLaughlin's successor revealed yet another trend that boards were exploring: the law school dean as president. Before becoming its President, James O. Freedman had been Dean of the Law School at the University of Iowa, one of the giant public universities with a formidable athletic program. That might have been enough to make him incompatible, but he had a Harvard undergraduate degree and a Yale Law School diploma, which made the pedigree acceptable. Harvard and Columbia had also selected law school deans as their presidents. It was time to have a good negotiator and skilled conflict resolver.

Trustees at the private universities, even in the Ivy League, were also looking for the skills they associated with managing large, complex organizations. They began looking for candidates with previous presidential experience at larger institutions, and they turned westward. Freedman came from the University of Iowa in 1987 to Dartmouth. Harold Shapiro, president of the University of Michigan for eight years and an economist, came to Princeton in 1988. Hunter Rawlings III moved from the presidency of Iowa to Cornell in 1995. All of these proved to be successful transitions from large public universities with big-time athletic programs to highly distinguished private eastern universities with academic priorities first and foremost. The only mismatch occurred in 1997, when Gordon Gee left Ohio State to become president of Brown University. This was his fourth university presidency. He was, in every sense, an experienced administrator and professional president, having also led the University of West Virginia and the University of Colorado. In fifteen months, he was gone from Brown, having been appointed Chancellor of Vanderbilt University, his fifth presidency. His compensation package at Vanderbilt made headlines in more than just academic journals.

American higher education had discovered the professional president, whose path from the start had been through the administrative channel rather than the academic. One of the most remarkable was Michael Hooker, who became President of Bennington College at age thirty-six, President of the University of Maryland-Baltimore County at age forty, and President of the five-campus University of Massachusetts system at age forty-seven. In 1995, after just two years at the Massachusetts post, Hooker returned to his alma mater, the University of North Carolina at Chapel Hill, and became Chancellor at the age of forty-nine. In thirteen years, he had been president or chancellor of four universities, and he was not yet fifty. He had a Ph.D., but his reputation was based on his higher education activities. He was a member of the Advisory Board of Presidents of the AGB and served on the American Association of State Colleges and Universities' Committee on International Programs. He chaired the American Council of Education's Commission on Leadership Development. Chancellor Hooker died tragically in 1999 of lymphatic cancer.

It was becoming increasingly apparent that the complexity of the American research university had reached a level where mere mortal academician presidents needed help, whether they thought they needed it or not. In the case of Jean Mayer at Tufts, the Board had two purposes in creating the position of Executive Vice President: second in order of importance was to bring a greater level of professional business organization and discipline to the increasingly complex operations of the university as the Information Age got going; but first, they sought a mechanism to control a dynamic but undisciplined president. I have chronicled the incumbents in the Executive Vice President's position at Tufts in earlier pages. Although Michael Hoffman lasted less than a year, he set the stage for the extraordinary career of Steven Manos, who assumed the position of Executive Vice President on July 1, 1981, and at this writing remains in that post, although with an altered mandate and a less extensive span of control. The creation of this super, nuanced corporate vice presidency was not a phenomenon that occurred only at Tufts in the early 1980s. There might have been a special need for the position reflecting the Mayer presidency, but something else was happening that made the "EVP" necessary in the eyes of the trustees. When Steve Manos came to Tufts, there was not one personal computer sitting on a desktop on the Medford campus. Today, one would be hard-pressed to find a desk without one.

The explosion of technology and information associated with computing has been a phenomenon that has marked the last decades of the twentieth century. There has been a revolution in teaching and research affecting all of us who make our way in the classroom, library, or laboratory. But, what trustees saw was a potential cost that would have an impact on every aspect of life in the university, academic or nonacademic. This was pervasive, threatening, and would cross boundaries in a way unseen in the academic community's history. Technology would affect colleges and universities at all levels, from the first moment of interest shown by a potential student applicant, faculty hire, maintenance worker, or dining service employee. The bottom line–oriented trustees were among the first to grasp the implications. Nelson Gifford, Chairman of the Tufts Trustee Committee on Administration and Finance and not yet Chairman of the Board, told Manos to acquire "a couple of hundred" personal computers and start getting the faculty involved, but under no circumstances should they be placed in charge of computing. The Boston-based health scientists had the rudimentary beginnings of computational data, but they were far ahead of their Medford and Grafton colleagues. No one else seemed able to get moving with personal computing. The university's Digital Corporation DEC-20 computer, which actually was two DEC-10 machines yoked together and barely serviceable, was bursting at the seams and at the same time inadequate as a research instrument, when you could use it at all. It was difficult enough just to get the payroll done, and the faculty could only gain access after that. The last Provost at Tufts to be responsible for academic information systems was Kathryn McCarthy. All computing—academic and nonacademic—had shifted to the newly created position of Executive Vice President after her resignation. No dean seemed capable of developing any sort of strategy for computing for the faculty. There was no idea of the budgetary implications for the schools or university. Clearly, here was something that needed *managing,* and Gifford had little hope of finding appropriate skills among the faculty, who, he believed, would make a financial disaster if given responsibility for academic computing. The economy of the situation demanded that academic and nonacademic computing be combined and placed in the hands of a powerful executive. This was the building block on which the position of Executive Vice President was set. In the minds of Nelson Gifford and his fellow board members across the country, the running of the university required a stronger hand than ever before, and that hand would be guided by corporate values of management and economy. There was risk. If the faculty came to the conclusion that what it needed in the way of resources was being limited because some other part of the institution—student information systems or financial information systems—was getting priority treatment, there would be a bloody war. It was essential that the faculty be served appropriately, but that they be led by others who, it was hoped, knew better and were wiser.

The corporate board members were the first to see the universal application of computers and technology across every aspect of university life. There would be systems for fundraising, payroll, enrollment, data gathering everywhere, dormitory life, and of course, research and teaching. Here was the future; and it was going to cost a lot of money.

Steve Manos had not been the first dominant Executive Vice President. When the Reverend Donald Monan, SJ, became President of Jesuit Boston College in 1972, he found some very savvy business people on the Board. BC was in terrible financial and academic shape. The endowment was pathetic; academically this mid-sized institution had neither distinguished undergraduate nor graduate programs. The new President had his work cut out for him, and he proved to be yet another of the transforming presidents of his generation. He stopped the decline, and his presidency from 1972 to 1996 will go down in the annals of the institution's history as the turning point. He needed one more strong management hand on the tiller, and his Board recommended that he concentrate as much authority and power as possible in the hands of the right man. The right man was Frank Campanella, a Professor of Business Administration who in 1973 was appointed Executive Vice President. The *Academic* Vice President, a position created in 1957, now reported to the *Executive* Vice President, a historical sea change in a world where, until now, the academic leadership was preeminent. Campanella had oversight of all aspects of information technology, strategic planning, and resource allocation to both academic and administrative departments. Institutional advancement and development was the only other department that reported directly to the President, but the Executive Vice President controlled their information systems and databases. EVP Campanella had it all. He supervised planning, budgeting, all matters related to new construction, major renovations, space planning, and capital expenditures. He also provided support and information to the trustees. Boston College had no Provost.

Frank Campanella served as a super Vice President for eighteen years, and together he and Father Monan brought about a revolution for Boston College. Perhaps it could only have happened in a church-affiliated institution that accepted a hierarchical order of things; or perhaps the Boston College faculty realized how serious the situation was in the early 1970s, just as the Tufts faculty was willing to risk much with Jean Mayer for the same reasons. At BC, no attempt was made to hide the role of this new and powerful position. There was no tradition of an academic Provost who was clearly the second in command behind the President. When a new EVP was chosen in 1991, Frank Campanella was happy to return to the faculty, but his successor did not have the emotional skills to deal with faculty that his predecessor had, and in 1993 Father Monan asked Campanella to return. He stayed on until 2001, having served in total for twenty-six years as Executive Vice President. He left a Boston College administration and institution profoundly changed from the one he encountered in 1973.

This all-powerful nonacademic administrator model worked if the incumbent had the emotional intelligence to make it work. Frank Campanella had no challenge to his authority from the academic side of Boston College, and his great strength came from not exercising his authority too overtly. He was courtly, deferential, and respectful of the faculty and its needs. He never made them feel subservient, even though board policy pumped as much as possible into endowment and placed faculty priorities somewhere down the line. He exercised his authority with a light touch. Steve Manos, on the other hand, had to deal with a Provost and Academic Vice President—my title from 1981 to 1985—at Tufts who did not report to him, and he had to live with a tradition of the Provost as the second officer of the university, next to the President.[2] Although Manos's span of control equaled that of Campanella, the Tufts Provost did not come out of the Catholic tradition of accepting authority, and he made it clear to the Board of Trustees that the success of this new administrative order depended on how well the Provost and the EVP worked together. From the moment Manos and Gittleman started in tandem on July 1, 1981, there already had been grumbling from the faculty when it became clear that the Provost did not have responsibility for academic computing. But I could give them assurances that faculty and student needs would be met best by keeping computing in one person's hands, and we would all be better off if that person was Steve Manos. For his part, EVP Manos knew that he had to deliver for the faculty, that he had to provide a level of service and material that would satisfy them, because he knew all too well how fast they would denounce an unsatisfactory performance. He was tough on deans who often did not have the first idea of how to build an academic information system for faculty or students. Over the years, Manos won the grudging admiration of the schools, their deans, and faculty for the

2. After Vice President for Health Sciences Bob Levy left in 1983, all the deans once again reported to the Provost, and the authority of that position was reconstituted. In 1985, I was given the title of Provost and Senior Vice President, further establishing parity in the eyes of the community with the Executive Vice President.

level of support and creative imagination he showed in making Tufts a reasonably mature Information Age university, while making certain that the budgets were balanced. We spent less on computing than our peer institutions, made fewer mistakes, and produced satisfactory results for the faculty and students. When this new and powerful administrative position is held by someone who has the respect of the faculty, it works. Manos has been at his post for over twenty years, at this writing.

Campanella and Manos understood that if you control the information technology (and its budget), you control the university. They were intelligent enough to keep the secret to themselves. Campanella, older, more patriarchal and benevolent, got away with his avuncular image with the BC community. He was, next to the President, the most visible university administrator. Steve Manos, the youngest of the Troika, cerebral, intellectual, insistently opinionated, in public was generally self-effacing, even reticent. He deferred to me because he knew that if he were perceived as too powerful, a raging faculty could bring down the entire structure. For more than twenty years, we preserved our special relationship. From time to time a dean would become aware that he was being squeezed by Steve Manos and would complain to me. When appropriate, I would lean on the Executive Vice President to back off, and over that time there were only a handful of occasions when we did battle. He remained a force with the Trustees throughout the Mayer and DiBiaggio years, but kept a low profile among students and faculty. People rarely got his title right; and they never understand the authority he had in his hands. He made it work.

Not every Executive Vice President accepted the need for subtlety inherent in the position. In 1995, John Fry was selected to become President Judith Rodin's first Executive Vice President at the University of Pennsylvania. The EVP position had been created in 1991 at Penn and had been filled, similar to the Tufts experience with Michael Hoffman, with people who were gone before it seemed they had arrived. A series of one-year appointments had frustrated the Penn Board of Trustees who wanted some management discipline brought to a very fractious campus where, it seemed to the nonacademic, the faculties of the twelve colleges went their own chaotic ways. Judith Rodin, a noted research psychologist, had been Provost at Yale before coming to Penn as President in 1994, and she personally hired John Fry, who by then at the age of thirty-nine had run educational consulting at KPMG Peat Marwick before moving to the national higher education practice at Coopers & Lybrand, where he was appointed partner-in-charge of the national practice. That was the extent of his academic experience. Fry stayed at Penn for seven years. In that time, he became a national celebrity of university change, the subject of articles in higher education journals, a frequent speaker, and a highly controversial agent of change. In July 2002, he became the President of Franklin & Marshall College.

Fry, next to the President, was Penn's most visible administrator. His span of control reflected the new reality of trustee policy: one all-powerful executive who, whether it looked that way or not, ran the university, including at times the academic enterprise. Fry, like Campanella and Manos, was responsible for finance, investments, human resources, facilities, real estate, public safety, all computing, technology transfer, corporate relations, auxiliary enterprises, internal audit, and compliance. He brought centralization to the budget process and, with trustee blessing, took charge. Unlike Campanella and Manos, he liked the center stage and made it clear that he had presidential ambition. By this time in the mid 1990s, the *Chronicle of Higher Education* had become the *People Magazine* of the profession, and the story it did on Fry for the September 3, 1999, issue distinctly had an attitude.[3] Both the magazine and the subject took particular pleasure in making Fry seem larger than life ("A Vice President from the Business World Brings a New Bottom Line to Penn"). The story was chiefly about Fry's decision to outsource the maintenance of all university buildings and real estate holdings to the Trammell Crow Company, a private developer and property manager. Fry announced a new day for Penn, introducing, said the reporter, "a range of cost-cutting practices commonly used in business. He embodies the new, corporatized Penn." The portrait that emerged was of a highly charged visionary who was remaking Penn, and nothing was going to stop him ("People at Penn have learned that what Mr. Fry dreams, he generally gets."). There was also a hint of ruthlessness and fear, with lay-offs and faculty not wanting to speak on the record. Fry was delighted that performance management was finally taking hold among Penn's employees: "They are taking less for granted in terms of their employment status . . . Is it the kind of thing that people have a hard time adjusting to? Yes, but over time, I think it puts us on the proper trajectory . . . I feel we do the institution a disservice if we all allow inefficiency to perpetuate because we don't want to rock the boat, or we don't want to deprive these poor people who have been working here for five decades from their jobs. I don't consider it cold-hearted. I consider it an absolute responsibility." He also took it upon himself to define the

3. The article, appearing in the "Money and Management" section, was written by Martin Van Der Werf.

office of the presidency: "The president is no longer this sort of person in the tweed jacket wandering around the campus with all sorts of free time, engaging in intellectual dialogue with students and faculty. I think the things that boards increasingly care the most about are the things that people like me know how to do."

It is for the Penn community to evaluate the impact of this remarkable Executive Vice President. The controversial outsourcing arrangement with the Trammell Crow Company was scrapped in September 2002, after Fry had left for Franklin & Marshall. It was generally acknowledged that it had not worked. What *is* certain is how his corporate persona and style were viewed within the academic community and that the Board of Trustees were willing to place him at the center of university life, immediately next to the President. The *academic* authority of Penn had been divided between the Provost—there had been two incumbents plus an interim during Fry's tenure—and a Vice President for the health sciences. While they made war on each other, Fry's authority was undiluted. He extended it to the complete control of information technology and could make policy that shaped the academic agenda of Penn. He did not care who knew this, because the message from the Board of Trustees was clear: The modern American university is too complex to leave it in the hands of the traditional academic keepers of the flame, who were apt to fly off in all directions. What was needed was a new discipline, one that spoke from the experience of the business world. At American universities all over the country, this new breed of executive vice president, encouraged by trustees, emerged out of the shadow of the presidents.

Some universities, those with deep academic traditions of faculty governance as well as very deep pockets, stayed the course with the traditional model of the Provost as the clear Deputy President, with responsibility for this new tool of information technology/computing as well as much of the day-to-day enterprise. At Princeton, the Provost, in addition to being the chief academic officer, has administrative oversight of the Vice President for Computing and Information Technology as well as the university budget, and is also responsible for long-range planning. She is in every respect second-in-command when the President is on campus and in the President's absence, in charge. After all, the position of Provost was created only in recent memory—in the 1950s—when responsibilities increasingly began to take the President off campus and another chief university-wide officer was needed to handle the activities that traditionally had fallen to the President. But in the age of fundraising, increased alumni nurturing, political hand-holding, and global travel, the President needed a deputy who could stand above the deans, the schools, the interdisciplinary centers, and manage the place. When the institution became too complex for one leader, they created another leader, but a little less so.

Now, in the 1980s, the trustees were saying that the universities had become too complex for academic people; enter the non-traditional, non-tenurable president with limited academic credentials, but strong management or fundraising ability, soon followed by the new position of Executive President to deal with the enormous complexity of information.

Above all, the creation and proliferation of the position of Executive Vice President and the search for new models of presidents reflected the muscular strategic planning of American boards of trustees, who, as higher education entered the last two decades of the twentieth century, aggressively took charge of what, in their view, was "the business" of higher education that was too important to leave to educators and, above all, to faculty. The publication lists of the Associated Governing Boards of Trustees reflect the expanding range of activities that boards saw as part of their new mandate: *Prioritizing Academic Programs and Services: Reallocating Resources to Achieve Strategic Balance; Honoring the Trust: Quality and Cost Containment in Higher Education; Strategic Leadership in Academic Affairs: Clarifying the Board's Responsibilities; Best Practices Top to Bottom;* and the trustees' magazine *Trusteeship,* which had begun publishing in 1992, pulled very few punches. In an article entitled "Trash the Rubber Stamp," the chairman of the board at Syracuse University wrote, "A docile board is a luxury no higher education institution can afford."[4] As for seeking new models for the presidency, a *Trusteeship* article, "A Non-traditional President May Fit Just Right" suggested that "out-of-the-box leaders who come from corporations, the government, or nonprofits can bring needed practical skills to the academic presidency" and warned that "when faced with a final choice, trustees too often are unwilling to push for the nontraditional candidates in the face of faculty opposition."[5]

In much of this trustee literature, the single greatest obstruction to change was the faculty and the institution of tenure. To get a truly schizophrenic view of what was happening in higher education as the twentieth century was coming to a close, one should alternately read issues of *Trusteeship* and *Academe,* the principle publication of the American Association of University Professors. One could scarcely find an issue of either publication that

4. November–December 2002, 24.
5. March–April 2003, 24–26.

did not have some discussion of the merits, irrelevance, vital need, and destructive influence of tenure. The most aggressive and belligerent attack on the institution of tenure came from the public sector, university regents at Minnesota and Texas in the mid-1990s. Allan Bloom had prepared the ground in his 1987 assault on the American faculty in *The Closing of the American Mind,* in which he blamed the entrenched and protected tenured faculty for all of American higher education's alleged mediocrity. The original conditions that created the need for protection of free speech on the campuses no longer existed, he argued. Instead, what had emerged was a dogmatic orthodoxy that squelched any opinion other than the "politically correct" one. This argument resonated across the country. The battle cry to eliminate or somehow modify tenure was picked up by boards at private universities as well, claiming, as Bennington College in Bennington, Vermont, did, that financial exigency forced the elimination of tenure. The AAUP censured Bennington in 1995, and in spite of the frontal assault, no research university or other selective liberal arts college has abandoned tenure. But the mere fact that aggressive, articulate public intellectuals, boards of trustees and regents, and the public in general were taking a hard look at tenure forced the professional faculty to ask itself: Will tenure survive?

The 1980s and 1990s represented a period of considerable defensiveness for faculty, who saw hostility all around them. So many of their cherished institutions were collapsing or were under assault. Faculty were overwhelmingly and at times intolerantly liberal, had mocked Ronald Reagan as a nonintellectual second-rate actor who had somehow, miraculously, won the White House. They scorned Margaret Thatcher, routinely called "Attila the Hen," and ridiculed Great Britain for going to war in 1982 against Argentina. When she abolished tenure in the British universities, the American academic community predicted the greatest brain drain in world history. When President Reagan fired all the air traffic controllers in his first term in response to what he considered an illegal strike, academic experts believes that the country would be thrown into chaos.

What happened instead over the last twenty years of the century was the triumph of free market capitalism all over the world, even while some countries continued staggering in poverty, and gaps widened globally between the rich and the poor. In the United States, however, after a period of unemployment and deflationary recession, the Reagan tax cuts led to considerable economic growth. Later, the (early) Bush and Clinton economic policies were also driven by free market principles and tax cuts; the language of neoconservative public policy meant smaller government, citizen participation, and "volunteerism," instead of variations on the old welfare state. In foreign affairs, President Reagan took on "the Evil Empire," and, lo and behold, the Soviet Union collapsed. Marxist economists as well as a great number of American faculty were in shock, Francis Fukiyama announced the triumph of Western capitalist democracy, and by the end of the millennium the public dialogue was dominated by University of Chicago–trained intellectuals who had learned their lessons sitting at the feet of the economists Friedrich Hayek and Milton Friedman, the political theorist Leo Strauss, and the curmudgeon Allan Bloom. The liberal faculty at most of the other four thousand colleges and universities, overwhelmingly supportive of a Democratic Party that had, in their eyes, abandoned the principles of the left, looked on with despair as President Clinton's 1997 capital gains tax cut proved to be the driving force for more budget surpluses. Clinton also reformed welfare and led the nation into an extraordinary stock market boom. Faculty watched their TIAA-CREF retirement funds reach extraordinary heights. More than half the American population owned stocks, and faculty were becoming reluctant millionaires, at least on paper. However, the financial prosperity did not make the faculty any more collegial or friendly. Departments all over the country were going into receivership, because of internal battles, stalemates, and paralysis, unable even to reach consensus on hiring. The once-cherished idea of faculty civility was under assault. Tufts did not escape this misery. Sylvan Barnet was one of our most distinguished teacher/scholars. He had come to the English Department in the mid 1950s, became chairman, and was responsible for most of those colleagues who were there in the 1980s. He had recruited them, shepherded the tenure cases, and built a department, he thought, for the better times to come. Yet he walked into my office in 1982, coming directly from a departmental meeting, to resign. He could not stand his colleagues any longer, he said. During the 1980s and 1990s, Barnet's feelings about his colleagues did not represent an isolated case, either at Tufts and certainly not across the nation's campuses.

One might have thought that the college campus was the last, great, unchallenged stronghold of faculty and student liberalism. It was not the case. The undergraduate and graduate students of the 1960s and 1970s who had become the faculty of the 1980s and 1990s found themselves under assault by a renewed and energized conservative movement. The National Association of Scholars (NAS) rallied against what it perceived as a weakening of academic standards, speech codes, the silencing of disagreement on the part of dogmatic liberals, the denigration of the Western tradition in literature and history, and tenure, which it considered the single greatest reason for institutional mediocrity. Here was the equivalent of the free market in higher education. Libertarian student movements sprouted up everywhere to challenge the curriculum that they considered politically correct and without standards. They monitored faculty who advocated political ideologies or championed liberal ideas of feminism or sexuality in the classroom. Right in the middle of the argument was affirmative action and the whole issue of racial preferences. Here was the beleaguered faculty, surrounded by what they generally saw as the forces marshaled against them: boards of trustees looking for greater accountability, corporate business models, parents and students treating them like clerks, and technology demanding a willingness to innovate. As if that wasn't bad enough, now they find the enemy even inside their own bastions.

The ground seemed to be shifting underneath their feet. Where there had been a self-assured certainty, now appeared doubt. Faculty on both sides of the intellectual and ideological arguments had agreed since the end of the Second World War, even when they disagreed, that time and forces were on their side. Whether for Hayek or Marx, Strauss or Fanon, the majority of faculty had grown up intellectually in an age of secularism, where religion played no significant role. The celebration of science over faith reached its triumphant climax on April 25, 1953, when James Watson and Francis Crick published in *Nature* their brief paper announcing the discovery of the double helix, which Crick described as "the secret of life." There had been a spiritual school of scientists who firmly believed that revelations of new laws of nature, perhaps divinely inspired, would be necessary to reveal what only God could explain. Now, here were two rationalists proving that "life was just a matter of physics and chemistry."[6] The script of life was written not by God, but by scientists in laboratories. The double-helix discovery was the high point of rationalism in the academic community and in the intellectual world at large, which was not prepared for the events that were to sweep the world in the last quarter of the century and millennium. No public or academic intellectuals paid particular attention to the horrors of Jonestown, Guyana, in 1978, when a charismatic preacher named Jim Jones promised his flock imminent resurrection as he oversaw the mass suicide of more than nine hundred followers, all Americans, many of whom gave their children Kool-Aid laced with cyanide. In 1991, American troops were fighting on the banks of the Tigris and Euphrates rivers, near where pilgrims were seeking

6. See James D. Watson, with Andrew Berry, *DNA: The Secret of Life* (New York: Alfred A. Knopf, 2003), 61.

the site of the Garden of Eden. In February 1993, a powerful car bomb ripped through the underground parking garage at New York City's World Trade Center. The perpetrators were Islamic fundamentalists who viewed America as Sodom and Gomorrah. A few months later, self-proclaimed Branch Davidian Messiah David Koresh at Waco, Texas, having announced that the world, once destroyed by flood, would next be consumed by fire, died in a conflagration with eighty-six of his followers, seventeen of whom were children. In the same year as the Oklahoma City bombing in 1995, Sheik Omar Abdel Rahman and nine of his militant Muslim followers were convicted of conspiring to blow up the United Nations, a building they considered the home of Satan. In that year, a Doomsday cult in Japan released poison gas into the Tokyo subway system, in anticipation of the end of time. In 1997, thirty-nine outer space messianists of Rancho Santa Fe, California, called Heaven's Gate, committed suicide while waiting for their redeemer to appear with the Hale-Bopp Comet. This was not a world that American higher education anticipated or understood. What was happening?

These events signaled a fundamental shift in this country's and the world's preoccupation that had passed, for the most part, unnoticed by the universities. The year 2000 and the Millennium approached, and a wave of religiously inspired eschatology swept the world, as the three religions of Abraham awaited the coming of a Messiah. At the same time, the college campuses were also swept by a deep spirituality. There had been nothing like it at the mid-century, nothing of any great significance into the early 1970s, when colleges often closed their chaplaincies in budget-saving measures. No one had trained any number of generations of graduate students to be prepared to deal with students of deep faith in their classrooms. Most of us believed that such students would find their way to the evangelical colleges and universities that had sprouted up around the country, but we did not suspect that they would also appear in our classrooms. As the 1990s approached, religious life was alive and well on the American college campus, and it was a force to be reckoned with, even by an unsuspecting and ill-equipped secular academic community. Religious revivalism challenged the set ideas of a rational and generally skeptical faculty.

The academic enterprise that Clark Kerr had called "the City of Intellect" had evolved into an entity more complex than Kerr ever could have imagined. In what seemed to be no more than a twinkling of a moment, the Internet and other technologies had revolutionized teaching, learning, and how we do research. The American university had undergone a profound change. Trustees were looking at new business models, partnerships with industry, enormous scientific breakthroughs, technology transfer, and capital campaigns of a billion dollars or more, previously undreamed of. In addition to the technological revolution, we encountered a spiritual one, as well.

Tufts University, which stood a good chance of disappearing before the end of the 1970s, had emerged, miraculously, much stronger and focused as it faced the last decade of the twentieth century. On the edge of the Millennium, it was an institution that had, in every sense, been born again.

6

UNDERGRADUATE STUDENTS AND ALUMNI

While the search for a successor to Jean Mayer was underway in the spring of 1992, the *Tufts Observer* commented in the April 23 issue about some perceptions of its editorial board and characteristics it hoped to find in the next president of Tufts: "Undergraduate students do not hide their beliefs that Mayer has sometimes seemed a little out of touch with students . . ." Mayer never ceased his avuncular criticism of student attitudes when his opinion differed from the prevailing undergraduate tastes of the times. He remained skeptical about innovations such as the Experimental College, which the undergraduates enthusiastically embraced. He loved traditional jazz, was a Louis Armstrong and Charlie Parker devotee, adored the records of Billie Holiday, and had no use for the contemporary tastes in music of the American undergraduate. He was an ardent supporter of the Tufts equestrian team, an activity somewhat more toward the exotic end of the intercollegiate athletic spectrum. Near the end of his presidency, the student body had lost the sense of admiration that had characterized the wonderment felt by the first generations of Tufts students who saw what Mayer was doing to the reputation of Tufts and to the value of their degrees. The Arts and Sciences faculty never lost their admiration. Their memory was longer. Most of them had a clear picture of where Tufts had been before Mayer, and where it was in 1992. To this constituency, there was no doubt who deserved the credit for a newly gained eminence.

The undergraduates, however, now wanted something else. "A commitment to relations with students will, in the long run, benefit university fundraising activities," stated the editorial. They had no historical memory of Tufts fundraising before or during the Mayer years, but they sought someone who showed more concern for their needs, and they were convinced that this attention would convert into increased alumni giving. In the end, they were right.

Tufts was about to be blessed with something that had not been a part of its history over more than a century: a little serendipitous luck. The two presidents who succeeded Jean Mayer appeared in the right order and brought the appropriate characteristics of temperament and personality to their office. The sequencing was very important. If John DiBiaggio had succeeded Burt Hallowell, Tufts might have floundered. The strengths that he possessed in winning the hearts and minds of the Tufts alumni would not have translated into successful fundraising, since the alumni in the 1960s and 1970s were totally incapable of seeing their responsibility to give back. Mayer encountered an alumni temperamentally incapable of giving money. The fundraising strategies devised by him and Tom Murnane took this into account. The alumni gave a disproportionately small amount to the first triumphant $140 million campaign. It took some years to get them conditioned, and by the second capital campaign of the mid-1980s, they were ready, or at least more ready. The percentage of alumni giving had increased, there were several million-dollar gifts, and even the Board of Trustees stepped up in a much more visible fashion, as Mayer and Murnane began changing the character of the Board.

When President DiBiaggio spoke to the student press in September soon after his arrival, he left them totally delighted: Tufts was ready to move forward, said the editors, "now that we have John DiBiaggio, a President who will find time for personal interviews" and who announced an open-door policy. He stated publicly and repeatedly that he would be available to meet with any student at any time. This was going to be a student-centered and alumni-centered university. The President would be always available, and the President's House would be "the front door of the university, to help with fundraising," as his spouse Nancy DiBiaggio put it when interviewed in that first October of 1992.

This was going to be a new kind of presidency for Tufts, and Nancy DiBiaggio was clearly part of the package. Although she was a career woman and had a major regional sales responsibility for a line of upscale women's apparel, she made it clear that as the President's spouse, she would share the responsibilities associated with the regeneration of the President's House; this she undertook with a vengeance of energy, and the students applauded. The announcement of a $1.4 million renovation was greeted by total student approval. "Justified Expense" headlined the *Observer* editorial, and Mrs. DiBiaggio took charge. In the meantime, in his first year at Tufts President

DiBiaggio could be found eating in the dorms, speaking to student government, or driving students around campus in his antique Packard automobile. He was headlined as an auctioneer at charity events, went to football and basketball games, openly delighted in the small-time Division III athletic program, and yet impressed the student body when he went off to attend, as he did every year of his presidency, the Final Four NCAA basketball playoffs. He became an enthusiast for small-time college athletics that he discovered at Tufts, yet his most significant national recognition came as a member of the Knight Commission, which was established to address abuses in NCAA Division I athletic programs. As the former President of two athletic powerhouse universities, John DiBiaggio felt very comfortable in big-time intercollegiate athletics, but he never displayed condescension when watching games in Medford that never were mentioned in the sports pages of newspapers that provided the gamblers' point spread.

Tom Murnane saw what he had in the way of a people-oriented President, and went with the strengths. John DiBiaggio was immediately in his element with the Tufts alumni. He was tall, handsome, and comfortable with his Italian ethnicity, a down-to-earth "shmoozer," kisser and hugger. Mayer, who did not look forward to alumni events in the United States, preferring those Tufts graduates who had made their way to Europe or Asia, often talked down to the old-timers, talked globally when they were scarcely regional, and did not tolerate fools easily. Where Betty Mayer was retiring and reserved, Nancy DiBiaggio was ebullient and effervescent. Board Chairman Nelson Gifford made a considerable gift toward the house renovation, and it was renamed Gifford House in his honor. The refurbished President's home transformed fundraising at Tufts. Tom Murnane scheduled on average ninety events a year, some involving up to three hundred guests, either in the extended dining area inside the house or in heated enclosed tents attached to it. The dining and décor were sumptuous. Nancy DiBiaggio oversaw the often spectacular flower arrangements, table settings, seating assignments, and menus. She was, in every respect, the First Lady. When the renovations had been completed and Gifford House opened to the community, it was metamorphosed into a symbol of the DiBiaggios' style. The highlight of the academic year was the Christmas open house, with a huge floor-to-ceiling spruce beautifully decorated, electric trains, wreaths, and a cornucopia of refreshments. The DiBiaggios and their two white West Highland terriers welcomed students and staff as family in a scene filled with warmth and holiday cheer, right out of Norman Rockwell. I heard the same remark repeatedly from women who worked in the dining halls, custodians, and campus painters, many of whom were first-generation Americans: "This is what a President of a university and his wife should look like!" Although he looked patrician, John DiBiaggio was very much at ease with those nonacademics whom he welcomed into his home. These were his kind of people.

THE TROIKA

Each of us—Tom Murnane, Steve Manos, and Sol Gittleman—had individual responses to the events of Mayer's going and DiBiaggio's coming. Manos's future might have been the least complicated, because of the enormous authority that the Trustees had placed in his hands and their unshakable faith in his talent. The same people who had selected John DiBiaggio had also brought Steve Manos to Tufts, and they had no reason to regret their choice of the Executive Vice President. Nelson Gifford was the primary kingmaker, and I assumed that he had told DiBiaggio to keep Steve on board, that he would be an essential part of the new President's team. Manos had admired Mayer, but also understood the dynamic chaos caused by the Mayer style, and he was ready for whatever the Trustees wanted. He wanted to remain at Tufts, but he was eminently marketable. Neither Manos nor I had ever met John DiBiaggio before he accepted the presidency, so we had no expectations or knowledge. We knew nothing about him, other than the fact that he was President of Michigan State University and former President of the University of Connecticut. It seemed an odd match, but we had no Trustee conversations about this. In any case, Manos seemed secure, at least in my mind.

Tom Murnane, the architect of Mayer's fundraising successes, could have moved on to Washington with Cassidy or the Congressional delegation, or to Beacon Hill, where he was very well wired with the Democratic leadership in Massachusetts. He was Mayer's man, in every sense, and he could have expected that this would be the end of his time at Tufts. Although Murnane had had no meetings with any of the candidates for the Tufts presidency, he had known John DiBiaggio for more than twenty years in their capacity as Dental School administrators and during the time of the founding of the Vet School, when DiBiaggio was President of the University of Connecticut and was, according to Mayer, opposing Tufts. The last dealings had not been particularly cordial, and Murnane had every reason to think that he would not survive with the new president, who, after all, had the right to select his own team. As close as Tom Murnane was to some members of the Board's inner circle and power brokers, he was not part of that privileged few who had brought John DiBiaggio on board. The new President undoubtedly knew that Murnane was Jean Mayer's closest confidant, and that could seal his fate. Tom Murnane would no longer want to return to the Dental School full-time, so there was some uncertainty.

As for me, it was time to go back to the faculty, which actually I had never left. I still taught one class per semester, my enrollments for each class were in the hundreds, and I never dreamed my time as Provost would last eleven years, longer than that of any previous incumbent. In my first year as Provost, we lived in our house in nearby Winchester, until the President asked me to move into the Provost's House on campus. Thinking that I might last another year or two, we decided not to sell our house, but to let one of our children stay there. Now, in 1992, we had been out of our home for eleven years, a new president with a new broom was coming in, and I was ready. Inevitably, serving that long as Provost brought me some attention and some presidential interest from other institutions. Yet, somehow, I could never really generate enough enthusiasm to become a college or university president, though I did allow my name to be considered at a few places. Sometimes these things get out of control, and before I knew it, one of the chairmen of a search committee, himself the chairman of his board of trustees, short-circuited the process and offered me the presidency of a fine New England College. Fortunately, my wife said she would be delighted if I became a president, but would not give up her job as Director of the Experimental College at Tufts to become a full-time presidential spouse. Robyn needed an academic job with some substance, and this traditional search committee wanted a president's wife of the old model. My wife was prepared to accommodate by commuting several days a week. When my children heard of this possibility, they came over to the Provost's House for a family meeting. My oldest daughter Julia, very pregnant with her first child, led the "discussion," concluding, with her siblings, that they did not want us moving away, nor did they think that I was that interested in becoming a president. That really clinched it. We would stay in Boston, near our own three kids and our grandchildren, and play the game out whichever way it ran, moving back to Winchester, if I returned to full-time teaching. I was ready to give the new President the formal resignation so he could select his own Provost. But, first, we had to meet him.

The troika met first individually, then collectively, with President DiBiaggio. Each of us had been given the same message: no resignations required, we would go on as we had been. DiBiaggio laid out his philosophy of management and explained his style. He would delegate completely all authority in our areas of responsibility, wanted to be informed about any potential difficulties, never wanted to be "blind-sided," and would hold us accountable if anything went wrong. I had responsibility for the academic enterprise across the university. He would be available, but he felt that his university responsibilities would take him off campus much more, and he needed a trusted deputy in his place; that was to be the Provost.

It took a while for the effect of this first set of meetings to sink in. Having worked with only one Tufts president, I had no expectations about different styles of management. It gradually came to me that this President was a delegator, and that he would not be pressing on schools for new programs, would not be charging ahead with the creation of new institutions nor projecting a vision of intellectual innovation that would force the faculty to follow him as he led into new realms. He would manage the enterprise by finding people he could trust. John DiBiaggio was the first person I can recall saying, "This is not a business, but it has to be run business-like." The Trustees, who had become exhausted by Jean Mayer's creativity, had found their President.

I called an immediate meeting of all the deans of the Tufts' schools, before they had met with the President. My message was clear and direct: You as deans will have an unprecedented opportunity to set the agenda for your schools, you can lead as you never thought possible in the Mayer presidency. If I approve of your initiatives, we will jointly inform the President, and you may move forward. Steve Manos had informed the new President that for the past few years there had been a structural deficit, and President DiBiaggio made it clear that he would address this problem immediately. After that, they would have unprecedented latitude.

The deans' response was varied. Erling Johansen, Dean of the Dental School, was delighted to have a close professional colleague as the Tufts president. Medical School Dean Mort Madoff and Mel Bernstein of the Arts, Sciences and Engineering were on the search committee, saw the DiBiaggio appointment as a Trustee coup d'etat, shrugged their shoulders, and prepared to move their agendas.

Frank Loew, Dean of the Veterinary School and himself a finalist for the Tufts presidency, was quietly raging. He had discovered that the basic sciences faculty had got up a signed petition that was sent to the Board stating that Loew was not a suitable candidate to become the President of Tufts, so his bitterness toward the Medical School only increased. He was also dismissive of DiBiaggio's credentials, which he and members of the search committee had seen and passed over as academically unacceptable. Loew expressed outspoken contempt for ceremonial presidents who looked good, and he was infuriated by the appointment of John DiBiaggio. It was clear that Frank Loew could not work for this President. In spite of his love for the Tufts Vet School, Loew was gone in two years, accepting the deanship of his veterinary alma mater, Cornell School of Veterinary Medicine. The bitterness about the Tufts presidential search stayed with him for the rest of his life. But his opportunity came when he was appointed president of Becker College, a small two-year institution in Worcester, Massachusetts, in 1999. In a few short years before his untimely death in 2003, he transformed Becker into a vital little four-year college with all the energy that Frank Loew possessed. Everything that he touched, he made better. Like Mayer, he was a defining change agent.

As for the other deans, they were on board and ready to move. The Di-Biaggio presidency would provide unique opportunities to shape their schools in a manner rarely provided to deans.

The nine years of the DiBiaggio presidency also proved to be a very special time for the troika, in personal terms. During Jean Mayer's sixteen years as leader of Tufts, there was no question that only Tom Murnane enjoyed the full confidence of the President. As much as the President grew to like Steve Manos and me, he never fully trusted either of us. He knew that members of the Board would come directly to us on occasion. At times the Board would demand that loyalty to them take precedent. This continued right through the DiBiaggio presidency, as well, and ultimately became a problem for the three of us. Different Board members constantly look to one or another of us as a pipeline. It had begun with Jean Mayer. Board members had struck up very close and personal relationships with faculty, who at times felt no compunction about going to the Trustees with information, complaints, or whatever was on their minds. Some Trustees encouraged this behavior. As for the troika, routine calls from Board members were part of our ritual. Sometimes they dealt with specific Trustee issues. Often they just wanted to know "what was going on." As in the days of Jean Mayer, we each had several masters.

With the ascendancy of John DiBiaggio, we three drew closer together. Once the Board had voted in the new President and he had committed him-self to making no changes in his top leadership, we devised a plan to gain community acceptance of the new President. This became the highest priority for the three of us. We had no part in the selection, but we knew that it was up to us to make it work.

At the first meeting of the President's Cabinet, President DiBiaggio said the first order of business was to eliminate the structural deficit, which had

"I CAN'T REMEMBER IF THIS IS A MEETING, A CONFERENCE, A SEMINAR, OR A WORKSHOP."

© J. P. Rini 2003, originally published in The Chronicle of Higher Education.

been eating away at the university's free reserves for the past few years. He instructed Steve Manos to come up with a plan that placed the central university administration at the front of the issue, making the first and largest cuts in its operating budgets. All the schools would contribute in what was proposed as a sliding three-year solution. All of the deans came on board, and in three years the structural deficit was gone. When he informed the Trustees at the next Board meeting of the results, there was universal satisfaction. Here was their kind of President, business-like and orderly.

THE ARTS, SCIENCES AND ENGINEERING:
LEADING FROM WITHIN

When it came to dealing with the undergraduate student body, John DiBiaggio was a master. He did not meet with members of the student press until the first week in September as his first academic year at Tufts got underway. From that very first encounter, these hard-boiled student journalists were delighted with "the fine choice of John DiBiaggio as the new university president."[1] They were also ready to lacerate the search process, editorializ-

1. *Tufts Daily*, September 8, 1992.

ing that "in the final analysis, the process ended with a secret, hidden candidate being chosen as president . . . Using the word 'open' for the process only to betray this description, the Trustees showed unanimous disregard for the community's voice in the selection of a new president." These intrepid young investigatory reporters had also gotten to their counterparts at Michigan State and clearly liked what they heard. At this huge public university, DiBiaggio would be most remembered for his accessibility to students, his ability to mitigate disagreements, and for the sense of community he established during his tenure in East Lansing. Bob Allison, news editor of the Michigan State daily newspaper *State News,* summed up the general impression of the departing president: "He was always very open towards students. He visited a lot of classes, and went to games around campus a lot." It was this availability to the Tufts undergraduate students that would endear John DiBiaggio to them. Over his nine-year term of office he attended their endless senate meetings, ate in every dining facility, came to their clubs, invited them to his home, raised money for their causes, served as auctioneer, and took them seriously. They reciprocated with genuine affection. Intellectually, he did not make them uncomfortable. At his April 1993 inauguration, he articulated what he wished to be remembered for, and he never wavered from what he saw as his academic legacy for Tufts: "We have the opportunity today to make public service a defining feature of Tufts, to make the values and skills of active citizenship a true hallmark of a Tufts education." For a school like Tufts, with its strong tradition of community outreach embodied in the eight-hundred-member Leonard Carmichael Society, he had hit the right note. Alumni as well as trustees could resonate to this theme; and the trustees saw an idea that did not translate into high-risk, large, and new expenditures. Who could fault community service and citizen participation, and how much could it cost, anyway? Mayer's sudden bursts of heart-stopping entrepreneurial individualism were over. Chairman Gifford spoke to the students of DiBiaggio's "consensual style of management" and, as if to place a period after the Mayer era, the new President told the students: "Under Jean Mayer, the university experienced a necessary rapid growth. It is now time for stabilization . . ." Here was a President who would pay attention to the needs of the Tufts undergraduates. From the outset, there was no student dissent from that opinion or diminishing of their enthusiasm for John DiBiaggio.

Not so the faculty of Arts and Sciences. As I look back on my goals for the 1992–1993 academic year, the first leaps out: "Make the transition to the new President hassle-free; and keep any residual issues related to the search process under control." My greatest challenge was in keeping the Arts and Sciences faculty from running amok. A considerable number of them had followed Jean Mayer across the Jordan and had seen the Promised Land. They wanted no stabilization; they wanted more of what they had seen over the past sixteen years. Two weeks after the announcement of the new President, a rump group of about forty faculty met in the Coolidge Room in Ballou Hall on the Medford campus. They asked me to attend. As soon as I saw the make-up of the meeting, I realized the potential for serious trouble. Present were some of the most distinguished faculty in Arts and Sciences, and they were angry. The meeting had one agenda item: the drafting of a letter of no confidence in the new President of Tufts University. I asked: On what basis? They laid out a litany of criticism: President DiBiaggio had no serious academic credentials, his curriculum vitae was trivial, he had been a professional and ceremonial president of two second-tier state universities that are in no way comparable to Tufts. What provoked the Trustees, they asked, to make such an inappropriate selection? Somehow they had the idea that I was an insider with knowledge of the process, search, and selection.

Here was a clear and present danger. I have seen smaller groups than this one inside the Arts and Sciences faculty bring down deans and cause enormous mischief. This was an insurrectionist bunch bent on trouble, and they needed to be deflected. My instant strategy was to blame the executive search firm for doing a terrible job in finding good candidates. I knew that there was no great wave of enthusiasm among the faculty for any of the three finalists, and I told them that the Trustees shared that sentiment. In the end, the Chairman of the Board felt that Tufts could do better, and he went into action. If you want to criticize anyone, write Nelson Gifford a nasty letter, but do not vote no-confidence in the man who is coming, whether you like it or not. Give him a chance. He will raise money, I assured them, and provide you with the means to develop your ideas and plans. No doubt, I admitted, John DiBiaggio will be different than Jean Mayer. The emphasis will turn from the President to the faculty and deans. We can build even a stronger Tufts University on the foundation left us by Jean Mayer.

They wrote Gifford, strongly condemning his process in selecting a President for Tufts, and waited for their President to arrive. The insurrection never took place, although someone from the faculty or the search committee got to the *Boston Globe's* resident muckraker Anthony Flint, who headlined a column on September 20, "Presidential hunt at Tufts was 'horrible.'" Flint, using unnamed sources, said one "major player" involved in the search said, "It turned out better than the Trustees deserved." By this time, the President had diffused much of the anger, and the community was preparing for the DiBiaggio era. For the faculty, it was going to be very different. They had gotten accustomed to Jean Mayer running the faculty meetings, laying out his intellectual agenda. He had been an active, often unpredictable leader who had shaken the Arts and Sciences faculty loose from historical lethargy and brought it to an unexpected and exhilarating eminence. They liked it. The new faculty hired during Mayer's time were clearly superior in terms of scholarship and research, while holding on to the traditions of great teaching. The faculty had also become accustomed to the color of money, and saw what new facilities could do. They took pride in the new prestige of their university. They had to be assured that John DiBiaggio would only add to that prestige, but using a different calibration and style than Jean Mayer.

From the beginning, the difference was apparent. For all of his time at Tufts President, DiBiaggio chaired only the first ceremonial and social meeting of the academic year, and thereafter rarely sat in front of the faculty, unless for a special and specific reason. Mel Bernstein, Vice President for Arts, Sciences and Technology, chaired his faculty meetings. From time to time, President DiBiaggio would come to an Arts and Sciences or Engineering faculty meeting and sit in the audience.

Arts, Sciences and Engineering flourished during the 1990s. Mel Bernstein had succeeded Bob Rotberg as Vice President for Arts, Sciences and Technology, which also included engineering, and brought the interpersonal skills that the brilliant and often contemptuous Rotberg had lacked. Bernstein was an engineer, but wanted an opportunity to lead a strong Arts and Sciences, to prepare himself someday for a presidency. I was happy to give him the opportunity. His first step was to raise the bar on tenure and to let his community know that teaching was cherished and research was essential. Rotberg had given the same message, but in doing so informed them that they were not nearly as smart as he was. Bernstein worked on the Tenure and Promotion Committee, got them to understand the need for a stronger faculty, and he prevailed. He was also given all the slack he needed to run the Arts, Sciences and Engineering in his own style. Since I had nearly thirty years of Tufts behind me, I gave him the benefit of whatever wisdom I had, and let him run. He made some excellent appointments of directors and deans under him, gave the humanities what seemed to them to be equal attention while pushing hardest on the sciences and engineering. It was a tremendous opportunity for him: to run an operation almost as if he were the president of his own small university with a $150 million budget. Of course, the troika stood above him, with Steve Manos and Tom Murnane at times too close for Bernstein's tastes, but he had more room for maneuvering that any other leader of an Arts and Sciences/Engineering faculty in the country, and he knew it. My advice to him was to speak to the President from time to time, merely to keep him informed, and then to run his own show. I would manage the President, run all of the searches for school deans, maintain thin walls and low hurdles, take whatever heat and anger that might be directed toward the central administration on a denied tenure case, and get maximum synergy out of the university. But the center stage, in the Arts, Sciences and Engineering, would belong to Mel Bernstein, with no Tufts President or Provost casting a shadow.

My biggest problem was political and educational. First, how to make the faculty of Arts, Sciences and Engineering accept the reality that this was a different kind of President, one that Tufts had never experienced before, even for those ancients whose memory, like mine, went back to the 1960s of Nils Wessell and Burt Hallowell. Second, how to explain to the Chairman of the Board the fears of a faculty that never had a professional president before and worried that the style of governance he had known at an enormous public university would be alien to the Tufts culture. I had prepared him early for the letter of condemnation he received from the faculty group, which he happily dismissed.

John DiBiaggio did not routinely chair meetings of the Arts and Sciences faculty at the University of Connecticut or at Michigan State. The Tufts faculty expected this of their President. Wessell did; Hallowell did; and Jean Mayer, most of all, ran the A&S meetings. In the case of Mayer, he walked the campus, barged into departmental meetings, involved himself in searches, and let it be known very quickly that he knew as much about *any* field as any member of the faculty. For whatever reasons, the faculty loved this intrusion, this interest in their work, and the academic crossing of swords with their President. I tried to make it clear to Nelson Gifford and to the faculty at the beginning of the new President's first year that this was a different style, but faculties need to find fault, and they found it in what this President, in terms of philosophy and temperament, simply could not provide. By the November faculty meeting of President DiBiaggio's third year, chaired by Mel Bernstein and with me reporting on a recent Trustee meeting, it blew up. "It is as if we have an invisible president," one faculty member was quoted in the *Tufts Daily*.[2] The headline on the weekly *Tufts Observer* front page read "DiBiaggio Criticized by Faculty." The meeting, which had a published and long

2. *Tufts Daily,* November 15, 1994.

agenda, was taken over by the issue of presidential style. They complained that he did not visit their departments, did not show interest in their research activities. These complainers were not the members of the rump insurrection group of two years earlier. I made the same pitch, that John DiBiaggio was out raising money, getting the faculty the resources they wanted, and that they ought to stop whining and enjoy the fruits of Tufts' growing reputation. There was more grumbling, but basically this one session of open complaint ended the Arts and Sciences faculty fault finding. Gradually, they came to understand that DiBiaggio's strengths were not in the tradition of academic and intellectual leadership they so admired in Jean Mayer. The construction of facilities continued, Tufts was attracting better and better students, the much-scorned but much-read *U.S. News & World Report* college and university rankings placed Tufts in the top twenty-five national universities in 1995 and a year later Tufts was bumped up to twenty-second. I continued to tell them that it was the Arts and Sciences that provided this enhanced reputation (which was true).

Educating Nelson Gifford was still another issue. I doubt if Chairman Gifford ever fully understood the different characteristics required of a president who oversaw a fifty thousand-student campus and the leader of a university-college like Tufts. Gifford was looking for a manager who could "run" an enterprise. When John DiBiaggio met privately with a portion of the available search committee late in the process, he purportedly said that he could run Tufts with one hand tied behind his back. It was the management skills and smart business sense that the Chairman recognized in this candidate, characteristics that none of the public finalists had to his satisfaction. Nelson Gifford had said, many years earlier when he was being recruited for the Tufts Board, that he had no patience with or particular understanding of academic values. These were concepts that did not interest him. Gifford himself had been a CEO. It was time for a manager/CEO for Tufts, and when two eminent former Big Ten presidents, who had gone on to Ivy League universities, described John DiBiaggio as the finest sitting president of a university in the United States, that sealed it for Gifford. John DiBiaggio's scholarly reputation seemed to him as solid as the academic reputations of his candidate's two major supporters. Gifford gave no thought to the academic backgrounds of John DiBiaggio, Harold Shapiro, or James Freedman, the latter two eminent scholars, whose writing would have qualified them for tenure in any economics department or law school faculty. John DiBiaggio, an acknowledged professional president, had never established a scholarly reputation as a researcher in his chosen field, dental medicine. Chairman Gifford never understood the issue of presidential academic credibility with a faculty, particularly of Arts and Sciences. Nonetheless, the period of the DiBiaggio presidency was enormously productive for the Arts, Sciences and Engineering. The stars were aligned, and the right people were in place.

Whatever Tufts was destined to become, to continue on the upward course set by Jean Mayer, the Arts and Sciences would have to be in the forefront. Such was the nature of American higher education; the disciplines of the liberal arts and sciences carried the reputation of their universities on their backs, no matter how prestigious the professional schools became. Jean Mayer understood this as well as John DiBiaggio, but Mayer's strategy was first to lift a mediocre Arts and Sciences with the reputation of new and instantly prestigious professional schools. Mayer had no time to attack the problems of Arts and Sciences systematically.

For the nine years of John DiBiaggio's presidency, Mel Bernstein was the leader of Arts, Sciences and Engineering. He inherited a faculty that represented Jean Mayer's best efforts to break with the past while at the same time holding on to the traditions of Tufts College. The best of the appointments made during the Mayer years were not part of any specific plan or strategy, but they served as the foundation for Bernstein's building. Where Mayer had his eyes everywhere on many targets for improvement, Mel Bernstein could focus on the Arts and Sciences and know he could make an enormous difference; and he did.

When Bernstein arrived from Illinois Institute of Technology in 1991, the Tufts endowment sat at less than $200 million, which represented an astonishing growth under Jean Mayer, but still left Tufts very far back in the competitive pack. Bernstein realized that, although fundraising would continue, Tufts did not have the resources to raise all of the boats together in Arts, Sciences and Engineering. He would select his targets for eminence strategically and look for the biggest possible impact. As an engineer, he knew also that he had to convince a skeptical humanities and social sciences faculty that he was interested in their fate. It was also clear to him that the College of Engineering needed serious attention. Jean Mayer was already too distracted by his own woes to spend much time with Mel Bernstein, so we brainstormed together. The Arts and Sciences deans have always suffered from Provosts living in the same building and hanging over their shoulders. My personal style of management, if one could call it that, was to provide a long rope and to permit deans to dean. I talked, gave opinions, blessed the vision, made peace between combatants when necessary, and occasionally said no. My first advice to Bernstein, before he did anything, was to get his team in place in order to make change. Arts and Sciences faculty everywhere are extremely sensitive to the personalities of the nonacademic administrators who surround the deans, or, in this case, the Vice President for Arts, Sciences and Technology. If faculty do not like the people guarding the doors of the academic administration, they can turn very hostile. This phenomenon had helped ruin Bob Rotberg's tenure. Fortunately, Bernstein inherited a very capable Dean for Admissions, David Cuttino, who, besides knowing how to build an interesting class, was very nurturing of faculty and staff children trying to gain admittance to the undergraduate college. He gave them personal attention, and they liked his style. Bernstein needed nonacademic personnel whom the faculty trusted, particularly in a new position that Steve Manos had built into the schools' administrative structure: the Executive Associate Dean.

Manos wanted a person in each school who was authorized to take charge of all nonacademic activities and some historically academic ones as well, a mini-Executive VP. The deans liked the idea of a senior staff person who was in charge of all activities with even a hint of a business/management orientation, even those that had been run by faculty, such as the Dental School clinics, previously in the hands of traditionally incompetent dental faculty who had no idea how to manage anything, but believed that this was an academic area under faculty purview. For Arts and Sciences, this meant summer school or continuing education could be taken over by a genuine manager, someone who could stroke the faculty, soothe them, even put money into their pockets, while they were quietly losing authority, to their own benefit and that of the university. The deans did not seem to mind, because better-run schools meant a healthier bottom line. The Executive Associate Dean had the capacity to make the Dean of the school look better. Bernstein's first move was to promote a middle-level budget and finance officer, Wayne Bouchard, to this new and sensitive position. It was one of the three best appointments he made in his decade as the leader of his faculty. Bouchard was one of those rare, transparent communicators who talked to faculty and had their trust. He could explain accounting procedures, was infinitely patient, and enjoyed being with faculty. Bernstein had his man.

Next, he turned to the faculty, and showing very good instincts, first to the humanities. There was an opportunity in Classics. Harvard had a young Associate Professor named Gregory Crane, who was not going to be tenured. He was a Thucydides scholar, and Harvard already had one. Besides, he was a Harvard Ph.D., and they were loath to keep their own homegrown without first shipping them off around the world. Also, Crane was immersed in an online computer project called *Perseus,* which was an electronic database of the Classics: Latin and Greek culture and civilization available through this newly created tool called the Internet. Crane was looking for a home for himself and the *Perseus Project.* Harvard had informed him that his electronic brainchild would not make a wit of difference in his tenure case. There was no opening for another classicist at Tufts, but the departmental chair Steven Hirsch, along with colleague Peter Reid, went to Mel Bernstein with the faint hope that maybe an engineer would appreciate the possibilities inherent in *Perseus.*

After he had been given a demonstration of *Perseus,* Bernstein did not have to be persuaded. Crane and his project came to Tufts, and the *Perseus Digital Library at Tufts University* has established itself as one of the great computational humanities miracles of the Internet. By 2003, the number of daily visits to the Web site reached over three hundred thousand, and the annual volume was estimated at *sixty-seven million.* Gregory Crane, who was tenured at Tufts in 1995, is recognized worldwide as one of the giants in the field, with *Perseus* home sites in Berlin, Germany, and Oxford, England, as well as at Tufts. He has received the largest grants ever received by Tufts from the National Science Foundation. The reach of *Perseus* is astounding. There is scarcely an elementary school student with access to a computer who has not reached into *Perseus* for assistance in a classroom presentation, for a picture of a Greek vase or a Roman coin. High school and college students all over the world discovered in *Perseus* a massive library of primary sources, sculptures, sites, and buildings. The overview of the entire corpus of Greek and Latin literature is breathtaking, with thirty-three thousand pictures taken from links to libraries, museums, and collections in thirty countries.

Bernstein placed whatever resources he could find at the disposal of Crane and his project. A center was established, the facilities were provided, and Crane never looked back. Tufts had had a Web site for the ages, and the *Perseus Project* provided the University with a status in the humanities that was extraordinary and global. It also gained Tufts a place at the national and international table in digital libraries and informational technology.

Bernstein's first year at Tufts was 1991, but he still managed to get a sweet and sour taste of Jean Mayer's legacy. In the mid-1980s, Tom Murnane had found Dudley Wright, a Geneva-based philanthropist with a powerful interest in science education and inspiring young people to careers in science. Eventually, Wright met Jean Mayer, and their conversations led to the idea of establishing a Wright Center for Science Education at Tufts University. Initially $3 to 4 million of funding was made available to get the Center started, but Mayer, who now kept Dudley Wright close to himself, could not find a suitable director. The Center languished with acting directors, and Wright was getting increasingly impatient. At this point, Mel Bernstein joined Tufts, and I urged the President to turn the search over to him. Bernstein saw the potential for complete implosion and accelerated the search. Among the candidates was Eric Chaisson, who was at that time Director of Educational Programs at the Space Telescope Science Institute at Johns Hopkins. He had moved from Harvard to Haverford to Hopkins over a twenty-year career, where the word "adjunct" seemed to be permanently attached to his name. A Tufts search committee had seen various candidates, but there was no doubt in the Vice President's mind: this was someone on whom it would be worthwhile to take a chance.

Again, Bernstein struck gold. Chaisson, part entrepreneur, part anarchist, saw a once-in-a-lifetime opportunity to run an enterprise without interference. As one colleague put it, "He walked into a job that nearly vaporized before he ever arrived on campus. Rather than stand by and watch his job melt, he hopped on a plane to Switzerland and persuaded the Wrights to keep the Center at Tufts." Within a few years, Chaisson turned the Wright Center into an internationally recognized force not only in secondary education—Chaisson's particular expertise—but also in communicating science to the public. He poured himself into convincing Dudley Wright and the people at the Wright Foundation that he was the one person who could make the Center work at Tufts. From these beginnings, Chaisson grew the Center into a multi-million-dollar generator. He was everything that Wright had been looking for, and Tom Murnane also saw his potential. One of Chaisson's faculty cheerleaders, Mary Jane Shultz, who took over the Chair of Chemistry in 2000, described the Center as a place "on campus where the faculty can sit down next to secondary teachers and Nobel prize winners to discuss both understanding of broad science issues and how these issues are best communicated to all levels . . . It's a great place to enjoy noncompetitive, but intense science at all size scales, from the subatomic to the molecular to the geological to the astronomical. It's a fantastic place." Anyone who had seen events sponsored by Chaisson and the Wright Center at the Boston Museum of Science could echo Shultz's praise. Chaisson did not win any popularity contests on the campus with many of the other faculty. He could be haughty, arrogant, temperamental, and dismissive of lights he thought had less wattage than he possessed. I went down to the Boston Museum of Science to see one of his programs featuring a Tufts physicist, Chris Sliwa, and encountered an auditorium filled to bursting with high school physics teachers and students, completely mesmerized by the presentations of Chaisson and Sliwa. Bernstein took a great deal of criticism for his support of Chaisson, but he knew quality when he saw it, albeit packaged in that unique academic casing of uncollegiality. He teaches for the most part on other campuses. To this date, no department at Tufts has accepted Chaisson, an internationally recognized and published astronomer and science educator, as a full-fledged member.

Bernstein was willing to take risks and to take criticism, if he thought his actions produced stimulating educational experiences. He was an outspoken supporter of a Tufts program called Education for Public Inquiry and International Citizenship (EPIIC), run initially out of the Experimental College by yet another academic entrepreneur, Sherman Teichman, who had come to the Political Science Department in the late 1970s as a part-time, one-shot replacement, returned a few years later in another guise, and has remained a fixture, outside of the normal departmental structure. He had at least one Master's degree, could cause instant excitement with his programming among the international relations undergraduates, and the Ex. College decided to give him a home. His first symposium, conducted in 1986 as an undergraduate-run event, was on International Terrorism. Looking back, it is astonishing to see how far ahead of his times Teichman was. His second symposium, on the West Bank and the Gaza Strip Twenty Years Later, attracted, through his invitation, Israelis and Arabs who had never dared sit in the same room together. It was obvious that Teichman had a gift, but the faculty initially took an instant dislike to his program and prominence. He had very few allies in political science, the IR program, or history, especially when local television programs, when looking for expert opinion on the Middle East or terrorism, turned to Teichman. His face appearing on a screen with "faculty member, Tufts University" written as a description, caused apoplexy. But Jean Mayer liked him, and Mel Bernstein loved the stimulation he caused among the undergraduate—and eventually graduate and faculty—population. He could attract the most prominent international figures to the Medford campus. Deans Salacuse and Galvin of the Fletcher School took notice and gave their blessing. Gradually, the faculty began understanding what EPIIC could do. Teichman may have been a bit of a showman, but he produced quality results, and Bernstein gave him the support that he needed. When visited by the Ford Foundation regarding an EPIIC grant application, I was told by the senior Ford person, "At any other university, this guy would have been strangled in his crib." At Tufts, Sherman Teichman survived and flourished, and eventually reached out to the secondary school population all over the United

States. Yet he could only survive because the Experimental College gave him an academic home where he could teach his courses and run his symposium. No department gave him a door to walk through, yet Bernstein provided the resources.

Bernstein constantly looked for anything that made Tufts look different. He saw the uniqueness of what had proved to be one of the most enduring and few surviving innovative centers for education in the United States: the Tufts Experimental College. Most of the student-inspired experimental colleges—Evergreen State in Washington, Oberlin, and a few others—never had the support of the faculty. They were born during the heady student explosions of the mid-1960s and died by the 1980s. For whatever reason, Tufts had been different, and from its founding in the early 1960s, *before* the student tempests, under President Wessell, the faculty nurtured it. The Ex. College, as it was affectionately called, also had the great good fortune of finding the right administrative godfather (in this case, "godmother") in the person of Robyn Gittleman (my wife) who became Executive Director in 1972 and for more than thirty years provided the continuity and discipline so that the Ex. College succeeded where all others had failed. She herded the students, faculty, and staff together and provided the tough love that permitted the Ex. College to continue innovating and stimulating. It was not a "college" in any sense of the word, more of an informal department, with a governing board made up of equal numbers of students and faculty. The Ex. College offered courses that fell outside the academic expertise of the regular faculty but had the rigor that satisfied them. The students loved these opportunities to take hard-nose courses taught by lawyers, stock market analysts, labor organizers, physicians, and a host of professionals. The *Tufts Observer* editorialized: "The Ex. College is the perfect complement to the education provided at this university. Without utilizing this window into the happenings beyond the Hill, students may lose one of the few available chances of glimpsing a bit of their future."[3] The Ex. College took chances, trying out exotic languages that often became part of the traditional course offerings. It was not afraid of failure. Without it, creations such as Sherman Teichman's EPIIC or its sister program *Inquiry* would, indeed, have been strangled in their cribs.

Whether planned or serendipitous, Crane's *Perseus Project,* Chaisson's Dudley Wright Center, and Teichman's EPIIC program brought Tufts into contact with the idea of K–12 education. Tufts had made a start in this field

3. *Tufts Observer,* September 28, 1995.

in 1986, when physicist Ron Thornton created the Center for Science and Mathematics Teaching. The Physics Department was primarily interested in its high-energy research agenda, and Thornton's efforts to build a career on middle- and secondary school teaching of science left his colleagues indifferent. He successfully found funding during the early years, and eventually more than half of his center's work was at the university level. He went on to produce curricula, real-time data logging tools, and pedagogical methods that allowed students to participate in their own learning. These materials are now used by universities nationally and internationally. A few years ago, Thornton estimated that more than 20 percent of all beginning university students in the United States who took physics were using materials coming from his Center. When Bernstein came on board, Thornton found a sympathetic administrator. Thornton has continued to pay his own way and has turned his Center into a nationally recognized pioneer whose mission went beyond Chaisson's exclusively secondary-school focus. These two science education centers were outreach efforts that had a much greater impact off the campus than on. Bernstein's next appointment would shake up the Tufts community as well as the outside world. This was the appointment of a new Dean for Engineering.

It is fair to say that in the pre-Mayer days, the College of Engineering brought up the rear of all the other academic components of Tufts. In 1956, only one of seven Tufts engineering faculty members possessed a Ph.D. It had no graduate education or research until the early 1960s. ROTC courses could fulfill requirements in humanities and social sciences; there were no foreign language requirements. When Ashley Campbell resigned in 1968 as Dean after eleven years, a Visiting Committee came in to take a look, and the kindest comment it could make was that the undergraduate program was unimaginative and the graduate program too weak and too small to make any difference at all.[4] Ernest Klema, who came from Northwestern, succeeded Campbell, encountered an old entrenched guard of Tufts engineers, and quit after three years. He stayed long enough to oversee one re-accreditation visit that left the college barely qualified to continue. The curriculum was considered to be below minimum standards and the physical facilities were inadequate. By the time Jean Mayer arrived, the College of Engineering was sinking into irrelevance. The Dean at that time, Arthur Uhlir, begged the newly arrived President not to mention the College of Engineering in his inaugural remarks, for fear that his faculty would think that Mayer planned to

4. Russell E. Miller, *Light on the Hill*, vol. 2 (Boston: Beacon Press, 1986), 89.

close it down. He had no such intention. Mayer also had no particular resources available for engineering. He needed a new Dean who would not demand much, who had the confidence of the faculty, but who also could start
moving the dead weight of the College forward. He found his man in Fred
Nelson, a graduate of the College, long-time faculty member, and Chairman
of the Department of Mechanical Engineering. He could have been just another of the good old boys, but he proved to be more. Nelson saw that Mayer
meant business about raising money, and although the engineers never
had any, he threw himself into Mayer's vision of more research. During his
fourteen-year tenure as Dean, from 1980 to 1994, Nelson soothed the old-
timers who wanted no change and worked around them. He made some good
appointments, raised more money than the engineers had ever seen before,
and placed the College of Engineering, still with very much an undergraduate teaching faculty, little or no national visibility, but with a few bright
young researchers, on a springboard where, with the right leadership, it
could leap forward. Nelson had bravely gone as far as he could. Bernstein,
who had served for many years at Carnegie Mellon University in engineering and knew what a first-rate school looked like, clearly saw how far back
Tufts engineering still remained. Now, to make things happen, he needed a
transformer.

The two most extraordinary entrepreneurs and change agents in Tufts
history were both immigrants who never lost their accents. They both brought
with them the immigrant's enthusiasm for America and a willingness to take
risks. One was Jean Mayer; the other was Ioannis (Yannis) Miaoulis, whom
Mel Bernstein named Dean of the College of Engineering in 1994. Miaoulis
was thirty-three years old and had already spent nearly half of his life at
Tufts. In 1980, he arrived from his native Athens, Greece, with a high school
diploma and landed on the campus in Medford, an energetic, irrepressible
teenager who spoke so fast that many could not understand half of what he
said. Over the years, it got a little better. From that point on, Tufts dominated
his life. With a brief time-out to acquire a Master's degree in Mechanical Engineering at M.I.T. in 1984, Miaoulis spent the next twenty-two years in a
love affair with his alma mater. After his B.S., he took an M.S. in Economics
and a Ph.D. in Mechanical Engineering at Tufts, married his undergraduate
sweetheart, and named his dogs after buildings on the campus. Before he left
in 2003 to become President of the Boston Museum of Science, he had repo-
sitioned Tufts Engineering from the tail end to the heart of the University.
His nine-year deanship was a model of what every provost prays for. He did
for the College of Engineering what Jean Mayer did for the University, even

championing a name change to the *School* of Engineering, which occurred in 2000. He lifted Engineering out from under the shadow of Arts and Sciences and elevated it to the same stature as the other Tufts schools.

It was not merely symbolic name changing. He took the instrument that Fred Nelson had given him and retooled it. Miaoulis realized that the key was superb faculty, research, and uniqueness: the individuality of the Tufts College of Engineering. Tufts Engineering could not hope to compete with those schools with a long research tradition, deep pockets, and infrastructure. Miaoulis had his own ideas: work with the other schools at Tufts, solve real-world problems with the treasures that lie in the crevices between disciplines, change the attitudes of Americans about engineering, and find faculty who loved to teach and also could be creative in their research. A headline in the October 13, 1999, *Wall Street Journal* stated, "In the Name of Science, Tufts Students Abuse Musical Instruments" and highlighted Professor Chris Rogers, a mechanical engineer and one of Miaoulis's favorites who had his students baking piano keys and freezing trumpets with liquid oxygen, to demonstrate how extreme conditions affect tone and sound. Miaoulis himself would run a cooking class with ovens and stoves to demonstrate the principles of heat transfer.

First, he had to sell his faculty on his vision, which generally met with enthusiasm. Some were suspicious that Miaoulis was a self-promoter. Those who opposed him had no ideas of their own, so the Dean's energy and focus carried the day. The isolated griping never stopped, but saying "no" can only get you so far. He also looked for every opportunity to make crucial appointments, particularly of people who intersected several disciplines. Miaoulis wanted the floundering Biotechnology Center to move to the center of a cooperative synergy with science departments in Arts and Sciences and with the health sciences downtown and in Grafton. He needed a first-rate scientist, a personality who could communicate, and an intellectual freethinker. He found the right person at the U.S. Army research labs in Natick, Massachusetts. His name was David Kaplan. His energy and transparent enthusiasm for new ideas pushed aside all the obstructions inherent in the traditional organizational structure of engineering schools. Hired as a chemical engineer and put in charge of the Bioengineering Center, Kaplan was part of the force that changed the name of the department to the Department of Chemical and Biological Engineering. His collaboration with the Medical School led to the creation of the Department of Biomedical Engineering at Tufts. Kaplan now oversees a Center that represents the strongest research effort in the School. He is a superb teacher and collaborator and has brought in other outstanding people from engineering centers at Tufts and across the university. Kaplan built a research relationship with Electro-optics and electrical engineering through Sergio Fantini, a young Florentine who had come from the University of Illinois. Kaplan reached out to the Biology Department and to the Sackler School; and he showed them how important his program could be for them. That was all they needed to see.

Miaoulis convinced Vice President Bernstein that there were opportunities now to gain some senior people for Tufts engineering, unthinkable only a few short years earlier. This could be coupled with another of Miaoulis's personal and professional hopes: to get more women into engineering and to get them to Tufts. Some of the senior faculty still did not believe Tufts Engineering could attract recognized scholars at all, much less females. Diane Souvaine was tenured at Rutgers and had established herself as a leader in the field of computational geometry. The Department of Electrical Engineering and Computer Science had an opening, and when they saw her application, they passed it over: She would not come, they "knew" it. Miaoulis looked over the applicant pool and saw immediately that Souvaine was by far the best available. When he heard about the timidity of the search committee to go after her, he personally contacted Professor Souvaine and made the pitch for Tufts. She joined the department in 1998 as an Associate Professor and was promoted to the final rank the next year, the second female full Professor in engineering in Tufts history. Earlier, Miaoulis had recruited from M.I.T. another senior faculty member in Chemical Engineering, Maria Flytzani-Stephanopoulos, who brought her funding with her and made full Professor soon after her arrival in Medford. Another was Lenore Cowen, a brilliant computer scientist and mathematician well on her way to tenure at Johns Hopkins when the Tufts Dean of Engineering convinced her of the enormous opportunities in Boston. During his tenure, the number of female faculty members grew to four times the national average at engineering schools, and the number of women engineering undergraduates was double the average.

Miaoulis was an innovator in curriculum. Tufts became the only national engineering school with a net gain of transfers between engineering and the undergraduate liberal arts programs. He saw the opportunity created by Chaisson and Thornton and pushed hard on K–12 science and technology/engineering education. He spearheaded the formal introduction of engineering into the public school curriculum in Massachusetts and began working with other states to expand the effort nationally.

Inside Tufts, he found willing partners in the Medical, Dental, and Vet schools, as well as at Fletcher. Innovative joint and dual degree programs sprouted everywhere. By 2000, the School of Engineering was the center of the Tufts wheel and was receiving national recognition. Miaoulis now had some fully funded endowed chairs at his disposal, and could go after some genuine luminaries. In 1999, he recruited Steven Chapra for the Louis Berger Chair in Civil and Environmental Engineering from the University of Michigan. Chapra was a national and international figure in the field of water quality modeling and numerical methods of advanced computer applications in environmental engineering. Ten years earlier, he would not have dreamt of coming to Tufts.

Miaoulis had accomplished what he had set out to do: to make Engineering at Tufts distinguished and unique. He had done it through smart hiring of junior faculty and by finding the occasional star, without capitulating to the national trend of making celebrity hires who for the most part stayed away from the classroom. As the 1990s progressed and academic reputation was based increasingly on the star power of the faculty, many presidents, provosts, and deans became celebrity headhunters. The *Chronicle's* "Peer Review" column was a measure of this, a "Who's Who" and who is going where, with what graduate student, and leaving which spouse behind. Salaries for these free agents were generally off the charts. Hiring away a great academic star provided a two-fold benefit: It diminished one institution and gave instant reputation to another. It came down to how the *U.S. News & World Report* calculated its standings. Fully 25 percent of academic reputation was based on opinions garnered from presidents, many of whom by this time were professional CEOs without specific knowledge of what constituted academic excellence.

Bernstein was not a charismatic leader like Mayer or Miaoulis. There will be those who, when reading these lines, will find it hard to acknowledge what he accomplished in the Arts and Sciences. He was actually a shy person who had aspirations for leadership that never really meshed with his personality. He never got the university presidency he had hoped for, but he was a builder. Bernstein had led his deans to find the right mix of outstanding junior and senior faculty who bought into the Tufts philosophy: the teaching college where research is important and everyone does it. He understood that Tufts would never tolerate the sacrifice of teaching for research, and celebrity hiring was just not the way he wanted to go. He had to mold the right departments that had the capacity to advance a research agenda while maintaining the traditional Tufts standards of undergraduate excellence. Bernstein even helped the anomalous Physics Department, that research-driven group, to re-shape its thinking by bringing in two senior appointments in Peggy Cebe from MIT and Roger Tobin from Michigan, both of whom turned out to be terrific teachers and funded researchers who loved undergraduates. The key for Tufts would always be finding faculty who did not come with the expectation of a reduced teaching "load" or who sought to buy their time away from the classroom.

Some departments presented very special problems. In Economics, with hundreds of undergraduate majors, no Ph.D. program, and a field where high-quality research required lighter teaching assignments, serious administrative support and financial commitment, Bernstein had to figure out a way to create a first-rate department in the Tufts image. As you examine the benchmark or aspiration departments around the country, they all seem to have doctoral programs along with the problems associated with having Ph.D. students to mentor. As it was, Economics at Tufts never seemed to have enough faculty. Whenever there was contention among the undergraduate population about a shortage of faculty, historically the focus would fall on Economics. Bernstein was determined to rebuild the department and infuse it with needed new and enriched blood. He found Gilbert Metcalf at Princeton, where he had just missed receiving tenure in a ferociously competitive department. Metcalf was perfect for Tufts: a superb teacher who loved being in the classroom, with a nationally recognized expertise in taxation. He came as an advanced tenure candidate in 1994, was tenured and promoted twice to full Professor in a few years, took over the chairmanship of the department, and became an acknowledged campus leader. Trustee Joe Neubauer gave the department an incremental chair in international economics. The search resulted in two outstanding finalists. The chair was given to Yannis Ioannides, who became the first to be hired since Frank Holzman thirty years earlier at the full Professor level in the history of the Economics Department. Bernstein was so impressed with the runner-up that he authorized a second slot in economics for another full Professor, George Norman, who came from the University of Edinburgh. Never in Tufts history had two full professors joined a department in the same year! A few years later, another Trustee, Bill Cummings, endowed a chair in Business Entrepreneurship for Norman. Tom Downes came in with Metcalf on the traditional tenure track, made it, is an outstanding teacher, and has co-authored a frequently cited paper with an undergraduate. Even in a department that does not offer the Ph.D., Economics has been able to attract and keep a much deeper pool of superb teacher-scholars. The tenure-track junior faculty love their undergraduate teaching, and as departmental chairman Metcalf describes them, " publish in better journals, participate in better conferences, and network with top scholars in the discipline. Karen Eggleston's book [on reforming the health sector in Eastern Europe, written with Harvard's Janos Kornai] has now been translated into three languages." He also had some strong people from the Mayer era who had remained at Tufts. Drusilla Brown had helped in the writing of the NAFTA legislation and was a well-known econometrician. The Economics Department had never before in its history attained this overall level of excellence.

Well-informed and experienced academic administrators at other institutions have always been stunned when informed that the Arts, Sciences and Engineering at Tufts award no more than thirty-five doctorates annually. There are no Ph.D. programs in economics, political science, and international relations; in the social sciences, only psychology and child development give the doctoral degree. We did not need any more start-up doctoral programs that mirrored the mediocrity of the graduate efforts at Tufts of the 1950s and early 1960s, but if we could build on what we had that was already strong, research could expand. Bernstein targeted child development as a growth opportunity. This unique department was perfect for what he had in mind. It was an extraordinary interdisciplinary group of educators, psychologists, physicians, attorneys, social policy analysts, child life specialists, sociolinguists, and other professionals committed to early childhood issues. It attracted hundreds of undergraduate majors, offered a variety of Master's degrees, and in 1981 established the first Ph.D. in the nation in Applied Child Development. Technically, the department was called the Eliot-Pearson Department of Child Study (later changed to Child Development), named after two pioneering women who in the 1920s dedicated themselves to improving the quality of life of very young children. By the 1950s, Tufts was thinking of getting rid of this program that the faculty, particularly in Psychology, considered without standards, too applied ("What is a nursery school doing on a college campus?!"), and alien to a liberal arts education. But, in 1959, a new Director of the Eliot-Pearson School, Evelyn Pitcher, came to Tufts from Yale and the laboratory of Arnold Gessell, and saw the future, yet another example of the right person in the right place at the right time. In 1964, she oversaw the full integration of the school into Tufts and the creation of the Eliot-Pearson Department of Child Study, in the Arts and Sciences. Jean Mayer took a major interest in the department, because he saw issues of childhood public health and nutrition as critical to the nation's well being. The Department brought David Elkind from the University of Rochester to succeed Pitcher as Chairman in 1979. The Ph.D. program in Applied Child

Development granted its first doctorate in 1987. By 1991, Eliot-Pearson was named one of the leading childhood education programs in the nation.

Bernstein wanted to reach one more level of accomplishment for this unique department. Again, a Trustee played a major role. Like Joe Neubauer, who had been an economics major, Joan (Margosian) Bergstrom's choice of Child Study as her undergraduate major was destined to shape her life. She went on to a distinguished career in childhood education, became a Trustee, and paid back by endowing the Bergstrom Family Chair in Applied Developmental Science, in 1997 the nation's first professorship explicitly framed in ADS terms. Richard Lerner was appointed to the Bergstrom Chair in 1999 and quickly established the Applied Developmental Institute as one of the department's premiere laboratory and outreach centers.

The same search for uniqueness attracted Bernstein to Trustee Bernard Gordon, founder and chairman of Analogic Corporation. Gordon was a genuine contrarian who had nothing but contempt for the traditional engineering education that he found everywhere. He was creative, aggressive, opinionated, and a bold thinker with his own ideas about educating the next generation of engineers. With Bernstein's and Murnane's nurturing, Bernie Gordon funded the establishment of the Gordon Institute at Tufts, a Master's degree program in engineering management that promised something special in engineering entrepreneurship.

Bernstein's fingerprints were to be found on several other important activities in the 1990s. He found resources in the Arts and Sciences budget to increase dramatically the commitment to library acquisitions, both print and technological. The collection of the Wessell Library was perhaps the single greatest embarrassment to Tufts and a genuine impediment to progress. Bernstein had as a goal the creation of a very good undergraduate research library. This was brought to realization on his watch and through his will. By the time in the late 1990s when the Wessell Library had morphed into the Tisch Library, both faculty and undergraduate student body could view the facility with some pride.

His greatest challenge was replacing the generation of great faculty who were already retiring when Jean Mayer was still president, those dedicated, totally student-oriented "givers" whose presence permitted Mayer to make the kinds of changes that brought Tufts a national and international eminence. When it came to surveys of research and citations, these people were not very visible. But if you asked students who were the cherished faculty, you heard the names of Dan Ounjian, Jim Elliott, Seymour Simches, Zella Luria, Sylvia Feinburg, Ivan Galantic, Lucille Palubinskas, and many others who held this place together during the difficult years of the 1960s and 1970s, and continued to provide stability for Mayer's inventiveness. Bernstein grasped early on what Tufts had been all about and also understood what was needed. With his deans and department chairs, he found a new generation of scholars who still had the classroom fire to inspire the undergraduates, but who represented a higher level of scholarly productivity than Tufts had historically attracted before Mayer's arrival. Kevin Dunn in English, Metcalf and Downes, Marcello Bianconi, Dan Richards, and Lynne Pepall in Economics, Jeanne Penvenne and Gerald Gill in History, Andrew McClellan and Dan Abramson in Art History, Barbara Grossman in Drama, Malik Mufti and Rob Devigne in Political Science, outstanding teachers all, along with many others, yet rigorous scholars, intellectually engaged with the national and international guild to which they belonged. Even the legendary Tufts Hillel Director, Rabbi Jeffrey Summit, who arrived shortly after Mayer, not only became an inspirational teacher, but received his Ph.D. from Tufts in ethnomusicology and went on to an outstanding scholarly career.

Bernstein also knew how to nurture the giants whom he inherited. If there had been a Nobel Prize in Philosophy, it might have gone to Dan Dennett, this extraordinarily productive and inventive thinker who had come to Tufts in 1971 and chose to remain. Dennett had received offers for endowed chairs, funded centers, embellishments of all shapes and forms. Bernstein haunted the Development people and pressed efforts to secure proper funding for Dennett's Center for Cognitive Studies. He created the position of Distinguished Arts and Sciences Professor for Dennett and prevailed upon the Trustees to make him a University Professor. He was an ardent cheerleader for Tufts' most distinguished faculty member.

Another was David Walt, a brilliant investigator who had almost single-handedly turned the Chemistry Department into a productive research enterprise and was a major force in persuading David Kaplan to come to Tufts. Mayer had promised him the moon, and Walt had been provided with just enough resources to keep him hanging on. But, as his reputation grew, his dissatisfaction with Tufts increased, and he was on the verge of leaving. Bernstein put his arms around him, made major commitments to research space and to the Walt Group, which was centered at the chemistry-biology interface, clearly a breakthrough opportunity of significance. Walt paid back the university in multiples with the first $8 million of licensing fees that came from the sale of the fiber optical chemical sensor technology that his patents, held by Tufts, produced.

Finally, Mel Bernstein was also a street-smart kid from New York City who knew how to play the Game. When *U.S. News and World Report*'s College and University issue began to tyrannize administrators and trustees, Bernstein noted that an old friend from high school, Mel Elfin, was editor-in-charge of the special edition. He renewed the friendship, brought Elfin to Tufts for a schmooze or two. It was during the DiBiaggio presidency, while Bernstein led the Arts, Sciences and Engineering, that Tufts moved to visible prominence on the list. It was the reputation, success, and extraordinary rise in visibility of the Arts, Sciences and Engineering that brought Tufts to the attention of the competitive academic magazine world. Mel Bernstein was there for every step of the way.

He left after ten years at Tufts, cheered by some, unappreciated by most for what he had accomplished. He sensed that it was time to leave. Henry Rosovsky, the distinguished Dean of Harvard Arts and Sciences in 1980s, had heard that message once before. He had gone to see the movie *Amadeus,* the study of two musical lives, one an immature, vain genius (Mozart), the other a hard-working, decent but average talent (Salieri). After he came out of the movie, Rosovsky realized that he had been rooting for Salieri.[5] His faculty was filled with unappreciative Mozarts whom he simply could not stand any longer. It was time to go.

So it was also for Mel Bernstein. What he left behind was a vastly better faculty and enterprise. It was a great time to be the leader of the Arts, Sciences and Engineering at Tufts. At it happened, he was also the second and last Vice President for the undergraduate colleges at Tufts. A new president had a new vision that would take this faculty to still greater heights.

FLETCHER: LIVING WITHOUT THE COLD WAR

For schools of advanced international relations, the 1990s was an often confusing period. With the collapse of the Soviet Union on Christmas Day, 1991, the hawks and doves of the Cold War discovered a world much less Manichean, with shades of gray replacing the simplicity of black and white. The conflicts in Chechnya, Rwanda, Somalia, the remnants of Yugoslavia, and the Middle East left most Americans grasping for heroes and villains, as we tried to assess the players. Were Yeltsin and Putin good guys or bad? How do we assess the leadership of China? Were the Chinese partners or competitors? Saddam Hussein made it easier when he invaded Kuwait in 1990,

---

5. Henry Rosovsky, *The University: An Owner's Manual* (New York: W.W. Norton and Company, 1990), 241–42.

because it provided this country with an unambiguous demon. But Americans, notoriously lacking in geographic literacy, had to scratch hard to find Serbia, Croatia, or Bosnia on a map of Europe. When they turned to Africa, most had a memory of a colonial past contemporary with *The African Queen* and World War I. President Clinton seemed to reflect all of these uncertainties regarding America's position in the world, an uncertainty that bordered on disinterest. The mantra that won him the presidency over a fairly internationally oriented George Bush was "It's the economy, stupid." It was the economy that got Bush beaten, and it was to the domestic economy that Bill Clinton turned. Warren Christopher, his first Secretary of State, was not your typically imperial statesman. Clinton had two options, and seemed to want to avoid activism abroad. He did not press America's strategic, super-power advantage. In fact, he followed in the religious, born-again Christian Baptist tradition of Jimmy Carter and his running mate Al Gore and bought into the humanitarian mission of America. This was Jesus of turning the other cheek, not Jesus the warrior king modeled on King David, who was embraced by the next American president. Even though the Clinton presidency was drawn into conflict around the world, America went sometimes reluctantly and always as a cooperative part of a larger venture. "Peace keeping" and "humanitarian assistance" were phrases that fairly characterized America's attitude, even when we sent troops to Bosnia or Somalia, were bombing the Serbs or responding to terror attacks on our embassies in Kenya, Tanzania, and Saudi Arabia. In 1998, Osama bin Laden was named for the first time as the mastermind behind the embassy bombings. In the Middle East, it seemed that the President was asking, through Ambassador Christopher, "Can't we all be friends?" Madeleine Albright had more activist instincts, but it was too late for the Clinton administration to become really interventionist, even after the Dayton accords and the Oslo agreements. While al-Qa'ida was attempting to blow up the World Trade Center in 1993, and the FBI was uncovering plots hatched abroad that threatened America, there apparently never was a thought by the Clinton administration in the 1990s to press the American presence aggressively around the world, the policy embraced so totally by his successor.

The country's attention seemed riveted on the extraordinary performance of the stock market and the economic boom. In 1995, the Dow-Jones Industrial index topped 4000 for the first time in history. By February of 1997, it passed 7000; four months later it swept by 8000. In April 1999, the Dow-Jones crossed into what had been thought unreachable territory when it surpassed 10,000, and then in the *next month,* went beyond 11,000. The technology index, the NASDAQ composite, ended the year over 4000, two months after crossing the 3000 barrier.

The other great attention-getter was President Clinton's domestic difficulties and sexual adventures, which led to his impeachment hearing before Congress. But his approval ratings with the public were tied to the economy and not to his infidelity. The more difficult that Congress made it for him, the greater the percentage of Americans who approved of his performance as President. The domestic economy's success was all they seemed to care about. With budget surpluses in the billions and trillions being projected, the country was in a state of optimistic, domestic euphoria, and the Republicans were just glad that the President could not run for a third term.

Nonetheless, the United States had emerged out of the Cold War as the world's sole superpower, and our colleges were producing thousands of young men and women interested in international relations who envisioned a career with some form of global involvement. These interests took form in two very different arenas. The instinct toward humanitarian assistance led to the creation of many nongovernmental organizations determined to make this into a better and safer world. Groups such as Physicians Without Borders and Greenpeace had become clearly international. Students were drawn to international issues of health, nutrition, famine, human and animal welfare, and a host of other concerns. The second area of enormous student interest was the globalization of business and trade and the emergence of the multinational corporation. As we entered the last decade of the century, the curriculum of schools of international relations had to reflect these changes. These were students who were more mature than the average college graduate, because they had gone to work, had some international experience, and now, after perhaps three or four years of honing their skills in foreign languages and cultures, were ready; and the Fletcher School had to be ready for them.

When Jes Salacuse had first visited Medford in 1985 in connection with the search for a new dean to succeed Ted Eliot, we spent some time in head-to-head conversation. At one point he fell silent, and I could see that something was on his mind. "Shoot," I told him, "I need to hear everything that concerns you." Salacuse had asked a group of students about their greatest worry. They expressed a fear that Fletcher's academic reality was less than its reputation, and they were worried because that reality would inevitably catch up with the reputation. A small group of faculty had also expressed concern to him about the academic program and the need, as one member said, for "academic leadership." It was at this point that I told Salacuse, should he become the Fletcher Dean, he would have complete support from the President and the Provost. Major rebuilding of the faculty was vital. I knew this was a school living on its hump, and the comments made by these students to the candidate for the deanship made it clear that they recognized this fact, as well. Fletcher had little more than its past reputation. In 1986, only the security studies program really reflected the current international realities, but Ted Eliot had granted no one tenure, and there would be plenty of latitude for reconfiguring the faculty. After Salacuse accepted the deanship, I told him to build, and he knew I meant it. By the time he left in 1994, no one was expressing concerns about the quality of the faculty. A dean can have that kind of impact.

The appointments made during the Salacuse deanship formed the bedrock of Fletcher excellence for the rest of the century. There were a few high-quality holdovers: Bob Pfaltzgraff and Dick Shultz in security studies and Al Rubin in international law. But this was not a sufficient foundation for the future. Fletcher needed more than just friendly and available teachers. It needed scholars and practitioners who had a place in the best research centers of the changing world, and these were the people that Salacuse set out to find.

Fletcher had good fortune in the geographic interests of these most recent two deans. Ted Eliot was the last—and only—living former American Ambassador to Afghanistan, his successor having been assassinated in the course of his service. He had a profound interest in this abused part of the world and he pushed for the appointment of Andrew Hess, who joined the Fletcher faculty in 1984 as Professor of Diplomacy and Director of the Program for Southwest Asia and Islamic Civilization. Hess worked at the non-Arabic intersection of Islam and Asia: Turkey, Iran, and Afghanistan. He had a book published by the University of Chicago Press, was well connected with the Saudis and the Arabian American Oil Company (Aramco), and was already a cut above much of Fletcher scholarship. Jes Salacuse had a background writing legal systems for Islamic countries and experience in Africa and the Middle East. When he arrived in 1986, he immediately saw where the strength of Middle Eastern scholarship was in Medford and began courting Professor Leila Fawaz of the Arts and Sciences History Department, who took her first joint appointment in 1987 and has been a force at Fletcher ever since. With Hess and Fawaz, soon to become President of the Middle East Studies Association (MESA), Fletcher established credibility that represented the first serious increase in its academic reputation in years.

Salacuse had no patience with any of the arched detachment of former Fletcher administrations or alumni when it came to the relationship with

Tufts. He was quick to see what Mayer was up to, spotted the stars in Arts and Sciences who could help Fletcher, and realized that he needed a strategy for building Fletcher's reputation. He was also confident enough to build on himself, because he saw where the future of Fletcher and the APSIA schools lay: in a post–Cold War world of international business and trade, global negotiations and transactions. As the Soviet Union was in the process of collapsing, Salacuse was building a post–Cold War curriculum for Fletcher. Before coming to Fletcher, he felt very comfortable in two distinct academic environments: law and business. After a close examination of the Fletcher curriculum, the new Dean immediately recognized the threat from the increasingly international focus of law and business schools. His first two appointments—he did not need an academic dean for this essential and most deanly activity—were lawyers, one with a business focus, the other to replace Leo Gross, the great old Europeanist who bridged the League of Nations and the United Nations.

Joel Trachtman represented the perfect fusion of disciplines the minute he joined the faculty in 1989. At Harvard Law School he had been Editor-in-chief of the *Harvard International Law Journal* before graduating in 1980 and joining Shearman & Sterling, a law firm in New York City and Hong Kong with wide international business experience. Trachtman remained with the firm until 1989, when the academic bug bit him, and he looked around for the perfect match. He found it at Fletcher. This lawyer-scholar with research interests in international trade, international economic integration, and international business and finance regulation, was publishing in the best journals of international law and finance and eventually would go on to membership on the boards of the *American Journal of International Law, Journal of International Economic Law,* and *European Journal of International Law.* The duo of Salacuse and Trachtman gave Fletcher instant applied and academic reputation and laid the foundation for the model of a law and business program in a school of advanced international relations.

No one could forget Leo Gross. When he died in 1990, he left behind generations of Fletcher students who represented a link with the first half of the century, to the twin ideologies of fascism and communism in their European context that had dominated Gross's time on earth. Now, Salacuse looked for someone who understood the explosion of ethnicity that already was marking the disintegration of the Yugoslav federation and threatened every corner of the earth, from Tatarstan and Chechnya, to Sri Lanka and East Timor. He needed a Leo Gross for a new world, and he found him in Hurst Hannum, who developed a curriculum in human rights law, peacekeeping, nationalism, and ethnicity that prepared Fletcher students for the unforeseen complexities of a world that seemed out of balance. Hannum was another scholar-lawyer, author of a half-dozen volumes on self-determination, conflicting rights, and the relationship of international human rights and U.S. constitutional law. Like Gross, he worked closely with the United Nations. Now, there were scholars working at the interface of law, human rights, emerging nations, and global negotiations.

The makeover of the Fletcher faculty under Salacuse continued in the fields of economics and business. Lisa Lynch came from MIT's Sloan School of Management in 1993. She was a superb labor economist and outstanding teacher. Her applied talent almost lost her to government work, when in 1995 she went on leave to serve as Chief Economist for the U.S. Department of Labor, but Medford had greater pull than Washington, and she returned to anchor the economics program. Macroeconomist Michael Klein joined her in 1991 and together they began a process that should have occurred years earlier: the shaping of an economics effort on the Hill at Medford that included Arts and Sciences as well as Nutrition. In the aggregate, there was considerable strength, but it took new people with no memory to set aside the pettiness that had kept the walls thick and the hurdles high. With the arrival of Professor Laurent Jacque to teach international corporate finance and global financial services, the Fletcher effort in international law, business, and economics had reached a level of professional reputation unique in the school's history, under Salacuse's leadership.

The Dean wanted to drive one more stake into the ground in demarcating Fletcher territory. By the 1980s, the issue of environmentalism was reaching around the world by means of provocation and political action. Here was a field where advocacy seemed to capture the imagination of people on all sides but showed little success in converting this energy into a sensible global policy. The advanced schools of international relations were having a difficult time in getting a handle on such a political issue that seemed to generate more passion than reason. Salacuse, himself a deft international negotiator and a committed environmentalist, was ready to move into a field where no other APSIA school had tread.

He needed the right combination of scholarly reputation and interpersonal skills to make the Fletcher initiative in environmentalism work. The potential for failure in a discipline marked by partisan polemics was great. In addition, the normally consultative Dean, dead certain in all of his faculty instincts, took this one on alone. He did not want the back-and-forth of endless faculty discussions that he knew for certain an appointment of this kind, in a new area for Fletcher, would engender. His instincts alone guided him this time. This was an appointment whose time had come. Salacuse was looking for maturity, unimpeachable integrity, and diplomacy. He found it next door, in the person of William Moomaw, a final and ironic legacy of Jean Mayer.

In the early 1980s, the fact that the federal government was pouring dollars into environmental initiatives did not escape Cassidy & Associates. President Mayer met with Cassidy right after Love Canal and returned from Washington to inform me that Tufts would be making a major initiative in environmentalism with a grant from the Environmental Protection Agency for several million dollars of start-up funds and continuous funding. I was concerned. As I looked around the various faculties, there was no sighting of any particular strength in this field or promise of success. We had a couple of modestly reputed engineers in civil engineering working on ground water pollution and the public health people in the Medical School, led by Morton Madoff, who could not get along with anyone on the Medford campus. We needed to get a proposal in front of Senator Kennedy and Congressmen O'Neill, Conte, and Boland, but no one on the faculty knew enough about hazardous waste. Tom Murnane, who always had a name, found John Bewick, who was just stepping down as Secretary for the Environment. Bewick came on as a consultant, wrote the grant proposal, and Tufts got the funding. What I did not know was that the President—as was frequently the case— already had his eye on a Director. Anthony Cortese, who was stepping down as Commissioner of the Massachusetts Department of Environmental Protection, appeared at Tufts after a perfunctory search, along with the first $2.5 million grant from the EPA.

As usual with Mayer's personal intervention in hiring, something remarkable happened. Cortese came to Tufts in 1984, through the force of his energy created something he called the Center for Environmental Management (CEM), and with the federal money started paying faculty to get interested in environmental issues. He was himself less scientist and more policy advocate, an environmental Pied Piper who inspired the students and knew how to get his Center in the news. He initiated training programs on asbestos, got industry involved, traveled all over the world, and put Tufts on the map environmentally. In 1989, he was made Dean for Environmental Programs at Tufts. Cortese now had an opportunity to bring in an outstanding environmental scientist who could drive the programs forward without having to entice the faculty with financial rewards.

Tony Cortese brought William Moomaw to Tufts. He had spent most of his first twenty-five years of academic life at Williams College as a tenured professor of Chemistry who started one of the nation's first environmental centers in 1982. He had tasted policy implementation, as legislative consultant from 1976 to 1983 to Senator Dale Bumpers, and by 1990 needed a bigger environmental playing field than bucolic Williamstown. Cortese knew of Moomaw's scholarly reputation and brought him to Tufts as his Director of Research and Policy Development in 1989. It was in that capacity that he met Dean Salacuse, who saw in this tall, elegant, and dignified environmentalist with a worldwide reputation for fairness and scientific credibility the perfect instrument. In 1992, Moomaw accepted an appointment at Fletcher as Professor of International Environmental Policy, the first scientist ever appointed to a tenure track at an APSIA school. The Dean's agenda was complete. He resigned and returned to the faculty in 1994.

The success of the Salacuse deanship had silenced those now reasonably small number of old-time Fletcher alumni who still wanted distance between Tufts and Fletcher. It had become clear after the Mayer presidency and during the heady *U.S. News and World Report* days of university rankings that Tufts University sat among the very best institutions in the country, and the Fletcher School did not have to worry about its reputation being tarnished. There was no outcry from alumni, faculty, or students when I appointed myself chairman of the search committee for Salacuse's successor. We played by the same rules: I will take at least two candidates under advisement, consult with President DiBiaggio, and we would announce our choice. One final contribution that Jes Salacuse made was in opening up the curriculum in such a way as to make the extraordinarily interdisciplinary aspect of Fletcher more visible. In doing so, it also opened up the possibility of finding a dean from many different quarters of the international world.

I assisted by breaking the mould set by the Ambassadors Gullion and Eliot. We were not wedded to diplomats, particularly ambassadors. The search committee took its charge eagerly: cast the net as wide as possible; find scholars, career diplomats, people from business, law, journalism, nonprofit leadership, academia, any field that Fletcher touched. As almost an afterthought, Bob Pfaltzgraff asked, "What about the military?" We all agreed immediately: absolutely, yes.

That afterthought proved to be prescient. Before the visiting phase of the search was reached, the review of resumes of potential candidates shook some of us loose from our stereotypes. One could not help but be curious to meet four-star General John R. Galvin, who had served as NATO Supreme Allied Commander in Europe and Commander-in-Chief of the U.S. Army,

Navy, and Air Forces in Europe during the five years that ended the Cold War. Yet, when you peeled away the military life, there were two books on the American Revolution, a Master's degree in English at Columbia, and post-graduate study at Penn that was leading to a dissertation on William Butler Yeats when he took off for a couple of years to complete his military obligations, which led to a forty-year career in the Army. In 1971, he had done a year's fellowship at Fletcher. I wanted to meet him.

When Jack Galvin appeared at the required public interview for all Fletcher candidates before a packed auditorium that included some from a dubious Arts and Sciences community, there was a low-grade but palpable feeling of hostility. His first sentence was, "Do I look like Norman Schwarz-kopf?" Indeed, he did not, and his disarming question drew a spontaneous laugh. He was short, white-haired, and soft-spoken but warmly gregarious, and had an accent reminiscent of his native Wakefield, Massachusetts. He spoke informally for thirty minutes about his background and almost accidental career in the army. The first question came from a Fletcher student." What do you think of the military's position on homosexuals?" He handled it with diplomacy, humanity, and understanding. In an hour he had totally disarmed his audience without firing a shot.

Two months later, the final selection came down to a superb legal scholar at Georgetown, a woman; and Jack Galvin. I was genuinely torn, because a woman leading Fletcher would have provided a great opportunity to break out of the overwhelmingly male orientation of these APSIA schools. But I already had an eye on the future Dean after the one we were just about to select, and *she* was already on the Fletcher faculty. Galvin had told me he would give Fletcher no more than five years, but that was enough for me. President DiBiaggio concurred in my choice; John R. Galvin, General of the U.S. Army, retired, would become the sixth Dean of the Fletcher School of Law and Diplomacy. On September 1, 1995, he took office.

After his first year as Dean, Jack Galvin told me that managing twenty-nine generals from sixteen different countries had not prepared him for dealing with a faculty. He said it in jest, but he meant it. He also loved the challenge and was quick to see his own strengths and weaknesses. Two books on the Revolutionary War did not give him the scholarly credibility that the faculty demanded, and Galvin was quick to select an Academic Dean. He chose first the Middle Eastern scholar Andrew Hess, then, at my urging, turned to one of the most respected members of the faculty, Joel Trachtman.

"Jack" Galvin did not take on the Fletcher deanship so he could sit back in an academic rocking chair and smell the roses until retirement. At age sixty-five, he had all the retirement money he needed, and he overruled his wife, who was ready to spend time with the grandchildren and was not interested in her husband having another "command." He loved his earlier fellowship year at Fletcher and had not fully scratched the academic itch he acquired during his graduate years at Columbia and Penn. He also wanted to teach and to build. The NATO experience of integration served Galvin well at Tufts, and he moved expeditiously in aligning Fletcher more closely to the university. The Fletcher "Visiting Committee" took its name originally from the Harvard tradition, while the rest of Tufts' schools had "Boards of Overseers." Galvin worked closely with his chairman, Trustee Peter Ackerman, an energetic and creative venture capitalist, who had a son coming into the undergraduate college. Ackerman had two Master's degrees and a Ph.D. from Fletcher, appreciated what Tufts had become and was ready to move with his new Dean. Together, they converted the "Visiting Committee" to a Fletcher Board of Overseers, in line with the other schools, and looked for their best opportunity to draw closer to programs in the medical and veterinary schools, nutrition and engineering. In his second annual report, Galvin told the President: "Most important in the long run, Fletcher is linking with other parts of the University to a greater degree than ever before and will continue to do so . . . We envision a future of combinations on all levels that will offer students and faculty a rich tapestry of interdisciplinary teaching, learning, and research opportunities, which should continue to contribute to the impressive rise of the university over the past twenty years." Dean Galvin's experience in Bosnia and Iraq had driven home the idea of humanitarian assistance in his mind, and he fully appreciated the link between medical assistance, rebuilding social infrastructures, and military force. He had helped rescue 450,000 Kurdish refugees in Northern Iraq and had been intimately involved in negotiations in Bosnia to relieve the people's misery. He understood poverty from his childhood days in Wakefield and service in Latin America and Vietnam. Galvin wanted Fletcher to make a difference in a larger world beyond diplomacy or security. Humanitarian assistance programs that he advocated led to Fletcher and Nutrition School-trained Tufts veterinarians being the only outsiders permitted to cross the battle lines in the Sudan, where they were allowed to vaccinate cattle on both sides of the civil war—veterinarians who understood the art of negotiation and the nutritional needs of the indigenous populations; Fletcher graduates who were sensitive to the cultural nuances of native traditions: Galvin took Salacuse's bequest to the next level.

But, if there is one legacy for which Galvin's deanship will be remembered, it will, ironically, be associated with technology. On Jack Galvin's watch, the Fletcher School pioneered the first distance-learning graduate degree at any APSIA school. It was only fitting that the university made it happen.

I had mentioned earlier that Steve Manos had been a pivotal mover and shaker in making information technology available to a faculty who, in the early 1980s, had little idea where to go with this new tool. By the mid-1990s, with proprietorial for-profit universities popping up all over the country based on the distance-learning technology, experts were predicting the demise of campus-based education. Manos wanted Tufts to get involved with distance learning in some capacity. He put his hands on $1 million and went shopping, first to the Arts and Sciences. He asked Mel Bernstein if he was interested in a distance-learning project, but Bernstein saw no application for his school and turned Manos down. Manos went to Fletcher, and to Jack Galvin, who jumped at it.

The challenge was enormous. The very idea that you could teach anyone who was sitting somewhere else other than the classroom was particularly alien to the seminar-oriented Fletcher faculty, who cherished their small groups and intimacy with their students. Galvin would place himself on the line, work hard to convince the faculty that this was a path-breaking idea that would strengthen Fletcher, and lead the way for others. He needed an implementer and found her in the person of Associate Dean Deborah Nutter, an administrator with great organizational skills, a Ph.D. in international relations, and a prior career behind her as a tenured faculty member at Simmons College. With the million dollars in hand and Steve Manos as the cheerleader, Galvin and Nutter jumped into the battle. At first there were enormous faculty doubts. Galvin made himself vulnerable to criticism, Associate Dean Nutter needed a suit of armor and protective camouflage, but they pressed forward with the idea of a year-long graduate program in international affairs, combining short residency sessions, Internet-mediated collaboration, and faculty-produced multi-media content. The program would be designed specifically for mid- to high-level professionals who were unable to attend a traditional residence-based Master's degree. In addition, the program would be unlike the impersonal products of the big state universities or the for-profit institutions, which were functionally lacking in any human contact. While Nutter looked for the cutting edge of computer-mediated education technology, Galvin worked on overcoming faculty resistance. They built into their program two three-week residency sessions that would bring the participants together. By combining these short residencies and computer-mediated instruction, Nutter could show the faculty that they

"His final wish was that all his medical bills be paid promptly."

were not sacrificing the special quality of faculty-student contact that Fletcher had come to cherish. The first breakthrough came with his Academic Dean, Joel Trachtman, who was perfectly prepared to tell his Dean he would not participate; instead, he saw the light and bought in, which began an enormous faculty learning effort. There would be money, yes, but not all the remuneration in the world could compensate for the time and effort to make a faculty as computer literate as this effort would require. With Trachtman joining the effort, Galvin needed a senior convert, and he found him in the person of the former Dean, Jes Salacuse, who threw himself enthusiastically into the project. When Bob Pflatzgraff, the senior faculty member in term of service at Fletcher and a major force in the faculty joined up, the battle was won. In 2000, with the faculty completely trained and the marketing surveys complete, the Global Master of Arts Program (GMAP) was rolled out amidst anxiety and hope. The positive response was immediate. Applications came rolling in from all corners of the world. Jack Galvin stepped down as Fletcher Dean at the end of the year. He had taken the school into the twenty-first century and had bonded Fletcher to the university.

THE SCHOOL OF MEDICINE: A PROFESSION LOSES ITS WAY

In spite of enormous medical advancements that took place in the last quarter of the twentieth century, the crisis in health management in the United States deepened in the 1990s and affected every aspect of the medical profession. The pain was pervasive; there was no accepted diagnosis of the illness, and no cure in sight. The American medical community had for years been telling citizens that our system was the envy of the world and provided Americans with the best medical care anywhere. But as America entered the last decade of the century, people were beginning to have their doubts. How could a country, unlike any in the world in terms of generosity, giving nearly $200 *billion* in philanthropy, still not come up with a comprehensive national health plan? It seemed that any effort to solve the problem of health care was shot down immediately. The newly elected President's spouse, Hillary Rodham Clinton, had an office in the White House where she established a committee in 1993 to overhaul the nation's health care system. Regardless of the merits of her plan, she drew the ire of the insurance and pharmaceutical industries, the medical and hospital associations, as well as every other interest group that feared government regulation or, worse, price controls, and the effort collapsed. In the meantime, estimates ranged up to forty million Americans who were without health care coverage. Insurance companies were squeezing the health maintenance organizations, which in turn were pushing the hospitals to more efficiency. The hospitals and HMOs were pressuring the doctors to see more and more patients and to spend less time teaching. There was scarcely a moment even to think about research, and the National Institutes of Health were worried that the physician-investigator, considered the best in the world, would not have time to apply for grants. Pharmaceutical companies were driving up the costs of drugs, fighting the availability of cheaper generic products, while at the same time conducting massive advertising campaigns pushing their name brands. Even hospitals were getting into the act in the 1990s with television, radio, and newspaper marketing blitzes. Every newspaper seemed to describe a system in chaos that was broken. Routinely, stories appeared about resident physicians who were working 100-hour weeks to the point of exhaustion, or how the clinical aspect of medical training was in disarray because there was no time to teach. Worst of all, medical research came under scrutiny as never before, first as promise, then as peril, and finally as greed. In the 1980s, everything that could be done to help speed medical discoveries *was* done. But, in the 1990s, several high-profile patient deaths in gene therapy trials conducted by physicians who, it was alleged, had a financial conflict of interest, caused a deep loss of public confidence and raised suspicions about the morality of the doctors and the hospitals. The two most prominent medical journals, the *Journal of the American Medical Association* and the *New England Journal of Medicine,* produced self-lacerating articles about research results produced by investigators with financial interests in their own work and published in these journals. The integrity of the medical profession was under assault.

There seemed to be no national capacity for coming together in order to face these problems. As long as one segment's ox was being gored, there could be no solution. No single part of the health enterprise in America seemed willing to sacrifice for any other part; and everyone was suspicious of government. As the country aged, topics such as the future of Medicare, Medicaid, and Social Security were on the lips of millions, along with prescription drug benefits for senior citizens. We were a country preoccupied, and a little bit neurotic. It should not be surprising that the medical profession's health was not all that well off. It needed intensive care.

Boston Medicine

Whatever was happening nationally in health care and medicine was intensified in the unique environment of Boston medicine. With three medical schools, a dozen affiliated teaching hospitals, the *New England Journal of Medicine,* and more status consciousness than most country clubs, one major question was: which medical school was third? Number One was a forgone conclusion. The medical school of Harvard University, with its unparalleled financial resources, laboratories, and major teaching hospitals (before the mergers of the 1990s, Massachusetts General Hospital, Brigham and Women's Hospital, Beth Israel Hospital, and Deaconess Hospital) was in a class by itself and had educated many of the faculty at Tufts and Boston University Medical schools. Both of these very good runners-up got a major shot in the arm with their two presidents who came on in the 1970s. The John Silber era at Boston University from 1971 *may* be coming to an end in 2003. Jean Mayer brought his magic to Tufts in 1976, and, with his intense focus on the Medical School, took it to a position where, at least from the prejudiced perspective of the Tufts faculty, it was number two in the pecking order. Students seemed to validate that opinion, since it was rare for Tufts to lose an overlap medical school applicant to BU. The overall reputation of the university aided Tufts Medical School. As hard as he might try, John Silber could not gain the national recognition for Boston University that Jean Mayer managed for Tufts. It must have outraged him that *U.S. News & World Report* consistently by its measurements had BU in the second tier of American universities, while Tufts had shot past all the other universities in Greater Boston except Harvard and MIT into the top twenty-five and remained there all through the 1990s. Mayer and Silber, who were close to one another, also shared in the largesse provided by Gerry Cassidy. He was a great admirer of both Silber and Mayer and earned his considerable fees. The large federal earmarks that came their way also aided in making them the two most dominant education personalities in Boston through the late 1980s, until Mayer passed from the scene. With Mayer gone, Cassidy's loyalty shifted to Silber, and it was at this time in the 1990s when Boston University Medical School made a leap forward and became a head-to-head competitor with Tufts Medical School. Some would say it has that head in front.

On the Tufts health sciences campus, the 1980s had been dominated by the struggle between the New England Medical Center Hospital and Tufts Medical School as proxy for the university, because it was not a fight between hospital president and school dean; it was a battle between NEMC President Jerome Grossman and Tufts University President Jean Mayer, with the Medical School Dean, in this case Henry Banks, holding on for his life. This was one of the few struggles that Jean Mayer lost. There were just too many cards stacked against him. Grossman not only had consolidated total power in the hospital in his own hands, he could also count on his Boards of Governors and Trustees, several of whom sat on the Tufts Board of Trustees, consistently to give him the benefit of any doubts in confrontations with Mayer; he was also very good, in many ways as much a visionary in hospital administration as Mayer was in his world. Grossman's reputation soared. He was viewed as a health care innovator who was making the New England Medical Center a premiere hospital in this most competitive environment of giants like Massachusetts General and Beth Israel. Grossman was a creative hospital administrator who was on the cutting edge of technology and thought he saw where the future of managed care was going in America. Even if he was described by subordinates as a bully and tyrant, he was smart and articulate; the results impressed his boards. He also had immediate control of a great deal of money, had access to the hospital's grateful patients, and could make things happen quickly where Mayer, under the financial thumb of a Board that had become guarded after so many years of unnerving ventures by the university President, was often hamstrung in his ability to get his hands on resources. Grossman bought the loyalty of the Medical School's clinical faculty, particularly the extraordinarily productive Department of Medicine run by Shelly Wolff, renovated an entire building of research space for him, and took $4 million of grants away from the Medical School. Wolff, who would have preferred to stay with the Medical School authority, had no choice but to move closer to NEMC and to Grossman, who was one of the few people whom Shelly Wolff feared. He needn't have. Wolff's department was a national treasure as a research enterprise and also the money machine for the hospital's research effort, which Grossman wanted to expand and to capitalize on. Wolff had a fairly free hand to build, using his own departmental dollars as well as those provided by the hospital. Even while he was dying of cancer, Wolff recruited a brilliant and promising molecular cardiologist from Harvard, Michael Mendelsohn, like Wolff the quintessential physician-investigator. Mendelsohn, enormously productive in the grants game, established the Molecular Cardiology Research Institute funded by the NIH and the American Heart Association. After Wolff's death in 1994, Mendelsohn assumed the position of leadership in research in the Department of Medicine.

Grossman wanted to be the unchallenged boss of the downtown campus, an independent President/Provost of the health sciences complex that would include all the teaching and research functions of the medical, dental, and nutrition schools. Joined with the New England Medical Center, he hoped to create a power base that could be competitive with the other giants in Boston. Ultimately, he could see himself as President of the entire university. For Grossman and some of his allies on both hospital and university boards, it was not an impossibility. Mayer almost threw in the towel at one point, nearly allowing Grossman to gain a potential foothold. At a breakfast meeting with hospital and Tufts Trustee William Meserve, who was trying to bring some semblance of peace to the disorder, Mayer in desperation offered the Deanship of the Medical School to Grossman, who leapt at the offer. When Mayer saw how eager Grossman was to become Dean, he had second thoughts. He put it to a group of Trustees in such a way that made Grossman seem a threat to the Medical School, and they suggested that it might not be such a good idea. Mayer happily pulled the offer back, and Grossman was furious. That was the end of any possible compromise between these two adversaries.

The Medical School in the 1990s

Jean Mayer had handpicked his Medical School deans. After the failure of Bob Levy, who also attributed his demise to the hospital leadership's antagonism, Mayer looked for a loyalist, a clinician M.D. whom Grossman's dollars did not control or own. The only practice plan independent of the hospital and supported by the Medical School was in the Department of Orthopedic Surgery, chaired since 1970 by Henry Banks, a graduate of Tufts Medical School, class of '45.

Henry Banks represented all the best traditions of "Boston Medicine": the warm associations and friendships, the intimacy associated with people who practiced medicine, who knew and was known by every health professional in town. He was a graduate of Harvard College and Tufts Medical School. He started a surgical internship at Beth Israel, went into the army, returned to Beth Israel in 1947, and began his orthopedic education at Harvard in 1949. In 1953, after having served his residency at Boston Children's, Massachusetts General, and the then-called Peter Bent Brigham Hospital, Banks joined the full-time orthopedic faculty of the Brigham and Boston Children's Hospitals, where he spent the next seventeen years as a member of the Harvard faculty. In 1970, he was appointed Professor and Chairman of the Department of Orthopedic Surgery at Tufts. Professor Banks was one of Tufts' most eminent clinicians, in 1971 President of the American Academy for Cerebral Palsy, and in 1978 he was elected President of the American Board of Orthopedic Surgery. He was honored to be selected by Jean Mayer as Dean of the Medical School in 1983 and could think of no greater culmination to his career in Boston. Henry Banks was a gentle, sweet, and beloved bedside physician of the old school, who believed he could get along with anyone—until he became Dean and had to do battle with Jerry Grossman. He immediately found himself at war with the New England Medical Center and its President, a theme that opened every one of his seven annual reports to Jean Mayer. But he accomplished much. When Banks stepped down as Dean in 1990, he left behind a newly built library and communications center named for Arthur M. Sackler, an endowment that had increased from a miniscule $3 million in 1983 to $20 million—not enough to make a difference to a Medical School in need of many more millions, but at least on the road—and a rebuilt basic sciences. The Dean was convinced that the hospital President lived only to thwart him at every turn. He had taken the Department of Medicine and its grants away from the Medical School. Banks had been told that Dr. Grossman had poisoned the accreditation visit from the Liaison Committee on Medical Education (LCME), and there were tangible signs that he had separated the New England Medical Center name from Tufts in every sense: from the stationery and the buildings. If he could have found another academic partner, Grossman would have ended the affiliation between the Medical School and his hospital. The Dean was no match for him, and as it proved out, neither was the President of the university. Jean Mayer's own problems took priority in the early 1990s. He tried desperately before his retirement to recruit an outside dean, but any candidate who appeared interested suddenly lost enthusiasm after a conversation with the hospital President. From 1990 to 1992, a non-M.D. administrator named Richard Ryan served as Interim Dean, while Mayer tried to entice a candidate from outside. In one of his last acts as President, Jean Mayer again was forced to turn to an insider loyalist and friend who was not in the grip of President Grossman, and in July 1992, just before his own retirement as President and elevation to Chancellor, he appointed Professor and Chairman of Community Health Morton Madoff to the Deanship. Madoff, an innovator in managed care, had been the creative force behind the building of the Tufts Associated Health Plan (TAHP). Like Mayer, he had been active in public health and nutrition. Temperamentally, he was at the opposite end from Henry Banks. Madoff was pugnacious, irascible, and confrontational, but he did have a single-minded idea: to get away from Grossman by constructing a new research building to take the place of the garment factory. He raised funds, worked hard for basic sciences and clinical research collaboration, and was in a constant state of belligerency with everyone while the plans for the new research facility became a reality. He also built on two of his strengths to give the Medical School something unique. He wanted every medical student to have an opportunity to explore the public health implications of the profession and pushed hard to get through the faculty a combined M.D./M.P.H. degree, a Master's in Public Health. Madoff, the founder of the Tufts managed care health plan, also believed that the physician of the future needed business savvy and a grounding in the economics of health care. A Tufts M.D./ administrator, Norman Stearns, had excellent connections at local schools and put together a specialized kind of M.B.A. for doctors, using business faculty from Northeastern University and health care experts from the Heller School at Brandeis. The Tufts M.D./M.B.A. in Health Management was the first of its kind in the nation. Both these combined degree programs have remained very attractive to incoming students.

In the meantime, the first DiBiaggio capital campaign was moving along, and the oft-repeated notion of a new research building was actually taking form. Several more years would be needed, but Mort Madoff gave life to the idea, even though he exhausted everyone in his presence. He served as Dean for only three years, between 1992 and 1995, and in that period the health care world found itself on a track that ultimately would lead it to a train wreck. As fate would have it, one of the victims who emerged shaken and tarnished was Dr. Jerome Grossman. To make matters worse for the hospital and the Medical School, Sheldon Wolff, the intellectual glue and personal mentor who led the Department of Medicine to great research eminence, succumbed to cancer in 1994. His reputation alone had been enough to bring enormous visibility to Tufts medicine in the 1980s until his death.

What happened to the American health care system, and to Boston medicine in particular? All through the 1980s, Grossman and NEMC were making money hand over fist. He was a skilled and articulate definer of what public policy in health care for the nation should be. His expertise in information technology and health care delivery was universally acknowledged. He was also a visionary builder. To fulfill his dream of creating a rival medical center to challenge the Boston elite, Grossman made elaborate plans for expansion. What he had somehow not anticipated was the squeeze that started in the early 1990s and continued, when insurers and HMOs started pressuring hospitals to cut costs by getting patients in and out as quickly as possible. At the very moment when Grossman's grand scheme for a 750-bed NEMC was being proposed, he suddenly found himself, like every other hospital in the Boston area, swimming in a sea of red ink. The visionary proved to have no magic formula and nothing could stop the meltdown; the merger mania in Boston had begun, and no one wanted to merge with Jerome Grossman.

Whatever had existed in the way of good manners and civility among physicians in the medical community disappeared as "survival" became the watchword. The dog-eat-dog environment led to the MGH/Brigham & Women's merger, called "Partners," and Beth Israel/Deaconess ("Caregroup"). One might have expected that these most eminent Harvard teaching hospitals would have found an appropriate degree of that "shared culture" of an earlier time. Instead, there was blood all over the place before things settled down. Samuel Thier, a physician with a long and distinguished pedigree in and out of Boston, became head of the newly formed MGH/Brigham and emerged as the biggest shark in the dangerous waters surrounding Boston's hospitals. He was a kidney specialist in a town where nephrologists were an intimate circle. He had been chairman of the Department of Internal Medicine at Yale for eleven years, then served six years as president of the Institute of Medicine at the National Academy of Sciences. He was a close, personal friend of Shelly Wolff, and when Brandeis was seeking a President in 1991, Wolff told the search committee to stop looking, he had found the man they wanted. Thier stayed at Brandeis only for three years, before moving to the MGH in 1994. He oversaw the hospitals' merger and the evolution of Partners Healthcare System, Inc., made a great success, and left in 2003 to become the Chairman of the Commonwealth Fund. He had been considered a member of that unique Boston medical world, very much part of that great Boston tradition of collegiality among the M.D. community, where everyone would give the helping hand. But Jerry Grossman was not the kind of potential partner who other hospital heads reached out to, and finally, in 1995 he exited the foundering vessel that was NEMC. The physicians at the New England Medical Center took a leading role in seeking aid and comfort from their Boston colleagues. After all, managed care had gone so well in Boston because, as the Tufts Associated Health Plan CEO Harris Berman had expressed it, "Boston medicine was still a gentlemen's game." To their surprise and shock, they found little collegial and gentlemanly comfort, especially from Sam Thier, who told them that MGH would be willing to take over the Department of Medicine and absorb it, as well as the program in Rehabilitation Medicine. As for the rest, he recommended that the New England Medical Center Hospital should go out of business. From the perspective of the predatory monster mergers going on, there was no room for the likes of the New England Medical Center any longer in Boston. When what are arguably two of the best hospitals in the United States merged to form "Partners," everything in Boston medicine became destabilized, including the rest of the Harvard teaching hospitals, who were sent reeling. Physician practices were being swallowed up by the giant hospital merger of MGH and Brigham & Women's, who established market dominance in Boston that pretty much could dictate whatever terms they wanted and could extract more money from payers who wanted to do business with them. If they did not want to do business with you, you could quietly hide yourself in a corner and hope for a painless demise. This was not the aid and comfort that the NEMC physicians had hoped for. For the first time in Boston medical history, "betrayal" was a word used to describe events taking place in the culture.

After the shock wore off and the physicians at NEMC realized that no one in Boston was coming to their rescue, they turned back to the Medical School and the university. The Grossman era was over, love was again declared, and the Tufts name returned to the NEMC stationery.

It was during these frantic days of uncertain survival for the Medical School's primary teaching hospital that Boston University Medical Center found its equilibrium. Silber and Mayor Menino brokered a full asset merger of two public hospitals and the private academic medical center with its medical school that became the Boston Medical Center, in July 1996. With a very able President and CEO of the merged hospitals in Elaine Ullian (a Tufts undergraduate alumna) and long-term continuity in the Medical School administration in Dean Aram Chobanian, the Boston Medical Center enjoyed a period of uninterrupted stability and growth. Ullian and Chobanian both were wired completely into the Boston political scene, Gerry Cassidy was coming on to the Boston University Board of Trustees, and the Boston Medical School and the associated hospitals had survived the trauma of mergers that were still buffeting the Tufts Medical School and its wounded primary teaching hospital.

The Coming of the Irish

Considering the long and deep academic heritage of Boston that extended back to the founding of the colony, one knew that the shared and common culture of Anglo-Saxon Protestantism ran right through the colleges and universities of the Massachusetts Commonwealth. Walls were put up early to keep out the Catholics and Jews. The highest and thickest walls were in the medical schools, where the common culture made it clear that there was room at the top—department heads in medicine and surgery—only for the Brahmins with three names who wore their bow ties with traditional dignity, well into the twentieth century. A few Catholics and Jews were willing to pay whatever price was necessary to gain acceptance, and they often would emulate and honor their mentors by wearing the same bow ties and naming their children "Sumner" or some such appropriately non-ethnic appellation.

But Boston was a town that could not suppress the ethnicity of its people. As fast as many assimilated, more held on to their roots. As I mentioned earlier, the national medical authorities pressured Tufts for admitting too many Jews and Catholics in the 1920s and 1930s. The Medical School was a place where students with Italian, Irish, Greek, Armenian, and Jewish names felt comfortable. In the second half of the twentieth century, Tufts Medical School had four Jews and two Catholics as its deans.

In spite of instincts to assimilate, Boston remains an intensely ethnic community. I could go to the Belmont Country Club as a dinner guest and meet every prominent Jewish family associated with Tufts over the past fifty years. In the dining room would be found most of the living Jackson graduates of the 1940s who shared rooms involuntarily with their Jewish friends of a lifetime. Their children and grandchildren, also dining at the Belmont C.C., would have no such problems when they attended Tufts.

If the venue were to shift in the summer to Old Silver Beach on Cape Cod, a similar concentration of alumni could be found, but they would all be of Armenian extraction, with a Greek-American enclave nearby.

But the Irish always have had a very special hold on a city that was a Balkans of ethnic neighborhoods in fluid movement. At one point in the early 1900s, the famous Boston North End contained Irish, Jews, and Italians in almost equal numbers until it evolved into the definitive Italian neighborhood of today. The West End was Jewish until urban renewal removed them. But the Irish began to thrive in the 1840s, terribly dehumanized and stereotyped; yet they proliferated and were everywhere. They had South Boston pretty much to themselves, but the Irish-Catholic corridor extended from Boston down to Fall River, Massachusetts, and westward to Worcester. There was a strong and separate higher education tradition anchored by the College of Holy Cross and Boston College, with smaller colleges such as Providence, Stonehill, Assumption, Merrimack, Regis, and Emmanuel providing education for the sons and daughters of Irish immigrants.

As luck would have it, the Tufts University School of Medicine would be the beneficiary of this Gaelic presence. Mort Madoff wanted to establish the succession before he left. In 1994, he asked John Harrington, then Chief-of-Medicine at Newton-Wellesley Hospital in Newton and a long-time NEMC nephrologist, to serve as his Academic Dean. When Madoff announced his retirement, he lobbied intensely for Harrington to serve as interim Dean, and I agreed.

Several characteristics defined John Harrington. He came out of the ferocious loyalties of the Fall River, Massachusetts, Irish-Catholic community. He attended Holy Cross and then Yale Medical School. His long association with New England Medical Center and Tufts began in 1965 when he was a Clinical and Research Fellow in William Schwartz's renal lab. Bill Schwartz must have educated most of the nephrologists who trained in Boston. In 1968, Harrington started a three-year stint at Boston University, only to return to NEMC as a physician on the renal service and Director of the Hemodyalisis Unit in 1971. In 1979, he was promoted to Professor of Medicine in the Tufts Medical School. From 1981 to 1986, he was Chief of the General Medical Division at NEMC.

Before he was tapped in 1994 by Mort Madoff as his Academic Dean, he served for six years as Chairman of Medicine at one of the major community hospitals used by the Medical School, Newton-Wellesley. His life was defined by his family, particularly his seven children and wife Trudy, loyalty to his hospital and university, the Boston Red Sox, and the depth of his Irish heritage. He kept copies of Thomas Cahill's *How the Irish Saved Civilization* to distribute from his office. (I reciprocated when Cahill wrote his next book, *The Gift of the Jews*). He quoted James Joyce and William Butler Yeats in his annual reports. He cherished a photo taken of Ted Williams playing in an exhibition game against Holy Cross.

John Harrington was also the doctors' doctor. He was a legendary clinician, the physician for many of his medical colleagues, a role model for medical students, and a man of sunny disposition and irrepressible good humor. Madoff, his temperamental opposite, selected him because he could bridge the gap between clinicians in the hospitals and researchers in basic sciences. Harrington could talk to everyone, possessed the personality, intelligence, and transparent good will that provided him with access to the far-flung medical school affiliated hospitals, as far west as Springfield, Massachusetts, where the Bay State Medical Center had responsibility for the medical education of nearly 15 percent of the Tufts medical students. Madoff also intended to have Harrington succeed him as permanent Dean, when on November 1, 1995, he suddenly announced that he was retiring. Harrington was appointed interim Dean, and there was little doubt in my mind that he would succeed to the deanship. When I spoke to President DiBiaggio, I shared a conversation that I had had with the leadership of the Association of American Medical Colleges (AAMC). At that time, searches were going on at a dozen medical schools in the United States. The average length of survival as dean of a medical school was under five years, and for anyone coming in from the outside, it was less than that. The AAMC was making a recommendation: Do not go outside for a medical school dean. Given the state of uncertainty in hospital relations, clinical care, and medical economics, they urged us to find someone inside who could stabilize and calm the waters. We had that person in John Harrington, and President DiBiaggio concurred. Harrington was appointed Dean in 1995. He served for seven years, well beyond the national average.

Harrington inherited a hospital crisis. Jerome Grossman had left, no merger seemed feasible, and NEMC was in dire financial straits. The hospital board was seriously contemplating sale of the hospital to a for-profit organization, a shocking thought for the Boston medical community. The Medical School's problem was that so much pressure was being placed on the staff physicians to see more and more patients that they had little or no time for teaching: the great unpaid "living endowment" of the Boston medical schools where most of the teaching was done by clinicians. If the primary teaching hospital of Tufts Medical School crashed in flames, the viability of the Medical School itself would be placed in doubt. What were vitally needed now were Harrington's diplomatic skills and his great credibility as a long-time NEMC physician. He also needed a partner he could work with. He found him in Thomas F. O'Donnell, Jr., former Chairman of the Department of Surgery at NEMC who in 1996 took over the foundering hospital as CEO and President. The chemistry was perfect. The nephrologist and the surgeon had been colleagues and friends for years, trusted each other, shared a common style and values.

Harrington and O'Donnell gave the harried medical staff a renewed prescription of morale. They calmed nerves, gave assurances, and within six months the New England Medical Center had entered into an agreement with the Rhode Island–based Lifespan hospital and physicians network. The relationship with Lifespan, while never a perfect arrangement, stabilized the hospital and assured the Medical School that at least one-third of its students would have access to the teaching opportunities at NEMC. Harrington and O'Donnell made it happen. They calmed the troubled seas. O'Donnell allowed Harrington to reach out to other hospital systems in order to stabilize the teaching for the medical students. Tufts had a special relationship with Caritas Christi, the Catholic hospital system, whose CEO was Michael Collins, graduate of Tufts Medical School and the College of Holy Cross. Ten percent of the Tufts medical students were stationed at St. Elizabeth's, the flagship hospital of the system, and Caritas Christi's relationship to Tufts Medical School was critical. Harrington, O'Donnell, and Collins somehow could work out any aggravations. Dean Harrington's biggest diplomatic success, accomplished while not annoying any of his other hospital affiliates, was in reaching out to the Lahey Clinic in Burlington, a superb facility and physician base that now makes a major contribution to the teaching of third- and fourth-year Tufts medical students.

Dean Harrington had a good eye for finding talented administrative personnel who really made a difference. None made a greater impact than a Tufts undergraduate, a "local" first generation Chinese-American from Medford who went on to Tufts Medical School, joined the faculty, and was appointed Dean for Educational Affairs: Mary Lee. She turned her extraordinary energy and focus to a problem she identified before her dean's appointment: the need for major shifts in how health science course material was managed, kept current, and integrated into the curriculum. The students were being crushed by information overload in their courses. Mary Lee, working with health sciences librarian Elizabeth Eaton and her staff, Bruce Metz, Vice President for Information Technology, and other Tufts systems people and faculty, led the way in the development of a dynamic new educational model based on the latest advances in information technology. The team got startup funding from the National Library of Medicine and a project team orchestrated by Lee created the Tufts Health Sciences Database (HSDB), the first Web-accessible, multi-media database of health sciences curricula information. It combined course delivery, digital library, knowledge management, and curriculum management systems in such a way as to make sane the lives of the medical, dental, and veterinary students. The HSDB contained full-text syllabi, slides, lecture recordings (audio and video), and additional resources made available by the faculty of all the health sciences schools at Tufts.[6]

The Tufts HSDB was more than a university's knowledge management system applied to the transformation of medical education. The world of information technology saw immediately the possibility for other applications. Mary Lee had connected the technology to the curriculum, and the students immediately bought in. The business world saw the potential for increasing organizational efficiency, and the HSDB became a prize-winning phenomenon.[7]

Knowing that she had absolutely no time to do anything else, I appointed Dr. Lee Associate Provost for Health Sciences, in addition to her work as Dean in the Medical School, member of the Department of Medicine, and staff physician in the New England Medical Center.

One of the great benefits of the Harrington deanship was his dedication to and success in fundraising. Tom Murnane took him everywhere on the road. Donors laughed, warning others that it was time to zipper their pockets when the two of them showed up. But, the Tufts medical community gave as never before, Jerry Cassidy grudgingly made one more final effort to secure additional funds for the Tufts research building, and as steel girders rose on Harrison Avenue for the first purpose-built research facility in the history of Tufts medicine, Harrington's tenure was memorialized. As had seemingly become the custom with Tufts medical deans, he suddenly announced his retirement on November 1, 2002 (the day of the dedication of the research building), effective December 31 of that year. He had told me a few weeks ear-

6. See Mary Lee et al., "Tufts Health Sciences Database: Lessons, Issues, and Opportunities," *Academic Medicine* 78, no. 3 (March 2003).

7. See "Prescription for Learning," *CIO*, February 1, 2001, 102–10. The magazine presented Tufts the annual Enterprise Value Award.

lier of his intention, and I begged him to reconsider. Then he showed me his reservations on Aer Lingus, the Irish National airline. In his heart and mind, he and Trudy were already gone.

By the end of the century, a relative state of calm had settled over the Tufts Medical School, thanks to the effective bridge building that John Harrington and Tom O'Donnell had accomplished. New England Medical Center still floated in troubled financial waters, but at least both university and medical school were looking out for its well-being.

But the profession of medicine had not found its way out of the mess it was in nationally. No matter how much we tried to convince ourselves that American medicine was the best, the data were inescapable. The United States spent an average of $4,270 on medical care for every American—man, woman, and child—fifty-five percent more than the distant runner-up, Switzerland, and nearly 3.5 percent more of our GNP than the next country, Germany.[8] We also get a mediocre payback for our investment. The World Health Organization ranked the United States thirty-seventh in the world, with one Latin American and one African nation ahead of us. Our rank in terms of life expectancy was twenty-fourth in the world. With forty-one million people in this country uninsured, the profession was losing faith in itself and could not find a remedy.

THE SACKLER SCHOOL

But, the other part of medical school activity—basic science research—was exploding in a wave of research and discovery that produced eye-popping results across the nation. Here, the United States seemed unchallenged. Federal budgets were increased regularly, and scientists had little trouble maintaining and expanding their laboratories. At Tufts, the basic sciences, under the umbrella name given it by Jean Mayer, shared in the bounty.

Even placing the Sackler under the heading of "Tufts School of Medicine" will cause irregular heartbeats among some basic scientists. One of the great paradoxes of the basic sciences faculty, once they were taken out of the Arts and Sciences in one of Jean Mayer's coup d'etats and established as "the Sackler School of Biomedical Sciences," was an inexorable feeling on their part that they were indeed a separate school, independent from the Tufts University School of Medicine. One could hear them asserting: "We have our

8. See Fitzhugh Mullan, M.D., *Big Doctoring in America: Profiles in Primary Care* (Berkeley: University of California Press, 2002), xiiiff.

own eminent Dean. We do not train physicians; we do research. We should have our own budget, our own independence." Jean Mayer encouraged this sense of independence. He insisted that Lou Lasagna, who possessed a reputation as eminent as anyone in Tufts science when he joined the faculty in 1984, should have equal status with the other school deans. I insisted—and Mayer grudgingly concurred—that the Sackler Dean should nonetheless report to the Medical School Dean, as well as to the Provost. Sackler had no income and collected no tuition (all tuition was waived). But, most important, without the basic sciences, the Dean of the Medical School controlled—nothing. He had little of the loyalty of and control over the clinical departments, who got from Tufts their academic titles but no income or salary. The hospitals—New England Medical Center, St. Elizabeth's, and Baystate Medical Center primarily—put money in the pockets of the clinical faculty. If the basic sciences faculty were given the autonomy they wanted, it would be impossible to recruit a dean for the Medical School.

But once they were cut loose from Medford's Arts and Sciences faculty, they took Mayer's pressure to expand research seriously, and, led by the national visibility of Louis Lasagna, whose reputation admittedly was based on his clinical pharmacology work, these departments exploded in a fury of research activity. Still in the run-down garment factory but with money gradually becoming available, renovations of laboratory space began, and new scientists were recruited. Molecular and Microbiology under Elio Schaechter had established a funded research agenda before the coming of Mayer in 1976, but now it too leapt forward. Biochemistry, Physiology, and Anatomy/Cellular Biology needed rebuilding. Nothing was higher on Mayer's agenda. The last two decades of the twentieth century proved to be a period of astonishing growth for biomedical research in the United States, and for Tufts.

The Tufts part is remarkable because research in basic science departments came unbelievably far, from a nearly nonexistent base, through a period of modest growth in the 1960s, that was still most definitely separated consciously from clinical medicine. There has always been some degree of war between clinical and basic science research in this country, at medical schools and hospitals. It took time for medical schools to realize that graduate education was an integral part of medical research, and that medical schools could also train Ph.D.s who would go on to make enormous contributions in collaboration with clinical researchers. Harvard Medical School, from the outset, directed its main efforts at research. At Tufts, almost no research developed in basic sciences, although there were a couple of pioneers: David

Rapport became Chairman of Physiology in 1939, and along with Attilio Canzanelli and Milton Greenblatt published about a dozen articles in major journals through the 1940s. But the facilities at Tufts were dreadful for laboratory teaching and investigation. In 1948, Halvor Christensen became Chairman of Biochemistry and the June 1950 commencement counted among the graduates the first Ph.D. issued for investigative work carried out within the walls of the Medical School.

It was Dean Joe Hayman who took the research agenda of the Medical School to a level of competence in all five basic science departments. In 1956, he brought in Alton Meister in Biochemistry, Morris Friedkin in Pharmacology, Ted Park in Microbiology, Walter Hughes in Physiology, and Lauro Cavazos in Anatomy. These leaders recruited a faculty of young scientists interested in fledgling doctoral programs, even if the facilities were primitive and the relationship with "medical research" was something that basic scientists did not see as their mission. There was still a wall between these pre-clinical investigators and the clinicians in the hospital, who were doing research as well, but who were committed uniquely to the education of physicians. Here is where the anomalies of medical education and medical schools became evident. All through the 1960s, there were no clinical members in the Ph.D. programs in the Tufts Medical School. Any clinicians who had a basic science appointment got it because they were teaching, not for doing research collaboratively with their colleagues in the basic science departments.

In these pre-Mayer years before the Sackler School was established in 1980, the graduate students in the Medical School floated unnoticed and unwanted between the Graduate School of Arts and Sciences in Medford, where they were officially registered, and a Medical School administration interested almost exclusively in the education and training of physicians. Who cared about these Ph.D. students in a medical school? As it turned out, their real home was the basic science department, where the graduate students were nurtured and cared for. These departments quietly developed a sense of autonomy that eventually was to characterize their evolution into the powerful research component that did as much as anything to change the image of Tufts University as it moved toward the twenty-first century.

When Jean Mayer dropped his bombshell and announced that Tufts would have a new school, two parts of the title brought faculty out of their chairs. The first, naming the new entity the Sackler School caused a brawl at faculty meetings on both campuses, where Mayer vehemently had to defend the Sackler brothers from charges that they made their money in unsavory ways. The President did not back down an inch. Although the basic science faculty grumbled that they did not want the Sackler name attached to their school, they settled down, because they liked the rest of the name: Biomedical Sciences. Mayer, who was not a physician and had to live with this "deficiency," knew from his Harvard experience that basic science research had significant medical implications. Of course, he also had several other agendas. He was determined to make nutrition a visible force in biomedical research; and he wanted to make Boston the center of a revolution in the pharmaceutical industry. His grand vision also included the hospital-based physician-scientists who understood both clinical and basic science research.

Mayer could do what he wanted, but the Sackler School would still be made up of powerful departments and their chairs who would not yield authority in governance to anyone. Before my appearance as Provost, Mayer appointed the highly respected immunologist Sidney Leskowitz as Acting Dean, and then Mayer proceeded to get the Dean he wanted: Louis Lasagna, acknowledged as the father of clinical pharmacology, an M.D. investigator with very close ties to the pharmaceutical industry—and the Sackler brothers. Mayer's entire strategy would build on having Lou Lasagna as Dean of the Sackler School. Lasagna would be the link to both the Federal Drug Administration and industry. Mayer's intention was to attract first the FDA to Boston, then to bring pharmaceutical money and companies to a huge research facility run by Tufts. He would die before he could see his vision fulfilled.

For the Sackler faculty, Lou Lasagna, who came from the University of Rochester in 1984, was a perfect Dean. He left the departments alone, traveled incessantly to give testimony to Congress, sit on boards, or to appear as an honored guest at meetings. He was an articulate spokesman, an intellectual and elder statesmen with a great reputation that reflected well on the school, but he was not a basic scientist, no matter what he thought he was. He loved teaching medical students and spent the majority of his time in Boston working with problem-based groups of students who loved him. Lasagna was a truly gifted teacher, with all the fragility of the classroom performer who needs constant reinforcement. He would send his laudatory teaching evaluations to anyone who would read them. He was remote from the hiring process, which was now left to the faculty and the chairs. They did their job well. During Lasagna's seventeen-year tenure as Dean of the Sackler School, he saw it emerge as the creative research engine that provided the whole university with its energy. It also reached out across the street to the New England Medical Center and created some wonderful synergy. The scientists really did not care who the Dean of the Medical School or the Sackler School was. They found each other. The great breakthrough was the arrival of Shelly Wolff in the Department of Medicine. When it came to science, he was apolitical and encouraged hospital-based scientists to get involved in the basic science departments. Andrew Plaut, Barbara and Bruce Furie, and Robert Schwartz shared research resources with basic science colleagues and established collaborative projects that profoundly affected work on both sides of the street. Win Arias, Dave Stollar, Bryan Toole, Henry Wortis, Barbara Talamo, and just about everyone in Molecular and Microbiology created an environment where deans were irrelevant. The real power brokers were the basic science chairs, who met, established a consensus-style of governance based on Schaechter's commune model, made decisions, and hired great faculty. The administrative glue was provided by a small but remarkable administrative team led by an M.B.A./J.D., Peggy Newell, who came to Sackler in 1982 and stayed for sixteen years, until she was made Associate Provost for Research. It was she who provided the intelligence to keep this hothouse of scientists in the Medical School and hospital from beating up on each other. Even while the wars between the presidents raged, and research dollars were being fought over between hospital and school, the scientists continued to work together. Shelly Wolff and later Michael Mendelsohn were hospital-based scientists who were alternately respected and feared by the Sackler faculty when they prowled the political jungles of Harrison Avenue. Neither of them could stand the idea of someone else controlling their operations, yet they were very much inclined to take over the research of the Medical School's basic science, if it could come to that. But, in spite of the threat of lost autonomy, basic scientists and hospital scientists worked together in Mendelsohn's Molecular Cardiology Research Institute. Politically, everyone was wary; scientifically, they enjoyed a deep collaboration. Today, there are scientists who have tenure track appointments in basic science and full-time appointments in the Department of Medicine. Harry Selker, Matt Waldor, and Stuart Levy have deep roots in Medicine and basic sciences.

Nonetheless, the 1990s challenged the Sackler School. Even while Tufts was launching its biggest fundraising campaign that finally settled at $600 million, the research environment for basic sciences at Tufts was suffering. The National Institutes of Health, the single greatest source for university research, between 1995 and 2000 increased funding to medical schools by 64 percent. Tufts basic research grew by only 34 percent. They had the will, they had the quality; they lacked space and another dozen researchers. Basic science research at Tufts had made unbelievable strides in a very short time; but lack of critical research space in the 1990s held it back from even more impressive success. When President Bacow settled in in 2001, his first action was to provide funds to hire basic scientists.

But the Sackler School remains a miracle. It was created to give a research image to a university that had been characterized by its undergraduate college, and it succeeded wonderfully. It began the 2000–2001 academic year with 211 full-time graduate students, thirty-one pursuing combined M.D./Ph.D. degrees. For the forty-three seats in the entering class, it will have over one thousand applications. Twenty-three Ph.D.s were awarded, fully a quarter of all the doctorates granted by Tufts that year. In spite of the garment factory, research in the basic sciences topped $40 million for the first time in history. When coupled with the $60 million of research booked by the New England Medical Center–based Tufts faculty ($40 million in the Department of Medicine alone), Tufts Medical School would rank among the top quarter of medical schools in research productivity. Considering where we had come from in the previous twenty years, one can only marvel.

THE SCHOOL OF DENTAL MEDICINE: SMILES ALL AROUND

Even someone with the tenacity and endurance of Erling Johansen could, at times, become discouraged. He often expected the worst from his faculty, and they seemed to get particular pleasure in fulfilling his expectations. As dental schools all around him were closing in the 1980s and right into the 1990s, life could get somewhat grim, although the university and its President Jean Mayer gave total support to the School of Dental Medicine. Still, it was a profession that seemed unhappy with its lot in life, with its place in the health sciences order of things. As the 1980s came to an end and dental schools continued closing, the profession could not see the pinprick of light that was shining at the end of the tunnel.

But the lights lit up in every face in the Dental School when John DiBiaggio was named President of Tufts in 1992. He was one of the 0.4 percent of leaders who were dentists and had become a university leader; and other changes were taking place that were destined to affect the state of the dental profession specifically and the health sciences in general. They had to do with the mental health of the professions at large.

As we have just discussed, the 1990s represented a traumatic period for the medical professional. HMO managed care, hospital closings, sales to for-profit hospital systems, high-profile research scandals, and the loss of prestige that characterized the public's view of the physician through the first eight decades of the twentieth century had battered the image and self-esteem of the M.D.s. The message that was going out to the youth of America from doctors' offices, similar to that proclaimed by dentists a decade earlier, was: Go find another career. The medical profession definitely projected an attitude, and it was not a positive one.

This was the very same attitude projected by the dental profession in the 1980s, when all they could see was gloom, doom, and no cavities. Enrollments plummeted, dental schools were closing, research and respect were in short supply. Yet, even while Northwestern Dental School was not enrolling a class for 1998, one could see a dramatic turn-around in attitude and mental health. The dental profession was coming out of the doldrums. Ironically, it was basic science medical research that provided the fair wind. A few visionary dental researchers saw the implications that biomedical advances in the human genome project and biometrics suggested, and gradually it became clear that oral hygiene involved more than cleaning teeth and scraping gums. Scientists were beginning to discover the underlying relationship between oral and systemic health; that oral diagnosis had a relationship to the detection of cancer, diabetes, and cardiovascular disease. A growing body of research saw evidence of a connection between teeth and arteries. The dental profession of the 1990s gradually came out of its isolation. It needed scientists and basic researchers, because oral hygiene was becoming a profoundly important part of the American health care system. The days of "drill, fill, and bill" were over.

However, the professional practitioners of the late 1970s and 1980s had done their work too well. The fear of fluoridation, the certainty that there would be an oversupply of dentists in the 1990s and into the twenty-first century gave the Jeremiahs their temporary victory; dental school applications fell through the floor. When the surviving dental schools began looking around late in the 1990s, they saw a potentially disastrous shortage of dental professionals. The survivors also discovered a profession that had been reborn and was evolving into an unprecedented state of improved mental health. There had been a reversal of fortune. Here was a health profession that had not gotten overwhelmed by managed care and still allowed over 60 percent of its practitioners to work as individual chiefs of their own operatories, with staff and assistants. The health care bill for Americans had exploded into the hundreds of billions, and oral hygiene was now a top priority. In addition, financial compensation was proving to be exceptional, exceeding on average that earned by general medical practitioners, pediatricians, family medicine specialists, and psychiatrists. While the Northwestern Dental School faculty tried to figure out what led to the demise of its school in 2001, Florida and Nevada opened new dental schools. In fact, it was becoming increasingly difficult to recruit faculty for academic positions, because it was nearly impossible to match their potential compensation in private practice. In the year 2000, there were over four hundred vacant openings in American dental schools. That year also produced the first-ever Surgeon General's Report on Oral Health focusing on the public health crisis with particular attention to economically disadvantaged children. Fortunately, enrollment trends have reversed, applications were dramatically increasing, women were (and are) entering the profession in unprecedented numbers; and for anyone contemplating dentistry as a profession, whether beginning a career in private practice, academic medicine, research, or public health, the twenty-first century has emerged as the second Golden Age for dental medicine in the United States.

Tufts School of Dental Medicine and its redoubtable Dean had also weathered the stormy seas. His more than sixteen years as its leader had brought the school through the toughest of times, and it was inevitable, given the nature of academic leadership and faculty expectations, that Erling Johansen would have had to pay a price. During one particularly difficult patch, when he had faculty undermining him, students involved in what seemed to be the wholesale theft of equipment, and administrative disarray in his clinics, he sat in my office and stoically said, "I am sitting on a volcano, and that is the only thing keeping it from erupting." Increasingly over the years, Johansen had to resolve problems by making unpopular decisions that at times had an impact on the entire community. He was part dean, part policeman, and part truant officer. He demanded loyalty and found himself surrounded by a diminishing number of loyal supporters. He worked tirelessly, but with a grim determination that at times did not pay attention to the needs of a contentious faculty. Inevitably, he made enemies. When he turned seventy, we both began thinking that it was time for a change. I asked Vet School Dean Frank Loew in July 1994 to chair the search committee, but Loew would announce within a few months that he, too, would be leaving, and I assumed the chair of the committee for the Dental School Dean. Joining me was Professor Lonnie Norris, an Afro-American oral surgeon and Phi Beta Kappa graduate of Fisk University who, after getting his D.M.D. and M.P.H. degrees from Harvard, took his postgraduate residency in oral and maxillo-facial surgery at Tufts and in 1980 became a member of the faculty under Chris Doku's mentoring. After reading resumes and interviewing candidates, it did not take me long to realize that we had the best person right in front of us. I polled the search committee, got the President's approval, and after a six-month period as Interim Dean, Lonnie Norris became the thirteenth Dean of the Tufts School of Dental Medicine in February 1996.

The timing was right. The national climate was clearly improving for the profession, Dean Johansen's heroic efforts had pushed his faculty to a point where their grumbling now brought out the worst of their adversarial attitude, and it was getting to the students. Lonnie Norris was temperamentally a different kind of person, possessor of a just and generous mind, a person who anticipated the best from his colleagues, and they were quick to meet these transparent expectations. He also had the capacity to build on the platform left by his predecessor, and his disposition and intelligence got infinite mileage out of a team he more or less inherited. Under Steve Manos' directive, each school was to hire an executive associate dean who would free the dean from any serious management and business decisions. The deans, at first very guarded about this mandated appointment, gained confidence in it when Manos brought them immediately into the selection process. The Executive Vice-President had done the earlier screening and he was assured that all of the candidates for each of the schools were seasoned and skilled business managers. Johansen, who had a streak of suspicion in him, wanted this person tied completely to him, because so much of the dental enterprise was involved in clinical management, and this had proved to be the Dean's painful Achilles heel. The clinics were a mess, the faculty insisted (and the Dean had concurred) that this was their prerogative as an academic and pedagogical component of dental education, and wanted "hands-off" from central administration. The choice of the Executive Associate Dean for the Tufts University School of Dental Medicine was, both Manos and I realized, of more than critical importance; it could spell the future of the school. Patricia Campbell was a seasoned veteran of the health sciences wars at Albany, New York, where she was Director of Administration for the Capital District Psychiatric Center. Pat Campbell also understood the controlling culture of both medical and dental faculty and realized immediately that she would need more freedom to act than Dean Johansen was prepared to give her. Any dean can hobble anyone in the administration, and Pat Campbell needed more latitude to make the changes that were essential for the future viability of the Dental School. When Norris became Dean, he gave her all the slack she needed to completely revamp the clinics, institute appropriate business practices, and above all get rid of the incompetent faculty who were fine clinicians and dreadful managers. Within two years, the clinics were running smoothly, with timely billings and collections, happy patients, and delighted faculty. Pat Campbell became one of those university-wide resources who were called on at every possible occasion. Like Peggy Newell at the Sackler School and Martha Pokras in the Vet School, she was trusted everywhere and knew how to play in the sandbox.

Another one of Johansen's legacies was the appointment of a Dean for Research. The reader should be reminded that research died almost completely in the Dental School during the transition from the four-year to the three-year curriculum in the 1970s. When the Dean was forced back to the four-year curriculum as federal support disappeared, he tried valiantly to resuscitate a research life for his school. Scarcely any of the basic science faculty had a research program, but one young Associate Professor of Dental Materials, Gerard Kugel, had been examining the relationship between the use of nitrous oxide (laughing gas) and low birth weight in the newborn. Dean Johansen appointed Kugel Assistant Dean for Research, gave him very little other than the resources he already had and waited for results that did not come. Without an effort at engaging the basic science faculty there was little hope for progress, and the basic scientists kept their distance.

Norris knew that without basic science support and encouragement there would be little hope of creating a research agenda. He made it clear to Sackler School Dean Lou Lasagna that research would occur in dental medicine that would eventually have enormous impact on the health of the nation. Norris pointed to the work of Professor Athena Papas, Jean Mayer's early ally, who had been working collaboratively with nutritionists in the Human Nutrition Research Center and now was concentrating on the impact of drugs on medically compromised people who had undergone chemotherapy or radiation treatment, and as a result suffered from the loss of saliva flow: dry mouth. Papas' patient studies were much more than clinical trials; they had implications for drug usage and the whole range of issues associated with therapeutic pharmacology. The basic scientists starting paying attention. National recognition was coming to some young and promising Tufts dental researchers. In Norris's own department, the veteran Chris Doku was succeeded by a young and energetic practitioner and researcher, Maria Papageorge. Norris promoted Kugel to Associate Dean for Research and, with a strengthened research program in oral and maxillofacial pathology and surgery coming to life, he set out to hire himself a cadre of basic scientists with NIH/NIDCR support to work alongside the clinical faculty who were aggressively seeking corporate sponsorship. When Norris presented the credentials of Professor Jake Chen, a tenured faculty member recruited from the University of Texas Medical Center at San Antonio, to the Department of Anatomy and Cellular Biology, he was met with the stunned acknowledgement that this was a serious basic scientist with serious grant support. He was immediately given a rare secondary appointment at Sackler. The doors were opening. Carole Palmer and Tina Papas had continued their work in nutrition and were given appointments in the now-named Friedman School of Nutrition. Robert Goode, newly chaired in Oral and Maxillofacial Pathology, was welcomed into the Sackler Department of Pathology.

Dental students were also now arriving with significantly better grade point averages in science from their undergraduate colleges, and it was inevitable that increasing numbers, previously interested in getting their degrees and getting out, under this new kind of research leadership would turn to the laboratory, as well. In 1998, a D2000 student named Edward Lahey was the *only* dental student in the nation to receive a Clinical Research Training Fellowship from the NIH in Bethesda, Maryland. No one was more thrilled that Bruce Baum, D'71, member of the Dental School's Board of Overseers and at the time chief of the Gene Therapy and Therapeutics Branch of NIH's National Institute of Dental and Craniofacial Research. Baum had been urging the Dean to encourage research among the students. Norris was delighted to give Lahey a leave for the 1998–1999 academic year. He returned to Tufts and graduated. Matthew Rand, D2004, applied after his third year at the Tufts Dental School to the Howard Hughes Medical Institute and the NIH for a one-year basic science research fellowship that is generally considered the biomedical equivalent of the Rhodes Scholarship. He was one of two dental students in the program's history to be accepted and spent the 2002–2003 academic year as a Research Fellow in the surgery branch of the National Cancer Institute on a topic that raised all the eyebrows in the Sackler faculty: the role of chemokine signaling in effector T lymphocyte migration to melanoma in a murine model. Here was dental research at the cutting edge of basic science.

More than anything else, there had been a mood swing at One Kneeland Street. No matter what Erling Johansen could do after more than sixteen years as Dean, it was not going to be appreciated. He represented another time, and above all, the attitude of another age. When I first encountered large numbers of dental students, I was struck by what seemed to be a common theme: The faculty treated them miserably. I shared this information with several of the senior faculty who had been involved in dental education for upwards of forty years. Their collective reply stunned me. "Yes, our faculty made us miserable when we were in dental school, and we hand on that tradition. It's not supposed to be fun." This sentiment characterized most of the faculty and administration during the 1980s and on into the next decade. Erling Johansen tried to create a user-friendly school, but he could not change a faculty that got perverse pleasure out of being just plain mean.

Norris was determined to change the culture. He benefited from a series of retirements, and then put himself on the line. With the invaluable help of his administrative team led by Pat Campbell, Mark Gonthier, Kugel, and Professor Nancy Arbree, his Dean for Academic Affairs, he set about spreading a sense of optimism and satisfaction in the profession. As the only Afro-American Dean serving at a predominantly white institution, he could not accept the appalling fact that in the year he took over he was left with no black students in the school. Norris actively recruited minority candidates, spread the gospel of good cheer and wonderful career opportunities in the profession to the students and alumni and was paid back with joyous enthusiasm. In a very short time the volcano that Dean Johansen had been sitting on went extinct. Even the older, more contentious faculty responded to Norris' leadership. Some were completely renewed. Veteran oral pediatrician Athni Tsamstouris, who during the dark years was often a lone voice of optimism in the school, urging students into her field, became one of Norris' most devoted cheerleaders. She also led the continued effort of an international humanitarian commitment that had always characterized the school. Tsamtsouris led a team of Tufts oral pediatricians to work in Chernobyl on young victims of the nuclear meltdown and its aftermath.

As the millennium was coming to a close, the Tufts University School of Dental Medicine could look back on a fairly recent past that had seen troubled times, and now one felt satisfaction and accomplishment. It represented a profession that had hit bottom and bounced back, and their deans had led them. Johansen had the first unqualifiably successful accreditation visit in the early 1990s, but Norris's first accreditation in 2000 earned the Dental School an unprecedented positive report. The faculty felt a newly discovered pride in their profession. The Dean had recruited senior research faculty from distinguished dental schools in Tennessee and Texas. Students were turning toward research, and those who spoke to the accreditation team expressed an enthusiasm for their education that left the outside evaluators shaking their heads in disbelief. But you could believe it. It was a new day, not just for the American dentist, but for Tufts School of Dental Medicine, as well.

Deanship of a school may be the most complex and unnerving position in the academic hierarchy. You have to lead, but not by too much. You must create an image of strength, capable of making the difficult and at times unpopular decisions while remaining admired, reasonably liked, and capable of explaining your actions in a way that demonstrates your civility and modesty. In passing, it does not hurt to be a better scholar or teacher than most of your faculty, but do not brag about it. Jean Mayer never thought much of deans, since he saw himself as the "dean of deans" and in many respects the leader of each individual school at Tufts. Some deans are better than others, of course, have a more intuitive sense of human nature and a greater capacity to get mileage out of their faculty. A very few are unique and gifted with a special quality of leadership that produces something very rare in faculty: genuine affection and loyalty. For a successor, this can be a real problem. Frank Loew was such a dean, and it is a tribute to his successor, Phil Kosch, that he has survived and even managed to prosper. It was not so easy. Here was an institution that, to most of its inhabitants, was identifiable with one man. Even after Loew's death in April 2003, Dean Kosch wrote in his eulogy, "TUSVM is still and always will be Frank's school."

In spite of his profound disappointment at not being selected President of Tufts University, Frank Loew bravely kept a bright public face and continued cheering on his "dandy little vet school." He kept up his political activities on behalf of the state appropriation, drove the fundraising forward, and no one saw a diminution of his prodigious energy. He contained his rage against the basic scientists who had publicly worked against his presidential candidacy, although henceforth he wanted no part of the Boston campus. He had gotten three of his classes out to Grafton and would not be satisfied until he had all of the vet students on the rolling hills of central Massachusetts, along with his researchers, several of whom still used space downtown. He avoided any involvement with One Medicine in one sense as Jean Mayer had intended it, with students from all the health sciences schools in common classrooms. Ultimately, he hoped to have his own basic sciences department and a Ph.D. program independent of Sackler. However, he was too good a scientist not to see where Mayer was going with the *other* idea of One Medicine, that is, the synergy that could evolve from scientific investigation that had veterinarians and nutritionists in a mix with the other health sciences researchers, where orthopedic surgeons in the New England Medical Center learned from the skeletal structure of dachshunds and oncologists at the

Tufts-NEMC Cancer Center appreciated that treating cancer in dogs and cats could teach them something about treating cancer in humans. Still, he was a man of enormous pride, and none of us should have been shocked when he told the community early in 1995, in the middle of the academic year, that he had accepted the deanship of his alma mater, the Veterinary School at Cornell University in Ithaca. He would assume his new responsibilities on September 1, 1995.

Nonetheless, we *were* shocked, and also unprepared. Frank had gone to Ithaca for a weekend on what his closest friends thought was a social visit and called me when he returned. "I'm out of here!" he exploded over the telephone, and all of the pent-up anger and bitterness poured out. Cornell had been wooing him for some years, and why should he stay at a place where he was not wanted? He flayed the Tufts presidential search committee, the Board of Trustees, the new President, and the "spineless" faculty who had undermined his candidacy. He had also called his administrative Dean and other confessor Martha Pokras, and we commiserated and consulted next morning. Loew was a great mentor of junior faculty, staff, and a terrific communicator with everyone. He was one of the few deans I have encountered who genuinely encouraged the professional development and advancement of female faculty. But he did not mentor a potential successor. For most everyone, he was the heart and soul of the institution, and the idea of a successor, much less one from among the faculty, just never caught on, neither with Loew nor his faculty. The year before an anonymous donor had named the new library, classroom, and education building at Grafton the Franklin M. Loew Veterinary Medical Education Center. Naming a building after a sitting dean is extraordinary; it makes sense only if one thought that Frank Loew would be Dean forever. After the impact of his announcement sunk in, a couple of inside candidates soon came forward, but once the senior faculty recovered from the stunning news, most of them made it clear to me that no one was really qualified, and we would have to look outside. Loew, after he had calmed down, concurred. I would now be looking simultaneously for deans in medicine, dental medicine, and veterinary medicine. Where professional search firms would swarm all over you to win a consulting contract to seek a dean for medicine or dental medicine, the phones went dead when it came to looking for a veterinary school dean. I finally called three of the leading educational practices, and they informed me that, with only twenty-seven American veterinary schools, there was not a large enough pool for them to help. We were on our own.

Fortunately, we were blessed with a wonderful candidate for interim Dean.

Sawkat Anwer was a basic scientist who had been recruited in 1983 to the Vet School to conduct research and to teach Pharmacology. He was also appointed in basic sciences and had appointments in Biochemistry and Pharmacology in the Sackler School. He was a first-rate investigator, well funded, and one of the vet school faculty who won the respect of the Boston basic scientists. He was Grafton-based and because he held a Ph.D. and not a veterinary degree, he could not be a candidate for the deanship. There was a general consensus among the senior faculty and staff that he would have made a great Dean of the Vet School, but the American Veterinary Medical Association, the accrediting agency, stipulated in its bylaws that only a veterinarian could serve as dean of a school. While the search went on, we would be in good hands. Of all the schools of Tufts, the Vet School had, as a team, the very best and most experienced, dedicated nonacademic players. Martha Pokras was the Dean's right arm and conscience, his resident counselor on all matters of personnel, whether faculty or staff. She could have had any number of jobs in human resources. In fact, the Vice President for Human Resources had selected her as HR Director for the Medford campus in the 1980s, and Martha, seeing a more attractive career path, was about to accept the position, when President Mayer heard about it. He was furious and told the Human Resources Vice President that she was meddling with a school and putting the veterinary program in harm's way. The offer was rescinded. In another age and at another time, and maybe with another person with less love for the university, Mayer would have found himself in court. Pokras had great interpersonal skills, was admired by the health sciences deans because she could keep Loew under some constraints when he was frustrated, and was one of the great treasures that a university comes to appreciate. Joe McManus was Loew's youthful and talented financial person, and the faculty trusted him. He was flexible in finding ways to wrangle more compensation for his professors and was scrupulously honest. He also educated the faculty and students about veterinary economics and helped find funding for new electives in business and economics for veterinary students. Both of them often found themselves on university-wide assignments. Shelley Rodman was a Development Director whom the faculty actually *liked*. They enjoyed traveling with her, she had a great style and infinite patience when explaining what cultivating, asking, and closing a gift meant. Rebecca Russo was the perfect Admissions Director: open to all visitors, a patient respondent to all questions wise or foolish, tour leader, travel agent, hotelier, and guide. Her honesty and candor made application to the Tufts Veterinary School an experience with no trauma involved. The team also was willing to carry the burden of communicating with the far-off other schools and the Central Administration, when their mercurial Dean was out of sorts. They minimized the geographic isolation, which was always an emotional problem for the Grafton school. With or without Frank Loew, this was a well-run institution.

It was important to have Dr. Henry Foster on the search committee. He was there at the beginning to select Al Jonas, he had helped to recruit Frank Loew, and his blessing was important when we laid hands on the next Dean of the school in which this remarkable businessman/veterinarian had invested more than just his financial resources. Hank Foster had poured himself body and soul into the Tufts Vet School. He, Loew, and Mayer were the pillars on which this enterprise had been built. When the administration building at Grafton was named in 1995 for Jean Mayer, there were then three names engraved on buildings, names that would always be associated with veterinary medicine at Tufts: the Foster Small Animal Hospital, the Loew Education Center, and the Mayer Administration Building.

The search committee, which I chaired, understood one thing clearly: Don't look for another Frank Loew. Trying to duplicate those qualities would lead only to frustration. I would secretly look for one essential characteristic: Find an optimist who could deal with the unique liabilities associated with this remarkable veterinary school. Given the small number of veterinary schools in the country, any candidate would have considerable benchmarking knowledge of what vet school had resources and who did not. Almost exclusively, the twenty-seven institutions were all within large land-grant public universities. The University of Pennsylvania Veterinary School was part of a private university, but it received fully one-third of its revenue budget from the State of Pennsylvania, as well as some capital support. Cornell, a private land-grant university with a statutory veterinary college, received state capital investment as well as other public cost sharing. Both enjoyed considerable capital building support from their states. Tufts was and remains the *only* veterinary school to receive nothing in capital support from the public sector, while at the same time having agreed to accept a minimum of 51 percent of its class from Massachusetts, for which it receives the lowest state appropriation—when during hard times it is not zeroed out of the budget completely—of all vet schools in the country. On every appropriation chart listing state contributions to vet school budgets, Tufts was at the very bottom of the page. On national average, the schools received 36 percent of their budgets from the states. Tufts received 13 percent of its budget in the best of times from the Commonwealth of Massachusetts. We also had the only veterinary faculty that did not enjoy the availability of tenure. The Trustees wanted no part of it for either nutrition or veterinary medicine. There were not enough faculty, salaries were just on the low side of mid-range nationally, and the successful candidate would be following one of the most charismatic figures in American veterinary medicine. "Attitude" would be important: I wanted someone who could see opportunity, no matter how rugged the landscape appeared.

And there was opportunity. Against all odds and in spite of having the highest veterinary tuition *in the world,* Tufts Vet School had convinced applicants from all over the country that it was worth the difference, because it *was* different. The Signature Programs—International Veterinary Medicine, Ethics and Values, Wildlife Medicine, Biotechnology, and Equine Sports Medicine—were unique as a package. The school was not required to have these programs to be accredited, but they were essential in establishing the school's uniqueness. Loew had put as many faculty resources as he could manage into these nonessential but attractive offerings that singled out the Tufts School of Veterinary Medicine. Chances were, we would have to find someone who felt the same way about being "different," someone who was willing to take a chance in looking unlike any other veterinary school in the nation or the world. We found him in Florida.

Phil Kosch had the same itch that Frank Loew had: He wanted to run a vet school that could be different. Four veterinary schools were looking for deans in 1995, but Phil Kosch wanted to be Dean of the Tufts Veterinary School. Hints in his resume told me he might be seeking a school that moved well beyond the traditional role of veterinary medicine. After obtaining his veterinary degree from Ohio State, he did a three-year stint in the army, emerging as a captain. Instead of starting a practice, Kosch headed for the University of California and a Ph.D. in Physiology. He was still not ready to leave a campus, and in 1977 headed for Harvard and two years of study at the School of Public Health. This set off a bell in my head. Ever since I had met Jean Mayer, public health interest had signaled innovation and an interdisciplinary mind. Kosch came to the University of Florida in 1980, and over the next fifteen years had appointments in the Veterinary School, electrical engineering, and Physiology and Pediatrics in the Medical School. In 1987, he was appointed Associate Dean for Research and Graduate Studies. He had had an active, funded clinical and basic science research agenda that took him into neonatology in both animals and humans, dealing with fundamental questions in the general area of comparative and developmental respiratory physiology. While the search was underway, one of the most productive basic scientists came to me and quietly whispered in my ear, "Please get us a scientist this time." Frank Loew had not built his career in basic science research. Kosch was clearly a step up in terms of reputation as a bench researcher. Now he felt he was ready to run his own shop, and he liked the national and international stage. Tufts had none of the parochialism of state veterinary schools. Although more than half the students came from Massachusetts, 70 percent of the applicants were from outside New England. No doubt, the Massachusetts applicants had a vastly better chance, one-of-three gaining admission, while the out-of-state ratio was one-of-eleven. The applicant pool clearly had a national flavor, and the research agenda was visibly international.

There was nothing timid about Phil Kosch. He was a very large man, jovial, laughed as often and as loud as Frank Loew, and had an easy smile, and, like his predecessor, suffered from the occasional symptoms of Foot in Mouth Disease. He had known Frank Loew, spoke of him as a rare veterinary academic intellectual, unique in the profession, and understood the challenge of succeeding him. He was ready to fundraise, eager to build on Loew's accomplishments, and seemed suited to the task. The search committee was unanimous, and I brought the President one candidate. On July 1, 1996, the third Dean of Tufts Veterinary School took the reins.

The fact that at this writing, into his seventh year as Dean, Phil Kosch is still leading a flourishing Tufts Veterinary School, is a tribute to Kosch's own grit, his utterly committed staff, and to my unwillingness to accede to yet another well-meaning but misdirected faculty insurrection, which I think began about a month after Kosch took over the deanship.

What Kosch did *not* possess was a subtle understanding of faculty dynamics. This you learn on the job, and one prays that the learning curve can keep ahead of the bullets that are heading directly between the eyes. The new Dean thought of himself as a consultative colleague who wanted to share authority and responsibility with his faculty, and that this style would make the transition from the Loew era seamless, since he assumed that the astonishing affection that the previous dean had generated was due to this collegial style. It could not have been further from the fact. Frank Loew ran his school like a benevolent dictator, and the faculty loved it. They did not even notice it. He had a genuine contempt for faculty governance and would have rare faculty meetings, explain what life was like, and make it clear that he was prepared to carry the heavy burden of leadership that no one else in the school could possibly assume. It was also true that the faculty of the Tufts Veterinary School was made up of relatively young, sometimes immature professionals, who had careers to make, and they had other priorities than faculty governance. They were happy to let Frank Loew run the school. I would appear at what seemed to be annual general faculty meetings, underline the esteem in which the school and its dean were held by the university, promise that Tufts would be there at all times for them, and listen as no questions were asked or issues engaged. Loew would *tell* the faculty of his strategies, cheer them on, and they loved it. In his thirteen years as Dean, I never received a single call or word of complaint concerning his management style.

Now comes the consensus builder, who wants to take the faculty into his confidence, share governance, do it all right, make them part of the process. (How often have I heard this!) His first, and appropriate, order of business was the restructuring of the departments. The faculty was an amorphous organization of the whole. Kosch wanted a clean distinction between basic and clinical sciences, two separate departments. With a school like Tufts with limited resources, such an organization would permit efficiencies in teaching and research through easier collaboration. There would be more scientific contact with each other within the proposed two-department structure, better synergy and grant-writing opportunities. He felt that there was no fear of alienation of one department from the other, because everyone was close enough as it was. There was also destined to be a third department, Environmental and Population Health, which appeared to the faculty to be a catch-all made up of all the programs that seemingly did not fit into the other two, but was really part of the Dean's long-range vision. Deep down in his ample bosom, Phil Kosch was as much of a contrarian veterinarian as Frank Loew. He, too, wanted a different kind of vet school. For now, Dean Kosch started conversations with the faculty, initially met with some resistance, until he started talking about possible departmental chairs, and the resistance melted away. Here is where he dug his first hole for himself. With each individual conversation, the faculty member walked away with the idea that the Dean had tapped *him as the new chair of the department!* Unaccustomed as they were to sharing *anything,* the idea of suddenly becoming chair of a department sent an authoritarian thrill through every faculty member who came away with the wrong impression, because Dean Kosch was simply feeling everyone out as to possible candidates. The miscommunication resulted in resignations, raging telephone calls to me, disappointed faculty members who already were having visions of administrative careers, and a bewildered Dean who thought he had been doing the right thing. He had only managed to unify a disparate faculty. The only problem was, they were unified against *him.* Matters calmed down a bit when he picked his two candidates: Sawkat Anwer as head of the Department of Biomedical Sciences, a natural and popular choice and a loyal supporter of the Dean, having also served on the search committee; and Chairman of the Department of Clinical Sciences John Berg, a young clinician whose selection indicated that Kosch might indeed be a mentor for younger colleagues. Berg grew in this enormous administrative job, overseeing something like forty regular and clinical faculty and politically helping Kosch deal with the faculty demons. At the same time, he is a regular faculty member and continues as a surgeon. With the selection of Steve Rowell, V'83—one of the first graduates of the school to become a member of the faculty—as Director of Hospitals, he had the courage and wisdom to put two people in place who eventually could have the potential to be his successor. Rowell became the best faculty manager and problem solver in the school. He continued his work as a faculty member while running a large hospital complex. Under his stewardship, the hospital was transformed from a major financial drain into the *only* veterinary hospital system in the country that became a major base of financial support for its school. The rest of the academic veterinary hospitals lose money. Rowell, like Berg, grew into one of the most respected senior statesmen at a very young age.

Phil Kosch had no honeymoon. In his first year as Dean, he had to meet a very difficult deficit target—the school had from its inception *always* been in deficit—and salary raises were not given to faculty or to staff making over $40,000 annually. The faculty grumbled and blamed the Dean. But he persisted, pushed his agenda for a better faculty and departmental organization, and he made it happen. He remained true to Loew's and his commitment that Tufts had a different environment from other American veterinary schools. He took Frank Loew's vision, crafted his own pair of lenses with more focus on public health and research, and was able to accomplish what successor deans ideally hope for: to take the enterprise to the next level. Of all the Tufts deans of the DiBiaggio presidency, Kosch's task was the most difficult, because he followed in the footsteps of a legend. Whenever I heard the often-repeated refrain, "He's no Frank Loew," I would shoot back instantly, "So who is?" Kosch understood the culture that he inherited, bought into it, and advanced the enterprise. He could not charm or soothe faculty or staff who had the memory of their former boss. He was not forgiven for errors in judgment or displays of insensitivity that Frank Loew's admirers would shrug off, had he committed them. But, Kosch had the good grace to accept his lot and was not going to come in and undo those unique aspects of the school. Under Frank Loew, TUSVM had moved away from conventional protocols in the use of animals in the teaching program: in anatomy, surgery, and clinical courses. The students who came to Tufts were strong advocates of this protocol, and the vet school continued to attract students who wanted nothing to do with the traditional use of animals in experimentation or research. Kosch was committed to continuing this policy and advocated the elimination of terminal small animal surgery elective laboratories. He worked to complete the transition of the veterinary medical curriculum to one that excluded the use of healthy animals for invasive or terminal procedures that were not therapeutic. The client donation and willed body program for anatomy made this possible.

Kosch threw himself into support for the Signature Programs. Even after Andrew Rowan left, the Center for Animals and Public Policy remained an important part of his agenda. Gary Patronek was appointed Director without loss of momentum. Kosch was an enthusiastic supporter of the core curriculum courses in Wildlife Medicine and placed fundraising for a new wildlife center high on his agenda. To give three of the Signature Programs a stronger sense of parity with the clinical and basic research programs, Kosch created his third department: Environmental and Population Health, with a broad umbrella big enough to cover Mark Pokras's Wildlife Center, International Veterinary Medicine, and the Animals and Public Policy program. He championed the international commitments in the Middle East, where Tufts faculty led by George Saperstein were working frantically with Egypt, Israel, Jordan, and the Palestinian Authority to control Foot and Mouth Disease, as well as in Africa, where in Burkina Faso Tufts vets and engineering faculty were involved in meteorological information gathering to help pastoral livestock people find rain. He had his own passions, as well, and they fitted into the character of the school. His early interest in public health expanded into what Kosch called Conservation Medicine, a holistic team approach to promoting the health of all animals, humans, and their shared environments, part wildlife, part international veterinary medicine. This was an early benefit of putting these seemingly unconnected programs in proximity to one another. After September 11, 2001, diagnosing and mapping the incidence of highly infectious and dangerous diseases of wildlife such as anthrax took on a new importance for the world, and the Tufts veterinarians were in a unique position. Kosch was deeply committed to the relationship between sustainable ecosystems and public health through the balance of animal, human, and environmental sustainability, and he wanted this symbiosis reflected in the Tufts veterinary curriculum. Like Frank Loew before him, Phil Kosch lent his ample shoulders to the task of pushing the boundaries of the profession and defining new roles for veterinarians in society nationally and globally. By insisting that animals and humans share this common ground, Kosch gave public health preparedness a new definition, one that became all the clearer with the threat of global outbreaks of infectious diseases. He insisted that veterinary students at Tufts fully appreciate their responsibility to protect the health of the public; that their education has as much to do with humans as it does with animals. Although he had created two departments that rationalized how a vet school faculty should be organized, it was the "irrational" department that Kosch really loved. Some mocked the Department of Environmental and Population Health as "the Department of Everything Else." For the Dean, it was the future, the way that all the eco-disciplines dealing with world health would come together. For Kosch, this was population-based medicine, and veterinary practitioners, while understanding traditional individual animal medicine, had to understand how disease behaves in populations, whether it was a herd, a pod, a flock, or a kindergarten class. Those two years at Harvard's School of Public Health had lit Kosch's candle. He created the department in 1997, with Carol Reinisch, who was doing the research on toxins found in clams in New Bedford Harbor, as the first chair. She went to Woods Hole, and Kosch turned the Department over to George Saperstein, who broke down more walls and saw the relationship between old and new infectious disease outbreaks in man and animals around the world as well as the increased frequency of exchange of disease agents between man and animals. Saperstein, whose general research interest was cross-border disease control in the most contentious regions of the Middle East, was a model of the Tufts international veterinarian. Here is where Jean Mayer's One Medicine really went to work.

Getting his four classes together was as strong an urge for him as it had been with Loew. In the year 2000, first-year students matriculated on the Grafton campus, and the job was done. Kosch had energetically fundraised for new teaching facilities, and with the completion of the McGrath Veterinary Teaching Laboratory and the Varis Lecture Hall complex, the Barbour Wildlife Medicine Building, a new faculty office building, and a redesigned and enhanced computer laboratory in the Webster Library, he was ready to offer a historic welcome to all four classes. This made a tremendous difference to campus life, operational efficiency, quality of curriculum delivery, and everyone's morale. The Vet School was whole, and home.

And, yet, even as the last veterinary student left the Boston campus, the intellectual and scientific relationship of the vet school faculty and staff with the other health sciences continued. The relationship was never as strong as it could have been; it might have been a factor of distance. I was always surprised to see a more successful collaboration between the vet school and the University of Massachusetts Medical School in nearby Worcester. Nonetheless, the Vet School faculty continued to reach out to Medford and Boston for successful joint projects. One of the great builders of bridges was the Health Sciences Database, which the Veterinary School was eager to sustain and expand. In 2000, Tony Schwartz, the Vet School Academic Dean and a veteran faculty member, secured a USDA grant to convert and upgrade the entire system, enabling all faculty and staff to edit the database from their own desktop machines. The HSDB, ironically, has done more to bring the students of the Tufts health sciences schools together than any other aspect of what "One Medicine" originally meant. Similarly, one would expect that having its own Ph.D. program in Grafton would have further alienated the Boston basic scientists, but Sawkat Anwer was too smart for that. A Ph.D. program was not a high priority for Frank Loew, but it was for Phil Kosch. For him it was an essential component of a successful academic research enterprise. The timing was right for Kosch, when it had not been for Loew. Kosch had given the research effort his complete support; extramural funding grew, he had a superb administrator and respected scientist leading the department in Sawkat Anwer, who would make certain that the "other" Ph.D.-granting faculty in Boston would keep from getting alienated. The two areas of research concentration—comparative microbial pathogenesis and reproductive biology—were not in the Sackler mainstream; and the marquee theme over the announcement also extended a hand: "Advancing human and animal well being through research and discovery."

The Vet School had always been an attention-getter among the local and national news agencies. Frank Loew had a way of positioning the school and its unique approach. In the Kosch era, the faculty jumped forward and garnered extraordinary interest from the public. A 1998 NOVA program on Public Television dealt exclusively with the life of vet faculty in their teaching environment at Tufts and proved to be the most-viewed program in the series' history. No one attracted more national attention than Nicholas Dodman, who had come to TUSVM in 1981 and seemingly languished as an ordinary veterinarian until his 1996 book *The Dog Who Loved Too Much* exploded on the public's attention. Dodman had made a major contribution to the field of animal psychology and had written a blockbuster. This London-born vet followed in 1997 with *The Cat Who Cried for Help* and then two more best sellers that carried the name of Tufts Veterinary School to every corner of the small animal world.

Saul Tzipori's work was just as remarkable, but his audience was made up of his scientific peers at the Center for Disease Control and other such centers around the world. He joined the Tufts faculty in 1991 after working in Australia and Bangladesh, and within three years built the Division of Infectious Diseases. He was perfect for Tufts and Kosch's public health ecosystem approach. Tzipori's research was in the area of enteric diseases in humans and animals who share similar environments, both food-borne diseases and water-borne parasitic diseases. His research results were extraordinary, and he became the single most heavily funded faculty member at Tufts. After September 11, the threat of possible bioterrorist attacks on the country's water and food supply provided him with an even greater forum.

The Tufts veterinarians seemed in the 1990s and into the next century to be everywhere. They were saving the loons in New England, working to clean up the harbors, and when there was a potentially disastrous tanker foundering off Cape Cod, Flo Tseng, a junior faculty member and Assistant Director of the Wildlife Clinic, was called in to demonstrate her expertise in oil spill response.

The one great consistency that connects the two periods of deanships at the Vet School is the student body. It has been superb. Each year the Geraldine R. Dodge Foundation offers an innovative program (Frontiers in Veterinary Medicine) that provides funding for veterinary students to undertake projects that stretch the bounds of the profession, that take students beyond the imagination of even their teachers. In 2003, the foundation awarded twenty-six prizes to students across the country attending ten different veterinary schools. Of these, two schools had one student fellow, four schools had two, three schools had three, and Tufts Veterinary School had *seven.* One could look back over the previous ten years and discover similar results. These students were consistently highly intelligent, intellectually curious, and four out of five of them were women. The class of 2006, which matriculated in the fall of 2002, was 89 percent female. The phenomenal trend is similar to those at the other American veterinary schools.

Looking back on the failure of Harvard and Middlesex to sustain interest in veterinary medicine in the Commonwealth of Massachusetts and viewing with trepidation the political roller coaster of the modest up-and-down-and-even-gone state contribution, as the century came to a close the Tufts School of Veterinary Medicine proved to be a hardy survivor. But, more than that, it was *special.* In a state like Massachusetts, jaded with hundreds of academic enterprises, the Vet School gave Tufts a unique excellence and momentum. Fewer than thirty American universities could point to a veterinary school as part of their academic portrait. After September 11, 2001, the regional, national, and international reputation of the school took on a new urgency.

As the century came to a close, nearly thirteen hundred graduates—more than the combined total of all the previous veterinary programs in all the failed history of Massachusetts's efforts—had gone out with Tufts professional veterinary degrees. More than 40 percent were Massachusetts residents, and another 20 percent were from the other New England states. Nearly 40 percent came from all over the United States. The full-time faculty now numbered 100, there were another 150 part-time faculty, and they labored on behalf of 320 students, 80 in a class, seeking the terminal professional degree of Doctor of Veterinary Medicine. Jean Mayer's vision of a total university had been sustained even without him.

NUTRITION: FINDING RESPECT

Veterinary Medicine singled out Tufts as one among fewer than thirty higher educational institutions out of four thousand in the United States; the School of Nutrition made Tufts the *only* university in the country with professional school programs in medical, dental, and veterinary medicine, international relations, engineering—and nutrition. Tufts was one of a kind. These two academic adventures shared the survivor's tight-jawed determination to prosper. Created out of the restless imagination of Jean Mayer and left incomplete, they survived his passing, and thrived. Veterinary Medicine for Mayer was an idea; Nutrition was a calling, and he believed that it was connected to the well being of the nation. It would be up to his successors— to his students, in many cases—to fulfill his vision; and fulfill it they did.

It was the arrival of Irv Rosenberg from the University of Chicago, with his medical degree and reputation among nutritionists, clinicians, and basic scientists, as well as possessor of a less aggressive attitude than Mayer, that paved the rocky road and provided for the future synergy that came to be Nutrition at Tufts.

As the field of nutrition matured in the second half of the twentieth century, it gradually began to attract modest numbers of both Ph.D. basic scientists and M.D.s who saw the benefits of preventive medicine. During and immediately after World War II, progress had been made in winning over some members of the medical profession when they realized that not only classic nutritional deficiency diseases such as scurvy, beriberi, and pellagra could be cured by vitamins and prevented by adequate vitamin intake; they also became aware of the strong nutritional components in heart disease, cancer, diabetes, and osteoporosis. Even though the medical profession has to this day not given nutrition its proper place in the spectrum of health and disease, there was no way the physicians could resist the tidal wave of interest that the public placed in the importance of diet and nutrition in disease, ironically with the dubious assistance of those earlier popular exponents whom the medical profession and academic nutritionists like Mayer called charlatans. Jean Mayer saw the crest of public and political interest coming in the 1970s and 1980s. He was able to pull together elements of science and political elites, brought public opinion along by bringing hunger advocacy groups under the umbrella, and created the momentum that changed the landscape of nutrition programs and policies in this country; and he did it in spite of the entrenched opposition of traditional academic peer review panels, who lacked Mayer's vision. It was Mayer's cunning decision to go around the peer review process to seek funds for nutrition, and he did it because he knew he was right, and that he would get short shrift from the NIH panels. Jean Mayer saw nutrition as a public health requirement that was being ignored by those in scientific power in academic science. He did what he felt was necessary, and his name will forever be tied to the process. Two economic historians from MIT and the University of Toronto submitted in June 2002 a paper entitled "Academic Earmarks and the Return to Lobbying," in which they stated, "The birth of academic earmarks can be traced to the late 1970s, when Jean Mayer, President of Tufts University, engaged two lobbyists—Kenneth Schlossberg and Gerald Cassidy—to help secure funding for a nutrition and aging center."[9] In 2003, what is euphemistically known as "Academic Pork" topped $2 billion in congressional earmarks.

Mayer was a lightning rod for the agriculture bureaucrats in Washington, who did not like his nutrition advocacy and intimacy with congressional delegations and committee chairmen. It seemed as if the agencies sensed what kind of impact Schlossberg & Cassidy's success would have on other universities, and they were determined to make life as miserable as they could for Tufts, in order to make certain that the object lesson was understood. Mayer never quite accepted how obstructive a Washington agency bureaucracy could be. He believed that Gerry Cassidy could wave a magic wand at the appropriation committee, and all would be well. His close friend and ally Stanley Gershoff was equally dismissive of USDA officials. We were in a

9. John M. de Figueiredo and Brian S. Silverman, *National Bureau of Economic Research Working Paper,* No. 9064, 2002, 8.

state of war and little changed as long as Jean Mayer was President of Tufts. Steve Manos and I would make trips to Beltsville to smooth over ruffled feathers and soothe aggravated ARS regional directors. The scientific product coming out of the HNRC was superb, but it took an enormous political effort to keep everything in line. The Director of the Center after Hamish Munro, selected personally by Mayer, only made things worse, telling one Department of Agriculture official responsible for USDA personnel in the Center, "If you get in my way, I'll piss on your shoes and use you for a doorstop." Manos and I urged the President to make a change in the Center leadership, and he reluctantly did. The selection of the next Center Director would be critically important. Mayer turned to one of his early acolytes, Irv Rosenberg. It would be Rosenberg who, after Mayer's death, carried the flag of nutrition for Tufts and to a consideration degree, for the country.

From his arrival in 1986 as Center Director, Rosenberg would accomplish what Jean Mayer could not do: build a bridge to the clinical faculty in the Tufts hospitals. His credentials in biochemical nutrition were as deep as Stanley Gershoff's and his training in physiology as intense as Jean Mayer's. He also had been Chairman of the Food and Nutrition Board of the National Academy of Sciences and had held leadership positions in the World Health Organization. He did not recognize a line between nutrition and disease, and nutrition and health. For Rosenberg, it was a continuum. Like Munro before him, Irv Rosenberg was at home with Ph.D. and M.D. researchers in the HNRC and hospital. More than any of his associates and predecessors, he was able to extend the reach of nutrition from bedside, to populations in general, and finally to the research bench. His own continued research also reflected that range.

After Jean Mayer's departure from the scene, it was up to Rosenberg to keep the flame of nutrition burning bright. Mayer knew he wanted a School of Nutrition but did not see his way to organizing all the elements that went into the concept of nutrition. In his mind, the HNRC was to be a subsidiary of the School, the laboratory arm of nutrition at Tufts. Stanley Gershoff concurred; the United States Department of Agriculture did not. In the early 1990s, having further burnished the international reputation of the HNRC research, Rosenberg began creating the trademark of Tufts Nutrition, a more seamless coherence between School and Center. When he stepped down as Director of the downtown facility in 2001, by then named the Jean Mayer Human Nutrition Research Center by an act of Congress, he had created a single conceptual backbone that Center and School shared. Gershoff had stepped down as Dean of the School in 1993. The USDA adamantly refused to allow Rosenberg to be both Director of the Center and Dean of the School. After long negotiations and persistent pleading, they agreed that he could be called Dean for Nutrition. The Agricultural Research Service regional director, who did not trust anyone at Tufts, made a preposterous demand: He would go along only if *I* were named interim Dean of the School! For two years, while Rosenberg knitted the School and the Center together, established faculty governance, curricula, and degree committees and actually made a faculty of nutrition that felt at home in both sites, Sol Gittleman, Gantcher Professor of Judaic Studies and Provost of the University, was Dean of the School of Nutrition. This does not appear on my curriculum vitae.

The final piece that formed the special quality of Tufts Nutrition was to be found in the bedside component. Only Rosenberg could persuade Shelly Wolff, and that meant Jerry Grossman, to establish a clinical nutrition division in the Department of Medicine that would have some synergy with the long-established Frances Stern Nutrition Clinic run by Johanna Dwyer, another physician/nutritionist whom Wolff respected.

By the mid-1990s, attitudes began to change at both USDA and ARS. Rosenberg was a nonconfrontational scientist who had a following among the agricultural administrators in Washington, D.C., and Beltsville. He suggested that the nit-picking contract arrangement, which ran to hundreds of pages of detailed accountability, be changed to a much-simplified cooperative agreement that could be reduced to a couple of dozen pages. USDA agreed, and a new day had dawned. They were also prepared to close an eye to Rosenberg's increased activities at the School. We never changed his title from Dean for Nutrition; but in fact he became the Dean of the School, whose name was soon changed to the School of Nutrition Science and Policy, to make it clear that implementation of the scientific findings was an important component. Rosenberg wanted to grow the school into a viable size, and from the sixty to seventy students in 1990, he began moving the student body first into the hundreds and soon the two hundreds. He tripled the budget and developed a range of center programs that reflected his notion of leadership in all areas of nutrition. These included Nutrition Communication; Agriculture, Food and the Environment; Famine; Food Policy and Applied Nutrition; and Physical Activity and Nutrition.

No other university in the nation had become as identified with nutrition and all of its scientific and policy implications as had Tufts. By the year 2000, scarcely a day would pass without a reference to a Tufts nutritionist in the

Wall Street Journal, New York Times, or *Washington Post.* The national public's appetite for nutritional and dietary information was insatiable. Professor Miriam Nelson's series of books in the late 1990s and first years of the new century on the subject of well-being in women resulted in enormous attention for her, Tufts Nutrition, and wellness in general. Beginning with *Strong Women Stay Young* (1997), she became a one-author industry and took Tufts Nutrition across the country. *Strong Women Stay Slim; Strong Women, Strong Bones;* and *Strong Women Eat Well* were examples of solid research results that translated into bestsellers. With *Strong Woman (and Men) Beat Arthritis* (2002), she worked collaboratively with other HNRC scientists. Alice Lichtenstein was named as first holder of the Stanley Gershoff Chair of Nutrition in the School, and this HNRC scientist, who worked with the USDA to establish the nutritional pyramid guidelines, further cemented the relationship between School, Center, and government.

Jean Mayer's goal of joining his nutrition agenda to medicine and wellness was coming closer to reality. One of Jean Mayer's last efforts was to secure funding to move the School of Nutrition to the health sciences campus and to create a facility that would house biomedical research and nutrition. Nearly ten years after his death, Mayer's dream was fulfilled during Rosenberg's last years as the Dean for Nutrition. As the century drew to a close, one event made it perfectly clear how far nutrition had come at Tufts. A health-directed foundation, the Gerald J. and Dorothy R. Friedman New York Foundation for Medical Research, wanted to make a major investment in nutrition. The foundation knew Tufts already, having endowed a chair in Nephrology in the Department of Medicine. Its board actually did not want to give another gift to Tufts and was hoping to find another school where nutrition was significant. The director, Jane Friedman, niece of the founders, was a diligent researcher who went to hospitals, physicians, and nutrition organizations, asking the same question: Where do I go to make the best use of my money? When the American Dietetic Association gave its answer, the issue was settled for Ms. Friedman. The ADA said that Tufts Nutrition was the program at the cutting edge of science and policy. Jane Friedman approached the university with a proposition to name the Gerald J. and Dorothy R. Friedman School of Nutrition Science and Policy at Tufts University. The generous endowment guaranteed the future of Jean Mayer's creation. As if to punctuate the continued application of nutrition to the state-of-the-art fields of medical research, new laboratories were established that year at the HNRC in the field of Nutrition Genomics, under Professor Jose

Ordovas; and Brain, Nutrition and Aging, led by Irv Rosenberg; and Cancer Prevention and Cancer Biology, where Professors Joel Mason and Xiang Wang reinforced the synergy with the Department of Medicine that Rosenberg had nurtured so carefully.

It went further than just the Department of Medicine. The HNRC put together a fellowship program to train physicians in clinical nutrition. In the Department of Family Medicine and Community Health, Professor Aviva Must pushed her colleagues in the Medical School closer toward nutrition and public health. Out in Grafton, Professor Lisa Freeman was one of a handful of board-certified clinical nutritionists in veterinary medicine in the *world*. After completing her undergraduate and veterinary work at Tufts, she returned to the Nutrition School and in 1996 received her Ph.D. Freeman brought a strong nutritional presence to the Vet School faculty. We noted earlier the enormous role that the Dental School played in the development of a nutrition program there. Both Professors Carol Palmer and Athena Papas were involved from the very beginning of studies in nutrition and oral health. Fletcher became involved when its Institute for Human Security hired Peter Uvin as the first Henry J. Leir Professor of International Humanitarian Studies. His links to the School of Nutrition were forged early and strong. Nutrition had reached out to every school of the university.

As Tufts Nutrition was preparing to celebrate twenty years of a remarkable existence, I could still hear Jean Mayer's words ringing in my ears: "Nutrition is not a discipline, it is an agenda." He took science and shaped it toward the public interest. Even years after his death, his ideas were having an impact on generations of Americans and on peoples around the world. Tufts nutritionists followed our troops into Mogodishu and Kabul, fighting famine and trying to make a better world. Americans have notoriously short memories, and on university campuses, with complete generational changes occurring in what seems to be a blink of an eye, you can be gone and part of the vague and distant past in a remarkably brief span of years. The alumni will hold onto beloved teachers, but presidents do not have large constituencies. On our campuses in these early years of the twenty-first century, there are a few faculty and no students who remember Jean Mayer. He is no more than a portrait in the Coolidge Room of Ballou Hall and a name on a building at the Vet School. But, for Tufts Nutrition, embodied in the Jean Mayer Human Nutrition Research Center in Boston, and for a nation and world that still benefit from his vision, Mayer's legacy lived on after him. Few American university presidents can have as much said about them.

THE SUCCESSFUL ANOMALY

Tufts had never had a President like John DiBiaggio. He was the first who had previously led another institution. He was the first who came to his Tufts experience from a tradition of large land-grant universities. When he arrived in Medford, parts of the enterprise were strange to him. Here was Tufts, deeply committed to its Unitarian-Universalist roots, and the new President had no idea what to do with a University Chaplain. Religion and religious life had no formal representation at University of Connecticut or Michigan State, and John DiBiaggio was worried about what he would say to Chaplain Scotty McClellan and the several associate chaplains. His academic training had been in a professional school of health sciences, and he possessed no scholarly track record to speak of. All of these characteristics were different from anything in the Tufts academic memory. Nelson Gifford's choice could have been a disaster.

Yet, as different as he was from Jean Mayer and all of the Tufts presidents who preceded him, John DiBiaggio nonetheless had a successful presidency at Tufts and loved nearly every minute of it. He understood his own strengths and determined how he best could lead a university that was very different from his earlier presidencies. Nothing about his two former institutions—the University of Connecticut and Michigan State University—could be said to be similar to Tufts. Like other large public universities, they both had enormous commitments to big-time college athletics. He had special boxes and budgets to entertain donors who were more interested in athletics than academics. It was a world in which John DiBiaggio felt very comfortable. Both were basketball powerhouses, and President DiBiaggio, even during his Tufts experience, never missed the Final Four NCAA basketball weekend. His style was personal, and he had genuine warmth that could put people at ease who were normally not accustomed to deal with the academic elite. He was a "people" person, with an open door; in almost all academic respects he delegated responsibility.

Once he decided that there would be few administrative changes at Tufts, he turned the running of the university over to his key people, in this case, Murnane, Manos, and Gittleman. We each had our own style. For me, this meant the Age of the Dean. I selected the best leaders I could find, gave them what I thought was appropriate individual attention, kept them herded together for synergy, required thin walls and low hurdles between the schools, and let them loose. The Office of the Provost took on a new luster under the DiBiaggio presidency, one that became clear to Steve Manos, who had been the man to whom the Trustees turned during the Mayer era, simply out of fear that Mayer would spend the university into deficit. During the DiBiaggio presidency, they turned more to the Provost who was the chief academic officer at a time when the President, by temperament and background, would rather not be. It all worked to the institution's advantage. The bond rating agencies were delighted with the continuity. Standard & Poor's and Moody's would make periodic visits when Tufts went into the bond market, and they were always delighted to see the same university officers in place for fifteen and twenty years. That, plus stronger and stronger applicant pools in all of the Tufts schools was all they needed to see. Throughout the DiBiaggio presidency, the Tufts bond ratings continued to improve. *U.S. News & World Report* had also discovered Tufts during the DiBiaggio years. He never failed to mention our improved rankings in his reports to the Trustees, and the rating agencies never failed to mention Tufts improved status in their evaluations.

Most of all, they delighted in Tufts capacity to raise money. Here is where the DiBiaggio era took off and where Tom Murnane really hit his stride as a fundraiser and as an orchestrator, because he finally had a president for whom the community had real affection. Not since Nils Wessell did Tufts have as its President someone whom the students and alumni took to as they did to John DiBiaggio. Murnane aimed this cheerful, down-to-earth, and attractive man at the students, parents, and graduates of Tufts, and they embraced him. The President would take visitors for rides in his two antique Packards. He tirelessly told the newly arrived students the story of Jumbo, trustee P. T. Barnum's king-sized elephant and Tufts icon. John DiBiaggio indulged the local Tufts alumni whom Mayer mocked—"the Medford Mafia," Mayer called them. DiBiaggio also happily shared the stage with an attractive, effervescent, and dedicated spouse who turned her home—the former dowdy president's house of Betty Mayer—into a flower-filled residence of elegant style, heated tents, elaborate dinners, and exhausted staff who bent but did not break under the demanding schedule. President DiBiaggio gave Nancy DiBiaggio full credit for the high style. "This is all Nancy's doing," he would say. Visitors loved it; students delighted in their frequent visits, and Tom Murnane raised $450 million so quickly that he expanded the campaign to $600 million, and raised that, as well. The stock market and the boom years of the mid- and late 1990s went John DiBiaggio's way. There was also a generally agreeable Board of Trustees instead of the politically charged regents at Michigan State who turned on DiBiaggio in favor of an athletic director. The Tufts Board was willing and able to cultivate donors, ask for large amounts of money, and close gifts that a few years earlier would have been unreachable. Murnane was wired into the Board, into the European parents and alumni, he knew the color of money and went to it like a moth to light. From dead stop in the water when Jean Mayer arrived, with nothing but failure in its futile efforts to raise money, in twenty-five years Tufts had raised $1 billion, and the Gray Eminence behind it all was Tom Murnane, the dentist.

When necessary, John DiBiaggio stepped out of his ceremonial presidential style and grabbed the reins in his own hands. He did it with the structural deficit in the first weeks of his presidency; and his resolution to act emerged again in an admissions decision that caught the attention of the nation.

In April 1995, Tufts offered admission to an honors student from Cambridge Rindge and Latin School named Gina Grant. Sometime between the admissions decision and commencement of that year, anonymous packages of newspaper articles were dropped off at the *Boston Globe* and Harvard, informing officials that four years earlier Grant had pleaded no contest to the voluntary manslaughter of her mother, an abusive alcoholic who had threatened to kill her thirteen-year-old daughter. The teenager served eight months in a juvenile center in South Carolina, after which the judge ordered that her juvenile record would not be revealed unless she committed a future crime. The Lexington County sheriff did not agree with the court order and made public statements about Grant. No one ever discovered who dropped off the four-year-old news clippings to Harvard and to the *Globe.* The result of the sensational national news coverage was that both Harvard and Columbia University in New York rescinded their offer of admissions, saying that Grant lied in her application. It would have been very easy for Tufts to follow suit. But, it did not, mainly because John DiBiaggio refused to go along. The Tufts admissions people told him that no fraudulent statement was made in her application. At a meeting that included the senior university administration, general counsel, public relations, and alumni affairs, the President made his position clear: "She paid her penalty. That's supposed to be enough under our system. I like to think that this university is caring and forgiving." He was forceful in asserting his position, and opposition by some of his advisors who were reluctant to accept Grant melted away. President DiBiaggio never wavered. There was some outspoken student opposition ("Anyone want to room with a convicted killer?"), but Grant came to Tufts. After a few months, the local and national news coverage disappeared, and she enjoyed a quiet four years as an undergraduate until she graduated in May of 1999.

He also expressed decisively his long-term advocacy of volunteerism. He was deeply committed to the idea of citizen participation for the public good, and here he was a very good fit for Tufts. The Leonard Carmichael Society was by the far the largest student organization, and it was dedicated to those same principles that drove President DiBiaggio. When Mel Bernstein and Professor Rob Hollister closed the $10 million gift from Pierre and Pam Omidyar, the founders of *eBay* and 1988 graduates of the College, the DiBiaggio legacy was established. Hollister conceived of the idea of a University College of Citizen Participation and Public Service to formalize what John DiBiaggio had been preaching.

During the DiBiaggio presidency, the faculty went about its business. After the initial angry reaction, things settled down. From time to time there came some nasty comment about presidential academic leadership, but there was never a hint of any organized dissatisfaction.

The Trustees also had settled down. As they had with President Mayer, they gave President DiBiaggio a third-year review, which contained the responses of twenty-four Trustees. To make matters somewhat awkward, the senior administrators were asked to participate. We did, with considerable reluctance. The review confirmed all of the strengths we had seen: "Decent, warm, approachable." There was also some early dissent. When I received the first of several phone calls from Trustees expressing concern about "lack of boldness, too cautious, not an innovator," I became somewhat testy. "That's not what you hired him for," I replied once, with heat. But it was clear that there were within the Board of Trustees signs of early impatience and a sense that, yes, we needed a break from Jean Mayer, but we also need to regain presidential initiative. That sentiment gradually grew more vocal. Nelson Gifford stepped down from the chairmanship of the Board in 1995, and John DiBiaggio lost his strongest supporter. It was only a question of time before those more aggressive board members, who were invested in an assertive presidential style, were ready to look for new leadership.

There is some irony in the fact that three presidents—Carmichael, Wessell, and Hallowell—each walked away from a struggling institution on their own initiative. Even though Tufts was going nowhere, Carmichael and Wessell were begged to stay on by Trustees, alumni, and faculty. In the case of Jean Mayer, who would have happily remained to rival John Silber's more than thirty years at Boston University, he totally transformed the university and led it out of the wilderness. That did not prevent the Board from wanting a change. They made the change to John DiBiaggio, who never tired of saying that being President of Tufts University was the best job he ever had. But, boards of trustees have their own dynamic and memory. It was time, some felt, to find another Mayer, perhaps a little more disciplined, but an academic leader.

Not everyone on the Tufts Board agreed. The genuine affection felt by many alumni had translated into strong support for the incumbent president, and there was division. In the end, the President stepped aside at the end of the 2001 academic year after nine years, the longest term of his three university presidencies. In an unprecedented show of affection, the Tufts University Alumni Association awarded both DiBiaggios Distinguished Service Awards. *Boston Globe* columnist David Warsh summed up the perception of the general public: "No university president in Boston had a better decade than John DiBiaggio of Tufts."[10] One final acknowledgement of John DiBiaggio's place in the constellation of Massachusetts higher education came in October 2003, when he was appointed by Governor Mitt Romney as a new trustee for the University of Massachusetts governing board. The circle was complete. He had returned to the familiar environment of public education. His familiarity with the world of big-time collegiate athletics was confirmed in 2004, when he was brought in as consultant to the University of Colorado, where the athletic program was the center of a scandal that included allegations of rape and charges that football recruits were lured to the Boulder campus with sex and alcohol. This world of big-time intercollegiate athletics was the world in which John DiBiaggio himself was a player. His Tufts experience was an anomaly, yet he will be remembered by the alumni and students with deep affection.

10. David Warsh, "Coming Attractions," *Boston Globe*, June 5, 2001, D1.

Three powerful Trustees and their man. Howland, Callow, and Gifford, with Jean Mayer presenting an honorary degree to Allan Callow.

Nathan Gantcher, Chairman of the Board of Trustees, 1995–2003. The new face of Board leadership. Goodbye, Boston. Hello, New York City.

James Stern, Chairman of the Board, 2003 to the present. Smart, energetic, and a great fundraiser. The Board is transformed.

John DiBiaggio, President of Tufts,
1992–2001. Like Wessell, the alumni
loved him.

John DiBiaggio with his wife Nancy
and the two Westies. A Christmas card family.

Lawrence Bacow, President of Tufts
University, 2001 to the present. Back to
Mayer's ideas, but with discipline.

Adele Fleet Bacow, the President's spouse.
The perfect complement.

Peggy Newell, Associate Provost for Research. The perfect combination of talent for the new Tufts.

June Aprille, Professor of Biology and Associate Provost. The new faculty. She came because of Mayer.

Wayne Bouchard, Executive Administrative Dean, Arts, Sciences and Engineering. Like Pokras, Campbell, and other nonacademic Deans, he possesses the intelligence to make the faculty work.

Jamshed Bharucha, Provost, 2002 to the present. The perfect successor: scientist, musician, great people skills.

Mel Bernstein, Vice President of Arts and Sciences, 1992–2002. He was a benevolent ruler of his own little college.

A brace of Provosts. Bharucha and Gittleman, a perfect transition.

Susan Ernst, Dean of Arts and Sciences, 2001 to the present. Another biologist with people skills.

Yannis Miaoulis, Dean of Engineering, 1995–2003. Part Mayer, part Loew, all entrepreneur.

Linda Abriola, Dean of Engineering, 2003 to the present. From strength to strength in technology, and the future.

John Galvin, Dean of Fletcher School, 1995–2000. From four stars to Fletcher. "Do I look like Norman Schwartzkopf?"

Stephen Bosworth, Dean of Fletcher School, 2001 to the present. A diplomat with high academic standards.

Lisa Lynch, Academic Dean, Professor of Economics. The new Fletcher School. On to the future.

Frank Loew, Dean of the Veterinary School, 1982–1995.

Phil Kosch, Dean of the Veterinary School, 1996 to the present. Bravely trying to succeed a legend.

Morton Madoff, Dean of the Medical School,
1992–1995. A hard man for hard times.

John Harrington, Dean of the Medical School,
1995–2002. A good old boy and great decision.

Professor Sheldon Wolff, Chairman of
Medicine, 1977–1994. A great scientist
caught between hospital and school.

Michael Rosenblatt, Dean of the Medical
school, 2003 to the present. The new
generation of deans.

Irv Rosenberg, Dean of the Freidman School of Nutrition, 1997 to the present. Second Director of the Human Nutrition Research Center, 1986–2001. The future: The Nutritionist with an M.D. Passing Mayer.

Robert Russell, the third Director of the HNRC, 2001 to the present. He built a bridge to Medicine that Nutrition could cross.

Miriam Nelson, Faculty, Friedman School of Nutrition; Scientist, HNRC. Her books take nutrition and exercise to the public.

7

Something extraordinary happened at the first reception for the newly announced President of Tufts University in May 2001. Larry Bacow was going to be introduced at a general reception in the Coolidge Room on the Medford campus after the announcement of his selection had been made. There would be similar receptions downtown for the health sciences community and out in Grafton. President-designate Bacow was greeting the early arrivals when, to my astonishment, about one-quarter of the Fletcher faculty walked in and immediately mobbed him, not as their President, but as their colleague, one of the nation's leaders in dispute resolution in the area of environmental policy. A few minutes later, former Dean Jeswald Salacuse, now a Professor of International Business Law and himself a world-traveled international negotiator, asked me how soon the process could begin to give President Bacow a tenured appointment at Fletcher!

Fletcher offering a tenured appointment to a Tufts President. Now, I thought, anything was possible. But, matters did not stop there. Within a month, I had received inquiries from the Departments of Economics, Urban and Environmental Policy, and Civil/Environmental Engineering of Arts, Sciences and Engineering, asking if it would be appropriate for the new Tufts President to be given a professorial appointment in their departments. When the Medical School's Department of Community Health asked if the President would accept an appointment as Professor of Public Policy in Community Health, that added up to five different units of Tufts that wanted to lay claim to the new President's academic reputation. When President Bacow was elected to the American Academy of Arts and Sciences in 2003, he was the only faculty member so honored among the entire membership of those five programs. There is no record that any department ever offered Jean Mayer an academic appointment, either in the basic sciences or in the Biology Department of the Arts and Sciences, even though he had been for many years, since his Harvard days, an elected member of the AAAS. John DiBiaggio did not have an appointment in the Dental School. More than any previous Tufts President in recent memory, Lawrence Bacow came as a recognized academic leader, scholar, and peer.

When the Trustees selected Irwin Heller to chair the Trustee search committee, there was little doubt that they would be seeking a candidate to restore the appropriate historical balance to the presidency. Like Dartmouth after Kemeny, they would turn one hundred and eighty degrees. Harvard University, always showing the way even in presidential searches, seemed to have a peculiar predilection for seeking opposites. The most recent historians of Harvard, describing the presidential search process, wrote: "The most conspicuous dynamic in the Harvard presidential selection process— get someone as unlike his predecessor as possible—had once again kicked in. This was true of the choice of Eliot in 1869, of Lowell in 1909, of Conant in 1934; it was true of Pusey in 1953."[1] More recently, after Derek Bok, a law school dean and eminent scholar of labor law, Harvard turned to a generally ceremonial president of civil disposition with no particular academic distinction. When seeking a replacement for Neil Rudenstine, you could just feel it in the air that Harvard wanted a heavy-hitting academic intellectual who also could run that fractious university, where deans reported only nominally to presidents and ran their schools like independent baronial fiefdoms. Rudenstine had announced at his inauguration that one of his primary goals was to bring Harvard's schools closer together and to strengthen the central administrative accountability of this notoriously independent group of schools and deans. Within a few short years he was hospitalized with exhaustion. The next Harvard President would be surely of sterner metal. Indeed, he was.

Tufts would also now be looking for a strong academic leader, for another change agent. The faculty was aching for one. Heller, a 1967 graduate of the College, made it clear in all of his interviews that the committee was seeking someone who combined the best characteristics of the past two presidents: "We felt it was time to have a president who had academic standing that the

1. Morton Keller and Phyllis Keller, *Making Harvard Modern: The Rise of America's University* (New York: Oxford University Press, 2001), 175.

faculty would respond to, was not afraid to take risks, had a visionary's energy, but with some balance of prudence and judgment." Heller said that they had some very attractive candidates, but only one who had it all: the forty-nine-year-old Chancellor of the Massachusetts Institute of Technology, Lawrence S. Bacow.

Larry Bacow had the kind of credentials that the Boston academic community responds to. He earned a Bachelor's degree in economics from MIT, a law degree from Harvard, and a Master's and Ph.D. in Public Policy through Harvard's Kennedy School. He came to MIT as an Assistant Professor of Law and Environmental policy, authored four books, sat on the editorial boards of major environmental journals, and was a gifted teacher. In 1992, Bacow was promoted to full Professor, in 1995 he became the senior faculty spokesman at MIT by assuming the position of Chairman of the Faculty. President Charles Vest then asked him if he would serve in the newly created position of Chancellor, a title previously reserved for former MIT presidents, and in August 1998 Larry Bacow, the Lee and Geraldine Martin Professor of Environmental Studies at MIT, took the step that eventually led to the presidency of Tufts University. He served for three years as MIT's Chancellor, before being tapped for a position he did not seek.

Professor-and-now-Chancellor Bacow had no intention of becoming a college president or of leaving the institution that he had grown to believe, after thirty-one of his forty-nine years, was his permanent home. But, as he said at every one of his early get-to-know-me receptions, that coming to Tufts was "bescheert," the Hebrew word for a fated destiny. Someone mentioned his name to the firm assisting in the search; he met the committee once, then met with it again. As Heller said, "We had the perfect candidate."

THE TWO LARRYS

Harvard and Tufts share an academic universe of nearly sixty colleges and universities in the Boston area, but they exist in two different planetary systems. Harvard, the quintessential research university, certainly the wealthiest and perhaps the most eminent in the world, makes a deep genuflection toward undergraduate teaching, but it does a job no better than a dozen other large research universities. The same faculty cannot do both jobs superbly: engage in research that leads to a Nobel Prize, and teach undergraduates. Tufts, on the other hand, emerged out of an environment where research was looked upon with great suspicion and only with the coming of Jean

Mayer began to find its appropriate place in the academic research scheme of things. It could be truly eminent in a very selective number of research areas, but only in a few. As a teaching institution, however, it could excel.

There was some irony, therefore, to be noted in the aspirations of two new university presidents who appeared in Boston within months of each other, as the new millennium got under way. One wanted to reinvigorate the teaching at his institution. The other hoped to inspire a greater degree of research. For a moment, one might have thought that they had been switched at birth and were at the wrong institution.

In March 2001, the Harvard Corporation replaced Neil Rudenstine with Lawrence H. Summers. A few months later, Lawrence S. Bacow replaced John DiBiaggio. Both Larrys had strong ties to MIT's rigorous Economics Department as well as to Harvard, and they had known each other. They were academics from top to bottom. Both were succeeding presidents who had been extremely deferential to their faculties. Eager to get moving on issues they considered critical to their institutions, neither wanted a honeymoon.

Even though the two institutions were different in character, size, and emphasis, both new presidents felt a review of undergraduate education was a first priority. They also wanted to challenge the faculty after a period when some saw complacency taking hold both in Cambridge and in Medford. But, looking past the similarities, there were two distinct "Larrys." Both were Jews, but Summers was secular, somewhat less of a family man, and generally recognized as a bull in a china shop when it came to direct confrontations. He said exactly what was on his mind, as was noted in the celebrated contretemps with Afro-American Professor Cornel West, whose scholarship did not reach up to the standard his President thought appropriate for one of only seventeen extraordinary university professors at Harvard. Summers privately told him so; West told his five hundred best friends, and the incident made national headlines. West left for Princeton, Summers mended his fences with the Black community, took quiet congratulations from many of the Harvard faculty and alumni, and went on to make change in a very public fashion, as he did most everything. After his arrival at Harvard, it became known that he was going through a divorce, and soon after he began dating a member of the faculty. He dressed indifferently, was often seen with a shirt-tail hanging out, and could not have cared less.

Larry Bacow's Jewishness was part of his existence and inseparable from him. He might have been the third consecutive Tufts president whose parents were born in Europe, but he was the first whose mother survived Auschwitz. Jean Mayer, in the language of Nazi Aryan laws, was technically a

Jew but generally ran from any identification with Jewishness, which bothered his Jewish relatives on his mother's side when they would encounter him in America. For Larry Bacow, the Holocaust helped define his existence; he was an observant Jew, married to a woman from a traditionally pious southern Jewish family whom he had met when they were students in Boston. Adele Fleet Bacow was his partner in every sense. Equally as observant, the two of them jogged in the morning together, lit the Friday evening candles together, and made Gifford House, unostentatiously, a home where they and their college-age children could maintain a reasonable Jewish life. Within weeks of their settling in, they had a ceremony where four rabbis hung *mezuzahs,* the small parchment on which are inscribed the first two paragraphs of the "Hear, oh Israel" prayer from Deuteronomy, over the four doorpost entrances to Gifford House. It was at this point that I expected the murals in Alumnae Lounge, which depicted the Tufts' "Venerables" from the nineteenth and early twentieth centuries, to slide off the walls in shock and horror. But they stayed put.

The Bacows also demonstrated a very sensitive understanding of what Gifford House had become: a magnet for the Tufts community. They immediately threw open the doors of their home to everyone. In their first year, there were a series of senior dinners for the entire class. They even continued the tradition of the winter holiday celebration, without the sumptuous Christmas tree. Like the DiBiaggios before them, the Bacows came as a family package, and the community took to them instantly. They invited any member of the Tufts community to join with them in their early morning runs. In their second year, the Bacows helped train the Tufts contingent of students, alumni, and faculty who ran in the Boston Marathon. Here was a very specific instance where the Tufts "Larry" had the advantage.

But, when it came to issues dealing with students and campus life, from the very first minute Bacow showed the same transparently blunt opinions that characterized his Harvard counterpart. Before coming to Tufts, Chancellor Bacow of MIT had to deal with the death from alcohol poisoning of a first-year undergraduate, and he arrived at Tufts with zero tolerance for excessive student drinking. He made it abundantly clear in his first public pronouncements that he had no patience with anything that led students to drunkenness. He took on cherished student events, the fraternity system, and the alumni with the same determination, regardless of what it might cost him in popularity. He was resolute, and the faculty loved it.

His greatest support from the first moment he stepped onto any of the campuses was from the Tufts faculty. There were no doubts. Like Jean Mayer, he took charge at the faculty meetings, never diminishing the deans' authority, but making it clear that he was the President and ultimately responsible for their welfare. Within weeks of his arrival, he had won their hearts and minds. He started his post-jogging mornings by answering all of his overnight e-mail messages with long, thoughtful replies, no matter how trivial the issue or arrogant the sender. He had an instinct for dealing with faculty or school concerns. Sensing the issues associated with its distant location, President Bacow would frequently drive out to Grafton, had done his homework, and knew what was on the minds of faculty, students, and staff. He had taken on the problem of the Vet School bottom line as his personal challenge. President Bacow was not a pet owner or traditional animal lover like his two predecessors, but his energy, intellect, and creativity were evident to everyone in Grafton, and they knew he was working hard on their behalf. When Governor Romney zeroed out the school appropriation in the fiscal year 2003 state budget, the President leapt into action, and like Mayer before him, got the dollars restored. From the outset, he was deeply appreciated at the Vet School. For the Medical School, he opened up the university's pocketbook and authorized $10 million for nineteen new faculty positions in the basic sciences. He knew exactly what buttons to press. He told Dean Norris of the Dental School that he would wholeheartedly support his research initiative, gave Rosenberg and Rob Russell assurances that he understood the needs of Nutrition at Tufts, and was a champion of the kind of interdisciplinary research that the HNRC produced. The President cemented their loyalty and admiration when he brokered an arrangement with the John Hancock Insurance Company to fund the John Hancock Center for Physical Activity and Nutrition; and the Fletcher faculty actually went through the elaborate process from start to finish to award the President tenure by acclamation.

His greatest challenge, as with all presidents, would be with the Arts and Sciences, and there, too, his presence at the faculty meetings gave reassurance, even when he was provocative. He told the humanists that a published dissertation really should not be the measure of scholarship, that a *second,* independent research project really should be the standard, and that second projects should go far beyond the traditional boundaries of the discipline. The scientists and social scientists heard the same message: the future of research would be at the interface of the disciplines; faculty will want appointments in several departments and centers; be flexible, get ready, because Tufts will be moving ahead, once again. But he also made it clear that he understood that Tufts was not a traditional research university, but rather was a teaching institution where undergraduate education was the primary task of the faculty. Even here he demanded imagination, creativity, and some re-thinking. Within months of his arrival, he appointed Professor Gilbert Metcalf of the Economics Department as Chairman of the Task Force on the Undergraduate Experience. Bacow, in his charge to the committee, asked the key questions: Are we meeting the intellectual expectations of our students? Can we anticipate how technology might further enhance the overall educational experience, in terms of curriculum, pedagogy, and student support? How does the co-curricular and residential experience of our students complement their classroom education? He told the committee to find out our strengths and weaknesses, make recommendations on how to strengthen the undergraduate program, and get back to the faculty committees that are empowered with the responsibility to make change. At the same time, President Bacow appointed Chemistry Professor David Walt to establish a Graduate Council of all schools, to work on the interdisciplinary agenda of graduate education and research. Larry Bacow hit the road running.

What is all the more astonishing is that the calamity of September 2001 in no way deterred him. Ten days after he officially became President Bacow of Tufts University, the World Trade Towers collapsed, and America was a different country. He took grip of the community, organized the chaplaincy, and by 5:00 P.M. of that horrible day, President Bacow was reassuring the shaken Tufts community.

Like Jean Mayer before him, Larry Bacow was not lucky, and he did not need it. He would go against the grain of a weak stock market, declining fundraising in American universities, shrinking endowments, a numbing national tragedy, and a hostile Congress to have an extraordinarily successful first year as President of Tufts. As if to punctuate the events of that year, in the summer of 2002 a major breakdown of the Massachusetts Electric Company occurred, and the Medford campus was without power for seven days. Huge mobile generators provided energy for the campus, and the President kept morale high. So ended Year One of the Bacow presidency.

It was time for change, time for the President to build his own team. After twenty-one years, I felt that my contribution as Provost had run its course. He needed a younger, more focused academic leader, and I told the President to go and get the right candidate. He found him. On August 1, 2002, Jamshed Bharucha, Dean of the Faculty and Professor of Psychology at Dartmouth, began serving as Provost and Senior Vice President at Tufts. From a personal viewpoint, I was delighted. The Dartmouth academic culture is very similar to Tufts. Both are small teaching universities where everyone does research. The undergraduate liberal arts tradition is at the heart of both institutions, students are taken seriously and are empowered, and professional graduate education rounds out two very complex universities. The new Provost was born in Bombay, India, was an accomplished violinist, and his research on the impact of music on the nervous system was acclaimed. He had the right interdisciplinary stuff that Larry Bacow was looking for.

The changes came quickly, but appropriately. Mel Bernstein moved on, and this provided the President with the opportunity to reorganize. Engineering was given equal status with the Arts and Sciences, and Yannis Miaoulis had for the first time in the school's history full programmatic and administrative responsibility for all engineering education; and the College of Engineering officially became the School of Engineering. Within the next year, Dean Miaoulis would also move on to the Presidency of the Boston Museum of Science. Provost Bharucha's first search produced a diamond. It was a sign of the evolution of Tufts engineering that he was able to attract from the University of Michigan Linda Abriola, one of the world's top researchers in groundwater contamination and remediation. Tufts' first female Dean of the Engineering School, like the man who led the search, was a classically trained accomplished violinist.

The Arts and Sciences, still joined in admissions, financial aid, and in general academic administration with Engineering, was given a new administrative appearance. The Rotberg-Bernstein vice presidency was eliminated along with two deanships, and biologist and Associate Dean for Sciences and Social Sciences Susan Ernst was appointed Dean of Arts and Sciences.

For the first time in over twenty years, an outsider took over as Dean of the Medical School. In a sense, this was also a measure of progress made and reputation earned by TUSM, as well as infinitely more cordial relations with our primary teaching hospital, NEMC, now officially called Tufts-New England Medical Center. Michael Rosenblatt, M.D., was an internationally recognized researcher in bone and mineral metabolism, a Harvard Medical School professor who earlier had been connected with Merck Pharmaceuticals as a key investigator, and had impeccable credentials as a basic science researcher and clinician. He also had served as President of Beth Israel Deaconess Hospital, and was an important part of the Boston medical establishment. While many in the Medical School still preferred a Tufts insider as Dean, President Bacow believed it was time to get to the next rung of the ladder, and made the decision with Provost Bharucha. Michael Rosenblatt began his deanship on November 1, 2003.

Tom Murnane, who had spent nearly a half-century at Tufts and had left his fingerprints on almost every one of the billion dollars we had raised, re-tired at the end of the 2002 academic year. Brian Lee, his talented young deputy, would take over as Vice President for Institutional Advancement. Steve Manos remained as Executive Vice President. Mary Jeka was appointed Vice President for University Relations, a genuflection toward a hoped-for improvement in town-and-gown relations as well as the need for a reinvigo-rated relationship with the Washington, D.C., political establishment. David Cuttino, Dean of Admissions and the individual most responsible for the re-markable classes Tufts gathered into the undergraduate colleges, stepped down after sixteen years, and Dean Ernst brought in Lee Coffin from Milton Academy to fill his shoes. It was time for new faces.

ONE HUNDRED AND FIFTY YEARS OF TUFTS

In his first presidential year of 2001–2002 Larry Bacow and the Tufts community marked the sesquicentennial of the founding of Tufts College in 1852. The challenges that President Ballou faced one hundred and fifty years ago were unlike anything confronting the current President of Tufts Univer-sity. Hosea Ballou could look down Walnut Hill and see the horse path that soon would be called Professors Row. The property owned by his new col-lege stretched to the south as far as his eye could see toward Somerville and Cambridge, a lush expanse of green meadow with occasional trees and houses. The last thing on his mind would have been worries about becom-ing a land-locked institution hemmed in completely by the two neighboring communities. He would never have dreamed of a future with such a diverse faculty and student body, nor would it have been within the realm of his lib-eral Universalist imagination to believe that his college would some day have a Catholic priest as University Chaplain: Father David O'Leary, appointed in 2002; or a beautifully situated Hillel Center next to Wren Hall on the Hill. Larry Bacow was the President of a vastly different institution, unrecogniz-able even to the faculty who just twenty-five years earlier were dubious about the future of Tufts. The pre-Mayer college had evolved haphazardly into a very comfortable but indifferent institution, a university by this time, with no particular academic distinction, and had struggled with poverty during its first one hundred and twenty-five years. By the time, twenty-five years later, when it reached its one hundred and fiftieth birthday, Tufts had found itself an eminent place in American higher education. Now, the challenges for President Bacow were everywhere, and the educational instrument he controlled—this remarkably versatile and flexible Tufts University—would have to stand the test for the coming decades. Perhaps the greatest struggle was the one emanating from the national crisis in health care and medicine. With medical school applications plummeting all over the country, he faced a medical profession uncertain of its direction or mission and its place in the scheme of things. Internet use for medical data was shifting the doctor-patient roles; medical specialities were battling with one another over referrals, and the health care system in America seemed to be broken. No challenge was as daunting as the one the Tufts President faced regarding the future of the Medical School's primary teaching hospital, now once again officially named Tufts-New England Medical Center, but still with a separate board. When Thomas O'Donnell, M.D., announced his resignation in the late summer of 2003, amidst rising hospital deficits, that board turned to President Bacow to chair the critical search for O'Donnell's successor.

Space would be a constant problem. "The Cambridge Larry" had pulled off one of the greatest real estate deals of this or any century for a university in America when he acquired ninety-one acres of contiguous space in Allston, adjacent to the Harvard Business School and athletic fields. He had freed Harvard from its land-locked trap. "The Medford-Somerville-Boston Larry" faces a space crisis that threatened the viability of both urban campuses. There were also soaring undergraduate tuition costs, questions about the value of campus-based undergraduate education, the constant issue of the Vet School funding from the Commonwealth, and the pressure to provide for a student population accustomed to the latest in technology and innovations in quality of life that seemed to change by the minute.

Yet, he could delight in a university that had come a long, long way, and was ready to go wherever the President was prepared to take it. As these words are written in 2003, Tufts stands on a higher hill than ever before in its history. The Bacow presidency, beginning its third year, has lost none of the momentum that characterized its first two. No one can be certain what the next one hundred and fifty years will mean for Tufts. But the light shines brighter than ever before.

Where will the next Tufts chronicler begin? That question will be answered when he or she discovers the end point of this document. What does Tufts look like at this moment in the journey? The face of the institution has undergone an astonishing change. Although we may continue to struggle with the issues associated with the extraordinary diversity of a university that is truly multicultural, there is no doubt that we are much enriched by the dialogue. To walk the Tufts campuses today is to find a microcosm of the nation and the world. We are simply a *more interesting* place than we were when I arrived in Medford, forty years ago.

The next historian will be in a better position to answer the question of affordability in higher education. Right now, the President has as his highest priority the raising of sufficient funds to meet the needs of any student who wants to come to Tufts. But, who can win this race? When will parents decide that there are alternatives to traditional campus-bound higher education; or that the prestige frenzy is not worth it all? Right now, with applications to the premier American colleges and universities at all-time highs, our concern is focused on access for those who might not be able to afford this remarkable product. Tufts has never been more attractive to potential applicants; it also has never been more expensive. What will that next author confront, when that volume of Tufts history is begun? What will higher education look like in the America of 2030?

Finally, what *kind* of a university will that historian encounter? I think of Provost Leonard Mead stating, some fifty years ago, that research should be done in one's free time and should in no way interfere with the faculty's teaching commitment. That was clearly the Tufts of the first one hundred twenty-five years. Between 1976 and 1991, Jean Mayer shifted the paradigm to a teaching university where everyone does research. That general philosophy has remained in place through the turn of the century. Yet, at a meeting of the chairs of Arts and Sciences in late September 2003, the moderator asked the departmental chairs what they thought went into the tenure decisions at Tufts. The consensus was: 70 percent research, 25 percent teaching, 5 percent service. The deans were shocked, because that in no way reflected their or the administration's vision. But clearly faculty coming into higher education today feel the pressure of the research agenda much more powerfully than my or subsequent generations did. The challenge for Tufts over the next decades will be to balance the values of outstanding teaching, the values that got us part of the way to where we are, with those of significant research, which got us the rest of the way. This is a story of a great institution still making its way, a story not yet complete.

Baseball has often served as a metaphor for my personal thoughts, and it comes to my assistance at this point in the narrative. In the W. P. Kinsella novel *Shoeless Joe* (1982), the dead Joe Jackson miraculously returns to Iowa to join with ballplayers of his and other generations, all long gone. If I could have one magical moment like that, it would bring together Tufts first President Hosea Ballou, who would be invited to President Bacow's home on the Medford campus to share in the lighting of the Friday night Sabbath candles, in some future time twenty years from now. When the candles were lit, the small gathering of faculty would join in drinking a glass of wine, and a Tufts historian would present to Presidents Ballou and Bacow the *fourth* volume of the university's history. In one way or another, I would like to be there.

8

I began this book by admitting that the voice that you will hear belongs to me; indeed, the snapshots you have seen were taken through the camera of *my* mind. While trying to present the story of one particular modern university, I have touched on higher education as it presented itself to me in the larger community and nation; my own experience in this most satisfying of professions was never far from sight. That experience as a professor forms the continuity of my narrative. More than forty years at one institution is nearly a lifetime; it is certainly a career. For the sake of symmetry, let me close with some observations as this career winds down. I started as a faculty member, and end as one. In between, some things stayed the same; others changed.

No one in this country could be as privileged as a professor in an American college or university. It seems to me that I have been walking on one campus or another for most of my life, going from library to gym, roaming through the stacks, looking over the new acquisition shelves, or taking a little infield practice. So much has changed over this half-century, some of less significance, some of greater. The New York Marathon was run for the first time in 1970 with fifty-five participants. In 2002, thirty thousand runners finished the race. When my father was sixty-five, he was an old man, ready for retirement, which he hated. Within a very short time, we have made previously unimaginable changes in the process of aging. Molecular and microbiology, genetics, nutrition, and a revolution in health sciences interventions have us thinking of growing older in a different way. William Schwartz, former Chairman of Medicine at Tufts Medical School, has written a book called *Coping with Methuselah,* published by the Brookings Institute in 2003, that offers a startling view into the future of extended life. I need reading glasses now, and ground balls hit into the shortstop hole elude me, but a good memory provides enough continuity to look over the entire landscape of a life and make a few observations about change. My first-year advisees, born in 1985, are fifty-one years younger than I am; only three of them have ever seen a black-and-white motion picture. The staggering difference in age and attitude between undergraduates and me has perhaps the greatest effect on my view of the world we share and accounts for some of my occasional grumpiness. I wrote three books on a Royal portable typewriter, using carbon paper. None of my students know what carbon paper is or have ever seen a Royal portable typewriter. When new graduate students gather for orientation, I walk among them carrying a carbon copy of my doctoral dissertation, to show them the way it was. Yet, as much as the technology had altered their lives and mine, they still will have the same jitters and jumpy stomach that I have never been able to shake off, when they walk into their first class. They will be the professors of the future, so we share those experiences that never change, like walking into a classroom, terrified.

SOME THINGS NEVER CHANGE

On December 7, 1941, I was seven years old and sitting in my parents' Ford, listening to a National Football League game while my mother was buying a coat on the Lower East Side of New York City. The program was frequently interrupted with news reports about a place called Pearl Harbor. My brother, four years older and sitting next to me, asked, "Where's Pearl Harbor?" I did not know. When my parents returned to the car, I asked my father, "Where's Pearl Harbor?" He did not know. We returned to our candy store in Hoboken and Mr. Schulman, our butcher, was sitting in front of his store. I asked him, "Mr. Schulman, where is Pearl Harbor?" He had an answer: "It's near Long Island. They may be bombing Brooklyn."

This was one of my early encounters with geographic literacy among the average American. Class did not make much difference. A few years later, the following headline greeted readers of the *New York Times:* "Ignorance of U.S. History Shown by College Freshmen: Survey of 7,000 Students in 36 Institutions Discloses Vast Fund of Misinformation on Many Basic Facts." Reporter Ben Fine authored a series of articles that revealed a wondrous ignorance of items geographic and historical. Fine's reporting, based on research undertaken by eminent Columbia University historian Allan Nevins, offered some hilarious examples that reflected on the preparation of these students entering some of the best colleges and universities in the country.[1] One-third could not find St. Louis, Missouri, on a map; another third could not locate the Mississippi River. Half identified Will James as the brother of Jesse James. Thousands could not name the American presidents during the Civil War or World War I. Their knowledge of the Founding Fathers was equally abysmal. As for culture, over half identified Walt Whitman as an American band-leader. They confused his name with that of Paul Whiteman, George Gershwin's favorite conductor. Some of the institutions represented in the survey were: Boston University, Bucknell, Dartmouth, George Washington, Illinois Tech, Mount Holyoke, NYU, University of North Carolina, Penn State, Penn, Pitt, Washington University (St. Louis), William and Mary, and Yeshiva. A shaken Professor Nevins was concerned that a nation's youth, embarking on an unprecedented period of global involvement, fighting for American principles on all of the world's continents, could do so and yet be woefully ignorant of America's heritage, not to mention a lack of any familiarity with a map of the world.

Fine's article appeared on April 4, 1943. The Pacific Ocean was a blank to Mr. Schulman and to most of my young friends, yet within months we knew the names of every island group, archipelago, and atoll from San Francisco to the China mainland. Even Warner Brothers understood the needs of the average American, when they turned the opening moments of their 1942 film *Casablanca* into a history and geography lesson, complete with globe and lecture. Americans were about to invade North Africa, and it would be useful to know what Captain Reynaud meant when he welcomed Major Strasser to "unoccupied France." We might have been ignorant, but we were not stupid, and we learned what we had to when we needed it.

Every generation had its Allan Nevins, public figures decrying the lamentable state of American education, the woeful preparation of our students, and the failure of our schools. There have always been elders who somehow manage to convince themselves that their generation was more rigorously educated than "today's youth." The warning never changed: unless we reformed our educational system, Americans would remain buried in ignorance.

There is no reason to suspect that this sort of generational criticism will cease. When the distinguished literary historian E. D. Hirsch published *Cul-*

1. Nevins had published his findings in the *New York Times Magazine*, "American History for Americans," May 3, 1942. He wrote: "It is distressingly true that our young people are all too ignorant of American history when they leave high school or even college," 6.

tural Literacy in America: What Every American Needs to Know in 1986, he had joined that group of critics who claimed that universities were failing our students. At the end of his book, he added an appendix of lists, from A to Z, of what Americans needed to know about history, politics, geography, and general culture in America and the world. Missing from his alphabetized schoolroom was any mention of Bosnia, Croatia, or Serbia, or any reference to Shi'ite or Sunni, regions of the world and terms important to Islam that were about to explode on American consciousness. Today, with courses on Southeast Europe, Islam, and comparative religion proliferating on campuses all over the country, our students are much better informed than my generation, one that never heard of a Sunni or Shi'ite Muslim, or than those who relied exclusively on Professor Hirsch's lists. There is comfort in knowing with certainty that in twenty years some academic or public figure will step forward and decry the state of cultural illiteracy among "the nation's youth." In this respect as well as others, the university and its activities, as I prepare for my sixth and probably last decade in higher education, are very much familiar to me as I walk the campus of my mind and memory. Much of what I saw fifty years ago as a first-year student at Drew University is recognizable: looking at the new acquisitions shelves in the library stacks; having a cup of coffee with a favorite teacher; playing pinochle until 3:00 A.M.

Yet, other parts of the enterprise have been transformed and in no way resemble the shape of higher education in the 1950s. In many respects, it is a different world.

THE ENDOWMENT INDUSTRY

When Harvard began raising a few million dollars back in the early fifties, it started the machinery of higher education fundraising that has grown into an industry of staggering proportions across the country. Now, a half-century later, at least twenty American universities are each seeking to raise one billion dollars, and the overwhelming majority of American higher educational institutions, public or private, are engaged in a round-the-clock frenzy of "campaigns." Vice presidents of institutional advancement or development are in charge of enormous numbers of professional fundraisers who fan out across the country to ask alumni for money. University presidents are hired for their ability to cultivate, ask for, and close gifts. The ubiquitous *U.S. News & World Report* lists alumni giving as one of criteria for its rankings. The *Chronicle of Higher Education* has a separate section on Philanthropy. In its

"Career Networks" section, the job listings in development rival the number of academic vacancies.

In and of itself, these activities are only a part of the great American tradition of charity. Americans are generous as no others in their capacity and willingness to give to institutions of their own choosing. But the sheer scope of this academic philanthropy became the engine that drove higher education into the twenty-first century. It has led us into waters that at times seem remote from our familiar academic safe harbors. In preparation for an endless series of campaigns each lasting from five to seven years, marketing and branding materials are prepared, publications are generated, and academic administrators such as deans start carving out half of their time, which will inevitably be dedicated to raising money. This was a brave new world.

PRESIDENTS, BOARDS, AND THE CORPORATE CULTURE

At some point in the second half of the twentieth century, the American university bought into one part of the corporate culture that was totally alien to its tradition: the highly compensated CEO. American corporations, as in no other time in their history, were rewarding their chief executive officers with enormous financial incentives. These business leaders, ready to assume their appropriate philanthropic role in society, often turned to their alma mater when they were prepared to give back and would naturally gravitate to the position as Chairmen of the Board of Trustees. The strange chemistry between successful business CEOs, their corporate remuneration, and a desire to compensate university presidents who would lead massive fundraising campaigns led to an explosion of salaries and benefits for chancellors and presidents unprecedented in the history of higher education. The new Chancellor of the University of Texas System signed a contract worth nearly $800,000, and many public university presidents and chancellors approached this level of compensation. Others, even in the Ivy League, were inching toward $1 million. Multi-year contracts with incentives were becoming commonplace. Perhaps it was inevitable. When the *Chronicle of Higher Education* began to publish the pay and benefits of the five highest paid officers of the most distinguished American universities in the 1980s, it was soon apparent that at some institutions the president did not make the list. If it was an athletic powerhouse, you would find the basketball or football coach in the $1-to-2 million range, far ahead of the president. If there were health professional schools, the professor of cardiac surgery or orthopedic surgery routinely had compensation listed from the hospital practice, at times approaching $2 million annually. The figures for the outgoing former Dean and Executive Vice President of the University of Pennsylvania Medical School showed salary for 1999–2000 as $1,925,335, and benefits for the same year at $5,856,741. Within two years, the President of Penn received an annual compensation package of more than $1 million. By this time, twenty-seven private-college presidents were earning more than half a million dollars in salary, supplements, and benefits. The model of the first part of the twentieth century, when Professor "Chips" might reasonably expect to find himself someday as President "Chips" with a salary only slightly removed from his faculty, was broken forever. The American university president, more often coming from outside the teaching profession and brought into play by an executive search firm whose fee was often based on presidential compensation, looked more like a CEO of an industrial conglomerate than an academic president of the previous century. Academic credentials became less important as the institution's drive for increased endowment and resources placed fundraising as the top priority of the university's leadership. In this environment, it was inevitable that the Provost's position, as chief academic officer of the university, was strengthened. This was a new world for higher education.

CELEBRITY FACULTY

Faculty salaries were also improving, but newly minted Ph.D.s still had to manage in a range between $40,000 (English) and $70,000 (Economics, basic sciences, or Computer Science) at the best colleges and universities, often located in cities where housing costs were prohibitive. The same kinds of people and values were finding their way into the profession, although women were finally being given greater opportunity. Money was not a top priority, but making a living was not just important for self-esteem. You had to provide, male and female faculty alike, often for a family, and financial considerations took up a considerable amount of worry time. The egalitarian tradition in the profession assured that salaries in a department would be close to one another. Everyone—once female faculty were allowed to catch up—was at least in the same ballpark.

But, something happened. *U.S. News & World Report* gave the biggest percentage of its ranking, 25 percent, to "academic reputation," which was translated by university administrations trying to maintain or improve their rankings into hiring faculty with celebrity status. The wars had begun, and it was news. The *Chronicle* began a new column in the mid-1990s entitled "Peer Review" that kept a scorecard of which school and department was making wholesale raids on the competition. Faculty stars were being wooed with salaries ranging past $300,000, with additional embellishments, such as research funds, special housing arrangements, country club memberships, and then the final temptation: no teaching for two years. The impact on departmental morale was devastating. In all the history of the profession there had never been such wide salary discrepancies in departments.

PRESTIGE

When my high school baseball coach decided that I should attend Drew University in Madison, New Jersey, it took a big burden off my shoulders. Another New Jersey school had told me that I would be accepted: Princeton. But because the NCAA rules at the time allowed me to play varsity baseball as a freshman at Drew but not at Princeton, I was pleased with my coach's decision. Now I would not have to worry; a decision was being made for me. My Old World parents made no distinction between Drew and Princeton. Both schools were close enough for me to get home or for them to visit. No one in my neighborhood or among my circle of friends gave my decision a moment's thought. No one knew much about either of these colleges.

There was a different attitude toward colleges fifty years ago. Familiarity and proximity were the most important characteristics that went into a decision. My wife attended Abraham Lincoln High School in Brooklyn, a hard-nosed public school that routinely sent a huge percentage of its graduates on to higher education, primarily to local Brooklyn College, where *total* costs for a semester in 1956 was the $5 activities fee. When students wanted to show some real spirit of adventure, they would apply to Cornell University, the quasi-land grant university in remote upper New York State. To that date, there had never been more than a handful of applications to Harvard or Radcliffe College, or for that matter to any of the institutions that would eventually be called the Ivy League. It was an age when most parents and students made little of the distinctions and reputations that came to a near hysterical pitch in the next century, when "prestige" and college rankings came to dominate choice in American higher education.

No one contributed more to the race for eminence than *U.S. News & World Report.* In 1983, the year of its first rankings edition, few people in higher education realized what kind of frenzy would be generated among otherwise placid institutions. By the end of the century, one could scarcely find a university marketing publication that did not comment about some positive *U.S. News* mention it could refer to. *U.S. News* was smart enough to spin off regional rankings and other subsets of its original data, in order to give hundreds of additional institutions something to crow about. Before long, dozens of other magazines were describing rankings of boutique characteristics such as "the most outdoorsy campus," best college sports town (*Sports Illustrated*), the top college for activists (*Mother Jones*), or the top counterculture college (*High Times*). The glossy magazine competition—*Time* and *Newsweek*—attempted to keep up with *U.S. News,* and bookstores created special shelf sections for volumes providing the college rankings. It had become an industry, and it was driving some of the critical decisions made by institutions responding to a board of trustees who measured institutional excellence by these rankings.

CIVILITY

Civility is territory that may be difficult to survey accurately because nostalgia distorts the map. The academic world that I remember from my earlier days seemed more civil, less aggressive. We were the student generation of the 1950s and were generally docile, submissive, and ardently wishing to please our teachers. As for the faculty, they seemed to accept each other's company, and even if battles and hostility seethed beneath the surface, they never reached the ears of the student body. Few ideological battles spilled over into the seminar rooms or the convention halls of the Modern Language Association. The older generation of faculty who were in the best tradition of the American Historical Association's Carl Bridenbaugh had given way to the newcomers. The conquering and victorious faculty were my mentors, and they were thoroughly delighted to be part of the great tradition of American higher education. As different as they were from their predecessors, they were not eager to make *that* much change. When I was told, as a doctoral candidate at the University of Michigan, that Frank Wedekind was an inappropriate subject for my dissertation topic, *everyone* on the faculty agreed, and I accepted that collective wisdom. Graduate teaching assistants taught 60 percent of the courses in the German Department, accepted their stipends with gratitude, and the idea of being represented by the United Auto Workers in a graduate student union would have never crossed our minds. Undergraduates and graduate students were a docile lot.

The late 1960s changed all that, and there has been no letup since. At first the issues centered on national politics—the Vietnam War—but soon added race, gender, and generational conflict, and today the issues of confrontation, which spill over onto the campus, are global. By the 1980s, the older faculty was already back on their heels and acting defensively, as a new mood of student advocacy took hold of a curriculum that, from the student perspective, should reflect *their* interests and not necessarily the faculty's. The hyphenated studies programs proliferated; courses were created to celebrate subjects, rather than to analyze them. Inevitably, by the mid-1980s the Allan Blooms gathered their forces to stop what they saw as the barbarians at the gates, and the *Kulturkampf* was underway. Civil dialogue and detached discussion among colleagues occurred less frequently, and in their place came some fairly ugly assaults from all sides. The *Chronicle of Higher Education,* which had started out as a docile trade journal dedicated to printing articles on developments in higher education and helping people find jobs, turned into the profession's version of tabloid journalism, routinely describing departments and even campuses tearing themselves apart, going into receivership, and generally falling into anarchy; as a member of one such department described her situation in the *Chronicle:* "We were the Afghanistan of philosophy departments in America." The hostility grew so great that it became impossible to come to any agreement on new faculty. An Ivy League English department had to make all of its hires by means of a committee of faculty from *outside* the university. Tenure decisions became so contentious that the courts became involved to an unprecedented degree. Was collegiality dead, asked *Academe,* the journal of the American Association of University Professors? Has the profession given up on civility? The picture presented to the public, unhappy at the skyrocketing cost of sending their children to college or university in the 1990s, was grim. Lawmakers complained about a pampered faculty that did not teach, but were quick to take ideological sides. Nothing became as heated as issues associated with the Middle East. Charges and counter-charges of pro-Palestinian or pro-Israeli faculty, courses, and teach-ins on hundreds of college campuses polarized opinion and led to ugly confrontations. Web sites proliferated with lists of suspect faculty who had been identified as inappropriately pro-Israeli or pro-Palestinian. There was not much evidence of civility, but plenty of paranoia, as faculty grew suspicious of students who might turn them in or say something nasty on an anonymous teaching evaluation.

Something else was happening with the student body and its relationship to the faculty. The marketing frenzy caused by the ratings game of *U.S. News*

& World Report and similar publications led admissions officials to pressure their institutions to provide better and more attractive services and amenities. "Pleasing the customer" became one of the mantras handed down from trustees to administrators. Food courts began offering a breathtaking array of dining possibilities for students; hard-wired dormitories provided all-in-one entertainment opportunities that allowed for choices that would not have seemed possible to an earlier generation. By the end of the twentieth century, students had left their traditional electronics at home and were using state-of-the-art computer technology to get all their instant gratification and super-fast Internet access through their desktop PCs. The thirst for digital entertainment was limitless, and the universities were providing whatever was necessary to satisfy the consumer.

It was not all entertainment. First universities rushed toward a wired future, and the faculty coped as best as it could with the dazzling potential of the Internet. For someone of my generation, the changes were stunning. For those more up-to-date faculty who put their curricula and handouts online, students could opt for attending or not attending class. Today, as we move toward a wireless future, the next generation of faculty will have to fight for student attention as never before. It is a brave new world, and students do not have to be in the lecture room any longer, if they do not choose to. It is not unusual for a faculty member to be standing in front of an 8:00 A.M. lecture hall, expecting hundreds of students to show up, and finding a handful of loyal listeners present. The absentees would not be penalized, because the class had been videotaped and was available on the Internet.

Inevitably, the idea of student-as-customer led to the notion, quickly passed on from parent to child, that the university and its employees were clerks, serving at the pleasure of the consumer. Committees were formed at some of our most distinguished universities to handle and mediate student complaints about grades. Many of my colleagues were very discomforted by what they sensed as "an attitude" on the part of an increasing number of students: they believed that they were entitled to an A grade in a class, and it was up to the faculty member to see that this is the result. "I don't like the grade I received" became a frequently heard opening line at an office hour appointment with an indignant student.

Here my age works in my favor. I can act grandfatherly, demand respect, and generally get it. My griping about students' irritating sense of entitlement is mitigated by their intelligence, willingness to learn, and, at least at this university, an enormous energy.

The September 29, 2003, online *Chronicle of Higher Education* announced that James B. Holderman, who had been President of the University of South Carolina from 1977 until he was forced to resign in 1990 over issues of questionable expenditures, was convicted in Miami, Florida, on credit-card fraud and money-laundering charges arising from a federal sting operation. In the previous five years, the *Chronicle* offered harrowing stories of at least a dozen college and university presidents whose fall from grace was marked by acts of fraud, misappropriation of funds, and similar activities that led to criminal charges and indictments. Holderman looked very much like the CEOs at Enron and Tyco International, whose high-living life styles also preceded a humiliating public disgrace.

Faculty were not sheltered from a similar lurid exposure. The *Chronicle* front page of August 16, 2002, looked and read more like the *National Enquirer* than the flagship publication dealing with American higher education. Two professors were staring at the readers over a large-print headline that read: HOW THEY FELL. The caption next to the first professor read, "A star professor at Duke suffered a breakdown and was swindled of his savings. Huge federal grants he supervised can't be accounted for" (story on page A12). The front-page text next to the second professor announced: "A top physicist at Lawrence Berkeley Lab may have cheated in the race to find new elements, leaving his reputation destroyed and his colleagues devastated" (story on A16). Hardly an issue of the *Chronicle* appears that does not have a similar story of academic fraud, misconduct, and criminal conflicts of interest. It was inevitable that stories dealing with vaulting ambition and greed in Academia found their way into the national press, as well. "Ambition can combat the purity of physics" ran one such story in the *Boston Globe* and suggested that ambition was killing research in physics. The story was about a promising young physicist who had dazzled the scientific world with brilliant results, only to have his data proved to be fraudulent.[2] "What is happening to our field?" lamented one Physics Department chair in the *Globe* story, which described the academic world of big-time grants, global media attention to high-profile research, and the increasingly competitive pressure cooker of high-visibility academic personalities involved in huge financial stakes.

2. *Boston Globe*, September 28, 2002, A3.

Nowhere is the issue more volatile than with faculty involved in biomedical research. At stake is nothing less than the public trust. Former Harvard President Derek Bok has examined the whole issue of big money and higher education in his book *The Commercialization of Higher Education.*[3] The potential for corrupting the faculty was an idea that the public accepted, and media attention in the most prominent nation newspapers has zeroed in on scientists and their undisclosed relationship to pharmaceutical companies.[4] About one-quarter of university-based medical researchers were receiving funding from drug companies in 2003, and the number is growing. Between 1980 and 2000, industry share of investment in U.S. biomedical research increased from about 32 to 62 percent, as the government encouraged private sector involvement. One study alleged that almost half the medical faculty serving on boards that review clinical trials and standards of patient safety were consultants to the health industry.[5]

Even the most sacred texts, the almost canonical journals *Science* and *Nature,* were embarrassed. A group of scientists criticized both of them for publishing articles and reviews written by scholars who did not reveal their financial stake in a procedure or a drug. Medical-research ethics and practices were under the public microscope as never before.

There is a danger that our delightfully quirky profession, under circumstances associated with grander life styles, could begin to look like everyone else.

AND YET . . .

For the 2002 Commencement issue of the *Tufts Daily,* I wrote a short piece entitled "Looking for a Good Life?" The article urged anyone in the graduating class who was looking for the perfect career to consider my job: being a professor at an American college or university. Sure, there were some aggravations, but the positive side far outweighed the irritations. You were not going to be measured by how much money you made or how you dressed or what kind of a car you drove. If you liked your freedom, there were not too many authority figures giving orders. Anarchists and nonconformists were welcomed into the profession. You had, if you wanted, the summers to

3. Derek Bok, *The Commercialization of Higher Education* (Princeton University Press, 2003).

4. See Sheldon Krimsky, *Science in the Private Interest: Has the Lure of Profits Corrupted Biomedical Research?* (Lanham, Md.: Rowman & Littlefield, 2003).

5. *Wall Street Journal,* August 19, 2003, D3.

travel, read, or write, and you could spend the rest of your lives surrounded by books. Also, you were always near a gym. What could be better?

The answer is: Nothing could be better. In spite of the fear and trembling, the occasional pain and suffering of the profession, there have been many occasions over the past forty years when I found it difficult to believe that we actually got paid for this life on a campus. Sometimes the public face of the profession—and its voice projected in newspapers, journals, and magazines— will sound and look like a perpetual lamentation, reporting on the misery, decline, and fall of the American professoriate. But we delight in the secret truth of renewal in generations of young men and women who, at first hesitantly (because they previously had never given it a thought), begin to ask themselves about the quality of life led by their mentors. Slowly, it creeps up on them, as they see the freedom to shape thoughts and ideas, the life of the mind, the exhilarating pleasure experienced at the first taste of teaching a class in the Experimental College. We do not push them; but when they come to ask us, "Is this the good life?" I have yet to hear any of my colleagues give an answer other than "Yes, it does not get better than this." Hard as it may be to admit, we *are* truly blessed.

SELECTED BIBLIOGRAPHY

BOOKS

Banks, Henry. *A Century of Excellence: The History of Tufts University School of Medicine, 1893–1993.* Boston: Tufts University Press, 1993.

Barrett, Stephen, and William T. Jarvis, eds. *The Health Robbers: A Close Look at Quackery in America.* Buffalo: Prometheus Books, 1993.

Benjamin, Ludy T., Jr., ed. *A History of Psychology: Original Sources and Contemporary Research.* Boston: McGraw-Hill, 1988.

Bennett, William J. *The De-Valuing of America.* New York: Simon and Schuster, Inc., 1992.

Black, Herbert. *Doctor and Teacher, Hospital Chief: Dr. Samuel Proger and the New England Medical Center.* Chester: The Globe Pequod Press, 1982.

Bloom, Allan. *The Closing of the American Mind.* New York: Simon and Schuster, 1987.

Bok, Derek. *The Cost of Talent: How Executives and Professionals Are Paid and How it Affects America.* New York: The Free Press, 1993.

———. *Higher Learning.* Cambridge: Harvard University Press, 1986.

Carpenter, Teresa. *Missing Beauty.* New York: W.W. Norton and Company, 1988.

Cohen, Michael D., and James G. March. *Leadership and Ambiguity: The American College President.* Cambridge: Harvard Business School Press, 1974.

Crotty, Shane. *Ahead of the Curve: David Baltimore's Life in Science.* Berkeley: University of California Press, 2001.

Deutsch, Ronald M. *The New Nuts Among the Berries: How Nutrition Nonsense Captured America.* Palo Alto: Bull Publishing Co., 1977.

Field, Marilyn J., ed. *Dental Education at the Crossroads: Challenges and Change.* Washington, D.C.: National Academy Press, 1995.

Freeland, Richard M. *Academia's Golden Age: Universities in Massachusetts, 1945–1970.* New York: Oxford University Press, 1992.

Friedland, Martin L. *The University of Toronto: A History.* Toronto: University of Toronto Press, 2002.

Graham, Hugh Davis, and Nancy Diamond. *The Rise of the American Research Universities.* Baltimore: Johns Hopkins University Press, 1997.

Hacker, Andrew. *Two Nations.* New York: Charles Scribner's Sons, 1992.

Higham, John. *Strangers in the Land: Patterns of American Nativism, 1860–1925.* New York: Atheneum, 1965.

Hirsch, E.D., Jr. *Cultural Literacy: What Every American Needs to Know.* Boston: Houghton Mifflin, 1987.

Hofstadter, Richard, and Walter Metzger. *The Development of Academic Freedom in the United States.* New York: Columbia University Press, 1955.

Keller, Morton, and Phyllis Keller. *Making Harvard Modern.* New York: Oxford University Press, 2001.

Kennedy, Donald. *Academic Duty.* Cambridge: Harvard University Press, 1997.

Kevles, Daniel J. *The Baltimore Case.* New York: W.W. Norton and Company, 1998.

Klingenstein, Susanne. *Jews in the American Academy, 1900–1940.* New Haven: Yale University Press, 1991.

Lasch, Christopher. *The Culture of Narcissism.* New York: W.W. Norton, 1978.

Loeb, Paul Rogat. *Generations at the Crosswords.* New Brunswick: Rutgers University Press, 1994.

Ludmerer, Kenneth M. *Time to Heal: American Medical Education from the Turn of the Century to the Era of Managed Care.* New York: Oxford University Press, 1999.

Mencken, H. L. *Prejudices.* New York: Alfred A. Knopf, 1926.

Miller, Russell E. *Light on the Hill,* vol. 2. Boston: Beacon Press, 1986.

Nizel, Abraham E. And Athena S. Papas. *Nutrition in Clinical Dentistry.* Philadelphia: Sanders, 1960.

Novick, Peter. *That Noble Dream.* New York: Cambridge University Press, 1988.

Readings, Bill. *The University in Ruins.* Cambridge: Harvard University Press, 1996.

Reisman, David, and Verne A. Stadtman, eds. *Academic Transformations: Seventeen Institutions Under Pressure.* New York: McGraw-Hill Book Company, 1973.

Reuben, Julie A. *The Making of the Modern University.* Chicago: University of Chicago Press, 1996.

Rhodes, Frank H. T. *The Creation of the Future: The Role of the American University.* New York: Cornell University Press, 2001.

Rosovsky, Henry. *The University: An Owner's Manual.* New York: W.W. Norton, 1990.

Rudolph, Frederick. *The American College and University.* New York: Alfred Knopf, 1962.

Smith, Page. *Killing the Spirit.* New York: Viking Press, 1990.

Steinberg, Stephen. *The Academic Melting Pot: Catholics and Jews in American Higher Education.* New Brunswick: Transaction Books, 1974.

Synnott, Marcia Graham. *The Half-Opened Door: Discrimination and Admissions at Harvard, Yale and Princeton, 1900–1970.* Westport: Greenwood Press, 1979.

Talese, Gay. *The Kingdom and the Power.* New York: Anchor Press/Doubleday, 1978.

Veysey, Lawrence R. *The Emergence of the American University.* Chicago: University of Chicago Press, 1965.

Watson, James D., with Andrew Berry. *DNA: The Secret of Life.* New York: Alfred A. Knopf, 2003.

Wechsler, Harold S. *The Qualified Student: A History of Selective College Admission in America.* New York: John Wiley & Sons, 1977.

World Almanac Book of Facts, 1929, The. Facsimile Edition, American Heritage Press, 1971.

Young, James Harvey. *The Medical Messiahs: A Social History of Health Quackery in Twentieth Century America.* Princeton: Princeton University Press, 1967.

ARTICLES

Bridenbaugh, Carl. "The Great Mutation," *American Historical Review* 68 (1963): 315–31.

Fine, Benjamin. "Ignorance of U.S. History Shown by College Freshmen," *New York Times,* April 4, 1943, 1ff.

———. "U.S. History Study Is Not Required in 82 of Colleges," *New York Times,* June 21, 1942, 1ff.

Nevins, Allan. "American History for Americans," *New York Times Magazine,* May 3, 1942, 6, 38.

REPORTS

Tufts: The Total University in Changing Times. A Report to the President by the University Steering Committee, January 1973.

INDEX

Page numbers in italics indicate illustrations.

Abramson, Dan, 224

Abriola, Linda, *289*, 300

Abu-Moustafa, Adel, 115

Academe, 191, 313

"academic entrepreneurship," 18

academic freedom: Tufts University's presidents, boards, and, 9–11

academic research: federal funding of, 21–22

Acapulco, xiv

Acheson, Dean, 86

Ackerman, Peter, 234

Adams, Charles Francis, 57–58

Adams, John, 57

Adams, John Quincy, 57

admissions: student, 60, 62, 66

Africa, 60, 93, 95

African Americans, 36, 74; "historically black" institutions and, 3; veterinary program for, 23

The African Queen, 226

Afro-American Studies, 63

Agricultural Research Service (ARS), 31, 140, 141, 144

Aidekman, Shirley, 149

Alabama A&M, 3

Albright, Madeleine, 226

Alexander II (czar), 5

Alexander III (czar), 5

Algiers, 86

Alice and Nathan Gantcher University Professor, xvii

Allison, Bob, 205

Amadeus, 225

Amelia Peabody Large Animal Pavilion, 129

American Academy of Arts and Sciences, 85, 293

American Association of State Colleges and Universities' Committee on International Programs, 184

American Association of University Professors (AAUP), 10, 60, 168, 191, 192, 313

American Bar Association, 45, 82; academic committee, 81

American Cancer Society, 165

The American Hebrew, 6

American Historical Association, 1, 6–7, 312

American Institute of Nutrition, 138

American Journal of International Law, 229

American Medical Association (AMA), 12

American Saudi Commission on Economic Cooperation, 115

American Veterinary Medicine Association, 110

Americans for Democratic Action, 89

Anderson, T. J., 74

Angell Memorial Animal Hospital, 27, 40, 129, 131

Anglo-Saxons, 3

Ann Arbor, xv

annus terribilis: Jean Mayer's, 35–39

anti-Semitic Laws of 1881, 5

Anwer, Sawkat, 133, 264

Aprille, June, 78, *287*
ARA Services, Inc., 149
Arabic, xvii
Arabs, 214
ARAMARK, 149
Arbree, Nancy, 261
Argentina, 192
Arias, Irwin, 115, 254
Armstrong, Louis, 197
Arnott, Peter, 73, 74
Arrango, Placido, 148, 149
Arthur M. Sackler School of Biomedical
    Sciences, 50, 110–12, 114, 115, 124, 172
Arts and Sciences: deans of, 37, *153, 154*;
    engineering and, 204–25; faculty, 37,
    47, 63, 64, 69–80, 197, 206
Asch, Bob, 76
Association of American Medical
    Colleges (AAMC), 247
Association of Governing Boards
    (AGB), 175
Association of New England Deans, 7
Association of Professional Schools of
    International Affairs (APSIA), 86
athletics: coaches, 178–79, 309–10;
    higher education and, 178–81; SAT
    scores and, 179, 180; scandals in,
    179–80
Atomic Age, 76
atomic bomb, 79
Atomic Energy Commission, 77
atomic weapons, 4
Auschwitz, 296
Austria, 88

Bacow, Adele Fleet, *286, 297*
Bacow, Lawrence, 255, *286*; coming of,
    293–95; 150 years of Tufts and,
    301–4; two Larrys, 295–301
Bakke decision, 60
Ballou, Hosea, 301
Ballou Hall, 49, 206, 304
Balmuth, Miriam, 74

Baltimore (Maryland), 86
Baltimore, David, 164, 165
Banks, Harry, 114, *159*, 163, 164, 239, 241
Baptists, 2
Barcelona, 76
Barnet, Sylvan, 8–9, 73, 193
Barrymore, Lionel, 100
Bartlett, Ruhl, 84, 85
Barzun, Jacques, 4
Battle Creek, 136
Baum, Bruce, 260
Baylor College of Medicine, 117
Baylor University, 117
Beard, Charles A., 9
Bedau, Hugo, 73
Begin, Menachem, 59
Behnke, Michael, 65
Belmont, 54
Beltsville, 141
Benedict, Robin: murder of, 166
Benedictine monastery, 33
Bennett, William J., 69, 70, 71
Bennington College, 184, 192
Beowulf, 73
Berenberg, Roslyn, 150
Berenguer, Angel and Joan, 76
Berenson, Bernard, 33
Berg, John, 131, 269
Berger, Louis, 147, 220
Bergstrom, Joan, 223
Berkeley, xv
Berlin, 212
Berlitz, 63
Berman, Morton, 73
Bernstein, David, 148
Bernstein, Irene, 147, 148
Bernstein, Mel, 202, 207, 208, 210, 212,
    214, 216, 220, 221, 223, 224, 235, 283,
    288, 300
Berry, Jeff, 74
Best Practices Top to Bottom (Associated
    Governing Boards of Trustees), 191
Beth Israel Hospital, 113, 239, 300

Betty Mayer Campus Center, 67

Bewick, John, 231

Bharucha, Jamshed, *288,* 299, 300

Bianconi, Marcello, 224

Big Ten Conference, 179

bin Laden, Osama, 226

Black Forest, 75

Black Friar monk, 9

Blake, Caesar, xv

Blanchard, Harold, 9

Bloom, Allan, 70, 192, 193

Blumberg, Jeffrey, 139, 140

Board of Trustees, 37, 40, 57–58; geography lesson, 146–50; Management Committee, 41, 42, 43, 44, 45, 51, 57; Mayer, Jean, veterinary school and, 22–24, 25–26, 27, 40, 127–36, 160–61; presidents, academic freedom and, 9–11, 16; presidents, fundraising and, 13–16, 55; presidents, job turnover rate and, 35. *See also* Tufts Trustees

Bok, Derek, 80–81, 294, 316

Boland, Edward P., 231

Bolt Hall, 97

Bombay, 300

Bosnia, 226, 308

Boston, xiv, xv, 12, 13, 16, 19, 26, 27, 28, 30, 33, 38, 42, 44, 46, 50, 56, 64, 69, 73, 74, 75, 81, 99, 100, 102, 104, 107, 113, 145, 146, 295; dental schools in, 118; medicine, 238–45

Boston Brahmins, 57, 91, 97, 245

Boston Braves, 91

Boston College, 2, 51, 69, 180, 186, 187

Boston Globe, 36, 39, 65, 127, 170, 172, 173, 206, 282, 284, 315

Boston Herald, 173

Boston Red Sox, 90–91, 247

Boston Redevelopment Authority, 31, 107

Boston School of Occupational Therapy, 81

Boston University, 31, 60, 61, 70, 145, 168, 178, 307; dental school, 119; medical school, 102, 238

Boston Veterinary Institute, 23

Bosworth, Stephen, *290*

Bouchard, Wayne, 211, *287*

Bowdoin College, 7, 10, 18

Brademas, John, 180–81

Braintree, 7

Branch Davidian, 195

Brandeis University, 89

Brennan, Jack, 60, 161

Bridenbaugh, Carl, 1, 3, 4, 5, 6, 7, 8, 59, 312

Brigham and Women's Hospital, 99, 113

Brookings Institution, 87, 305

Brooklyn, 90, 306, 311

Brooklyn College, xv, 311

Brooks, Harvey, x, 58

Brooks, John, 180

Brown, Drusilla, 222

Brown, Timothy, 83

Brown University, 1, 2, 183

Bryant, "Bear," 178

Bucknell University, 307

Bulger, William, 132, 161

Bumpers, Dale, 232

Burger, Warren, 60

Burnim, Kalmin, 74

Burns, Matthew, x

Burstein, Bobbie, 147, 148

Burstein, Maxwell, 147, 148

Burto, William, 73

Bush, George, 192, 226

Butler, Nicholas Murray, 9, 10

Butterfield, Fox, 168

Cabot, John, 149

Cabot, Paul, 33–34

Cabot Intercultural Center, 77

Cahill, Thomas, 247

California, xv, 39, 94, 105, 150, 195

Calisti, Louis, 119, 120

Callow, Allan, x, 10, 13, 15, 19, 25, 32, 37–38, 39–40, 41, 42, 43, 51, 57, 67, 148, 149, *153, 285*

Cambodia, 67

Cambridge, 64, 69, 71, 74, 83, 88, 104, 139, 177, 296, 301

Campanella, Frank, 51, 186, 187, 188, 189

Campbell, Ashley, 216

Campbell, Patricia, *158,* 258, 261, 287

Canzanelli, Attilio, 252

Capen, Elmer Hewitt, 6

Caritas Christi, 248

Carleton College, 92

Carley, Warren, 38, 41, 43, 51, 57

Carmichael, Leonard, ix, 8, 14, 15, 283; presidency of, 12; resignation of, 13

Carnegie Foundation, 14

Carnegie Mellon University, 217

Carson, Johnny, 138

Carter, Jimmy, 59, 60, 226

Carzo, Rocco ("Rocky"), 74

Casablanca, 307

Cassidy, Gerald, 20, 21, 56, 162, 200, 231, 239, 249, 275

The Cat Who Cried for Help (Dodman), 272

Catholic Church, 9; academic institutions founded by, 2

Catholics, 103, 149, 245; Irish, 2, 5; students, 147

Cavazos, Lauro, 103, 108, 109, 252; resignation of, 41

Caviness, Madeline, 74

Cebe, Peggy, 221

Center for Drug Development, 110

Center for Science and Mathematics Teaching, 216

Century of Excellence, 30

Chaisson, Eric, 213, 214, 215, 219

Chamberlain, Joshua Lawrence, 10, 18

A Changing University in a Changing Times, 173

Chapra, Steven, 220

Charles River, 8

Charles River Labs, Inc., 130

Chaucer, Geoffrey, 73

Chechnya, 225, 229

Chen, Jake, 259

Cheney, Lynne, 69, 71

Chicago, 1, 45

Children's Hospital, 113

Chinese, xvi

Christensen, Halvor, 252

Christians, 115

Christopher, Warren, 226

Chronicle of Higher Education, 35, 172, 175, 189, 220, 308, 309, 311, 313, 315

Church Women United, 177

CIA, 87

civil rights movement, 60

Civil War, 10, 307

Clark University, 3

Clayton, Alan, 74

Clinton, Bill, 192, 193, 226, 227

Clinton, Hillary Rodham, 237

The Closing of the American Mind (Bloom), 70, 192

coaches, athletic, 178–79, 309–10

Coffin, John, 103, 104

Coffin, Lee, 301

Cohen, Benjamin, 88, 89, 90

Colati, Gregory, xi

Colcord, Frank, 77, 79, *154,* 167

Cold War, 85, 87, 92; Fletcher School of Law and Diplomacy and end of, 225–37

College of the Holy Cross, Worcester, 180

college rankings: higher education and, 181–82

Collins, Jerry, 72

Collins, Michael, 248

Columbia Point, 103

Columbia University, xiv, xvii, 9, 98, 181, 183, 306; Jewish student population at, 6; School of International and Public Affairs (SIPA), 86

Combat Zone, 107, 165

The Commercialization of Higher Education (Bok), 316

Conant, James, 83, 294

Congo, Republic of the, 85, 87

Conklin, John, 74

Connecticut, 27, 129

Conrad Hilton Hotel, 1

Consortium on Financing Higher Education (COFHE), 14

Conte, Sylvio, 231

Coopers & Lybrand, 188

Coping with Methuselah (Schwartz), 305

Cormack, Alan, 67

Cornell University, 20, 134, 183, 311; veterinary program at, 23, 26, 203

Cortese, Anthony, 231

Cotter, Sue, 130

Cousens, John, 12, 13, 82, 83

Cousens Gymnasium, 93, 175

Crane, Gregory, 211–12, 215

Crick, Francis, 194

Croatia, 226, 308

Croix de Guerre, 18

Crowley, Zachary, xi

Cuba, 129

Cultural Literacy in America: What Every American Needs to Know (Hirsch), 307–8

Cummings, Bill, 149, 221

Cuttino, David, 211, 301

Daniels, Norman, 73, 74

Dartmouth College, 16, 75, 171, 182, 294, 307; trustees, 183; Tuck School of Business Administration, 97

Dartmouth Review, 69, 70

David (king), 226

Davis, Adele, 136, 137–38

Dawson-Hughes, Beth, 140

Deaconess Hospital, 113, 300

deans, 13, 27, 37, 38, 50, 78; arts and sciences, 37, *153, 154*; Banks, Harry, 114, *159*, 163, 164, 239, 241; Behnke, Michael, 65; Calisti, Louis, 119, 120; Campbell, Patricia, *158*, 258, 261, 287; Cavazos, Larry, 41, 103, 108, 109, 252; Colcord, Frank, 77, 79, 154, 167; Eliot, Theodore, 90, *155*; Engineering School, 41; Gershoff, Stanley, 19, 32, 107, 141–42, *155*, 275; Gullion, Edmund, 85, 86, 87–90, 92, *155*, 232; Harleston, Bernard, 36, 41, 42, 66, *153*; Johansen, Erling, 28, 123, 124, 125, 126, *157*, 202, 255, 257, 258; Jonas, Albert M., 26, 110, 129–30, *156*, 265; Lasagna, Louis, 110, 115, *159*, 172, 251, 253, 259; Levy, Robert I., xvii, 28, 29, 49, 52, 53, 106, 125–26, 130, 141, *158*, 241; liberal arts, 47; Loew, Frank, xvii, 93, 129, 130–34, 135, 136, *157*, 160–61, 202–3, 257, 262, 263, 264, 290; McCarthy, Kathryn, 36, 38, 39, 40, 42, 47, 66, 67, 94, 121, 152, 153, 185; Medical School, 31, 41, 53; Murnane, Thomas, xi, 25, 27, 38, 47, 49–50, 53, 55–56, 77, 94, 119–20, 127, 146–47, 148, 154, 160–61, 172, 177, 198–200, 203, 207, 213, 231, 249, 280, 282, 300; Nelson, Fred, 77, *155*, 217; Norris, Lonnie, *157, 158*, 257, 258, 261, 298; Pokras, Martha, xi, 128, *156*, 259, 263, 287; provosts and, 46, 52; Roche, John, 89–90, 91, 92, 94, *155*; Salacuse, Jeswald, 94–97, *156*, 163, 214, 227, 228, 229–30, 232, 234, 236, 293; Shira, Robert, 40, 42–43, 48, 120–22, 125, *157*; Stewart, Robert, 84, 86; tenure for medical school, 101

DeGaulle, Charles, 18, 34, 173

degrees: academic, 29; doctoral, 13

Delaware State University, 3

Democratic Party, 193, 200

Dennett, Daniel, 73, 74, 224
Dennison Corporation, 38, 43
dental schools: applicants to, 124; Boston, 118; fundraising and, 125; history and closure of, 116–17
departments: anatomy, 103, 165; arts and sciences, 204–5; biochemistry, 32; biology, 77, 78; chemistry, 77, 78, 79, 224; child study, 222–23; drama, 74; economics, 72, 293; engineering, 77; English, 72, 193; geology, 72; German, 9, 78, 312; history, 79, 83; molecular and microbiology, 26, 29; pathology, 111; philosophy, 73; physics, 36, 47, 77, 216, 220; political science, 74; preventative medicine, 103; Russian, 78; sociology, 74
Depression. *See* Great Depression
Detroit, 165
Development Division, 38, 43
Devigne, Rob, 224
Dewald, Bob, 72
Diabetes: Its Cause, Nature and Treatment (Macfadden), 136
DiBiaggio, John, 170–71, 172, 173, 188, *286*, 294, 296, 297; arts, sciences, engineering and, 204–25; Fletcher School of Law and Diplomacy and, 225–37; Sackler School and, 250–55; school of dental medicine and, 255–61; school of medicine and, 237–50; school of nutrition and, 274–79; school of veterinary medicine and, 262–74; students, alumni and, 197–200; successful anomaly and, 280–84; Troika and, 200–204
DiBiaggio, Nancy, 198, 199–200, *286*
A Diet for Living (Mayer), 138
Din, Gunga, 101
Dingell, Charles, 164, 165, 166
Divinity School, Tufts, 12
Dixon, Linda, xi
doctorate programs, 13

Dodman, Nick, 134, 272
The Dog Who Loved Too Much (Dodman), 272
Doku, Hristo (Chris), 123, 257, 259
Dominican Republic, 142–43
Douglas, William, 165; murder conviction of, 166
Dow-Jones Industrial index, 226
Downes, Tom, 221, 224
Drew University, xiv, 308, 311; Brothers College at, 80
Dudley House, 24, 63, 176–77
Dukakis, Michael, 127, 161
Duke University, 179
Dunn, Kevin, 224
Dwyer, Johanna, 30, 107, 121, 122, 277

East Hall, 9
Eastern Europe, xvii
Eastern Mediterranean Studies, 77
Eaton, Elizabeth, 249
eBay, 283
Ebert, Karl, 135
education: "historically black" institutions and, 3; religion's influence in higher, 1–3; secularization/democratization of higher, 3
Education for Public Inquiry and International Citizenship (EPIIC), 214
educators: attitude toward immigrants by American, 6
Eggleston, Karen, 222
Egypt, 95
Elfin, Mel, 225
Eliot, Charles W., 3, 98, 294
Eliot, Pat, 94
Eliot, Theodore Lyman, 91–94, 96, *155*, 156, 227, 228; Fletcher School of Law and Diplomacy and, 90–94, 96
Eliot-Pearson Department of Child Study, 222–23
Elkind, David, 222

Elliott, James, 72, 223
Emory University, 28, 116
endowments, 44, 53–54, 83; history of, 308–9; shrinking, 13, 14
energy crisis, 60
English, xiii
Enron, 315
Ernst, Susan, *289*, 300, 301
Euphrates River, 194
Europe, 18, 87, 150, 226; college preparatory schools in, 33; immigrants from, 2, 5
European Journal of International Law, 229
European Study Center at Talloires, 37, 74, 75, 126
executive vice presidents, 183–84, 186–92
Experimental College, 63–64, 91, 214, 215, 317; director of, *154*

"Face the Nation," 68
faculty, 15, 28, 29, 32, 39, 58, *151*, 158, 168, 304; arts and sciences, 37, 47, 63, 64, 69–80, 197, 206; Boston University, 60; celebrity, 310–11; dental, 53; diversification of, 8–9; Harvard, 18; hiring and promotion of, 77–78; job security for, 10; Medical School, 29; Medical School's Basic Sciences, 27, 29; Massachusetts Institute of Technology (MIT), 64; research fund for, 75; salaries of, 14, 55, 310–11; school of veterinary medicine, 128–29, 131; students, changing times and, 58–62; tenure for, 77–78, 88, 90, 94, 96, 101, 207, 293; unions, 60–61
Faculty Research Fund, 75
Fairleigh Dickinson University, 116
Fanon, Franz, 194
Fantini, Sergio, 219
Fares, Issam, 148
Fawaz, Leila, 69, 228

FBI, 226
Federal Army, 10
federal funding, 72; academic research and, 21–22; USDA/Tufts human nutrition research center on aging, 31, 62, 107; veterinary school and, 25–26
Feinburg, Sylvia, 73, 223
Fenway, 33
Ferguson, Alan D., 24
Fernald, Mason, xi
Fine, Ben, 306, 307
Finn, Chester, 71
FitzGerald, Edward, xv
Fixler, Michael, 9
Flax, Marty, 111
Fleming, Robben, 178
Fletcher, Austin Barclay, 47, 82, 132
Fletcher Board of Visitors, 57
Fletcher Ginn Library, 93
Fletcher School of Law and Diplomacy, 12, 19, 37, 46–47, 56, 57, 65, 69, 76, 77, 80, 97–98, 155, 163; Cold War's end and, 225–37; Eliot, Theodore Lyman, and, 90–94, 96; founding of, 81–85; Gullion, Edmund, and, 86–90; history and development of, 86–97; Mayer, Jean, and, 80–97; Salacuse, Jeswald, and, 94–97, *156*, 163; student council, 93
Flint, Anthony, 206
Florence, 33
Florida, 315
Flytzani-Stephanopoulos, Maria, 219
Ford Foundation, 92, 95, 214
Foreign Policy Research Institute, 88
Foster, Henry, x–xi, 148, *156*; school of veterinary medicine and, 127, 129, 130–31
France, 18, 33, 34, 176
Frances Stern Nutritional Center, 30, 107, 121
Frank W. Olin Foundation, 68
Franklin & Marshall College, 189

Fredericks, Carleton, 137, 138
Free Speech Movement, xv
Freedman, James O., 171, 183, 209
Freeland, Richard, 8, 12, 15, 80
Freeman, Lisa, 279
French underground, 18
Friedkin, Morris, 252
Friedman, Dorothy R., 278
Friedman, Gerald J., 278
Friedman, Jane, 278
Friedman, Milton, 193
Fry, John, 188, 189–90
Fukiyama, Francis, 193
Fulbright scholarship, xiv, 75, 76
fundraising, 15, 38, 41; business of,
    53–57, 145–50; dental school, 125;
    presidents, board and, 13–66, 55
Furie, Barbara, 254
Furie, Bruce, 254
Fyler, John, 73

Galantic, Ivan, 223
Galbraith, Kenneth, 160
Galvin, John R., 214, 232, 233, 234, 235,
    237, 289
Gandhi, Indira, 33
Gantcher, Alice, xvii
Gantcher, Nathan, xvii, 149, 150, 277, 285
Gardner, Isabel Stewart, 33
Gardner Museum, 33
Gee, Gordon, 186
Geiger, Jack, 103, 119, 120
George Washington University, 307
Georgetown University, 28, 86, 98, 116,
    179
Gerald Cassidy Associates, 22, 56
Germans, 17, 34, 65
Germantown, 2
Germany, xiv, xv, xvi, 75, 133, 212; Nazi,
    18, 33, 84, 85, 123, 149, 176, 296; uni-
    versity model of, 3–4
Gershoff, Stanley, 19, 32, 107, 155, 275;
    school of nutrition and, 141–42

Gershwin, George, 172, 307
Gessell, Arnold, 222
Gettysburg, battle of, 18
G.I. Bill, 10
Gibson, Count, 103, 119, 120
Gibson, John, 72
Gifford, Nelson, xi, 38, 41, 43, 45, 51, 57,
    148, 149, 150, 152, 153, 167, 168, 170, 171,
    172, 173, 185, 200, 206, 208, 209, 280,
    283, 285
Gill, Gerald, 224
Gilman, Daniel Coit, 3
Gittleman, Julia, 201
Gittleman, Robyn, xi, xiv–xv, 201, 215
Gittleman, Sol, 29, 49, 154, 172, 187, 200,
    201, 203, 246, 276, 277, 280, 288,
    305–6
God, xvi, xviii, 58, 194
Goldberg, Eddie, 103
Goldberg, Jeanne, 143
Golden Globe, 65
Gonthier, Mark, 261
Goode, Robert, 260
Good Morning America, 143
Gordon, Bernard, 223
Gore, Al, 226
The Government of Science (Brooks), 58
Grafton, xvii, 43, 112, 129, 134, 161, 293,
    297
Grafton State Hospital, 24, 25, 27, 127
Grant, Gina, 282–83
Grant, Ulysses S., 47
Great Britain, 192
Great Confrontation, 27
Great Depression, ix
Great Manipulator, 72
Greek and Aegean Studies, 77
Greek Orthodox, 8
Greenblatt, David, 115
Greenblatt, Milton, 252
Greenpeace, 227
Griffin, Merv, 138
Gross, Leo, 84–85, 87, 229, 230

Grossman, Barbara, 224

Grossman, Jerome, 50, 53, 113–14, 115, *159*, 162, 164, 239–40, 241, 247

Gullion, Edmund A., 85, 92, *155*, 232; Fletcher School of Law and Diplomacy and, 86–90; office firebombing of, 88

Guyana, 59, 194

Haber, Fritz, 4

Hale, Audrey, xi

Hale-Bopp Comet, 195

Halifax, 176

Hall, G. Stanley, 3

Hallowell, Burton, ix, 16, 17, 34, 36, *152*, 198, 208, 283; presidency of, 14–15, 41; resignation of, 15

Halm, George, 84, 85

Halm, Lore, 85

Hanham, Harry, 69

Hannum, Hurst, 229–30

Hanover, 16, 75

Haq, Aysha, xi

Harleston, Bernard, 42; resignation of, 36, 41, 66, *153*

Harrington, John, 103, 116, 246, 247, *291*

Harvard Club, 16

Harvard Community Health Plan, 113

Harvard Corporation, 34, 295

Harvard International Law Journal, 229

Harvard Square, 66

Harvard University, 2, 3, 9, 18, 21, 33, 34, 64, 98, 106, 112, 144, 145, 166, 183, 294, 295, 296, 302, 308, 311; alumni, 42, 73, 74, 80, 90, 95; arts and sciences, 58; deans at, 46; Dudley House at, 24, 63, 176–77; fundraising and, 53–54; Jewish student population at, 6; Kennedy School of Goverment, 58, 295; law school, 80, 82, 83, 229; medical school, 98, 102, 104; quotas against Jews at, 7; school of dental medicine, 118–19; school of public

health, 19, 20, 31, 32, 63, 80, 107, 138–39; teaching hospitals, 113; tenure at, 71; treasurer, 57; Veterinary School at, 23; Widener Library at, 83

Hauser, Gayelord, 137, 138

Haute Savoie, 33, 34

Haviland, Field, 87

Hayden, Tom, xv

Hayek, Friedrich, 193, 194

Hayman, Joseph, 102, 103, 252

Health Sciences: academic pecking order, 30

Hebrew, xvi

Heidrick & Struggles, 169

Heller, Irwin, 294, 295

Helsinki, 86

Henry and Lois Foster Hospital for Small Animals, 131

Herschbach, Dudley, 169

Hess, Andrew, 228, 233

Hicks, Edward, 58, 59

higher education: administrative vs. academic presidents in, 183–84, 186–92; college rankings and, 181–82; faculty reaction to changing climate in, 192–94; Mayer era of, 175–77; religion and, 1–3; role of athletics in, 178–81; technology and, 184–85; world events and, 194–96

Hill, Percy, 75

Hillel Center, 301

Hirsch, E. D., 307, 308

Hirsch, Steven, 212

Hitler, Adolf, 85, 153

HMOs, 101, 102, 112, 237

Hoboken, xiii, 306

Hoffman, Michael, 20, 42, 43, 44, 45, 51, 52, 184, 188

Holderman, James B., 315

Holiday, Billie, 197

Hollister, Rob, 283

Holocaust, 297

Holy Cross, 2

Holzman, Frank, 72, 221
Honduras, 143
Honoring the Trust: Quality and Cost Containment in Higher Education (Associated Governing Boards of Trustees), 191
Hooker, Michael, 184
Hopkins, Ernest Martin, 182
Hoskins, Halford L., 83, 84
Hospital for Large Animals, 127
hostages, 59
How the Irish Saved Civilization (Cahill), 247
How to Gain Weight (Macfadden), 136
How to Reduce Weight (Macfadden), 137
Howard Hughes Medical Institute, 79
Howland, Weston, xi, 38, 41, 43, 51, 57, 148, 150, 285
Huber, Brigitte, 104
Hughes, Walter, 252
Human Rights and Conflict Resolution, 96
Humanitarian Studies, 96
Hunter, Howard, 73
Huron Bowling Lanes, xv
Hussein, Saddam, 225
Hutchins, Robert Maynard, 180

I Tatti, 33, 34
Iberian Studies, 77
Illinois Institute of Technology, 210, 307
Imanishi-Kari, Thereza, 164, 165, 166
immigrants: American educators' attitudes toward, 6; Chinese, 5; European, 2, 5; Japanese, 5; university enrollment by, 5–7
immigration: laws restricting, 5, 7
India, 300
Indochina, 87
Inquiry, 215
Institute of Medicine, 118
Institute for Foreign Policy Analysis, 88

International Advisory Board of Overseers, 77
International Business Transactions program, 88
International Congress on Nutrition, 66
International Environment and Resource Policy, 96
International Minerals and Chemical Corporation of Boston, 42
International Relations program, 76
International Security Studies Program (ISSP), 88, 92, 95, 96
Ioannides, Yannis, 221
Iowa, 303
Iowa State University: veterinary program at, 23
Iran, 59
Irish, 2, 5, 90, 245–46
Islam, 59, 195, 308
Israel, 59, 214, 313
Istanbul, 59
Italy, 5, 34
Ivy League, 21, 46, 81, 183, 209, 309, 313

Jack the Ripper, xv
Jackson College: bigotry and, 147
Jackson, Joe, 303
Jacque, Laurent, 230
Jaharis, Michael, 107
Jaharis Family Center for Biomedical and Nutrition Sciences, 107
James, Jesse, 307
James, William, 3–4, 8, 307
Japanese, xvi, 65
Jeddah, 115
Jeka, Mary, 301
Jesuit Boston College, 186
Jesus, 226
Jews, xiii, xiv, 9, 33, 49, 85, 90, 115, 176, 182, 245, 296, 297; anti-semitic laws and, 5; first faculty hiring of, 8; "standards of conduct" of, 6;

students, 147; universities and quotas against, 7, 103; universities and student population of, 6; U.S. population and increase of, 5; women, 147

Johansen, Erling, 28, 123, 124, 125, 126, 157, 202, 255, 257, 258, 260

Johansen, Inge, 126

Johns Hopkins School for Advanced International Studies (SAIS), 86

Johns Hopkins University, 3, 16, 74, 86, 130

Johnson, Lyndon, 89

Jonas, Albert M., 26, 110, 129–30, 156, 265

Jonas, Dean, 128

Jones, James (Jim), 59, 194

Jonestown, 194

Joplin, Scott, 74

Jordan, 95, 206

Journal of International Economic Law, 229

Journal of the American Medical Association, 238

Joyce, James, 247

Junior Year Abroad program, 76

Kanarek, Robin, 32

Kansas, 73

Kaplan, David, 218, 219

Kellogg, W. K., 136

Kemeny, John, 182, 294

Kennedy, Donald, 165

Kennedy, John (Jack) F., xv, 155

Kennedy, Ted, 68, 127, 231

Kennedy School of Government, 58

Kenya, 226

Kerr, Clark, 178, 195

Khomeini, Ayatollah, 59

Kildare, Richard, 99, 100

Kimball, Roger, 71

Kindler, Jeff, 64–65

King Abdulaziz University, 115

Kinsella, W. P., 303

Kipling, Rudyard, 101

Kissinger, Henry, 19

Klein, Michael, 230

Kleine, Larry, 130

Klema, Ernest, 216

Klingenstein, Susanne, 7

Knight, Bobby, 178

Kool-Aid, 59, 194

Koresh, David, 195

Korn Ferry International, 169

Kosch, Phil, 262, 266, 267, *290*

Kramer, Hilton, 71

Krinsky, Norman, 32, 103

Kugel, Gerard, 259, 261

Kumar, Amarendhra, 134

Kuwait, 225

Lahey, Edward, 260

Lake Annecy, 33

Lambert, Joseph, 43

Land, Edmund, 92

land grants, 23; institutions and, 64

Landes, David, 69

languages: foreign, 63, 74, 95; modern, 75

Las Vegas, 180

Lasagna, Louis, 110, 115, *159*, 172, 251, 253, 259

laws: anti-Semitic, 5; May, 5; restricting immigration, 5, 7

Layfayette College, 168

League of Nations, 82, 84, 229

Leav, Irv: school of veterinary medicine and, 128, 130

Lebanon, 95

Lee, Brian, 301

Lee, Mary, 248, 249

Legion of Honor, 18

Leir, Henry, 37

Leonard Carmichael Society, 205

Lerner, Richard, 223

Leskowitz, Sidney, 253

Let's Eat Right to Keep Fit (Davis), 138

Levy, Robert I., xvii, 28, 29, 49, 52, 53, 106, 125, 126, 130, 141, 241; resignation of, 50–51, *158*

Levy, Stuart, 254

Liaison Committee on Medical Education (LCME), 104, 114

Liberal Arts, 47

Libya, 126

Lichtenstein, Alice, 139–40

Light on the Hill (Miller), 61–62

Lincoln, Abraham, 47

Lincoln University, 36

Little, Brown and Company, 73

Little Roundtop, 18

Loew, Frank, xvii, 93, *157*, 202–3, 257, 262, 264, *290*; school of veterinary medicine and, 129, 130–36, 160–61, 263

London, 86

Long Island, 306

Looby, George, 129

"Looking for a Good Life?" (Gittleman), 316

Los Angeles Times, 150

Loutfi, Martine, 72

Love Canal, 231

Lovett, Robert A., 86

Lowell, Abbott, 7, 294

Loyola University of Chicago, 28, 116

Lubarsky, Ruth, 147

Luce Foundation, 89

Ludmerer, Kenneth, 101, 103

Lumumba, Patrice, 87

Luria, Zella, 72, 223

Lydon, Christopher, 112

Lynch, Lisa, 230, *290*

Macfadden, Bernarr, 136–37

MacJannett, Charlotte, 33, 34

MacJannett, Donald, 32–34

MacJannett School for Young Americans, 32

Madison, xiv

Madoff, Morton, 103, 164, 202, 231, 242, 246, *291*

Madrid, 59, 76

Maine, 27

Maine Twentieth Regiment, 18

Making Old Bodies Young (Macfadden), 136

Malamy, Michael, 104

Mali, 142

Management Committee, 41, 42, 43, 44, 45, 51, 57

Manos, Steve, xi, 45–46, 49, 50, 51, 52, 94, 145, *154*, 172, 173, 184, 185, 186, 187, 188, 189, 200, 202, 203, 207, 211, 235, 258, 275, 280, 301

Marcopoulos, George, 8, 73

Marcos, Ferdinand, 65

Marcos, Imelda, 65

Marcus, Danny, 70

Mariner, Jeff, 133

Marseilles, 86

Marshall, Thurgood, 60

Martin, Geraldine, 295

Martin, Lee, 295

Marts & Lundy, 15, 54, 55

Marx, Karl, 194

Maryland, 141

Mason, Joel, 279

Massachusetts, xv, 7, 22, 23, 24, 31, 54, 88, 118, 127

Massachusetts American Cancer Society Chair, 103

Massachusetts General Hospital, 50, 99, 113, 239

Massachusetts Institute of Technology (MIT), 31, 32, 64, 84, 108, 112, 121, 139, 144, 164, 168, 217, 221, 295, 296, 297

Massachusetts Society for the Prevention of Cruelty to Animals, 27

May Laws, 5

Mayer, André, 17

Mayer, Betty, xi, 67, *154*, 175, 199, 281; background of, 176–77

Mayer, Jean, ix, x, xi, xvii, 152, *153*, *154*, 155, 157, 159, 197, 201, 202, 203, 206, 207, 216, 217, 220, 223, 224, 229, 231, 239, 250, 252–53, 274, 281, *285*, 287, 295, 296, 297, 299, 303; "academic entrepreneurship" and, 18; acceptance of presidency by, 16; annus terribilis and, 35–39; background and history of, 17–20; consolidating presidency of, 45–49; dark years of transition before, 12–16; death of, 173; end of era and, 175–79; faculty and, 58–61, 69–80; Fletcher School of Law and Diplomacy and, 80–97; fundraising under, 53–57; Great Confrontation and, 27; Great Manipulator, 72; independent action and, 20; mountain-top and, 144–50; "one medicine" and, 27, 109, 110, 124, 133, 262; presidency (1987-1992), 160–74; Priory at Talloires and, 32–35; Schlossberg & Cassidy and, 20–22; school of dentistry and, 116–26; school of medicine and, 97–116; school of nutrition and, 28–32, 136–44, 274–79; school of veterinary medicine and, 22–27, 40, 127–36, 160–61; shock to system and, 16–20; students and, 58–61, 62–68; troika and, 50–53; trustees and, 39–44, 57–58

McCabe, Bernard, 9

McCarthy, Joe, 49

McCarthy, Kathryn, 36, 38, 40, 42, 47, 67, 94, 121, *152*, 153, 185; resignation of, 39, 66

McClellan, Andrew, 224

McClellan, General George, 47

McClellan, Scott, 280

McFarlane, Alexander, 147

McGandy, Robert, 122

McKay, Gordon, 58

McLaughlin, David T., 182, 183

McManus, Joe, *157*, 264

Mead, Leonard, 8, 303

Medford, ix, xvi, xvii, 8, 28, 39, 40, 44, 45, 75, 83, 296, 303; campus, 62, 66, 67, 76, 81, 112, 184, 206, 293, 299, 304

Medical Information Technology, 113

Meister, Alton, 252

Mencken, H. L., 69

Mendelsohn, Michael, 240, 254

Merrin, Ed, 149

Meserve, William, xi, 240

Metcalf, Gilbert, 221, 224, 299

Methodists, xiv, 2

Metz, Bruce, 249

Mexico, xiv

Meydani, Mohsen, 139

Meydani, Simin, 139

Miami, 315

Miaoulis, Yannis, 217, 218, 219, 220, *289*, 300

Michigan, 136, 221

Michigan State University, 170, 171, 173, 200, 208

Middle East, 60, 91, 95, 149, 225, 226, 228, 313

Middlesex University, 23

The Miracle of Milk (Macfadden), 136

Miller, Russell, ix, x, 13, 61, 119, 147

Milton Academy, 301

Mississippi, 73, 103

Mississippi River, 307

Monan, Donald, 186, 187

money management, 37

Montreal, 74

Moomaw, William, 231

Moravian College, 2

Morehead, James, 103

Morrill, Congressman Justin Smith, 23

Morrill Land Grant Act of 1862, 3, 23

Moscow State University, 76

Mound Bayou, 103

Mount Auburn Cemetery, 107

Mount Holyoke College, xv, xvi, 307

Mozart, Wolfgang Amadeus, 225

Mufti, Malik, 224
Munro, Hamish, 108, 121, 276; school of nutrition and, 139, 140, 141–42, 143, 155
Murnane, Thomas, xi, 38, 47, 49, 50, 53, 77, 94, 119, 120, 146, 147, *154*, 172, 177, 198, 199, 200, 203, 207, 213, 231, 249, 280, 282, 300; fundraising and, 55–56, 148; Veterinary School and, 25, 27, 127, 160–61
Myrick, Kenneth, 9

Nablus, 59
Najjar, Victor, 103
NASDAQ, 226
National Academy of Sciences, 108
National Association of Scholars, 71, 193
National Collegiate Athletic Association (NCAA), 178, 179, 311
National Endowment for the Humanities (NEH), 69, 70, 78, 89
National Enquirer, 315
National Institutes of Health (NIH), 28, 50, 53, 100, 105, 111, 118, 128, 133, 164
National Labor Relations Board, 60
National Public Radio, 143
National Society for the Prevention of Blindness Award, 68
NATO, 88, 232
Nature, 194, 316
Nazis, 18, 33, 84, 85, 123, 149, 176, 296
Nelson, Fred, 77, *155,* 217
Nelson, Miriam, 278, *292*
Neubauer, Joseph, 149, 221, 223
Nevins, Allan, 306, 307
New England, xv, 12, 13, 18, 23, 26, 38, 40, 55, 72, 102; colleges and universities in, 14, 54, 177; veterinary school students from, 24, 62
New England Board of Higher Education (NEBHE), 23–24

New England Governors Conference, 25
New England Journal of Medicine, 238
New England Medical Center (NEMC), 30, 50, 53, 99, 102, 103, 111, 113, 114, 115, 139, 162
New Hampshire, 16
New Jersey, xiii, xiv, 311
New Mexico, 4
New York, 23
New York City, xv, 5, 15, 61, 138, 181, 195, 224, 306
New York State College of Veterinary Surgeons, 23
New York Times, 5, 144, 150, 168, 169, 173, 278, 306
New York University, xiv, 137, 180, 181, 307
Newell, Peggy, 254, 259, *287*
Newsweek, 175, 312
Nickerson, Norton, 73
"1940 Statement of Principles on Academic Freedom and Tenure," 10
Nixon, Richard, 20
Nizel, Abraham, 121, 122
Nobel Prize, 295; chemistry, 4, 169; medicine, 67
Norman, George, 221
Norris, Lonnie, *158,* 257, 258, 261, 298
Northwestern University, 28, 116, 179, 216, 257
Norway, 123
Notre Dame University, 2, 179
Nova Scotia, 176
Novick, Peter, 6
nutrition: history of, 136–38
Nutrition in Clinical Dentistry (Nizel), 122
Nutrition in Preventive Dentistry: Science and Practice (Nizel), 122
Nutrition Institute, 32
Nutter, Deborah, 235
NYU. *See* New York University

Oberlin College, 168
Observer, 64, 66, 67
O'Connell, Brian, 170
O'Donnell, Thomas F., 248, 250
Ohio State University, xiv, 183
Oklahoma City bombing, 195
O'Leary, David, 301
O'Leary, Jim, 73
Olin Center for Culture and Language, 68
Omidyar, Pam and Pierre, 283
"One Medicine," 27, 109, 110, 124, 133, 262
O'Neill, "Tip," 108, 231
OPEC, 60
Oral Roberts University, 28, 116
Ordovas, Jose, 278
Ounjian, Dan, 72, 223
Overstrom, Eric, 135
Oxford University, 180

Pacific Ocean, 307
Pakistan, 59
Palestine, 313
Palmer, Carol, 121, 122, 260, 279
Palubinskas, Lucille, 73, 223
Papageorge, Maria, 259
Papas, Athena, 121, 122, 259, 260, 279
Paris, 17, 33, 75, 76
Park, James, 103
Park, Ted, 252
Parker, Charlie, 197
Pattullo, Pat, xi
Peace and Justice Studies, 64
Peace Corps, xv
Pearl Harbor, 306
peer-reviewed grants, 21
Pennsylvania State University, 307
Penvenne, Jeanne, 224
People magazine, 189
Pepall, Lynne, 224
Perlman, Ben, 73
Perry, John, 92
Perseus Project, 212, 215

Pfaltzgraff, Robert, 87–88, 89, 90, 96, 228, 232, 236
Ph.D. programs. *See* doctorate programs
Phi Beta Kappa, 37, 45, 182, 257
Philip (prince), 33
Philippines, 59, 65
Physicians Without Borders, 227
Pierce, Benjamin, 58
Pitcher, Evelyn, 222
Plaut, Andrew, 104, 254
Plessy v. Ferguson, 3
Pokras, Mark, 135, 270
Pokras, Martha, xi, 128, *156,* 259, 263, 287
Polaroid, 92
population: rise of Jewish, 5
Port Huron Doctrine, Students for Democratic Action, xv
Post, Charles W., 136
Pound, Roscoe, 82
Pradal, Georgette, 72
Presbyterians, Evangelical, 2
presidents, Tufts: Bacow, Lawrence, 255, *286,* 293–304; board, academic freedom, and, 9–11, 16; board, corporate culture, and, 309–10; board, fundraising, and, 13–16, 55; Capen, Elmer Hewitt, 6; Carmichael, Leonard, ix, 8, 12, 13–15, 283; Cousens, John, 12, 13, 82, 83; DiBiaggio, John, 170–71, 172, 173, 188, 197–284, *286,* 294, 296, 297; Hallowell, Burton, ix, 14–15, 16–17, 34, 36, 41, *152,* 198, 208, 283; job turnover rate of, 35; Mayer, Jean, ix, x, xi, xvii, 12–44, 45–150, 152, *153, 154,* 155, 157, 159, 160–74, 175–79, 197, 201–3, 206–7, 216–17, 220, 223–24, 229, 231, 239, 250, 252–53, 262, 274–79, 281, 285, 287, 295, 296–97, 299, 303; Wessell, Nils, ix, 8, 12, 13, 14–15, 34, 104, 119, 147, *151, 152,* 208, 215, 281.

President's Commission on World
  Hunger, 66
Primary Source, 69–70
Princeton University, 2, 7, 79, 98, 171,
  183, 190, 221, 296, 311; Jewish student
  population at, 6; Woodrow Wilson
  School at, 86
*Prioritizing Academic Programs and
  Services: Reallocating Resources to
  Achieve Strategic Balance* (Associated
  Governing Boards of Trustees), 191
Professors Row, 301
Profscam (Sykes), 70
Proger, Sam, 111
Protestants, 1, 2, 3, 5, 147; non, 8
Provost of Tufts, x, 16, 17, 20, 26, 28, 29,
  37, 50, *288*; assistant, xi; council, 52;
  deans and, 46, 52; Gittleman, Sol, 29,
  48, 49, 51–53, 72, 77, 90, 94, 105, *154,*
  172, 187, 200, 201–2, 203, 246, 276,
  277, 280, 288, 305–6; McCarthy,
  Kathryn, 36, 38, 39, 40, 42, 46, 47,
  48–49, 66, 67, 94, 121, *152,* 153, 185;
  Mead, Leonard, 8, 303; selection of,
  46–49; Shira, Robert, 40–41, 42, 43,
  48, 120–21, 122, 125, 157
Pusey, Nathan, 34, 294
Putin, Vladimir, 225

al-Qa'ida, 226
Quaker Haverford, 89

Ra'anan, Uri, 87, 88, 96
race: college admissions and, 60
Radcliffe College, 176
Rahman, Sheik Omar Abdel, 195
railroads, 5
Ramalah, 59
Rancho Santa Fe, 195
Rand, Matthew, 260
Rapport, David, 251
Rawlings, Hunter, 183
Rawls, John, 74

Raytheon Corporation, 57
Reagan, Ronald, 59, 68, 69, 70, 108, 160,
  192, 193
Reed College, 73
Rehnquist, William, 60
Reichlin, Seymour, 128
Reid, Peter, 212
Reinisch, Carol, 130, 271
religion: higher education influenced
  by, 1–3
Remis, Ruth, xi, 147, 148
Remmers, Virginia, 76
Republican Party, 227
research degrees: history and literature
  fields influenced by, 4; Ph.D., 3, 4
Resistence Medal, 18
Restrictive Immigration League, 7
Reuss, Bert, 73
Reyes Syndrome, 78
Rhodes, Cecil, 168
Rhodes scholar, 180
Ricci, Carla, 133
Richard II (Shakespeare), 173
Richards, Dan, 224
Rinderpest, 93, 133
riots, 59
Roche, John, 89–90, 91, 92, 94, *155*
Rockefeller, David, 34
Rockefeller University, 165
Rockwell, Norman, 199
Rodin, Judith, 188
Rodman, Shelley, 264
Rogers, Beatrice, 142, 143
Rogers, Rosemarie, 88, 89, 90
Romance languages, xvi
Rome, 9
Romero, Christiane, 74
Romney, Mitt, 284, 298
Ropes & Gray, 38
Rose Bowl, 179
Rosenberg, Irwin, 143, 274, 276, 279, 292,
  298
Rosenberg, Naomi, 104

Rosenblatt, Michael, *291, 300*
Rosenmeier, Jesper, *73*
Rosovsky, Henry, 225
Ross, Jim, 130
Rotberg, Robert, 207, 211, *300*
ROTC, 64, 216
Rowan, Andrew, 131, 134, 270
Rowell, Steven, 127, 269
Rubaiyat of Omar Khayyam
    (FitzGerald), xv
Rubin, Alfred, 88, 89, 90, 228
Rudenstine, Neil, 294, 295
Rupp, Adolph, 178
Russell, Robert, 122, 139, 140, *292, 298*
Russia, xvi, 5
Russo, Rebecca, 264
Rwanda, 225

Sackler, Arthur M., 110, 241
Sackler School: history of, 250–55.
    See also Arthur M. Sackler School of
    Biomedical Sciences
Sahel, 93
Saigon, 86
Salacuse, Jeswald, 214, 227, 228, 229, 230,
    232, 234, 236, *293*; Fletcher School of
    Law and Diplomacy and, 94–97, *156,*
    163
salaries: athletic coaches, 178–79,
    309–10; college presidents, 309–10;
    faculty, 14, 55, 310–11
Salieri, Antonio, 225
Salonika, 86
Salter, Ron, 74
Saltonstall, William, xi, 149
San Francisco, 307
Sand, George, 78
Santa Fe, 127
Saperstein, George, 129, 270
Sardinia, 74
Sargent, Frank, 25
Sargent, Hester, 149
SAT scores, 179, 180

Satan, 195
Saudi Arabia, 95, 115, 226
Sauer, Anne, xi
Schaechter, Elio, 103, 105, 251
Schaechter, Moselio, 115
Schaefer, Ernie, 140
Schlossberg, Kenneth, 20–21, *275*
Schlossberg & Cassidy Associates,
    20–22, 25, 30, 37, 55, 76, 139, 142, *275*
Schneider, John, xi
School of International and Public
    Affairs (SIPA), 86
Schulman, Mr., 306, 307
Schwartz, Robert, 254
Schwartz, Tony, 130, 272
Schwartz, William, 111, 246, 305
Schwartzkopf, Norman, 233, 289
Science, 316
The Science of Nutrition and its Applica-
    tion in Clinical Dentistry (Nizel), 122
Scovil, Carl, xi
Secretary of State, 19
Security Studies program, 88
Sedgwick, Chuck, 134–35
Selker, Harry, 254
Senelick, Laurence, 74
Serbia, 226, 308
Settingnano, 33
Shader, Richard, 115
Shah of Iran, 59
Shakespeare, William, 73, 173
Shapiro, Harold, 171, 183, 209
Shapiro, Neal, 66–67
Sheer, Roberta, 147
Sheraton Commander Hotel, 66
Sherwin, Martin, 76, 79
Sherwin, Susan, 79
Shi'ite Muslim, 308
Shira, Robert, 40, 42, 43, 48, 120–21, 122,
    125, *157*
Shoeless Joe (Kinsella), 303
Shore, Dinah, 138
shtetls, 5

Shultz, Mary Jane, 213
Shultz, Richard, 96, 228
Sicily, 5
Silber, John, 60, 61, 112, 145, 178, 238, 239, 283
Sills, Dean, 7
Simches, Seymour, 34–35, 72, 75, 223
Sliwa, Chris, 213, 214
Smith, Page, 72
Smith, Tony, 74
Society for American Baseball Research, 91
Sociology Department, 74
Sollod, Al, 93; school of veterinary medicine and, 130, 132–34
Solomon, Howard, 8
Somalia, 225, 226
Sonnenschein, Abraham, 103
Sorbonne University, 17, 18
South Africa, 65, 67
South America, 59
South Hadley Center, xv
Southeast Asia, 87
Southern Methodist University, 95
Soviet Union, 87, 88, 95, 193, 225, 229
Soweto, 59
Spain, 149
Sputnik, xvi
St. Cloud, 33
St. Louis University, 28, 116
Stalin, Joseph, 89
Stanford University, 9, 165, 179
State News, 205
State Street Research, 34
Stearns, Charles, xvi
Stearns, Norman, 242
Stem, "Chip," 134
Stern, James, 149, 150, 285
Stewart, Robert, 84, 86
Stollar, David, 103, 115, 128, 254
Strassbourg, 75
Strategic Leadership in Academic Affairs: Clarifying the Board's Responsibilities

(Associated Governing Boards of Trustees), 191
Strauss, Leo, 193, 194
Strength from Eating (Macfadden), 136
Strong Women (and Men) Beat Arthritis (Nelson), 278
Strong Women Eat Well (Nelson), 278
Strong Women Stay Slim (Nelson), 278
Strong Women Stay Young (Nelson), 278
Strong Women, Strong Bones (Nelson), 278
Stryker, Dirck, 93, 132, 133
students, 58, 306–7; activists, 47; admissions, 60, 62, 66; campus mood and, 62–68; Catholic, 147; committee, 47, 168; council, 93; dental, 27; DiBiaggio, John, alumni, and, 197–200; faculty, changing times and, 58–62; Jewish, 147; junior year abroad, 76; medical, 27, 128; minority, 60; veterinary, 27, 40, 109, 127–28
Students for Democratic Action: Port Huron Doctrine of, xv
Sudan, 95, 134
Summers, Lawrence H., 296
Summit, Jeffrey (Rabbi), 224
Sunni Muslim, 308
SUNY, xv
Supreme Court, 3, 61; Bakke decision, 60; Yeshiva decision, 61
Swap, Walter, 72
Sykes, Charles, 70–71
Syracuse University, 191

Talamo, Barbara, 115, 254
Talloires, 145; European Study Center at, 37, 74, 75, 126; Priory at, 32–35
Tanzania, 226
Taylor, Allen, 139
technology: higher education and, 184–85
Tehran, 59

Teichman, Sherman, 214, 215
Tennessee State University, 3
tenure, 10, 84, 88, 90, 94, 96, 211, 293;
abolishment and survival of, 192;
Harvard University and, 71; medical
school deans and, 101; raising stan-
dards for, 77–78, 207
Tenure and Promotion Committee, 96,
207
Texas, 195
Texas Tech University, 108, 109
Thailand, 59
Thatcher, Margaret, 192
Third Reich, 75, 124
Thornton, Ron, 216, 219
Three Mile Island, 60
TIAA-CREFF retirement funds, 193
Tiant, Louis, 90, 91
Tigris River, 194
Time, 175, 312
Tisch, Jonathan, 149
Tobin, Roger, 221
Today Show, 143
Tokyo, 195
Toole, Brian, 115, 254
Tosteson, Dan, 99
Trachtman, Joel, 229, 236
"The Treaty of Packard Avenue," 91
Treaty of Versailles, 82
Troika, 50–53, 167, 188; DiBiaggio, John,
and, 200–204
trustees. *See* Board of Trustees; Tufts
Trustees
Trusteeship, 191
Tsamstouris, Athni, 261
Tseng, Flo, 273
Tuck School of Business Administra-
tion, 97
Tuebingen, 75, 76
Tufts Alumni Association, ix
Tufts College, xvi, 13, 37, 72, 85, 147;
founding of, 301
Tufts Daily, 208, 316

Tufts Friedman School of Nutritional
Science and Policy, 19
Tufts Health Plan (HMO), 112
Tufts Human Nutrition Research
Center on Aging, 26, 32, 43, 108, 114,
121, 163, 298; director of, 139, *155*;
Gershoff, Stanley, and, 141–42;
history of, 274–79; search for legitimacy, 136–44
Tufts Luck, 125
Tufts Observer, 62, 197, 198, 208, 215
Tufts School of Dental Medicine, 27, 28,
47, 115, 141, 294; deans, 40, *157, 158*;
DiBiaggio, John, and, 255–61; history
of, 119–26
Tufts School of Medicine, 28, 32, 43, 163,
298; 1990s and, 241–45; Arthur M.
Sackler School of Biomedical Sciences, 50, 110–12, 250–55; Boston
medicine and, 238–40; deans, 49, 53,
158, 159; DiBiaggio, John, and,
237–50; faculty, 29; Irish and,
245–50; Mayer, Jean, and, 97–116;
new view of health and, 107–12;
nutrition and, 30; rebuilding,
97–106; two scorpions in bottle
and, 112–16; veterinarian students
and, 27
Tufts School of Nutrition, 35, 55, 106;
dean, *155*; establishing, 28–32;
Mayer, Jean, and, 28–32, 136–44,
274–79
Tufts School of Veterinary Medicine,
23, 35, 43, 44, 53, 93, 112, 141, 145, 148,
156, 298; chief financial officer, *157*;
economy and, 160–61; Foster, Henry,
and, 127, 129, 130–31; Leav, Irv, and,
128, 130; Loew, Frank, and, 129,
130–36, 160–61, 263; lost leader and,
262–74; Mayer, Jean, and creation of,
22–32, 40, 110, 127–36; Murnane,
Thomas, and, 25, 27, 127, 160–61;
will to survive, 127–36

Tufts: The Total University in Changing Times (University Steering Committee), 15, 16

Tufts Trustees, 10, 13, 15, 19, 25, 32; Callow, Allan, x, 37–38, 39–40, 41–43, 51, 57, 67, 148, 149, *153*, 285; Gifford, Nelson, xi, 38, 41, 43, 45, 51, 57, 148, 149, 150, *152*, 153, 167, 168, 170, 171–73, 185, 200, 206, 208, 209, 280, 283, 285; Jaharis, Michael, 107; presidents, academic freedom, and, 9–11; presidents, fundraising, and, 13–16; Priory at Talloires and, 32–35; voting record of, 16–17

Tufts University, xvi, xvii, 18, 147, 305–6; alumni, 54, 55, 56, 64, 77, 198; Bacow, Lawrence, and, 255, 286, 293–304; Cabot Intercultural Center, 77; civility and, 312–14; dark years of transition at, 12–16; DiBiaggio years at, 197–284; early 1960s at, 8–9; endowment industry and, 308–9; European Study Center at Talloires, 32–35, 37, 74, 75, 126, 145; Experimental College, 63–64, 91, *154*, 214, 215, 317; faculty, 8–9, 10, 14, 15, 27, 28–29, 32, 37, 39, 47, 53, 55, 58, 59, 60–62, 63, 64, 69–80, 128–29, 131, *151*, 158, 168, 197, 304, 310–11; Fletcher School of Law and Diplomacy, 80–97; founding of, 2; Friedman School of Nutritional Science and Policy at, 19, 26, 35; fundraising at, 13–66, 15, 38, 41, 53–57, 55, 125, 145–50; great mutation of, 4–7; innocence and, 315–16; Jaharis Family Center for Biomedical and Nutritional Sciences, 107; Jewish student population at, 6; Mayer, Jean, presidency at, ix, x, xi, xvii, 12–44, 45–150, 152–55, 157, 159–74, 175–79, 197, 201–3, 206–7, 216–17, 220, 223–24, 229, 231, 239, 250, 252–53, 262, 274–79, 281, 285, 287, 295, 296–97, 299, 303; name change of, 13; new American university's shared culture with, 1–3; parents, 77; presidents, boards, and academic freedom at, 9–11, 16; presidents, boards, and corporate culture at, 309–10; prestige and, 311–12; research octopus and, 3–4, 8; some things never change, 306–8; Troika at, 50–53, 167, 188, 200–204; Tuebingen and, 75; what kind of light on hill?, 8–9

Tufts University Development Corporation (TUDC), 162, 163

Tufts University Diet and Nutrition Newsletter, 142, 143

Tufts–New England Medical Center, 302. *See also* New England Medical Center (NEMC)

tuition, increase, 38, 65

Tupper Building, 114

Tuskegee University, 3; veterinary program at, 23

Twareg, 93

Tyco International, 315

Tzipori, Saul, 273

Uhlir, Arthur, 216

"Undergraduate Bioscience Education Initiative," 79

UNICEF, 177

United Auto Workers, 312

United States, xvii, 10, 18, 33, 59, 70, 71, 85, 86, 112, 117, 134, 136, 192; aging population in, 139; economy, 59; energy crisis, 60; immigrant history of, 5; post-secondary growth in, 1–3

Universalist Church, 2

Universalist Tufts, ix

universities: Catholic, 2, 5; first American research, 3, 4; immigrants' enrollment in, 5–7; quotas against Jews in, 7

University of Alabama, 137, 178

University of California, Berkeley, 136, 179; Bolt Hall, 97

University of California, Davis: medical school, 60

University of Chicago, 4, 9, 180, 193; Jewish student population at, 6

University of Colorado, 179, 183

University of Connecticut, 170, 172, 200, 208

University of Edinburgh, 221

University of Florida, 134

University of Illinois, 219

University of Indiana, 178

University of Iowa, 73, 171, 183

University of Kentucky, 170, 178

University of Maryland-Baltimore County, 184

University of Massachusetts, 184

University of Michigan, xiv, xv, 171, 183, 312

University of Minnesota, 45

University of Munich, 85

University of North Carolina, Chapel Hill, 184, 307

University of Pennsylvania, 2, 87, 134, 188, 189, 307; veterinary school, 23, 26

University of Rochester, 13, 110, 123, 222

University of South Carolina, 315

University of Southern California, 136

University of Toronto, 275

University of Vienna, 84

University of Virginia, xvi

University of Washington, 179

University of West Virginia, 183

University Press of New England (UPNE), xi, 75

University Steering Committee, 15, 16

U.S. Congress, 25, 26, 107, 180

U.S. Department of Agriculture (USDA), 20, 21, 30, 31, 107, 140, 143

U.S. Department of Health, Education and Welfare, 25

U.S. Department of Treasury, 115

U.S. Energy Research and Development Administration, 77

U.S. Environmental Protection Agency (EPA), 135, 162, 231

U.S. Fish and Wildlife Service, 135

U.S. Food and Drug Administration (FDA), 138

U.S. House committees, 31

U.S. News & World Report, 175, 181, 209, 220, 225, 232, 239, 281, 308, 310, 311–12, 314

U.S. News & World Report College and University Rankings, 182

U.S. Senate committees, 31

U.S. State Department, 84

U.S.S.R., 86, 92, 96

Uvin, Peter, 279

Van Camp, Rosemarie, 173

Vanderbilt University, 183

Vannevar, Bush, 4

Vassar College, 176

Vermont, 23, 27

Vest, Charles, 295

vice presidents, 50; academic, 183–84, 186–92; executive, 183–84, 186–92; health sciences, 28; Manos, Steven, xi, 45, 46, 49, 50–52, 94, 145, *154,* 172–73, 184–200, 202, 203, 207, 211, 235, 258, 275, 280, 301; Murnane, Tom, xi, 38, 47, 49, 50, 53, 57, 77, 94, 119, 120, 146, 147, *154,* 172, 177, 198, 199, 200, 203, 207, 213, 231, 249, 280, 282, 300

Vietnam, 66, 85, 89, 234

Vietnam War, 59, 313

Virginia Commonwealth University, 170

Vogels, Helmi, 123

Waco, 195

Waldor, Matt, 254

Wall Street Journal, 150, 218, 278
Walnut Hill, 301
Walt, David, 79, 224, 299
Walter Reed Medical Center, 120
Waltham, 23
Warsh, David, 284
Washington, D.C., 20, 30, 32, 74, 86, 89, 123, 141, 165, 301
Washington Post, 150, 278
Washington University, St. Louis, 28, 90, 116, 307; *Record,* 30
Watson, James, 194
Wedekind, Frank, xv, xvi, xvii, 312
Welby, Marcus, 99, 100
Weld, William, 161
Wellesley, 64
Wesleyan University, 2, 14
Wessell, Nils, ix, 8, 15, 34, 104, 119, 147, *151, 152,* 208, 215, 281; presidency of, 12, 13; resignation of, 13, 14
West, Cornel, 296
West, Robert, 87
West Bank, 59
White House, 89, 192
White House Conference on Food, Nutrition and Health, 20, 136, 137, 138
Whiteman, Paul, 307
Whitman, Walt, 307
Whitten, Jamie, 142
Wicklum, Ellen, xi
Widener Library, 83
William and Mary College, 2, 307
Williams College, 70, 232
Williams, Ted, 247
Wilson, Harold, 60
Wilson, Woodrow, 6
Winship, Thomas, 65
Wolf, Maryanne, 80
Wolff, Sheldon, 50, 53, 111, 114, 162, 240, 243, 254, 277, *291*

women, 115, 116; class of 2006 and, 273; club for, 126; Jewish, 147
Women's Studies, 63
Woodrow Wilson School, 86
Woods Hole Institute, 130
Woodstock, 129
Woolf, Harry, 16, 17, 145
Worcester, 24, 132, 180
world events: higher education and, 194–96
World Trade Center, 195, 226; collapse of, 274, 299
World War I, xiii, 4, 7, 9, 10, 17, 226, 307
World War II, xix, 4, 10, 17, 53, 65, 82, 84, 85, 86, 89, 99, 100, 102, 118, 123, 194, 274
Wortis, Henry, 115, 254
Wren, Frank G., 7
Wren Hall, 301
Wright, Andy, 103, 104
Wright, Dudley, 212, 213

Xian, Wang, 279

Yale University, 2, 18, 80, 98, 106, 188; law school, 183; medical school, 26, 110; quotas against Jews at, 7
Yeats, William Butler, 233, 247
Yeltsin, Boris, 225
Yeshiva decision, 61
Yeshiva University, 61, 307
Yiddish, xiii, xvii, 90
Young, James Harvey, 137
Ypsilanti, xv
Yugoslavia, 34, 225

Zaire, 95
Zarker, Jack, 73
Zeitlin, Marian, 142, 143
Zelin, Marty, 73
Zwerling, Sidney, xiv